BECOMING TRANSNATIONAL YOUTH WORKERS

Latinidad

Transnational Cultures in the United States

Matt Garcia, Series Editor, Professor of Latin American, Latino and Caribbean Studies, and History, Dartmouth College

This series publishes books that deepen and expand our understanding of Latina/o populations, especially in the context of their transnational relationships within the Americas. Focusing on borders and boundary-crossings, broadly conceived, the series is committed to publishing scholarship in history, film and media, literary and cultural studies, public policy, economics, sociology, and anthropology. Inspired by interdisciplinary approaches, methods, and theories developed out of the study of transborder lives, cultures, and experiences, the titles enrich our understanding of transnational dynamics.

For a list of titles in the series, see the last page of the book.

BECOMING TRANSNATIONAL YOUTH WORKERS

Independent Mexican Teenage Migrants and Pathways of Survival and Social Mobility

ISABEL MARTINEZ

RUTGERS UNIVERSITY PRESS
New Brunswick, Camden, and Newark, New Jersey, and London

Library of Congress Cataloging-in-Publication Data

Names: Martinez, Isabel, 1979– author.
Title: Becoming transnational youth workers : independent Mexican teenage migrants and pathways of survival and social mobility / Isabel Martinez.
Description: New Brunswick, New Jersey : Rutgers University Press, [2019] | Series: Latinidad: transnational cultures in the United States | Includes bibliographical references and index.
Identifiers: LCCN 2018032220 | ISBN 9780813589800 (cloth) | ISBN 9780813589794 (pbk.)
Subjects: LCSH: Foreign workers—United States | Foreign workers—Mexico. | Teenage immigrants—United States. | Teenage immigrants—Mexico. | Mexican-American Border Region—History.
Classification: LCC HD8081.M6 M35 2019 | DDC 331.3/470973—dc23
LC record available at https://lccn.loc.gov/2018032220

A British Cataloging-in-Publication record for this book is available from the British Library.

∞ The paper used in this publication meets the requirements of the American National Standard for Information Sciences—Permanence of Paper for Printed Library Materials, ANSI Z39.48-1992.

www.rutgersuniversitypress.org

Manufactured in the United States of America

For my beloved mother and father, Belia and Ramiro

CONTENTS

BECOMING TRANSNATIONAL YOUTH WORKERS

1 • IN THE SHADOWS OF SKYSCRAPERS AND IVORY TOWERS

Almost two decades ago, I found myself gearing up for yet another Martinez family reunion in Harlingen, a South Texas town approximately thirty miles north of the U.S.-Mexico border. Prior to this event in July 2000, I had never inquired into, nor knew about, the history of our family. Yet laid out before us by my uncle, Tio Felipe Salazar II, was the history of the Martinez family from my paternal grandparents' early twentieth-century emigration from Mexico to the beginning of the twenty-first century, a narrative printed in its entirety in a slim, gray, Kinko's-bound volume.

Central to this family history is the story of a young girl—my paternal grandmother—who, by the age of sixteen, would flee violence and poverty in Mexico and cross the U.S.-Mexico border without her parents. Born poor in 1902, Josefa Cermeño Luna was brought into the world in El Molino, Guanajuato, to a *campesino* (farm worker) and an *ama de casa* (housewife). Subject to early twentieth-century rural gender norms and without nearby schools, she would be taught how to become a good woman, skilled in the ways of the home. She would learn how to cook and clean and care for her brothers.

By the time Josefa turned twelve, her older brother's twenty-two-year-old friend, Baltazar, took notice of her, and in 1915, as she approached her thirteenth birthday, she wed. The ceremony was, according to her account, "a simple but solemn" occasion with only a few family members serving as witnesses (Salazar 2000). After the ceremony, Baltazar would take her to his family's *jacal*, or mud and straw-thatched home, where, not much unlike rural areas of Mexico today, they would live, and he would work from sun up to sun down in the fields, and she would help rear her sister-in-law's children.

Josefa came of age in poverty amid the violence of the Mexican Revolution. Although El Molino was not yet a site of conflict, by the time Josefa was approximately sixteen years old, rumors had reached the small town that both Villistas and Federales were coercing men to join their armies and were forcibly seizing food, women, arms, ammunition, and horses from campesinos. These reports worried both Josefa and Baltazar. Left with little recourse, they made plans to leave and go to *el norte*. On a brisk October or November day in 1918, the barely sixteen-year-old wife and now mother would wrap Margarita, her infant daughter, in her *rebozo* (scarf), hug her parents good-bye, and leave the only home she knew to travel more than four hundred miles in an ox-driven cart, or *carreta*, with her husband; her eleven-year-old brother, Victoriano; and another family, the Colungas. This young girl—now affectionately known as Mama Chepa to more than a hundred U.S.-born children, grandchildren, and great-grandchildren—would arrive two months later in Reynosa, Tamaulipas, and cross the Rio Bravo River to Peñitas, Texas, a town founded in the sixteenth century by a splinter group of survivors of the Pánfilo de Nárvaez expedition—a priest, five military officers, and their slaves. Nearly four hundred years after that expedition, Josefa and Baltazar encountered a new group of "explorers," a campsite of Mexican families who had crossed in the days and weeks before them. Joining them, Josefa would care for young Margarita and prepare meals with the other women while Baltazar would seek backbreaking labor with the other men.

When told today, this story is usually met with loud gasps and questions about why my grandmother would engage in such grown-up actions at such a tender age. The short answer is fairly uncomplicated. Born a poor girl, young Josefa was simply following her community and her family's understandings of age, class, and gender norms. She was not precocious; rather, young Josefa was simply abiding by the social time, or the "set of norms that specify when particular life transitions or accomplishments are expected in a particular society or social milieu" (Clausen 1986: 2). Shaped by her community's and family's socioeconomic conditions, as well as the broader sociohistorical and political contexts in which her community and family were located, Josefa's acts, for her time and place, were deemed perfectly "on-time" (Burton 1996; Neugarten and Hagestad 1976). Early marriage, early childbearing, and eventually migration without parents were simply "normal."

But what about in contemporary times? One hundred years later, why would teenage Mexican minors *continue* to leave their parents to seek better lives in el norte? A century after the crossing of Josefa Cermeño Luna, this book focuses on a group of Mexican teenage minors, albeit mostly male and unmarried, who followed Josefa's lead and, indicative of new destinations of Mexican immigrant settlement that extend beyond the U.S. Southwest, sought "better" lives in New York City. Challenging the characterizations of immigrant minors as "luggage" or "appendages"—inanimate objects whose own migration is determined by their parents—this book illuminates how this particular class of post-NAFTA Mexican teenage minors, pre- and postmigration, actively observes and reacts to the socioeconomic conditions and shifts in their communities and households as well as to ideas about family interdependence and social mobility (Bhabha 2014a; Boehm et al. 2011; Kandel and Massey 2002; Terrio 2015; Thorne et al. 2003).[1] They are not the more recently discussed Central American unaccompanied alien children (UAC) or commonly named "unaccompanied minors" leaving their homes due to violence and poverty and/or to reunify with parents (Chavez and Menjivar 2010; Department of Homeland Security 2002; Haddal 2007).[2] More accurately referred to as *independent teenage migrants*, these minors not only travel and cross the U.S.-Mexico border alone; they have left their parents behind to ensure their own and their families' survival and social mobility (Bhabha 2014a; Martinez 2016a). Acting much like adults, they "make choices that express their views about their future preferences" (Bhabha 2014a: 5).

Similar to Josefa, these youths begin their transitions to adulthood long before entering the United States. As children, these Mexican youths learn to balance household and paid labor and schooling to help support their households. By their preteenage and teenage years, many of the youths leave school and work full time to offset their families' financial woes. Like their adult counterparts, by ages fourteen, fifteen, sixteen, or seventeen, these Mexican youths set out for New York City, enticed by the stories of higher wages and abundant work and frustrated by the low wages and sporadic employment that characterize informal work in their communities and elsewhere in Mexico. Once in New York, independent Mexican teenage migrants encounter a socioeconomic context that exploits undocumented adult and underage workers, and they are able to blend in without detection. As undocumented *underage* target earners and independent teenage migrants, the youths dedicate their waking hours to work, not traditional school, so that they may financially support themselves as well as their families back home (Martinez 2016a; Suárez-Orozco and Suárez-Orozco 2001: 29).[3]

A case in point is young Pedro's story. The scars on his caramel-colored hands betrayed the occupational hazards associated with working as a grill cook seventy hours a week at a popular *taqueria* near Columbia University. Nineteen years old at the time of my interview with him, Pedro was approximately the same age as the students who would come in at all hours for lunch, after classes, after parties, and on weekends to avoid bland dining-hall food. Here they would relax and enjoy the semiautonomous statuses that are associated with and deemed appropriate to college-age youths in the United States (Arnett 2004; Goldscheider and DaVanzo 1985). Many of these students carried money that they received from their parents, financial aid, or part-time campus jobs that were often located minutes from their dormitory rooms. While waiting for Pedro, I overheard their discussions about returning home for the Thanksgiving holiday, grateful for the short break during which they would be subject to their parents' questioning and scrutiny before returning to the round-the-clock studying and writing that accompanies the end of a semester. Conversely, Pedro had not been in school since he was twelve, nor had he seen his mother in more than three years: he had left Oaxaca at age sixteen to work and live independently in New York City. Recalling the final days with her before he left for el norte brought an abrupt halt to our interview as his voice broke and tears tumbled down his face.

At the start of the twenty-first century, few New York City residents question seeing young Mexicans such as Pedro on staff at the lowest positions in New York City's service industries. Assumed by most to be baby-faced adults, the youthfulness of these workers has been all but ignored in the name of inexpensive food, clothes, and childcare. While employers extend their "don't ask, don't tell" policies about their employees beyond legal status to include age, the minors themselves operate on their own notions of social time, deeming it appropriate to be out of school, living without their parents, and working full time. Unlike the university students whose responsibilities include attending class—many on their parents' dime—these youths learn at early ages that their responsibilities include making good on their promises to help support their parents and families left behind in Mexico. To honor this, the youths simply keep quiet about their ages and blend in with New York City's newest underclass: undocumented Mexican immigrants.[4]

But in this modern era where international conventions and national as well as state and local laws promise minors particular protections and rights based on notions of protracted dependence associated with those under the age of eighteen, how and why do some Mexican teenage minors both learn to be and become independent by immigrating to work so as to support themselves and their families? Examining the intersections of social reproduction, transnationalism, and age, this book transcends nation-state borders and explores how and why recently arrived Mexican youths such as Pedro leave their parents and schooling in Mexico as teenage minors to arrive in New York City and enter low-status, poorly protected, and exploitative jobs normally reserved for immigrant adults. Caught between both modernization policies that have exacerbated poverty in Mexico—especially among southern rural families—and discourses that have promoted children's extended periods of dependence, Mexican families and minors have adapted and pursued socioeconomic strategies to both survive and secure social mobility for themselves and their families, including youths' extreme relocation to New York City for work (Aitken et al. 2006; Bhabha 2014a, 2014b; Fernandez-Kelly and Massey 2007; Jennings et al. 2006).

Paying attention to critical notions of time and space, this book illustrates the processes and strategies that independent Mexican teenage migrants undertake across their brief lives to pursue survival and social mobility for their households and themselves across borders. With globalization and modernization as backdrops, this book draws upon social reproduction theory, transnational theory, and life course theory to reveal how these Mexican youths come to occupy the interdependent statuses they hold in New York as minors, including teenage migrants, household benefactors, undocumented workers, school leavers, and ultimately, in the words of some, "adults."

UNACCOMPANIED MINORS OR INDEPENDENT MEXICAN TEENAGE MIGRANTS?

During the summer of 2014, nearly seventy thousand mostly Central American child and teenage migrants were apprehended crossing the U.S.-Mexico border—something that brought the issue of unaccompanied minors, or children and teenagers who immigrate to the United States without their parents, to the forefront of the nation's attention (U.S. Customs and Border Patrol 2015b). Although they are officially labeled "unaccompanied" at the time of apprehension, for many youths who were eventually reunified with at least one parent, this label is "confusing" and inaccurate (Byrne and Miller 2012: 19; Department of Homeland Security 2002; Women's Refugee Commission 2009: 7). For instance, in the years just prior to the surge, approximately 35 percent of the unaccompanied minors apprehended by the Department of Homeland Security were reunited with a parent, stepparent, or a parent's partner (Byrne and Miller 2012: 19). This number was closer to 60 percent during surge years (Kelly 2017). In short, while youths immigrating to reunite with parents are unaccompanied for the duration of their journeys and during apprehension and detention, many will most likely resume at least somewhat of an accompanied and dependent status if and when released to at least one parent.[5]

Unlike this aforementioned group, the independent Mexican teenage migrants in this book not only go undetected but also go unaccompanied in a more permanent sense—from the start of their journeys to their arrivals in New York City until they transition to adulthood. Immigrating not to reunite with parents, these youths instead leave them behind so that they can provide financial support for them and their siblings. For one group of youths, this requires living with adult relatives. Arguably, joining these adult kin, including older adult siblings or adult aunts and uncles, could be considered reversing their independent status due to the presence of older, adult individuals who can provide care and assistance in times of need. However, several conditions shape this "care" that precludes the dependence often associated with parental proximity. For one, rules in New York households are already in place as to how expenses are to be divided by employment status but not age. More than just "helping the family out," as long as they are working, youths are expected to divide the costs of rent with other adult members. Second, these adult relatives do not seek sponsorship or legal guardianship.[6] Undetected and lacking legal statuses, both adults and youths prefer to remain out of the purview of the legal system and do not formally petition for either in family courts. Unlike their counterparts who are detected and detained, these immigrant youths are not subject to intervening processes that situate them in tracks of sponsorship or legal guardianship, nor do adult relatives encourage these processes. Lastly, adult relatives may leave or ask the minors to leave the household at any time. Adult kin may return to Mexico without arranging for the minors' care or may even ask them to find alternative accommodations, especially if they fear eviction. In these cases, youths either may remain living with other relatives, some older and some younger, or must find alternative arrangements.

A much smaller group of youths strike out on their own. These minors not only enter the United States without parents or lawful guardians, but they live in New York City with nonkin. Wholly independent, these youths either attach themselves to adults during their journeys to New York City or possess wrinkled slips of paper with the names and phone numbers of people who their parents or other relatives have shared with them who might be able to house them upon arrival in New York. From there, they improvise their living arrangements. For these reasons, both groups of youths—those who live with kin and those who live with nonkin—are referred to as independent Mexican teenage migrants in this book.

Unfortunately, determining their numbers at any given time in New York City, much less the United States, is difficult. Using American Community Survey (ACS) data, other indicators have been utilized as proxies, including matching Mexican nativity and age with (a) incomplete schooling or absence from formal schooling (Fry 2003, 2012; Hirschman 2001) or (b) household composition (i.e., youths living in households with or without their parents; Treschan and Mehrotra 2013).[7] Estimates based on 2010 ACS data placed approximately five thousand independent Mexican teenage migrants in the New York metro area (Fry 2012; Treschan and Mehrotra 2013). Paradoxically, during a period where *overall* Mexican migration declined due to the economic recession, the increased militarization of the U.S.-Mexico border, and deportation, records of apprehended immigrants showed little evidence that Mexican teenagers were deterred from attempting to cross the U.S.-Mexico border (Chishti and Hipsman 2014).[8] Rather, between fiscal years 2009 and 2012, approximately 55,580 Mexican minors attempted to cross but were apprehended. Fiscal years 2013 and 2014 saw the highest numbers of Mexican minor border apprehensions since 2009—17,240 and 15,634, respectively—followed by a drop to 11,926 in 2016 (Kandel 2017; Passel et al. 2012; U.S. Customs and Border Patrol 2013). Reflecting the persistence of Mexican *teenagers'* mobility, in 2013 and 2014, approximately 97 percent of these youths were ages thirteen and older (Krogstad and Gonzalez-Ibarra 2014). Although the Trafficking Victims Protection Reauthorization Act of 2008 (TVPRA), in accordance with the United States' agreement with contiguous countries such as Mexico, mandates a thorough screening of Mexican youths to determine whether repatriation places them at a risk for trafficking, persecution, or overall harm, in far too many cases after apprehension, the youths are oftentimes simply deported, with some dropped off just across the border in dangerous cartel strongholds. In effect, they are simply left to cross the border again (American Immigration Council 2015; Cavendish and Cortazar 2011).

GROWING UP AMID PARADOXES OF MODERNIZATION

And cross again they do. It is wholly unsurprising that independent Mexican teenage migrants attempt this as many times as they need to. Coming of age amid modernization efforts in Mexico, these youths were on the losing end of a bundle of economic policies that, once touted as the panacea to its economic woes, instead disparately impacted Mexico's different regions (Delgado-Wise and Cypher 2007). In particular, NAFTA's bundle of policies, whose broad impact continues to be the subject of argument today, largely benefited the industrialized north, while in the southern states from which most of the youths hail, the economic reforms only increased economic hardships and worsened poverty (Fernandez-Kelly and Massey 2007; Kelly 2001). Simultaneously, the universalization of extended, modern childhoods has been espoused and implemented first through international laws and more locally through educational reform and labor policies, with the law often mandating longer behavioral and financial dependence of children on their parents. Intersecting with traditional, class-based ideas about the organization of life courses in existence in poor Mexican families, the result has pulled the youths in two opposing directions: on the one hand, youths are obliged to assist in alleviating the worsening poverty in their households caused in part by so-called economic reforms. Paradoxically, this does not promote their dependence but rather promotes underage independence—namely, through the performance of waged work (Bey 2003; Jennings et al. 2006). On the other hand, shifting and evolving educational and labor reforms extended youths' periods of dependence with their official mandates demanding compulsory education and youths' exclusion from labor markets. Coming of age in the midst of these "paradoxes of modernization," Mexican youths are forced to make decisions about their households' and their own survival and social mobility—decisions that, for some, promote early immigration.

The following section provides a brief overview of how these paradoxes of Mexico's modernization have affected the lives of poor Mexican youths. While the origins of the policies and laws, as well as their disparate application and impact, will be discussed in further detail in the following chapters, a general discussion of the two diverging forces is provided here.

ECONOMIC MODERNIZATION AND ITS IMPACTS ON POOR MEXICAN YOUTH

The last half of the twentieth century saw Mexico's leaders embrace tenets of modernization. Entering into a series of agreements, these leaders would restructure Mexico's economy through the removal of tariffs and protections afforded to Mexican farmers and workers and by facilitating further penetration of U.S. and other foreign capital into its markets (Alarcon-Gonzalez and McKinley 1999). According to its supporters, this series of economic reforms, including the 1982 General Agreement on Tariffs and Trade (GATT) and 1994 North American Free Trade Agreement (NAFTA) would create millions of jobs for its citizens. It would "lift all boats," or improve the lives of all Mexicans (Delgado-Wise and Cypher 2007).

A more honest assessment is that the results have been lopsided, with successes mostly occurring in Northern Mexico targeted to a small, select group of binational elites and professionals, while southern Mexicans and, in particular, campesinos have witnessed growing rates of underemployment or unemployment, declines in wages, and an overall collapse of their local economies (Delgado-Wise and Cypher 2007; Fernandez-Kelly and Massey 2007; Helper et al. 2006; Kelly 2001; McKinley 2008). While northern Mexico, due in large part to its proximity to the United States, enjoyed increased investment in *maquiladora* (Mexican factory) and commercial sectors, southern Mexico instead endured deepening poverty, the displacement of more than 4.9 million Mexican farmers, and the out-migration of millions of the rural poor (Jennings et al. 2006; Weisbrot et al. 2014).

Critics blame the stipulations of these economic policies, in addition to Mexico's economic crises of 1982 and 1995, for inducing negative outcomes for southern rural Mexicans (Fernandez-Kelly and Massey 2007; Fitting 2011; Kelly 2001). For one, President Salinas's repeal of Article 27 of the Mexican Constitution facilitated the privatization of thousands of previously communally owned hectares of farm land, or *ejidos*. By allowing the purchase of ejidos by foreign investors, these changes meant that poor and indigenous Mexicans were increasingly displaced and local economies destabilized (Perramond 2008). Second, state support for agricultural subsidies, including fertilizer, seed, and feed, were reduced, redirected, or outright eliminated (Fernandez-Kelly and Massey 2007; Kelly 2001; McKinley 2008). Without these subsidies, campesinos could no longer carry out the subsistence farming that had fed their families for generations. For the few who had been able to continue producing small amounts of surplus crops, the last bit of irony arrived in the form of deregulation and the removal of price supports and tariffs. With tariffs lifted, heavily subsidized and industrially produced fruit, grain, and vegetable imports from the United States—including the "long time symbol of *lo mexicano*," corn—flooded the Mexican agricultural market at lower prices (Fitting 2011). Simply outpriced, the remaining small, local Mexican farmers were increasingly unable to compete in the marketplace (Alarcon-Gonzalez and McKinley 1999; Fernandez-Kelly and Massey 2007; McKinley 2008). With rapidly unraveling safety nets, millions of poor southern Mexicans were thrust deeper into economic insecurity and forced to abandon generations-old practices of subsistence and survival (Fernandez-Kelly and Massey 2007).

Born just prior to and during the introduction of NAFTA and hailing from the most affected regions, most of the youths with whom I spoke have firsthand experiences with these injurious outcomes. In these regions already exhibiting high rates of poverty, these so-called economic reforms only exacerbated conditions for many of Mexico's young southern, rural citizens (Fernandez-Kelly and Massey 2007; INEGI 2005). While national poverty rates in Mexico have stubbornly hovered around 50 percent between 2000 and 2012, or during the years in which the majority of the youths migrated, the states from which most of the youths originated—Puebla, Oaxaca, and Guerrero—suffered higher poverty rates of 64 percent, 61 percent and 69 percent, respectively, in 2012 (CEPAL 2013; CONEVAL 2013; Ixel Gonzalez 2013; Verdusco 2013). Other youths resided in municipalities and districts adjacent to Distrito Federal that have received high levels of internal migration from southern areas and exhibit admittedly lower but still alarming rates of poverty. In these areas, including Iztapalapa and Ciudad Nezahualcóyotl, poverty levels have hovered around 37 percent and 38.8 percent, respectively (Ascencio 2004; SEDESOL 2010a, 2014). To subsist, households diversified their survival strategies and incorporated not only women into waged work but also minors (Aitken et al. 2006; Alarcon-Gonzalez and McKinley 1999; Bey 2003; Cos Montiel 2000; Fernandez-Kelly and Massey 2007; Fitting 2011; Jennings et al. 2006; Malkin 2004; Parrado 2005). Whereas youths have generally worked only for their families in the past, the aforementioned neoliberal economic policies obligated youths to increasingly insert themselves into the waged labor market (Cos Montiel 2000; Jennings et al. 2006). But even waged work has not been enough to stave off extreme poverty and/or facilitate social mobility. Surrounded by scarce, low-paying labor opportunities and privy to the wage differential that sits just on the other side of the U.S.-Mexico border, emigration for work in the United States has become a survival strategy not only for adults in previously nontraditional regions of emigration but also for teenage minors (Martinez 2016a; Zenteno et al. 2013).[9]

MODERNIZING DISCOURSES OF CHILDHOOD AND ADOLESCENCE IN MEXICO

As neoliberal economic policies have taken effect, modernizing discourses of childhood and adolescence have also gathered, albeit unevenly, greater traction globally and in Mexico (Bianet-Castellanos 2010; Jennings et al. 2006; Parrado 2005; Ruddick 2003). Eager to show off their commitment to various so-called modernizing efforts and models of childhood as constituted in international children's rights treaties—including the United Nation's 1989 Convention on the Rights of the Child—Mexican officials are restructuring how childhood is experienced in Mexico by extending childhood dependence, even if regions and families lack the resources to support them (Levinson 2001; Ruddick 2003; Zapata 2013). Established through a variety of social institutions and means, including educational and labor reforms, modern discourses of childhood and age-graded dependence have been taking root in recent, as well as not-so-recent, years in Mexico (Levinson 2001).

Parceled into structural adjustment policies, the 1992 National Agreement on the Modernization of Basic Education (ANMEB) and then, a year later, the 1993 *Ley General de Educación*, or General Education Law, have perhaps been most effective in "recreat[ing] child subjects" and reshaping contemporary life rhythms in Mexico (Cole and Durham 2007: 8; see also Gutek 2006; Levinson 2001). The expansion of compulsory education from six to nine years in 1993 (or from the completion of *primaria*, the equivalent of elementary school, until the completion of *secundaria*, the equivalent of junior high school in the United States) extended the years in which Mexican youths were legally obligated to spend time away from both the household and the full-time labor market to ensure that two objectives of modernity would be met.[10] For one, expanded schooling would guarantee a skilled labor force for rapidly expanding maquiladora and commercial industries (Levinson 2001). Second, although discussed less frequently, this mandate also ensured the fulfillment of rapidly diffusing global discourses of childhood by requiring youths' school attendance through approximately age fourteen. This continued attendance would most likely ensure their absence from the full-time labor market and safeguard continued dependence on adults (Levinson 2001; Mayer and Schoepflin 1989).[11]

Mexican child labor laws are also essential to shaping extended periods of dependence and protection in the lives of Mexican youths. In the 1962 federal labor law reforms, the age of labor market eligibility was increased from age twelve to age fourteen, with youth workers between the ages of fourteen and sixteen subject to special vigilance, including prohibition from employment in dangerous or immoral conditions.[12] Total daily and weekly work hours were also regulated, with youths under the age of sixteen prohibited from working (a) more than six hours a day (which included one hour of rest), (b) on Sundays, and (c) overtime (CONAPRED 2010; de Buen 1980). Emphasizing the youths' lack of autonomy, the reforms also required youths under the age of sixteen to obtain the written permission of their parents or legal guardians in order to work. For youths older than age sixteen but younger than age eighteen, restrictions still exist. These youths are forbidden to work without proof of secundaria completion and medical examination and are forbidden from working in dangerous settings (Ley Federal de Trabajo 2015). Then, until age eighteen, Mexican minors are subject to laws shaped by modern, age-graded presumptions about their physical and emotional strengths, need for protection, and dependence.

However, much like Mexico's economic reforms, these educational and labor policies are unequally enforced and result in unequal outcomes. While better-resourced regions, including urban areas, have been able to enjoy higher rates of secundaria completion and lower rates of child labor, high-poverty areas such as the rural south continue to lag in both. Official national dropout rates for youths ages fifteen and over in Mexico are approximately 36 percent, but the states from which the youths highlighted in this book and their families largely originated—Puebla, Oaxaca, and Guerrero—all possess dropout rates approaching or surpassing 50 percent, or 44.6 percent, 51.8 percent, and 50 percent, respectively. Distrito Federal and its surrounding districts also possess high dropout rates; this metro area ranked third highest in dropout rates among Mexico's urban areas (CONAPO 2010a, 2010b, 2010c; SSP 2011). Unsurprisingly, youths from the rural south also appear in the labor market at higher rates and younger ages than their northern counterparts. With a national total of approximately 3.6 million child laborers, roughly 70 percent hail from rural regions (Perez-Garcia 2009). Puebla, Oaxaca, and Guerrero exhibit among the highest official rates of child labor: 17.3 percent, 17.5 percent, and 20.0 percent, respectively, or more than double the rates of northern states such as Chihuahua and Baja California. Distrito Federal's districts and surrounding municipalities also possess high rates; in 2015, Iztapalapa exhibited the highest rates of child labor, while 9.2 percent of all Neza youths under the age of seventeen worked (Perez-Garcia 2009; Suarez 2015; UNICEF 2010). With insufficient resources to support both extended school going and the foregoing of child labor, especially in the face of exacerbated poverty, Mexico's modern discourses of childhood seem sadly irrelevant for many poor rural and urban youths.

This is the paradox in which poor Mexican youths find themselves. Those who become independent teenage migrants grow up between contradictory sets of modernization policies and discourses—between the proverbial rock and a hard place, as it were. On the one hand, in the name of economic integration, neoliberal economic policies have left poor Mexicans with little choice but to increase their reliance on all household members, young and old, as wage earners. On the other hand, recent universalizing calls for extended, modern childhoods have mandated increased stays in schooling and delayed entry into labor markets. In a general context of increasing rural and, in some cases, urban poverty, the social programs and cash transfers meant to offset the costs of lost child labor (a consequence of the extension of mandated "free" basic education into upper grades) are simply insufficient to guarantee families' and youths' adherence to these laws. Instead, forced to reconsider their strategies of survival and social mobility, households rely on the early entry of minors into the waged labor market, early exit from schooling, and in the case of some poor Mexican youths, early emigration. Simply stated, poor Mexican youths are excluded from the promises of modernized childhoods and adolescences; "opting" to actively facilitate their families' survival and social mobility, some youths instead leave to continue their early transitions to adulthood in New York City.

THEORETICAL FRAMEWORK

This book puts a transnational life-course spin on social reproduction theory to illustrate how, beginning at young ages, these youths are disrupting, both voluntarily and less voluntarily, imitations of *their parents'* class positions and what this means for their survival and social mobility within and across two bordering nation-states. In doing so, I promote an understanding of social reproduction as it occurs in the youths' lives and across nation-state borders and demonstrate how—unlike those examples provided in the seminal studies of youths and social reproduction in Paul Willis's *Learning to Labor* and Jay MacLeod's *Ain't No Makin' It* that look no further than their immediate contexts—independent Mexican teenage migrants end up not in the work their parents filled in Mexico but rather in exploitative, low-paying service jobs typically reserved for adults in the United States.

Usually considered separately, the three distinct theories that I draw from—life course, social reproduction, and transnational theory—each partially explain the processes that lead to the youths' statuses as independent Mexican teenage migrants in New York City. First and foremost, social reproduction theory attempts to explain how social relations of society and inequalities are reproduced from one generation to the next (Bourdieu 1977b; MacLeod 1995; Morrow and Torres 1995). Moving beyond economic determinism, one of the leading reproduction theorists, Pierre Bourdieu, suggests that social reproduction is predicated on cultural reproduction and vice versa and that by examining everyday cultural practices and how individuals and structures interact to produce them, we can better understand how and why social classes are reproduced. To illustrate this argument, Bourdieu has demonstrated that by rewarding the dominant classes' cultural capital with superior academic placement and credentials—something that in turn translates into better jobs and higher economic wages—educational institutions both honored and reproduced upper-class culture; simultaneously, the cultural capital of lower classes was devalued, and they were provided with inferior rewards (MacLeod 1995: 12).

To theorize the ways in which these youths experience social reproduction, I focus less on cultural capital and instead draw from Bourdieu's repertoire of other concepts, including habitus and fields, that along with other forms of capital, economic and social, help trace how youths' undertake practices such that [(habitus) (capital) + field = practice] (Bourdieu 1985). To begin with, habitus can be thought of as sets of class-based, durable, and long-lasting socialized and socializing systems of perception, conception, and action that provide templates for people's future actions and ways of doing. Organized previously by other structures and agents, these systems are internalized and embodied by persons and then acted upon in ways that appear natural to themselves and others (Bourdieu 1990, 2002; Pallas and Jennings 2009; Swartz 1997). Individuals' habitus then orient them toward the acquisition or exchange of particular types of capital or resources as well as the fields in which they will be exchanged and over which they struggle.

For the youths highlighted in this book, economic and social capital appeared to hold high values. While economic capital can be converted directly into money and institutionalized into property rights, social capital—although also convertible into economic capital—is a resource that exists in individuals' social networks that, "when activated, enable[s] [individuals] to accomplish their goals or empower themselves in [some] meaningful way[s]" (Bourdieu 1977b; Portes 1998; Stanton-Salazar 2001: 265; Valenzuela 1999). Acting on their habitus, these Mexican youths acquire, assess, and then activate this capital as well as gravitate toward particular fields, or hierarchically structured social spaces across which capital is exchanged, accumulated, and even struggled over (Atkinson 2016; Bourdieu 1984). These feats of activating, exchanging, and contesting capital and its values and meanings across fields are largely considered as *practice* (Friedmann 2002; Pallas and Jennings 2009). As a result of these practices, class positions in the field overall then become reproduced or disrupted.

Characterized as games, the exchanges of and struggles over capital within fields are preceded by doxa (or presuppositions toward particular fields and positions over others, such that these "games" are worth playing) and then, subsequently, illusio (or the actual "playing" or investing in the games; Bourdieu 1990; Bourdieu and Wacquant 1992: 98; Swartz 1997). Doxa, Bourdieu (1990) states, is where habitus meet fields, or where one subscribes to the particular orders and rules at hand so that activities in particular fields appear to be natural. For example, although a six-year-old will not even ask about employment in the United States, in Guerrero, still one of Mexico's poorest states, more than 12 percent of children ages six to thirteen in 2011 sought underage access to the labor market. While some may have been forced to engage in child labor against their will, others may possess doxa or find it to be a "natural activity" and, as in the cases of the youths with whom I spoke, actively sought employment for themselves. It is the externalization of this internalized, natural activity, or *acting* on the belief that the rules are worth following, that defines illusio. Here is an example of illusio: Some Mexican youths, now provided with information about potential jobs or capital, decide to use the information to seek and then obtain employment (Rosati et al. 2012). Once in this labor market field, these youths invest in the labor, or demonstrate illusio to obtain particular types of work. By engaging in this labor, the youths are exhibiting a belief that these particular rules, positions, and ultimately fields are worth engaging with at their ages.

The struggles across fields or "games" that occur after investment are serious and either won or lost (Bourdieu 1977b, 1984, 1990; Levinson 2001). While individual fields and their positions are usually examined separately, overall "winning" and/or "losing" of these games, or upward and downward mobility, must take into account the *entire tournament*, or the multitude of fields in which individuals interact, from start to finish. Considered in this way, victory across the games denotes upward mobility or a disruption of current class positions, whereas class stagnation or, worse, downward mobility signifies an inability to acquire and exchange valued capital across the fields in which individuals "play" (Atkinson 2016; Bourdieu 1977b, 1990; MacLeod 1995; Swartz 1997; Young 2004).

By overlaying transnational theory onto social reproduction theory, just how *transnational migration* can and, for some, does, affect game play can be better understood. Some scholars suggest that migration, already deemed a cultural practice, "reproduces and even exacerbates class, gender, and regional inequalities" (Guarnizo 1997: 281). This may result from migration's potential by-product, "transnational living," or the conditions in which independent teenage migrants are locally embedded and where they engage in a matrix of relationships (social, cultural, economic) across borders before, during, and after migration (Glick-Schiller et al. 1992; Guarnizo 1997, 2003; Kandel and Massey 2002; Smith 2006). By focusing on the youths' realities of migration and transnational living and the practices generated by their own as well as others' mobility, this group's particular experiences of social reproduction are brought into focus, permitting a better understanding of their relationships and the ways in which the youths engage in them across borders to disrupt or reproduce their class positions (Guarnizo 1997, 2003).

Lastly, life course theory seeks to explain how people live out their lives from birth to death, specifically emphasizing how time impacts and is impacted by age-graded relationships embedded in social, cultural, and historical contexts (Clausen 1986; Elder et al. 2003; Fry 2003; Fussell 2005; Pallas 1993, 2007). These age-graded relationships also shape the elements of social reproduction, such as habitus, capital, doxa, and illusio, as well as field positions. All may be experienced dissimilarly at different times in the youths' lives. For example, a poor, five-year-old Mexican may be oriented toward learning the alphabet so as to be rewarded with a sticker at school, whereas a sixteen-year-old may be interested in learning information about local *coyotes*, or human smugglers, in order to prepare to migrate.

Although all three theories utilize history, time, and/or space to explain individual and group outcomes, they have mostly remained separate from each other in dialogue (Bourdieu 1977b, 1990; Bourdieu and Passeron 1990; Elder 1994; Guarnizo 1997; Swartz 1997). By considering them together, a more complete picture emerges of the youths' efforts to "get ahead" and how they are informed by age and class norms developed in and carried across both Mexico and the United States. As such, we gain a better understanding of how and where and at what ages and in what spaces immigrant youths may simultaneously disrupt and replicate local and transnational class inequalities (Levitt and Glick Schiller 2004; Malkin 2004). By focusing on a group of Mexican youths growing up in this particular era of aggressive globalization, this book demonstrates how age- and class-context-based ideas about survival and social mobility influence the important, life-altering decisions that take them to their positions in New York City.

INSERTING IMMIGRATION AND THE LIFE COURSE INTO SOCIAL REPRODUCTION THEORY

By bringing these three theories together, game playing and, by default, winning and/or losing are reconfigured. For one, the time during which individuals "play"—from start to finish, or throughout their life courses, including childhood—is more closely considered (Boehm et al. 2011: 11; Hirschfeld 2002). While the game may start as early as birth or one's early years, the game's end occurs predominantly with the stabilization of class positions, as determined through an assessment of capital accumulation and statuses, over time (Bourdieu and Wacquant 1992: 99). This often coincides with adulthood, a life-course stage that, for the youths discussed here, occurs in a context different from their origins in Mexico, under different legal circumstances, and possesses different meanings.

Second, although critics argue that Bourdieu does not sufficiently consider agency or the significance of "individual autonomy" in relation to structure, he does not deny that "agents face options, exert initiative and make decisions *within contexts of domination*" (Bourdieu and Wacquant 1992: 24; see also Bourdieu 1977b; Kitossa 2012; MacLeod 1995; Shanahan et al. 1997; Swartz 1997). Instead of imagining classes of individuals acting in accordance with rules or, alternatively, their own unrestricted agency, Bourdieu instead asks us to consider that they are planful "choice-makers" who *strategize*, or engage in, particular actions in relation to the age-graded dispositions (habitus) and capital that they possess and the opportunities or constraints (fields) that they encounter (Bourdieu 1977b, 1990; Clausen 1991; Dinovitzer et al. 2003; Elder 1994; Swartz 1997; Shanahan et al. 1997). Class-based and interest-oriented, as well as age-graded and contextualized, the enacted strategies may be preferred or understood by those within them, not by those outside of the milieus where the individuals find themselves (Bourdieu 1977b; Kitossa 2012; MacLeod 1995; Young 2004).

For independent Mexican teenage immigrants, this detail is particularly important. Traditionally, underage immigrants have been characterized as dependents simply following adult plans and are often ignored as "potential migration decision makers [and doers] in families" (Tyrell 2011: 23; see also Boehm et al. 2011). They have not been sufficiently discussed as planful, or possessing and enacting their own agency or "ability to exert one's will and act in the world" (Boehm et al. 2011: 7; see also Bhabha 2014a). Given various choices, including remaining in their home countries, engaging in internal migration, or even delaying immigration until adulthood, these independent Mexican teenage migrants have arguably exerted some agency, albeit within structural constraints, toward developing and acting on strategies that allow them to seek "various key elements of a rights respecting life absent in home countries"—namely, economic survival and social mobility (Bhabha 2014a: 5).

It is one's habitus, shaped by class as well as region and understandings of social time, that also orients individuals toward certain types of capital, or differentially valued forms of power, as well as doxa and illusio. In existing sociological literature about children and school-age teenagers, cultural and social capital are predominantly regarded as resources based in networks (which include parents and teachers as well as peers) and activated and exchanged within age-appropriate school settings (Brittain 2002; Leonard 2005; MacLeod 1995; Stanton-Salazar 2001; Valenzuela 1999). In the cases of independent Mexican teenage migrants who are seeking to migrate and enter into the labor market, however, discussions of capital, especially social capital, include as their topics membership and investment in networks mostly composed of adults *outside of school*—adults who, in turn, are able to provide them with information and resources so that they may perform "unchildlike" behaviors and acts (i.e., working in Mexico, migrating without their parents, and obtaining full-time employment in both Mexico and the United States). For example, a fourteen-year-old in rural Mexico may believe that earning money by performing strenuous labor at his age is perfectly normal and, as such, will do so. Meanwhile, a fourteen-year-old who, although from the same town and class, left Mexico at age two and now resides in Brooklyn, New York, may regard these same activities, due to differences in age norms in the United States, as inappropriate (Bourdieu and Passeron 1990; Friedmann 2002; Guarnizo 1997).

GAME-PLAYING IN LOCAL AND TRANSNATIONAL FIELDS

Whereas previous considerations of social reproduction, especially in the lives of youths, have conceptualized game-playing and fields as mostly context bound (nation-states, cities, communities), immigration provides another dimension to class replication or mobility by introducing cross-border game-playing (see MacLeod 1995; Stanton-Salazar 2001; Valenzuela 1999). For youths who arrive in New York at later ages, "place-bound" approaches become less relevant. Prior to migration and then as immigrants afterward, the youths are instead transnational actors who not only receive and send social and economic remittances across differently structured contexts but physically move across spaces themselves (Golbert 2001; Guarnizo 1997; Levitt 2001; Maira and Soep 2005). Instead, immigration forces one to consider social reproduction as occurring both simultaneously and separately in and across disparately structured fields located across and within nation-state borders. Pointing out these practices is essential to understanding the reasons behind the behaviors and practices that independent Mexican teenage migrants perform.

The first issue to consider regarding immigrant youths' transborder social reproduction is whether the fields in sending and receiving communities are synchronous or asynchronous, or more specifically, whether the ages at which individuals are expected to enter particular fields, employ particular strategies, and achieve particular statuses or positions—not to mention the values of capital—are the same or different in both contexts. If social time for the two contexts in which the fields are located is different, individual success or failure may be compromised. For example, although it is illegal, engaging in waged work at age ten is often overlooked in Mexico; although also illegal in the United States, it is far less acceptable and could result in, at the very least, a call from New York's Office of Children and Family Services. The same situation applies to teenage minors. Although restricted by official labor laws in Mexico, enforcement at these ages is often lax. It can be argued that similar levels of enforcement exist in New York City, yet for younger teenagers, tougher enforcement does indeed exist. As a result of these differences in social time across contexts after migration, some youths may not only be unable to immediately enter fields and employ strategies that they have employed in the past, but they may also face serious consequences if found acting on their previous understandings of social time rather than those practiced within the local fields.

Second, we must also consider how immigration and, in this case, independent and undocumented minor immigration reconfigure the fields engaged with, including how they are played and the positions available within fields. For undocumented and independent immigrant youths who remain connected to their homelands and households, how they maintain their relationships and, more specifically, how capital is accumulated and exchanged, both across and within nation-state borders, are all important in explaining social reproduction. One can consider this in two ways. In the first, immigration may extend the boundaries of what is considered a field beyond nation-state borders, and new class positions found in receiving communities are incorporated into the fields of the original class positions—that is, the fields become transnational. This has been captured in the nicknames given to geographies, such as "Puebla York," "Neza York," or "Manhatitlan" (Kugel 2004; Smith 2006). Building on the idea of transnational fields, the new class positions that migration brings may also be considered in reference to those available in the environments that are left behind (Lee and Zhou 2014; Shanin 1978; Vermeulen 2000). Hailing from communities where high out-migration has extended the boundaries of the fields across nation-state borders, even stay-at-home youths believe themselves to be no longer limited to the class positions and related pathways found in their immediate communities (Brittain 2002; Glick-Schiller et al. 1995; Golbert 2001; Malkin 2004). For example, while the rural youths who still resided in Mexico often named being a campesino as the most likely, albeit undesirable, job in their communities, they increasingly viewed the restaurant industry jobs found and largely held by nearly 1.4 million undocumented immigrants in the United States as attainable or possible future, "better" occupations for themselves (Passel and Cohn 2015; Tareen 2017). As discussed in chapter 5, this notion of "better," however, is complicated by the conditions in which they work.

We can also consider the ways in which immigration enables youths to pursue or not pursue survival and social mobility for themselves and their families in either their origin or their settlement communities or both. As will be further discussed in chapter 2, independent Mexican teenage migrants not only support themselves in New York City but also support their families in Mexico. In doing this, the youths make important decisions about how and where (doxa) they will engage in illusio. Youths may bypass particular fields and positions associated with social mobility in the United States, such as the educational field, and remain in lower positions in order to facilitate their families'—and in the future, their own—higher field positions in their Mexican locales. For example, whereas some Mexican youths may bypass schooling in New York City, their remittances may pay for the schooling of their younger siblings back home or even their own schooling upon return. Conversely, decisions to invest in or pursue social mobility in New York may adversely impact the survival and social mobility of their families in Mexico. Simply put, the youths' game playing in one national context affects the game playing in the other.

Of course, the youths' legal statuses significantly impact their ability to play the game and the positions they can acquire across multiple fields. For example, ideas about and then actual entry into the U.S. labor market are shaped by the youths' legal status, as they are relegated to only a limited set of positions in the secondary labor market. This also restricts their access to only particular types of lower-valued economic, social, and cultural capital that can be exchanged in other fields. For example, low wages in the U.S. labor market impact the type and conditions of housing they can access, the amounts they can send back home, and when including the long hours necessitated by low salaries, even whether they can attend school in New York.

TRANSITIONING TO ADULTHOOD ACROSS BORDERS

Their game playing also has significant implications for their transitions to adulthood and the outcomes of those transitions. Transitions to adulthood—commonly understood as comprising five markers—may also be considered in relation to the entry of and exit from particular fields, the transitioning from one position to another in those fields, and ultimately the experiencing of social reproduction or mobility. The five markers long associated with transitioning to adulthood—completing school, entering the labor market full time, leaving one's parental home, marrying, and having children (Fussell and Furstenberg 2005; Hogan 1978; Jackson and Berkowitz 2005; Marini et al. 1987; Marini 1984a; Osgood et al. 2005; Pallas 1993; Shanahan et al. 2005)—may correspond to varying degrees of participation and capital accumulation in fields. For example, leaving school can also be understood as leaving the educational field. Transitioning from unpaid intern to paid, full-time employee may denote not only a marker of completion but also a transition in position and in one's labor trajectory.

However, not all marker completions of transitions to adulthood are equal. Rather, the amount of capital one possesses at the time of marker completion bears great consequences for not only the speed and quality of completion of one's transition to adulthood but also whether it will be accompanied by social mobility. For example, compared to an individual who "completes" school (or leaves the educational field) prior to concluding high school, concluding one's schooling with a college degree not only increases the chances of completing another marker, entering full-time work, but is also associated with greater valued amounts of human, social, and cultural capital that may be exchanged for a better full-time job and/or higher wages or a higher position in the labor market and greater chances of occupational and social mobility across the life course (Gandara and Contreras 2009). However, those leaving high school without graduating may find difficulty securing employment and may be burdened with suppressed, stagnant wages over the course of their lives. To this day, college graduates are more likely to earn higher wages and at a steeper slope over the course of their lives than those with less education (Day and Newberger 2002).

As such, how and when youth transition to adulthood, or the sequences and timings of marker completions, also vary by class and context. Considered in light of earlier discussions about the impact of age and migration on capital acquisition and exchange, or illusio—especially as they relate to field participation—independent Mexican teenage migrants not only begin their transitions to adulthood at earlier ages than youths in the United States but also experience them differently (Fussell 2004b; Giorguli Saucedo 2011; Settersten 2003). For example, until 2015, the Mexican labor market was organized so that fourteen-year-old youths could obtain full-time employment in certain sectors with proof of a secundaria degree and medical records, a feature that is all but unheard of in the United States (U.S. Department of Labor 2010). Encountering social institutions in New York that operate on differently timed exits and entries—namely, schools and labor markets—the experiences of independent Mexican teenage migrants continue to diverge from those of many similarly aged youths, especially those who are native born in New York City. In the United States to work and committed to sending significant amounts of money back home, these youths have little interest in reversing previously completed markers—such as, for example, school completion—that may have been "normal" in their communities but are "off-time" in New York City (Burton 1996; Hagestad and Neugarten 1985).

The transitions to adulthood of independent teenage Mexican migrants versus youths found in the United States may also differ in other ways. For example, independent Mexican teenage migrants discussed an additional marker to depict their transitions to adulthood: wealth transfer to their parents.[13] Seemingly in accordance with the values of interdependence and familism found in Mexican families, this marker has been excluded from sociological discussions about transitions to adulthood in Mexico and the United States, and instead, sociologists have mostly adhered to the Western model of the five aforementioned markers (Fussell 2005; Parrado 2005; Salas and de Oliviera 2009; Wong 2008).

Additionally, as life-course scholars have reported decreased standardization of twenty-first-century transitions to adulthood, independent teenage Mexican migrants generally completed the first three markers in sequential order without experiences of marker reversal—such as reentering full-time schooling after leaving it—and appear on track to complete the final two markers in order: marriage or *juntando* and children (Shanahan 2000; Waters et al. 2011). Complementing these sequences and reflecting trends in the United States, youths also draw from subjective interpretations of adulthood, such as possessing feelings of responsibility and so on, to describe their transitions to adulthood (Arnett 2004; Gonzales 2011). A further discussion of their subjective understandings of becoming adults follows in chapter 6.

To understand if, how, and why these youths disrupt or do not disrupt social reproduction, all the aforementioned must be taken into consideration. The age structuring of the various contexts in which independent Mexican teenage migrants pursue social mobility must be considered in relation to their communities of origin as well as within the United States. Much like Lee and Zhou's (2014) recent methodological recommendation that second-generation immigrant status attainment be measured not by where the generation in question ends up but where, in relation to their parents, they started, this book recommends that one consider the "entire tournament"—not only the multitude of fields but also the geographies where independent teenage Mexican migrants and their parents start these "games" (Mexico) and where the youths currently live (New York City)—when regarding their own survival and social mobility.

Using a telescope metaphor, if the scope of practices under consideration is simultaneously broadened and narrowed—broadened to consider class relations as spanning across the U.S.-Mexico border and narrowed to consider only the range of class positions in Mexico or the United States—two different conclusions emerge. In the former, not only are these teenagers not occupying the same jobs or class positions as their parents in Mexico, but they also face, in their own words, despite undeniable exploitation, better pay and conditions than those found in their communities. Due to higher pay, they also calculate that when and if they return to Mexico as young adults, they can occupy higher-class positions than their parents had in their communities. Coming full circle, these youths believe themselves to be disrupting social reproduction.

However, considering the life trajectories of previous generations of Mexican immigrants, it is worth narrowing the scope of vision to examine class relations as they exist only within the context of the United States. In doing so, we see that this wave of independent Mexican teenage migrants occupies positions that have historically been filled by previous waves of unskilled, undocumented adult Mexican laborers. Emigrating from and arriving at new locales, these youths enter a more recently enlarged occupational niche for immigrants: the service industry. However, the ranges of class positions that they occupy are not new, and independent Mexican teenage migrants will join the United States' newest "underclass" (Massey 2007; Portes 2007). In other words, much like the "working class youths who obtain working class jobs," poor undocumented Mexican youths are obtaining the types of jobs that have been reserved for poor adult Mexican immigrants for over a hundred years: low status, low paying, and exploitative (Willis 1977). With current struggles over pathways to citizenship and aggressive deportation tactics further dashing the hopes that these youths, now young adults, could obtain legal relief, independent Mexican teenage migrants had no reason to believe that they would enjoy certainty regarding residency and life in the United States at any time in the future. Aware of the steel ceilings that limited their ladders of social mobility in New York City, they instead viewed their ladders as arching back to their communities in Mexico, where the money as well as other capital they gained while working in New York, they believed, could guarantee them and their families improved lives, careers, and social positions. As they age, however, their movements often become less certain. After receiving news of low salaries and/or chronic unemployment in Mexico and prepared to embark on family formation, youths are compelled to rethink their original plans regarding return to their homeland.

RESEARCH SETTINGS

This book is based on data collected within and across the sending-receiving context of Puebla and New York but also in New York City with youths from additional states in Mexico. Well documented in Robert C. Smith's groundbreaking ethnography *Mexican New York*, migration from Puebla to New York began in the 1920s and accelerated in the 1990s, as did migration from other locales (Galvez 2010: 11; Smith 2006). Since then, more than 50 percent of the foreign-born Mexican population in New York City hails from Puebla, while other largely rural southern states, including Guerrero and Oaxaca, as well as the urban metropolis known as Distrito Federal, account for the remaining numbers of foreign-born Mexicans (CONAPO 2010; Cortina 2003; Martinez-Leon and Smith 2003; Smith 2006).

Within Puebla, I conducted fieldwork in Valle de San Benito de los Lagos (the name of the site is a pseudonym), which, unlike the more often-discussed region of Mixteca Poblana, did not experience accelerated migration to New York City until *after* the passage of the Immigration Reform and Control Act of 1986 while implementation of NAFTA was intensifying (Binford 2003; Marroni 2003; Smith 2006). While Mixteca had exhibited signs of accelerated migration since the 1960s, Valle de San Benito de los Lagos and its communities lagged behind and instead remained agricultural centers (Binford 2003; Marroni

2009). By the 1980s, however, economic restructuring abruptly began to change the generations-old practices of small farm production (Binford 2003). The erosion of subsidies, as well as the arrival of cheaper foreign imports, all but erased the prospect of maintaining long-held family practices, and parents increasingly understood that times were changing. By the mid-2000s, the catchphrase "un migrante en cada hijo te dio," or "you were given an immigrant in each son," underscored the region's transformation. No longer able to survive on family crops, families looked to sons to become immigrants and send remittances home (Dominguez 2006, qtd. in Marroni 2009).[14]

Within Valle de San Benito de los Lagos, the two fieldwork sites, San Pedro (pseudonym) and San Valentín (pseudonym), are representative of other rural sending communities in Mexico; they exhibit noteworthy quantitative and qualitative indicators of high levels of poverty and out-migration.[15] Both communities rank highly in relation to levels of social exclusion, such as populations over the age of fifteen with incomplete basic education, populations without access to health care, and households without access to clean water or electricity and with dirt floors (SEDESOL 2010a, 2010b). Although San Valentín possesses a slightly longer history of out-migration to the New York City metro area, in both communities modern houses constructed with *migradolares*, or remittances, were immediately visible and stood in stark contrast to houses that appeared to be untouched by migration. Immigrant households were made of concrete with linoleum floors and often possessed covered patios and iron gates, while households that were noticeably less developed did not seem to enjoy an influx of economic remittances. Most of these homes were composed of one or two large rooms made of mud-caked walls and dirt floors and were covered with aluminum roofs.[16] Because of its lengthier history as a sending community, it also appeared as if San Valentín residents were more able than San Pedro residents to extend remittance investments beyond household needs and apply them toward small businesses. These small businesses included restaurants, an internet center, and countless small grocery stores. Lastly, the absence of teenagers and young adults, especially males, was palpable in both towns. Supplementing my observations, several teachers confided that the town would lose many of its young males in the days after secundaria graduation. Finished with compulsory school, these youths would leave their homes to seek their fortunes in el norte.[17]

New York City has seen dramatic increases in its foreign-born Mexican population, from Puebla as well as the other aforementioned states and regions, for the last thirty years (Rivera-Batiz 2004; Binford 2003; Marroni 2009; Smith 2003; Zuñiga and Leon-Hernandez 2006). Whereas in 1990, the total Mexican population in New York totaled a little more than 58,000, by 2010, official U.S. Census estimates of the Mexican population totaled nearly 350,000, but due to its significant undercounted, undocumented population, scholars place the population numbers as being closer to 600,000 (Bergad 2013; Galvez 2010; Treschan and Mehrotra 2013).

Arguably, however, this migration could not have occurred without earlier waves of migration that began some seventy years prior. As early as the 1920s, Mexican immigrants were arriving from the Yucatan to settle in New York City (Smith 2006, 2003). Nearly twenty years later, substantial flows of migration from Mexico began in earnest, lasting until the mid-1960s. These flows were composed predominantly of Mexican males who hailed from a handful of southern towns in Puebla found in the Mixteca region (Smith 2006). During the next phase, from the mid-1960s to the mid-1980s, Robert Smith (2006: 21) writes, the "first appreciable number of women" joined the pool of sojourners from Mexico to seek a better fortune.

By the third phase of migration, spanning from the mid-1980s to the mid-1990s, Poblano migration had spread from Valle de San Benito de los Lagos (Marroni 2009; Smith 2006). A failing Mexican economy, combined with the passage of comprehensive immigration legislation—that is, the Immigration Reform and Control Act (IRCA)—more mature social networks spanning transnationally across the New York and Mexico border, and an elastic New York City labor market all converged to create the ideal conditions for Mexican migration and settlement in New York City (Galvez 2010; Smith 2006). Several scholars cite the amnesty provision included in the 1986 IRCA legislation as the most important reason for this growth. With numbers trailing those of foreign-born Dominicans, Mexicans composed the second-largest group of ethnic immigrants in New York to apply for amnesty under these provisions. As a result, southern Mexican towns and communities witnessed an unprecedented exodus of women (and their children) to New York City, sponsored by their husbands, who were already living there (Smith 2006). Followed by NAFTA-driven migration IRCA facilitated the creation of a sizable Mexican community in New York City. Comprising approximately 14.3 percent of the Latino population in New York, Mexicans are poised to surpass both Puerto Ricans and Dominicans as the largest Latino population in New York City and the northeastern region by the 2020s (Bergad 2011a).

While being careful not to turn the Mexican population in New York into a monolithic entity, it is important to note that 42.4 percent of the population is U.S. born, while 57.6 percent of the Mexican-origin population is foreign born, with 6.1 percent naturalized citizens (Bergad 2011a). In 2010, Mexican foreign-born mothers accounted for the second largest numbers of births, falling ever so slightly behind Dominican mothers, something that also helps account for growth in U.S.-born Mexicans. Settling mostly into areas with other Spanish-speaking residents, Mexicans have established communities in all five boroughs, with ethnic enclaves found in Corona–Jackson Heights, Queens, and Sunset

Park, Brooklyn, followed by smaller enclaves in the Bronx, Manhattan, and Staten Island.

RESEARCH METHODS

The findings in this book are drawn from a qualitative case study conducted between 2006 and 2009 and 2013 and 2015 in and across two high-out-migration communities in Puebla, Mexico, and New York City. Originally designed to interrogate why some recently arrived, unauthorized Mexican immigrant teenagers remained outside of traditional school systems and others did not, over time the study evolved so as to better explain and understand the reasons a particular cohort of Mexican teenage minors immigrated without their parents. As unaccompanied status and independence distinguished those who remained out of school from those who dropped in, the focus of the study shifted to research as to how and why these Mexican teenagers—those who had arrived without their parents—challenged Western notions about age by immigrating, working, and ultimately remaining outside traditional schooling.

In both Puebla and New York City, the primary mode of data collection consisted of life history interviews, but in Puebla, I also performed participant observations.[18] In addition to conducting my own data collection in Puebla, I hired and trained a high school student there, and in New York City, several university students and a community worker were retained who, except for two individuals, were not eligible for the study but generously volunteered to help recruit and/or conduct interviews. Together, we completed eighty-one interviews with Mexican teenagers and adults who either planned to immigrate to New York City without legal authorization as minors or had immigrated as undocumented minors.

The first stage of the case study was conducted during the summer of 2006 in Puebla. During two and a half months, I shuttled between San Pedro and San Valentín, spending at least eight hours a day and six days a week in either town or the closest urban center where some youths were employed. Across the sites and with the assistance of several youths, I interviewed and observed eighteen Mexican teenagers between the ages of thirteen and seventeen who identified themselves as prospective immigrants to New York City. Conducted in Spanish, our interviews lasted anywhere from one to two hours. Participants recounted their lives, both in their immediate communities and elsewhere, including schooling, work, family, and migration. Also recounted were visits, phone calls, and letters with family and friends residing in New York City. As a participant observer, I sat in on activities with the youths at secundaria and preparatoria (high school) graduation parties and elsewhere in more mundane settings where they performed housework or played basketball in the plaza. Findings from this stage of the study shed light on the ways in which a "culture of migration" shapes ideas about leaving Mexico to work or go to school in New York (Kandel and Massey 2002; Macias 1990). These findings allowed me to tweak my interview questions and methods in New York City so that I could more accurately capture the premigration factors that led to Mexican teenage migrants entering into the labor market or school system in New York City. In addition, living in Puebla and developing a familiarity with the area increased my credibility and helped me develop trust when recruiting and interviewing participants in New York City.

Between 2007 and 2009, I conducted the second stage of my study. My research assistants and I interviewed thirty-five recently arrived Mexican immigrant teenagers in New York City. Because the study had originally been designed around the question of school going—why some recently arrived Mexican youths dropped into school while others did not—I interviewed Mexican youths who were variously enrolled in education programs in New York City. The sample was stratified to include twenty youths who had never enrolled in schooling or who had attended adult education classes. By comparison, I also included fifteen youths who were currently enrolled in or who had just completed their high school studies in New York City public high schools. While the mean age of arrival for the never-enrolled youths was 15.8 years, for school-going youth, it was 13.8 years, or two years fewer. I did not intentionally recruit youths whose parents remained in Mexico, but I soon overwhelmingly found that youths who were not enrolled in schooling had left them behind and were working full time.

The interviews conducted between 2013 and 2015 significantly complemented the original two stages of this study. For this stage of data collection, I wished to find out what happened to the original youths whom I had interviewed as well as obtain a glimpse into young adulthood for these and other youths who had immigrated as independent Mexican teenage migrants. To do this, I followed up in Puebla with seven of the youths or their family members whom I originally met in 2006, six of the youths whom I originally interviewed between 2007 and 2009, and fifteen new youths and adults in New York City who had arrived as independent Mexican teenage migrants. These interviews allowed me to enhance what I had previously learned about these youths, especially as they were further transitioning into adulthood. Across all stages, special attention was paid to the messy, multidirectional, transnational processes of household and individual social mobility that spanned borders and, as such, dissimilarly organized geopolitical spaces and social institutions found in Mexico and the United States throughout their life courses.

PLAN OF THE BOOK

The succeeding chapters focus on the processes that lead independent Mexican teenage migrants to arrive at the various interdependent, adult-like statuses and roles that they hold in New York City as minors: independent immigrant, school leaver, and undocumented worker. The following section and each of the four chapters in it bring attention to the specific processes, both before and after emigration, that have produced these statuses and roles.

Chapter 2 begins by exploring the fundamental reason given by the teenagers to explain their pursuit of these statuses: to support their families. Acting on deeply rooted ideas learned and institutionalized in Mexico about family responsibilities and interdependence, these teenagers moved from being dependents, to helping support their parents' households in Mexico, and finally, to contributing to two households—their parents and either kin or nonkin households—across borders once in New York City.

Chapter 3 examines just how the youths began to learn about and then complete the steps needed to fulfill these obligations in Mexico and New York. Tracing back through the ways that children learn about and then fulfill immigration, this chapter demonstrates that youth immigrants are not necessarily "followers." Some, with the help of adults and peers, actively shaped their own departures without their parents. The chapter ends with a brief discussion of their crossings and their arrivals in the Big Apple. After leaving home and becoming "independent immigrants," subsequent statuses were continued or activated in New York City.

Focusing on how and why the majority of these teenagers became school "stayouts" in New York City, chapter 4 describes how the teenagers' developed and carried ideas about schooling from their home contexts in Mexico to New York City and, once there, found them reinforced. Once in New York City, the teenagers encountered an educational system that—while legally obliged to accept them—frankly had little incentive to provide appropriate schooling for them; as such, youths generally remained out of school.

Discussed at length in chapter 5, most independent Mexican teenage migrants were laborers in Mexico, and usually within hours of arrival in New York City, they were able to resume this status full time. Encountering a labor market that cared little about their ages and legal statuses, youths employed the skills and orientations they had observed and learned since early childhood to work in jobs that, while exploitative, were held in higher regard than those they left behind.

Taking all these aforementioned statuses into consideration, the last section examines how the teenagers became adults. Drawing from both the objective markers of transitions to adulthood and the youths' subjective evaluations, chapter 6 argues that although these teenage minors fulfilled responsibilities and independence associated with adulthood, they still held doubts about when and where they would achieve this life-course stage, either in New York or in Mexico. In the concluding chapter, final thoughts about the youths are shared as well as suggestions as to how policymakers can work toward providing options for improving youths' educational and labor statuses.

2 • "GIVING MY FAMILY A BETTER FUTURE"

Familism and Interdependence across Borders

> I had the weight of pulling them ahead. My papá had already helped me, and now it was my turn to help him.
>
> —Fidencio, age twenty-one; arrived at age fifteen

Since at least the colonial era, Mexican youths have been socialized in accordance with what Fidencio characterized as "pulling" families ahead, such that families are central to the lives of Mexican households and its members (Kuznesof 2005). As such, the most valued, internalized, and durable "frameworks" that, in turn, constitute independent Mexican teenage migrants' primary habitus reflect this idea, with base habitus constructed to privilege actions that reinforce the youths' relationships with their families (Bourdieu 2000, 2002; Bourdieu and Passeron 1990).[1] Alternately understood as familism, or "deeply ingrained" (Bacallao and Smokowski 2007: 53) senses of reciprocity within the family that are characterized by "obligations to care" (Blum 2009: 190), these frameworks suggest that individuals should place their families first and generate capital that can improve the entire household, not just themselves (Flores et al. 2009; Martinez 2016a; Punch 2015; Valdes 1996).

These are the unstated rules that independent Mexican teenage migrants follow in their households (Blank and Torrecilha 1998; Blum 2009; Juarez et al. 2013). Instructed through teaching and modeling (primary pedagogic actions, or PAs) by individuals and institutions, including their parents and other family members (pedagogic agents) possessing pedagogic authority (PAu), these rules follow families' ideas about dependence and the life course, including expectations about the ages at which individuals may contribute and/or exchange different types of capital to household members, the directions of the exchanges, the types and values of this capital, and even the social and geographical location(s) from which household members exchange capital (Bourdieu and Passeron 1990). Also understood by developmental psychologists as one aspect of narrow socialization, or socialization that occurs in less economically developed societies, families teach youths to adhere to strong senses of responsibility and practices that reflect interdependence (Arnett and Taber 1994).

These lessons begin as early as infancy or early childhood. For example, even though little was expected from Saúl or his brother when they were toddlers, at subsequent ages, his parents began modeling the ways in which the two children would be expected to contribute to their households. Without anyone else to care for them, Saúl's mother brought him and his younger brother to the fields to observe how she and his father harvested the corn that she would later grind for tortillas, atolé, and other Mexican food staples. Left in the shade on the side of the field, Saúl and his brother would watch as their parents stooped over to clean and rake their cornfields as well as plant and harvest corn. Protected from the sun by tall cornstalks, he and his brother watched as their parents performed tasks that ensured the family's livelihood. By the time he turned six, Saúl was no longer allowed to sit on the edges of the cornfields. Already acquainted with his parents' expectations of him, he began to perform tasks alongside his parents that, at first, did not require much strength or cognitive maturity. After some time, though, he would mimic the tasks his parents were performing.

By the time youths such as Saúl reach mid- to late adolescence, however, they learn to increase their family contributions, giving more to the household after working longer hours. They are also expected to decrease dependence on their parents. To fulfill both, some eventually undertake immigration. After immigrating, these youths encounter differently configured households that are headed by aunts and uncles, or "horizontally extended," or include older members of the same generation, such as siblings and cousins. In these household fields, independent Mexican teenage migrants are subject to, and adjust to, modified or "negotiated" rules of interdependence and resource transmission that bear little resemblance to those practiced in their households in Mexico or those commonly associated with mainstream adolescences or even young adulthoods in the United States (Glick et al. 1997; Hartnett et al. 2013; Langton and Berger 2011; Punch 2015; Schoeni and Ross 2005; Van Hook and Glick 2007).

This chapter discusses the ways in which independent Mexican teenage migrants learn and build these frameworks for participation in their "household fields" during childhood and adolescence and even at the advent of adulthood. With special attention to the extension of households across nation-state borders and the spatial changes during migrations that occur during their relatively short life courses, the youths discuss how and when their relationships to their households, natal and then migrant, changed across their life courses. Although perhaps not unique to Mexican youths, the timing and locations of these shifts are distinct from the cases of teenagers found in the United States (Fuligni et al. 1999; Hartnett et al. 2013; Schoeni and Ross 2005). Rather, across thousands of miles, a nation-state border, and at ages deemed "too young," Mexican youths begin to reverse and even cease their dependence on their parents and other adult family members for economic and, in many cases, emotional nurturing. Upon migration, youths endeavor more earnestly to fulfill responsibilities toward their parents and siblings back home in Mexico while simultaneously asserting a form of independence in New York City.

HOUSEHOLDS AS FIELDS

Although embedded in larger contexts of power, households or the family, however composed and defined, are arguably the first fields that individuals encounter and the primary fields where practices guide their actions in other fields.[2] In general, although theories of cultural and social reproduction place parent-child relationships at their centers, discussions of the household as more than a source of mostly cultural and social capital are scarce (Atkinson 2016; Lareau 2000, 2003; MacLeod 1995). Casting households—or rather, the family—as a site of struggle, British sociologist Will Atkinson sets the stage to more purposefully center Bourdieu's theories in an understanding of the sociology of the family and demonstrate how families "act" like any other field. Families, according to Atkinson (2016), possess forms of domination with their own boundaries, hierarchies, positions, rules, and so on. Furthermore, Atkinson argues, family-specific doxa, or unquestioned truths, exist. Ideas about who is considered family, what are appropriate actions between family members, and even which furniture is allocated and attributed to which family members (e.g., "Daddy's chair") circulate in the household field. With a nod to history, generation, and in the case of these youths, distance, Atkinson (2016: 67) reminds us that even though the impacts and effects of certain family members may become weaker and weaker, the present state of the field always "owes its structure to the past."

From young ages, independent Mexican teenage migrants learn and internalize these beliefs that the family is central and that all members should be useful in and to their households' reproductions. Additionally, they engage in illusio by learning which capital demonstrates their utility and actually obtaining and exchanging it in their households. As young household members, they are not supposed to stand idly by; rather, they are to help their parent(s) with tasks related to the smooth functioning of their households (Ramirez Sanchez 2015). Sensitive to household composition, transitions, and age, youths' contributions take on forms that will, even in small ways, ensure that the families' needs are met. In what could be considered an intergenerational contract, through cajoling and even punishment, parents make sure that youths are fulfilling their duties; at the same time, youths are learning age-sensitive forms of family obligation and household field participation.

Interdependence, understood as *ayuda mutual* (unpaid mutual help), especially in poorer Mexican families, is largely understood as a protective strategy to surmount poverty as well as one that demonstrates respect, obedience, and support between family members (Alcala et al. 2014; Bianet-Castellanos 2007; Blum 2009: 190; Coppens et al. 2014; Punch 2015; Ramirez Sanchez 2015). Institutionalized in the 1917 Mexican *Ley sobre Relaciones Familiares* and known as *alimentos*, these reciprocal obligations compel parents to shelter, clothe, feed, and educate their children but also to teach and expect their children to respect, obey, and support them by performing necessary labors in the house (Alcala et al. 2014; Blum 2009: 190; Coppens et al. 2014; Urrieta 2013). A Mexican civil code enacted in 1932 further defined the law's intergenerational dimension to include older siblings, who were also expected to support their younger siblings until they became legal adults (Blum 2009: 190). Still observed, this ayuda mutua to support the reproduction of the household begins as soon as youths possess sufficient motor skills and do not require as much supervision from their parents or older siblings (Alcala et al. 2014; Magazine and Ramirez Sanchez 2007; Ramirez Sanchez 2015). This labor (and later on, wages) helps alleviate the burdens of parents and/or siblings and supports the overall functioning of the home.

One hundred years later, these practices continue to exist in high-poverty households, including those to which independent Mexican teenage migrants belong. Between 1990 and 2010, many households in the states with the highest levels of out-migration to New York City would "not be lifted" by the North American Free Trade Agreement (NAFTA) but rather continue to see poverty rates stubbornly persist above 60 percent. By 2014, the three states from which the majority of the youths I interviewed originated—Guerrero, Puebla, and Oaxaca—each possessed among the highest rates of minors growing up in poverty: 77.1, 72.5, and 66.9 percent, respectively. Only Chiapas has a higher percentage at 81.7 percent (CONEVAL 2015). The rates of children in poverty were even starker when regions most negatively impacted by NAFTA, in the rural south, were compared to areas that benefited, in the north. By 2000, more than half of all children from birth to age seventeen living in southern Mexico were poor (52.9 percent), compared to 11.2 percent of children in northwestern Mexican states (Fernandez-Kelly and Massey 2007; Rivera and Whiteford 2009: xvi).

Characterized by these high levels of poverty as well as narrow socialization, independent Mexican teenage migrants recalled learning (as in Saúl's case) and then performing ayuda mutua as both simple and more complex chores inside and outside of the home, with and without adult supervision. Tasked with sweeping, washing dishes, making food, washing clothes, and watching younger siblings, as well as cutting wood, getting water from the town well, working in the fields, and feeding and taking care of the family's animals, youths discussed being expected to help, with parents often obligating them to complete time-consuming and sometimes strenuous chores before undertaking anything else. Consequences for not helping ranged from scolding to punishment to physical violence. Rodolfo recalled being hit for resisting certain tasks: "[I] was there working from morning until afternoon, and there were times that they [my father and older brother] would hit me because I did not want to go to work because it was very difficult."

Challenging popular ideas about age, gender, and domestic labor, Carlos eloquently stated that in the Mexican household, "responsibilities trickle down to whoever is left in the house." In other words, ayuda mutua is sensitive to the structure of the household and, regardless of age, was oftentimes further expected from members left in households in which fathers and/or older male siblings were absent due to death, irresponsibility, and even migration. With his father deceased and his older brothers in New York City, Manuel recalled being told to forego the age-appropriate activity of play so that he could help his mother even though he was only six years old:

> [I] asked my mamá, "Why don't you send me to go over there and play?" and she would tell me, "Because you do not have a papá, and you have to pay more attention and work and like that, always cultivating the lands over there. There is a big property like that, always cultivating," and I said, "And I will always be there too?" and she told me, "Yes, because you do not have a papá, you have to work for me. I am going to help you," and like that, and my mamá would tell me, "You have to learn how to be a man; you have to work." (And how old were you?) Like six, seven years old.

As the eldest, fourteen-year-old Genoveva subverted gender norms and was often called to engage in rigorous labor instead of the domestic labor often attributed to females. Although her father was present in the household, frequent drinking binges sometimes left him incapacitated and unable to work the mornings after. As a result, Genoveva and her younger brothers were forced to take turns cutting wood or else their family would be left without kindling for the household's daily necessities.

The entrance of older siblings into the labor market, in Mexico or the United States, also tended to shift the "intergenerational contract." Much like Manuel, whose brothers had left Mexico to work in New York City, Mexican youths experienced increases in responsibilities and changed schedules after their older siblings transitioned into providing waged financial assistance, both near and far. Although Carolina had been performing chores in her household since she was a toddler, when her older sisters began fulfilling their household obligations by giving their wages to their mamá, Carolina was relegated to performing the tasks that they had previously carried out, including helping prepare tortillas. Likewise, when Carlos's older brothers left for New York, he was forced to assume new responsibilities that disrupted his schedule: "Before, it was to work a couple of hours and then go out to play soccer; before the responsibility was on my older brother. When he left, we had to look and take on feeding the animals and such." With these new responsibilities, Carlos complained, he had little time left for leisure.

LIGHTENING THE LOAD: REDUCING AND REVERSING DIRECTIONS OF DEPENDENCE

For either the eldest child or the next sibling in line, the time (or age) would come when labor contributions were not enough to help sustain the family. Coinciding with the community age norms about paid labor, youths eventually obtained waged work to fulfill their obligations to their households. For most of the independent Mexican teenage migrants, the approach of middle childhood or adolescence, which coincided with the end of compulsory schooling and relaxed labor restrictions, was often accompanied by a transition to contributing pesos or learning to balance both household and waged labor. However, when youths begin working for and contributing wages, (a) dependence on their parents is reduced, and (b) their parents begin to depend on their children to pay for expenses related to household reproduction. In the former case, some youths discussed that, as has been widely documented in empirical studies of U.S. adolescent laborers, they began working so that they could engage in discretionary spending, or pay for their own items and/or stop asking their parents and/or guardians for money (Mortimer 2010; Palan et al. 2010). While some simply wanted autonomy in deciding what to buy and when to buy it, others actually paid for their own expenses, such as schooling, because their parents either could not or would not pay (Mortimer 2010). However, for the majority of Mexican independent teenage migrants who worked prior to migration, their wages—in almost their entirety—would go to their parents to spend on household necessities and expenses.

In the former case, youths worked to develop "consumption autonomy" (Palan et al. 2010: 1342). With her aunts remitting money to her grandparents, at age fifteen, Clementina no longer wanted to ask for things she wished to buy. She said she first started working eight hours a day as a cook "because [I] felt that I did not want to ask my sister or grandmother for my things. I wanted to buy them." She would later admit, however, that she only kept half of her wages for her own purchases. The other half went to supporting her sister by paying for her continued schooling.

Other youths used their wages from part-time jobs to reduce their dependence on their parents for money related to schooling. Whereas minors in the United States may begin to help pay for expenses related to extracurricular activities or to save for college, for prospective independent teenage migrants, school expenses begin much earlier, with essential fees charged at lower levels of schooling (Mortimer 2010; Shanahan et al. 1996). With parents who were unable to pay for their schooling beyond mandatory secundaria, Lazaro worked as a clown and Lalo worked in construction, and they used their earnings to pay for their preparatoria, or high school studies. In Lazaro's case, he said, "[I] worked only Saturdays, and well, I supported my own expenses, and so since then, I paid my own expenses for prepa." Likewise, Lalo started working when he entered into preparatoria: "That is what I had to do to support my expenses."

The majority of the youths who worked, however, did so to help support their families and did not have the luxury of keeping all their wages for themselves, either for leisure or for schooling. In time, the flow of money between parents and their children began to reverse. Absent from previous discussions of U.S. adolescents and familism, most of the youths discussed handing over all their earnings to their mamás to pay for household expenses and debts. They, in turn, asked their parents only for what they needed when they needed it, or they kept only a few pesos for necessities, such as school supplies (Fuligni et al. 1999).

Carlos's father was reckless with money, burning through his own earnings and the remittances his older sons sent from New York. Rather than paying for household expenses, he spent the money on gambling and extramarital affairs and soon fell deeply into debt. Not long after turning fourteen and distraught over seeing his mamá cry in shame night after night after being visited by debtors who came to collect money from his father, Carlos realized that he needed to secretly give money to his mamá for household expenses:

> It was [out of] necessity, to see [them] owing so much money to the people, that there were days that two or three people would arrive to collect their money, and my papá was never in the house, so it was my mamá who had to be in charge, and there were days that we did not even have enough money to eat because of my papá. All of the money that they sent us [from New York], he alone stayed with it, so I felt the necessity . . . to support my family because my papá [did not]. So then the little that I earned, I would give to [my mamá], hidden, because if my papá found out that I was giving money to her, he would automatically say that the money was his.

Even when their families' situations were less financially precarious, youths did not consider handing over all their money to be out of the ordinary; rather, it was an aged (age-bound) rule in their households. In Armando's words, "The normal was to give everything to them and for me not to keep anything." When he would need money, instead of dipping into the money he had already given them, he said, "I would tell them to let me stay home that day, and I would work the entire day, and at the end, I would give 50 percent. I would give them half and half." Whether the youths provided their parents with all their wages or a portion, in essence, the youths were beginning to reverse the directions of dependence, however slightly.

Some youths would further reduce their economic dependence on their families by discontinuing schooling and entering into the labor market full time. As one of the most significant state policies that structures family relationships and impacts economic interdependence between parents and children, the mandate of compulsory schooling requires that parents pay for youths' school-related costs, including registration, enrollment, and so on, and as such limits their household labor and/or waged work. As youths approached and/or aged out of schooling and compulsory schooling requirements—for reasons both perceived and mandated—the costs and mechanisms associated with their schooling, which had partially shaped and/or prolonged youths' dependence on their parents, were expected to decrease or even end. Whereas parents had found ways to support and pay for their children's schooling up to the point of secundaria completion and, for some, just to the end of primaria, the costs of schooling increasingly became too prohibitive, especially if younger siblings were also enrolled. As such, some parents very clearly told their children that if they wished to continue their studies, the youths would have to fund them themselves; parents simply could no longer shoulder this particular economic burden.

Like Lazaro and Lalo, mentioned previously, Clementina and Genoveva had been told in no uncertain terms by their grandparents and parents that after secundaria, their studies and, by default, some measure of their economic dependence, would be coming to an end. In Clementina's case, it had been her parents' sudden, tragic death in a car accident when she was eleven that unexpectedly placed her and her sister as dependents in her grandparents' care. Saddled with this unforeseen burden, after secundaria, she said, "[My] grandparents told me that if I wanted to continue studying that they wouldn't be able to support me economically." Genoveva's mother also began to prepare her for the inevitable before she even completed secundaria. After sharing her dreams with her mother of becoming a hairstylist after completing secundaria, Genoveva was crestfallen when she was told to forget about those dreams: "She [my mamá] told me no, that I could only complete secundaria, that they were not going to be able to help me study more, and she told me, well, that's it, that I should forget about school and continuing to study." She had, after all, two younger siblings who also needed to continue *their* schooling. In this way, she would be fulfilling the intergenerational obligations harkening back to 1932.

Although some youths had no choice but to reduce this type of dependence on their parents, others were not told "no" outright, but after deliberating and demonstrating significant altruism, the youths strategized and acted to alleviate this specific economic burden on their parents *on their own* (Fuligni et al. 1999: 1031; Nolle et al. 2012). Contemplating the costs to their families of their continued schooling as well as those associated with their foregone labor, youths considered completing two markers of the transition to adulthood: school leaving and full-time entry into the labor market. For some, it only played in their consciousness as a passing thought. When asked whether she ever thought that she should be doing something else other than remaining in school, Laura, a fifteen-year-old secundaria student in San Pedro, responded, "Instead of studying, maybe I should be helping my mamá to earn more money." Several youths, including seventeen-year-old Catarina, went farther and actually exercised their own agency by leaving and staying out of school to financially assist their families. Catarina made her decision to "lighten her mother's financial load" after completing primaria. With a father and older siblings in the United States who rarely sent money home to San Pedro, Catarina made the decision not to add to her mother's suffering after she had observed how she struggled on a daily basis. Although her mother wanted her to continue her schooling, Catarina lied, denying that she enjoyed school so that her mother would stop worrying and scrambling for money to pay for school: "My mamá wanted to send me to secundaria here . . . in the clinic, but I saw how we were at home, and I saw how we did not have money, and . . . I thought, 'How am I going to continue studying if we cannot?' And how I saw it, I told her that I was not going to study, and she asked me why not, and I told her because I did not like it, but I did want to continue studying. No other reason but the money." Fifteen-year-old Alejandro also decided that he would not continue on to preparatoria in San Valentín. He believed that the wages he could earn if he left school could help his siblings, two in primaria and two in secundaria, attain their own goals instead. Reflecting earlier discussions of birth order as well as obligations to his younger siblings, as the eldest child, Alejandro shared the following: "Well, I told my mamá, since I was the oldest—I am a little older—well, better that I help with work, [so] that my brothers study and that I help by working. It isn't a problem. [So] that they reach their dreams. . . . [It] was my decision, even if I wasn't very conscious of making the decision."

These purposeful decisions are made by prospective independent Mexican teenage migrants—some consciously, others not—to reduce their dependence on their parents by leaving and/or staying out of school. In cases such as these, working and contributing money not only influence, as in Alejandro's case, the school going of the youths' younger siblings but also is the difference between family nourishment and malnourishment. Like Alejandro, as the eldest, Mauricio decided that the costs to his family were simply too high, both because of school and because of his absence from the labor market: "[I left school] because we didn't have anyone who was going to give us [food] to eat anymore. Yes, at thirteen years old. So then, because of that, I left school. . . . Little by little, we went buying things for us." Unwilling to see his family starve, Mauricio instead ended schooling-related payments in order to work and assume the financial costs associated with feeding his family.

In addition to providing unpaid labor and/or actively giving money to one's family, youths believed that foregoing school and the accompanying costs helped diminish their burdens on their families. Whether understood as an idea or an actual fact, youths regarded involuntary or voluntary school departure as a means to reduce dependence on their parents. For youths who did drop out, some were simply unable to justify school going at the expense of prolonging their parents' financial anxiety as parents attempted to educate family members at the expense of food on the table. By dropping out, prospective independent Mexican teenage migrants ostensibly began to alter and reverse the directions of dependence on their families.

ACCELERATING INDEPENDENCE IN MEXICO

While some youths attempted more gradual reversals of dependence prior to emigrating, such as leaving school and working to help support their families, others demonstrated more explicit, marked breaks from parental economic and emotional support. Factors such as worsening conflicts with parents and/or preparation for immigration to the United States expedited some of these departures. Although he was still living at home and attending school in San Pedro, sixteen-year-old Mario had recently been inquiring about immigrating. Precipitated by several run-ins with the police in San Pedro, he was growing increasingly estranged from his parents. After being charged three times for different types of mischief, including fighting and breaking glass, Mario admitted, "Casi no con todo mi familia no me llevo" (I was not getting along with basically all of my family). Eager to leave for New York City, Mario had been gradually lessening his overall economic dependence and specifically his domestic dependence on his parents. When asked about whether he depended on his parents financially, he responded, "No; in reality, no." To ensure that I was well aware that his growing independence extended beyond the economic, he continued, "Well, I wash, I iron, sometimes I make my food, and I buy my own things." When asked why he was doing these things, Mario recalled, "When [I] go there [to the United States], [my mother] told me that if I go over there, they are not going to make food for you, so I am learning how to make food."

At age fourteen, Rodolfo went several steps further than Mario. After being advised by his mother as early as age seven to "work and earn . . . money so that [he] would not have to depend on anyone" and after enduring a turbulent relationship with his father, Rodolfo left his home to work in a nearby town. After dropping in and out of school and working with his father and elsewhere in his hometown, Rodolfo finally left Jaltepec to work first with his cousin's boyfriend, Pedro, and then with a friend of his cousin, Jorge, about an hour away in Apan, Hidalgo. He no longer lived at home with his parents; rather, he said, "When [I] worked with Pedro, [I] slept in his house. He gave me a room and a bed, but with Jorge, I slept in his truck." During this time, Rodolfo's dependence was redirected to a certain extent, as he would first depend on his cousin and his boss for meals when he was invited, but he was also paying for his own food. When he returned home on weekends, his mother would wash his clothes and cook for him, but come Monday, he would depart again and return to this semiautonomous state (Goldscheider and DaVanzo 1986).

Reflecting literature on adolescence that contends that youths begin to assert autonomy and independence during this life-course stage, as prospective independent Mexican teenage migrants approached the middle of their adolescences, it appeared as if a bundle of structural mechanisms—including the end of costly compulsory schooling, an attractive informal labor market that beckons underage workers, the plight of economically challenged families, and problematic family and personal dynamics —all worked to accelerate the reversal of economic and also emotional dependence on their families (Dornbusch 1989; Furstenberg 2000; Roche et al. 2014). However, as they renegotiated their economic relationships with their parents and transitioned toward financial self-sufficiency at these ages, the extent of their own independence exceeded those of youths in oft-cited literature about teenagers in the United States, including other Mexican immigrant teenagers (Fuligni et al. 1999; Gonzales 2015). Accompanying this self-sufficiency was also a gradual move toward decreased emotional dependence by virtue of strained relationships and, in Rodolfo's case, part-time physical residences away from their childhood homes. These actions could be interpreted as preparation for what was to come once they left for *el norte*: increased financial self-sufficiency and modified emotional dependence on their parents. Moving their family relationships across borders, youths began to draw from their surroundings to learn how they would maintain engagement with their families from afar.

LEARNING TRANSNATIONAL FAMILISM

Mexican youths in the United States tend to be depicted in scholarly literature as residing within nation-state borders and adhering to more traditional (read Western) models of age in which their demonstrations of familism are related to school going and academic achievement (Desmond and Lopez Turley 2009; Fuligni and Pedersen 2002; Gonzales 2015; Nolle et al. 2012). Prospective independent Mexican teenage migrants, however, grow up to observe and understand families and acts of familism that are not necessarily limited to members with whom they share space—that is, familism can exist outside the home and even outside nation-state borders. Youths understood that by migrating, they would continue to engage in familism, albeit transnationally, by virtue of sending remittances that are understood as "proof of sacrifices and a serious commitment to the migrants' loved ones left behind" (Castañeda and Buck 2011: 85; Falicov 2005; Wilson 1993). Youths echoed these ideas by describing migration as an act they needed to undertake to uplift their natal households and then themselves and their future sanguine families. When asked how they learned this, Rogelio stated, "Maybe [sending remittances] is the culture that we have there. . . . I also saw people who said, 'My son sends me money from Mexico so that here, we don't live such a hard life.'"

This culture of transnational familism, however, does not merely appear but is taught by a variety of pedagogic agents, both outside and inside of their families, who possess pedagogic authority (Bourdieu and Passeron 1990; Kandel and Massey 2002; Swartz 1997). By growing up in communities where they continuously observe and receive remittances (a.k.a. pedagogic works, or PWs) and then witness their household's (field's) receipt and exchange of them, independent Mexican teenage migrants develop an understanding that one immigrates to financially uplift one's family (Cohen 2004; Garip and Asad 2016; Kandel and Massey 2002; Swartz 1997). Like Rogelio, Armando, a seventeen-year-old, explained how he was inspired to leave Tecomatlán, Puebla, after seeing how remittances could alleviate his parents' burdens: "I noticed that when they [my friends] would arrive, they would, some here [help their parents]. . . . I wanted to help my parents, or . . . I didn't want for them to continue how they were, because sometimes . . . my father was under a lot of pressure, and I would see him and I would talk to him. . . . I obviously wanted to come over here." In the families of prospective independent Mexican teenage migrants, older adult siblings are often the first to immigrate and send money home, and as such, they are the pedagogic agents with pedagogic authority who demonstrate how remittances can be used to support younger siblings. For example, Manuel related that when he was still in primaria, his eldest brother left but then returned to Mexico during the last days of December. Returning to New York City after New Year's

Day, his brother called home to reassure the family that money would be arriving there by January 15. Recalling the backpack that he had used for as long as he could remember—one that his mamá had sewed for him—Manuel shared that after his mamá received money, she used the funds to purchase Manuel a larger, sturdier backpack that could better hold his notebooks. From then on, his brother's remittances helped him pay for school expenses associated with both his primaria and secundaria studies. Now Manuel would do the same for his siblings left behind.

Examples of individuals demonstrating continued economic support after immigration extend beyond the youths' natal households. Even in absentia, adult family members—including uncles, aunts, and cousins who possess pedagogic authority—also act as pedagogic agents by modeling migration and remittance sending. Since he was age nine or ten, Rodolfo noticed the dramatic changes his cousin's remittances were bringing to his aunt's property. Over time, he observed not only the construction of a fence that enclosed his aunt's property but also the addition of a second floor to their home. After comparing his home made of mud with aluminum sheets for a roof to his aunt's concrete house with two floors inspired his idea to immigrate "a little." In Rodolfo's words, "It was like I was envious, but . . . it motivated me to do it [immigrate] too."

Clementina also shared several examples of adult aunts and cousins who had immigrated and were helping not only her ailing grandmother but also their younger siblings. Converted into remittances, a portion of Clementina's aunt's earnings from working in domestic services and selling household products off the books in New York City were earmarked for the medicines her grandmother relied on for her various ailments. Alternatively, her twenty-one-year-old cousin, who worked as a janitor in a New Jersey school, sent remittances home that not only helped support her mamá (Clementina's aunt), who remained in San Valentín, but also her sister (Clementina's cousin), who needed the money to complete her bachiller studies in the town. Wishing to imitate the examples set by her aunts and cousins, Clementina admitted that she wished to immigrate to do the same. She too wanted to "send money to help my grandmother and my sister with her schooling."

Observing and experiencing the economic benefits of transnational familism, youths began to imagine the reproduction of these practices so that they too could improve their households' and their parents' lives. Repeatedly, youths discussed contemplating or actually immigrating after witnessing these acts of familism within their families. In fewer cases, however, prospective independent Mexican teenage migrants observed how unforeseen and uncontrolled household circumstances could also force transnational familism. Citing "need and life" as reasons for immigration and remitting, youths sometimes believed that transnational familism was not brought about by "choice" but rather was the inevitable by-product of the hand that life dealt you. In the case of Miguel's eldest brother, who also left around sixteen or seventeen, poverty, birth order, and his father's death were the "hand that life [had] dealt" him, which prompted him to leave and send money home. Indirectly referring to him, Miguel explained, "There are many people who . . . their papá dies, you know? [And], like, the oldest has to take charge [and immigrate] even if he needs to break his dreams, his studies, [to] help his siblings, his family." Also as the eldest brother, Mauricio felt as if he had no other choice but to immigrate to help his younger brother. His father's absence and mother's death left him in charge of his younger brother's care, and he felt that he had done an inadequate job while still in Mexico. Echoing Fidencio's language, after being asked what he had hoped to achieve when he immigrated to New York at age seventeen, Mauricio replied, "To pull my little brother [ahead] because I left him when he was five years old. Well, I came over here to get him ahead, but . . . I did badly. I did not get him ahead. I feel bad . . . because I was not responsible with him."

Lastly, youths both voluntarily and involuntarily engaged in modified relay immigration, or a staged approach to migration traditionally understood as beginning with fathers or adult parents and then extending to their children to honor familism (Arizpe 1982: 37; Wilson 1993). In the cases of the majority of independent Mexican teenage migrants, however, relay migration occurred first with uncles, then with older siblings, and then with persons within the same generation—first with older siblings and then the youths themselves. Having never thought about immigrating himself, sixteen-year-old Miguel learned that it was now his turn to leave school and join his brothers in New York City to continue supporting their mamá. Reflecting the ways in which transnational familism is sensitive to the life course, Miguel's older brother not only believed that Miguel was old enough to migrate and send money home, but he had also recently begun to form his own family with his wife and baby and would not be able to be the sole remitter any longer. As a result, Miguel said, "[I came] to [help] my brother a little, [since] he had always sent us [money] weekly" and "so that it would be the two of us pulling the family ahead." Under these new arrangements, they would take turns, with each brother remitting every other week instead of once a week.

Prior to migration, prospective independent Mexican migrant minors first observe transnational familism and then learn how to actually carry it out. Studying their adult relatives, including siblings as well as extended family members, the youths learn that money is sent back home to pay for household necessities such as food, medicine, education, and even upgraded shelter. Youths witness both the foreseen and unforeseen markers of life—birth order and age, older siblings' (not their own) family formation, and parental deaths—and understand that immigrating and sending money home are beneficial and even obligatory actions. Sensitive to the life course, transnational familism is simply understood as a household strategy that their families and community members employ for the survival and/or uplift of their families.

LEARNING HOUSEHOLD OBLIGATIONS IN NEW YORK CITY

> I do not depend on anyone. I pay my bills, for... rent, food, my cellular phone, for myself. That is why it is difficult. I thought it was different.
>
> —José Maria, age twenty-two; arrived at age seventeen

Although privy to what transnational familism looks like in their home communities and households, prior to their arrival in New York City, independent Mexican teenage migrants know very little about their obligations in their future homes. While some relatives inform youths that the privileges afforded to minors elsewhere will not be taken into consideration and that they cannot become *cargas*, or burdens, to their relatives, others arrive unaware that they are expected to support themselves. Their ignorance of this, however, is short lived.

Unlike in Mexico, the social and economic organization of the housing market in New York City, along with the economic precariousness of new and older immigrant arrivals, compels independent Mexican teenage migrants to enter into renter households. Shortly after their arrivals—much like adult newcomers—most independent Mexican teenage migrants, such as those in this study, joined uncles, aunts, cousins and older brothers in cramped apartments and were informed that after short grace periods, they were expected to find work so that they could become full, rent-paying members of the household (Van Hook and Glick 2007). For most youths, the grace periods lasted up to a month, but after receiving their first week's pay, these arrangements ceased. José Maria discussed how she began to fulfill these arrangements by working two jobs to pay rent and the $3,500 her aunt loaned her to migrate: "Well, first I arrived with my aunt, and in the first month, she took me to an agency where she worked and I started working. And there and then she began to charge me ... $200 in rent, for food. I also ate in the room with her that we shared the first month.... I also had a job at the laundry, and I went with her. [I] also [paid] close to $180 ... for food, besides the light [bill], and little by little, we divided it [the bills] among ourselves." Even the three independent Mexican teenage migrants whose time in New York City briefly overlapped with that of their fathers found themselves subject to similar demands of financial independence. In fact, Rogelio recalled that when he arrived, his papá, although telling him to "rest as long as [he] want[ed]," added, "after you start working, you will become independent, and you will pay for your clothes, your food, everything. You will become independent." Within a month of his arrival from Mexico, Rogelio was paying his first rent payment, his expenses, and the debts from his passage that he owed his uncles.

It was rent, youths discovered, that significantly altered their relationships within their local households, regardless of whether they shared an apartment with kin. After arriving at age sixteen to live with his brothers in New York, Miguel quickly learned, "The first thing one puts aside is your rent. Any leftover money after that can be sent home and used for additional expenses." When pressed about the consequences of not paying rent, Miguel continued, "They [landlords] are hardly ever going to wait until you have it. He is not going to understand if you have or do not have the money. He wants his money." Joining other tenants—sometimes family, sometimes not—the youths were charged the same amount as other adults once the rent was divided among the total number of people living in the apartment. For the independent Mexican teenage migrants I spoke with, this amount averaged approximately $270 a month.

Similar to adult immigrants who moderated the risks associated with independence, most youths who lived with family (or even friends who were "like family") could rely on "conditional" safety nets that prevented their homelessness even if they could not pay their rent on time (Blank 1998; Van Hook and Glick 2007). None of the youths seemed particularly concerned when asked whether they faced dire consequences if they ever did not have rent money. Instead, speaking in hypothetical terms, one youth, Martín, explained that if he approached his uncle and said, "'You know what, uncle? I am not going to be able to pay today.' I think that he would support me and . . . tell me, 'Yes, it is OK. That is not a problem.'" Sheepishly admitting that they had been short on rent only a few times, youths such as Rogelio and Miguel pointed to their friends and siblings who were able to loan them the difference. By the following week, they said, they repaid the loans.

These safety nets, however, were not guaranteed. Symptomatic of a troubling and illegal housing practice in New York City, undocumented relatives without leases were at the mercy of landlords who could create unstable and tenuous situations for them (New York State Attorney General 2016; Pratt Center for Community Development 2008). Unable to pay rent after deciding to return to school, Rodolfo relied on the charity of his brother and girlfriend and joined them in renting a room. After discovering that three, not two, people were living in one room, their landlord gave them an ultimatum: either Rodolfo would leave or they all had to leave. Unable to find other arrangements, Rodolfo opted to leave, but with nowhere else to go, he took to bathing and storing his possessions at his brother's apartment and then sleeping on the subway trains. After two weeks of this, he shared his situation with the executive director of The Door, a nonprofit organization that had helped him in the past. The director allowed Rodolfo to sleep there that evening and helped him begin the process of entering into the foster care system the very next day. On Christmas Day 2009, Rodolfo officially became a foster child and no longer lived with his brother: he had learned that familism had its limits.

NEGOTIATING INDEPENDENCE IN NEW YORK CITY HOUSEHOLDS

Restructuring relationships of interdependence in their new and natal households that reflected adult, not minor, statuses, youths also found themselves possessing stronger feelings of autonomy. Discussing the fact that they were now working and managing all their money themselves, most youths discussed feeling more and more independent. Even though he was living with his father, seventeen-year-old José Luis observed this almost immediately after he arrived: "Because I am working more for my own sweat, that money is already for me, and I don't have to account for what I do with it. [I feel like an adult.] Yes, because if I like something, I do not have to tell my papá to give me money."

Other youths experienced delayed transitions to financial autonomy. Youths whose first jobs were with older relatives, including uncles and siblings with whom they were living, were subject to the relatives' management and negotiation of the money they earned in the months immediately after they started work. Both Carlos and Miguel discussed how their salaries were negotiated by their older brothers and then given to them at the time of their first jobs. In Carlos's case, "They gave my salary to him [his brother], and he kept the money, and the owner started paying me . . . some three months after."

There is also the question of how their newfound financial independence and distance from their parents translate into behavioral autonomy, or the ability to make independent decisions (Haase et al. 2008). Although the youths are charged the same amount as other adult immigrants living in the apartments and are expected to become financially independent, when living with relatives, they are not necessarily guaranteed the behavioral autonomy afforded these other adults. Rather, the youths' older relatives still feel responsible for them and regard them as minors in need of protection. Carlos, in particular, struggled with this when he arrived in Queens at age sixteen and lived with his older brothers. Used to making his own decisions about his comings and goings in Mexico, when he arrived in New York, he said,

> They [my brothers] treated me like a little [kid]. Since I was always more rebellious than them—well, I always gave them more problems—they always tried to give me advice, like what was bad, especially at my age, like sixteen or seventeen. I would go on the weekends with my friends and not appear until Monday, and they, like adults, would worry because they did not see me. [I would go] on

> Friday and [they would] not [see] me until after work on Mondays at night. I got used to that in Mexico, since my papá was hardly ever at home, so after I would tell my mamá that I would be back in a little while, or "I'll be back after." I was not used to having to ask permission. (And did your brothers make that rule to have to ask permission?) [*laughs*]. They tried to [make] that rule!

Fifteen-year-old Marco also discussed experiencing an abrupt limit on his freedom after arriving to live with his older brother. Fearful that Marco could be arrested for truancy, Marco's brother told him that he was to remain inside the apartment until after school let out. Marco said, "I would not go out to the street [outside] until after 3 p.m. in the afternoon. If the police would see me, they would arrest me." Growing bored with having to stay in the house all day long watching television, after a month, Marco eventually convinced his brother to let him seek work during daytime hours.

Whether out of fear of unknown dangers or the police, Carlos's and Marco's statements are reminiscent of Smith's (2006) discussion about adolescence and generation in his investigation of the influence of transnational life on second-generation New York Mexican youth identities. Life stages such as adolescence had particular social meanings in New York City, but visits to their parents' hometowns provided levels of freedom and autonomy not allowed in New York, such as staying out later, drinking, and so on—pastimes unavailable to them in New York City due to grave consequences. In Mexico, youths are more autonomous by virtue of both community understandings about age and citizenship and family-level factors, including the absence of parents or being the eldest left at home. However, New York City recognizes a different age organization and criminalizes both underage behaviors and undocumented statuses. Living with older siblings who are aware of both and feel responsible for their security and safety, at first independent Mexican teenage migrants experience diminished independence.

These sorts of negotiations were foreign to youths who were unable to live with kin. They were, however, subject to other types of household dynamics. Fully independent youths unable to live with known family members or friends experienced vulnerability and greater exposure to risky behaviors and expressed feelings that ranged from discomfort and distrust to outright lack of communication with the adults with whom they lived. Before his brother arrived, fifteen-year-old Rodolfo lived six months with adult men and women who drank excessively and used cocaine and marijuana, and they introduced him to these same practices, which his brother would not accept in his own home. Pedro also spoke of being uneasy living with older Mexican men with whom he rarely spoke and with whom he had little in common. After arriving at his previously unseen brother-in-law's home at age sixteen, he was asked to leave when the landlord threatened eviction due to overcrowding. Knowing no one else, Pedro looked for a room for rent and had to live with strangers. One of his roommates, he said, made him uncomfortable because he was oftentimes drunk when he arrived home. It affected the sense of security he felt in his home:

> It has not been very good because I did not know him. There are times that I did not want to arrive there [go home] because I did not know them; I did not want to talk with them. Well, I did talk with them, but only a little, about work. . . . Also, I went over there with the other man, but we talked very little, since he drank a lot. When I arrived, he was drunk. We barely talked—only sometimes, when he was more or less [sober]. Daily he was drunk, and we talked about where we were from, about that and the other.

Although none of the males explicitly discussed feeling physically insecure, several female participants insinuated or outright expressed considerable distress while living with male relatives. Upon her arrival in New York City, then sixteen-year-old Hilaria lived with her brother-in-law in Sunset Park, Brooklyn. Not related to him by blood, and not as close to him as one of her brothers, she felt uncomfortable living with him and accepting his help: "I lived with my brother-in-law after he helped me. Yes, it was something difficult, because he was not my brother like that. . . . It is something strange to be far from your family." She grew so uncomfortable that she went to live with an unrelated older female whom she met at work. Herminda was more candid in discussing the problems she experienced after moving in with her sister's family. Her brother-in-law propositioned her sexually, and she did not know what to do. After telling her other sister, she believed that the best thing to do was to live with her aunt and uncle. She had not told her sister (the wife of the brother-in-law who had propositioned her) and did not intend to.

Without fully considering the household dynamics that await them when they immigrate, independent Mexican teenage migrants arrive and encounter settings that are significantly different from those they left behind. Although paying equal amounts in rent, when joining older kin, youths are often subject to rules and supervision that they had outgrown in their home contexts. Due to their ages and tenuous statuses as undocumented minors, youths must become accustomed to an initial loss of autonomy and independence when renting with relatives, something that does not go uncontested. Youths who cannot join older kin, however, face significant discomfort and, in the case of some females, challenges to their personal safety. All in all, youths arrive in New York City to find that they must negotiate their household relationships in ways they had not previously anticipated.

PRACTICING TRANSNATIONAL FAMILISM: SENDING MONEY HOME

Once they find employment in New York City, youths are able to more actively engage in transnational familism by starting (or continuing) to contribute money to their households in Mexico (Martinez 2016a). From New York City, the youths assert—or in some cases, reassert—and strengthen the direction in which economic capital will flow, not from adult parent to children (Dreby 2010) or adult child to parent (Wong 2008) but rather from minor child to parent (Martinez 2016a). Although these vectors already began to shift prior to their departures from Mexico, once the teenage minors are settled in New York City, it is firmly established that they will send money to their parents and not vice versa.

This money totals hundreds of dollars sent either every eight days, every two weeks, or monthly. Independent Mexican teenage migrants discussed sending an average of $326 USD a month to their natal homes, an amount that could vary in times of unemployment or, as will be discussed in chapter 4, if youths returned to school. The uses of the youths' migradolares were not much different than those oft-discussed in relation to adult remittances (Cohen 2001; Massey and Parrado 1994). Their money paid for a variety of endeavors tied to household reproduction and social mobility, ranging from basic household necessities, such as food and clothes, utilities, medicine, and medical treatments, to their siblings' schooling and the construction of sturdier family homes. When asked, seventeen-year-old Julio simply responded, "[I knew] that she [his mamá] uses [the money] to continue eating." Carlos, on the other hand, discussed sending money home first for his mamá but then, after her passing, for his siblings' studies. Although Carlos only completed secundaria in Mexico, his remittances were specifically able to extend one brother's studies, but with mixed results: "The youngest one, yes, he arrived all the way to high school, but the same, he came over here."

Fidencio and Martin also discussed fulfilling their dreams of acquiring and/or constructing their parents' homes while in New York City. The now twenty-one-year-old Fidencio discussed how the $350 that he had sent every eight days since he had settled in New York City at age fifteen had paid for the construction of not one, but two, houses—one for his parents and one for himself—made of plaster and not the aluminum and wood of his natal home. Martín accomplished a number of the objectives he had set forth for himself when he arrived four years earlier at age sixteen. For one, he had already bought two properties—one for his mamá, on which he had already paid for the construction of a house (not a "big one, but it was something"), and another one for himself. Additionally, he had been able to help his papá acquire an apartment in Mexico City.[3]

Other youths shared that their remittances were being used in times of crises, including to help pay for expenses related to life-threatening medical conditions and family separations. Rodolfo began sending money to his mamá six months after arriving in New York City at age fifteen. His mother had just left his father, and he began to support her by sending her $100 every eight days. He would send it "so that she can buy her food, each thing she needs for the house." Carlos's mother was also facing a crisis after he left: she was diagnosed with cancer exactly one month after he arrived in Queens. He and his brothers paid for her medical treatments: "The treatment was very expensive, so my two older brothers returned to Mexico, and no one other than my other two brothers and I had to work here to pay for the treatment."

Occasionally, however, the independent Mexican teenage migrants encountered challenges and were unable to consistently send remittances. Like adults, they were susceptible to changes in the labor market and their lives, and they sometimes found themselves unemployed or injured and unable to work and earn money to send home (Walter et al. 2004). In these cases, the flows of remittances to their parents' households either decreased or were temporarily halted.

Although Armando began to send money home immediately after his arrival at age sixteen, nine months later, he had encountered financial difficulties. During his first three months in New York, he had saved and sent more than a thousand dollars to his parents after working in the city's higher-paying construction industry. With the onset of winter, construction had halted, and he was visibly frustrated that he had been forced to take a hiatus from sending remittances. He assured his parents that he would continue sending money home as soon as he resumed working: "Right now, since I have not worked in two months, well, the truth is that I am a little broke. I have debts, [and] what I have sent home is very little. . . . I have sent maybe eighty, maybe seventy . . . because construction is outside, and sometimes it rains and I have to stop one day and . . . don't get to work the full five days. I haven't earned that much."

Samuel also reported regularly sending hundreds of dollars home to his mother in Mexico, but like Armando, the amounts he could remit and how often he could do so depended on his employment. He had been unwilling to take lower-paying temporary jobs that employment agencies customarily offered and instead was looking on his own for a job with improved pay and consistent hours:

> Yes, when I work and it goes well for me, I send them money. (Is it regular, like a particular day each month?) Like that, let's say some three times [a month], because then the week to pay rent arrives, and I cannot send them anything. My mamá already knows. And when I do not have work, just two times a month. (How much do you send?) It also depends on the salary. If it goes well for me, then I send them, like, $300 [a month]. If it goes badly for me, I don't send them more than $100 [a month].

Unforeseen illnesses or injuries also affected the rhythms of remittances to the youths' homes. After a respite of several months due to injury and his subsequent recovery, now seventeen-year-old Marco had only recently resumed sending money home to his mamá every fifteen days. After falling and breaking his arm at work, he had to pay his medical bills out of his savings and was forced to stop working.

Returning to high school also interfered with youths' remittance-sending behaviors. For youths who resumed their studies in New York, enrollment and full-time attendance, even in nontraditional programs for older students, negatively impacted their abilities to continue sending the same amount of money—if any—to their homes. Rodolfo, Martín, and Herminda's entrances into high school and then later college resulted in decreased work hours and increased expenses, impacting their abilities to send remittances. Still obligated to support themselves, the youths simply could not send the same amounts home.

After entering into the ninth grade at Liberty High School Academy for Newcomers, Rodolfo related, "There was a time that I did not work, and there was [a] time that I did not send, and then after—for example, from the ninth to the tenth grade—I did not work and I did not send, but once I entered into eleventh grade, I started working part time, and I started earning money again, and I started to send money again." Likewise, after Martín enrolled in Flushing International High School, his uncle and cousin decided that he would pay less for rent: "They see that I am putting forth the effort and I am indeed trying." He also began to send less money home, missing some weeks and then making it up at later times.

Eventually, school-going youths begin to think about and even actively attempt to renegotiate the terms of their transnational familism. Herminda began to adopt more individualistic goals that threatened to rupture her commitment to her natal household. After matriculating into Manhattan Comprehensive High School, she increasingly needed money for school and, as a result, could not send as much money: "It isn't like [I tell them], 'Figure out how you are going to fix it, or fix it however you can,' but [I need] to make them see that I have my own needs, my own dreams here, and in that way, I cannot [send] anymore. She [my mamá] cannot depend on me all of the time." Martín also noted a change in his thinking after he attended high school in the United States. Before he attended high school, he said, "[I had] only wanted to have money and buy my mamá a house and all of that, [but] now [my] mentality has changed, and now I think that I do not only want that, but rather I want to be someone in life." Exposed to "American" norms and values in their high schools that emphasized individualism over familism, these youths were, as will be discussed in chapter 4, experiencing fine-tuning to their habitus and, as such, were renegotiating the agreements they had established with their natal households.

I was surprised to hear that these renegotiations were typically not contentious. In spite of the fact that the youths' families were using the youths' migradolares for necessities and, in some cases, emergencies, the youths said that they did not feel "obligated" to send money home and were not facing familial consequences for these interruptions and decreases in remittances. Rather, when faced with the news that their children would be decreasing the money sent home, parents continually told them, even if they needed the money, not to worry about sending funds. Perhaps due to remittances from older siblings, youths did not express being subject to penalties from their families for not sending money home.

Although the youths did not experience repercussions when the flow of remittances was disrupted, they themselves still felt as if they were failures and were falling short of their objectives when they arrived in New York. They were failing to uphold an aspect of, as Rogelio stated earlier, their "culture"—an obligation that had become integrated into their habitus. Being unable to fulfill this "natural act" caused the youths discomfort. As Armando shared, "That's what I feel bad about, that I came here to pull them forward, and it feels bad to not be able to." Martín, in particular, was distraught about being unable to send remittances back home or being forced to reduce the amounts he sent. After resuming his studies, he was unable to work as many hours and had also incurred new schooling expenses. Although his uncle lowered his rent while he attended school, the new amount, as well as the costs of his other personal expenses, including his phone bill and food, prevented him from sending money home weekly. When asked whether this bothered his parents, Martín replied, "They do not get mad . . . because they tell me . . . , 'No son, no already.' And they tell me that if I want, not to send, but I feel bad [about] myself. I know that they need, you understand me?" Rather, his mamá told him, "It is OK not to do it [send money] anymore." Likewise, in spite of her financial need after her separation from his father, Rodolfo's mamá also did not ask him for money or make him feel guilty when the amounts of money he could send home decreased after he started attending high school.

SHIFTING FAMILISM IN EARLY ADULTHOOD: FROM NATAL HOUSEHOLDS TO CONJUGAL HOUSEHOLDS

These gradual changes in remittances to their natal households also occurred when independent Mexican teenage migrants completed the last two markers of the transition to adulthood—that is, marrying and having children, or establishing conjugal households. When they were no longer minors, the youths began to consider present and future expenses and reevaluated how much they should continue to send in remittances or if they should stop altogether. As will be further discussed in chapter 6, aside from returning to school, the start of their own consanguine families most impacted the youths' remittance sending patterns. Carlos, Rodolfo, and Ignacio all discussed how committing to their partners and having children effectively ended their remittances.

After his mother's death, Carlos continued to send money home to help his father pay off his debts, but as he approached his wedding day at age twenty-seven, he stopped sending money. The last straw was learning that his father spent the money he had sent him to obtain a visa to attend his wedding. Disillusioned by his father's reckless spending and now forming and beginning to lead his own conjugal household, Carlos felt it was time to direct all his economic resources to his wife and future children. Likewise, Rodolfo stopped sending money to his mamá after obtaining an apartment, where he lived with his pregnant partner. Compounded by attending college, he simply had no money to send. Rodolfo felt bad, however, because he knew his actions negatively affected his mamá: "There was a lot of pressure. . . . Now my mamá is suffering from a lot of depression, since I have not sent money for the past two years. And the worry of whether or not I am OK or bad, more than anything . . . because sometimes I did not even have enough [money] to call her."

Alternatively, for Saúl, the formation of a conjugal household led to increases in remittances. Already sending money to his younger siblings who were without living parents, he extended his web of obligations to his wife's family (his wife was not employed) and began to send money to her parents whenever he could. Since he turned twenty-two, Saúl had been sending them

> like, $200 a month since 2004—like, $50 a week. We send money because her papá is sick. . . . [It's] to have them taken care of, more than anything. I decided to send because they do not have jobs over there, and not because they told me that they are very needy—but I know that they are needy. . . . I do not send them every week, but I send them $50 every time that I can. It may be every fifteen days, or a week, but it is not obligatory. (Why did you decide if it is not obligatory?) I just decided, that's all.

CONCLUSION

Not unlike other accounts of Mexican familism, independent Mexican teenage migrants possess relationships and positions in their families that contribute to the reproductions of their households. From very young ages, they observe, learn about, engage in and are beneficiaries and benefactors of the practices and resources that demonstrate primary commitments to nuclear and extended families. They thereby develop an understanding of how to exhibit these commitments and what resources are needed and valued, and these ideas become part of the internal frameworks that guide their actions.

In their case, however, their households are multilocal, located both in and across Mexico and the United States. As children, the youths contribute labor and/or wages to their natal households while observing and even benefitting from the flow of resources from older relatives residing in el norte. By the time they reach mid- or late adolescence, however, many independent Mexican teenage migrants shift from being mostly beneficiaries to being mostly benefactors as they begin to engage in familism across two households and two nation-states, Mexico and the United States. Contributing hundreds of dollars monthly to two households, youths negotiate and renegotiate simultaneous membership in two household fields in which they are members.

The youths are also slowly, quietly modifying the directions of interdependence that exist between their parents and siblings and themselves. As children, and then early teenagers, youths engage in household labors and then waged work whose outcomes gradually alleviate the youths' dependence on their parents and, rather, increasingly compel parents to depend on their children for household reproduction. In New York City, the reversal of the flow of resources and, as such, dependence—formerly from parent to child and now from child to parent—appears complete. As a result of this reversal, the youths' families in Mexico are able to survive and, in some cases—at least in terms of increases in education and material wealth—enjoy social mobility.

These shifts, however, are not without hiccups. Unaware of the rules that govern the households they enter upon arrival in New York City, the youths are surprised but do assume roles as renters while negotiating and renegotiating their economic and emotional independence with older relatives, who see themselves as their protectors. Youths who live with strangers and even unscrupulous relatives are more vulnerable to risks and even harm. Regardless, as minors with and without economic and emotional safety nets, independent Mexican teenage migrants navigate through their newfound independence, managing their multiple responsibilities to both their natal and local households as they march toward adulthood.

Lastly, the youths' relationships to familism mirror their advance through the time and space of migration. From being the beneficiary of their parents' and other older relatives' economic support, to migrating and sending *migradolares* to their parents and siblings in Mexico while residing and establishing a form of economic self-sufficiency in the United States just prior to adulthood, to focusing on their own individual needs in New York City and reducing the money sent back home in their late teens and early twenties, independent Mexican teenage migrants become sensitive to their own and their families' understandings of their aging and the cultural and structural demands that accompany family membership in dissimilar, multilocal contexts.

3 • "WE ALL COME YOUNG"

The Migration of Mexican Independent Teenage Migrants

> We all come young; we all come at ages fourteen, fifteen, sixteen years old. Because the journey is easier, you understand? Because if you are older than thirty, the journey that you have—to cross the border yourself—is more difficult than what you can endure, that big journey and all of the challenges that you see in the course. So then it is better if you come at a young age.
>
> —Martín, age twenty; arrived at age sixteen

Leaning forward as if describing the latest box-office hit action movie, now seventeen-year-old Luis proudly recounted how he, just as he was turning fifteen, managed to plan his entire departure from Mexico without his father's knowledge or consent. His father himself had never immigrated to the United States and instead regularly engaged in internal migration between Oaxaca and Mexico City for work. After Luis fell behind in his courses and refused to complete his secundaria studies in Oaxaca, he accompanied his father on one of his trips. Unemployed, Luis would meet up at night with older friends from his hometown who had also immigrated to Mexico City for work. Before long, their late-night conversations turned to planning their journey to *el norte* and "checking everything [they] had to do." With thoughtful deliberation, Luis described their planning as "well thought out, like a process." The youths discussed and negotiated their course of action: "We would agree on what we could do: we need this amount of money, we need an agenda too, we need to find a way to get the papers to take." The youths soon determined that they could "count on some people over there [in the United States] too" in order to arrive safely: "We thought about it—we know this is what we need, search for this and search for that, try to gather that." His older friends were able to acquire money as well as identification papers and a coyote, or human smuggler, from Oaxaca with whom they had made arrangements. As for telling his family, Luis replied that in all honesty, he had felt a tinge of guilt that he was doing this behind his father's back. He knew that his father deemed him too young to emigrate with his older friends to work, and his preparations and plans would not be met with his father's approval. But he could not help it. When he was planning his departure with his friends, all of whom were at least three to four years older than he and already legal adults, he admittedly became caught up in the excitement and felt older, not like a minor: "When I was making the plans with my homeboys, well, I felt like, you know, I was here with my friends, . . . I felt like that over there, like one of them, already big. . . . There was not a problem. I had decided to do what I had thought."

Soon he found that his predictions about his father's reaction were correct. Luis's revelation left his father feeling angry and betrayed. His father responded, "How could you do all of this behind my back? You are still not an adult, you cannot do what you want, you still depend on me. How is it that you did this?" His father's response left him confused, and he thought maybe, just maybe, his father was right. At age fifteen, maybe he *was* too young to leave without his parents to assume greater independence.

Luis had surprised his father and arguably himself in planning his own migration. He had asserted his own agency and activated the social capital found in the relationships he held with older friends in Mexico City to embark on his new life. These actions, however, did not come without significant conflict, but he continued to believe that "age does not matter" and that by "doing what he wanted," he would ultimately win his father's consent.

Immigrants' agency, generally attributed only to adults, is often omitted from accounts of youth immigration. This chapter *ages* immigration and places these independent Mexican teenage migrants front and center as active agents who, with the assistance of individuals found in their social networks in both Mexico and the United States, pursue migration without their parents and, in the process, complete one of the markers of the transition to adulthood: leaving home. With influences including personal observations, obligations to families, and relationships with older relatives and friends, in many cases, the youths' decision to immigrate progresses from first thinking about it, to deciding to do so, to preparing to do so, and finally, to actually embarking on the journey across Mexico to New York City. Exhibiting neither the spontaneity nor the impulsiveness often attributed to adolescents, they instead demonstrate *planful competence*—that is, the employment of a thoughtful, assertive, self-controlled process that underlies engagement with particular social institutions and interpersonal relationships—and enact their agency in arranging for emigration after evaluating their surrounding conditions and determining, much as Luis did, "that here [in Mexico], I do not have a future" (Clausen 1986, 1991; Dinovitzer et al. 2003; La Jornada 2017; Shanahan 2000).[1] In other words, at young ages, they refuse to be relegated to a lifetime of barely making ends meet in their parents' fields in Mexico. They instead wish to earn more capital, enter into new fields, and obtain new positions—a future guaranteed, they believe, if they only immigrate to New York City. Hoping to avoid their poverty-stricken parents' fates in Mexico and anticipating a better future for themselves and their families, they leave.

Focusing on the interplay of habitus, social capital, agency, and the influences these possess on the lives of independent Mexican teenage migrants as they begin to consider and then complete one of the markers of the transition to adulthood—that is, leaving home—this chapter argues that the youths challenge mainstream age norms as they seek to disrupt their families' poverty and achieve their own social mobility. By taking it upon themselves and relying on mostly older friends and relatives in planning their departures, the youths recount alternative narratives to popular discourses that usually characterize them as followers, not leaders, in decision-making about immigration (Boehm 2008; Dobson 2009; Farrow 2007; Hashim 2006; Orellana et al. 2001; Punch 2007; Thorne et al. 2003). The following section places independent Mexican teenage migration into a larger context of Mexican migration, including recent analysis of youths intending to leave Mexican sending communities and the reasons they report doing so.

MEXICAN TEENAGE MIGRATION AMID MODERNIZATION

During Mexico's economic restructuring at the end of the twentieth century, the emergence of newer migration circuits and the mobility of adults therein—many of whom were relatives, neighbors, and friends—did not go unnoticed by poor Mexican youths. The convergence of these examples, the lack of opportunities in their hometowns, and increasing economic insecurity juxtaposed against examples of remittance-induced social mobility were, and continue to be, translated into aspirations and actions (Kandel and Massey 2002). In one of Puebla's highest sending communities, Cuautlancingo, the reported number of secundaria and preparatoria students who intended to migrate reached 60 percent (Velazquez 2015).[2] Other sources have also noted the *actual* migration of minors at young ages. On February 21, 2012, Puebla's newspaper, *El Popular*, documented the increase in younger-aged migrants from Puebla in a news story titled "Migración afecta cada vez a personas mas jovenes" (Every time, migration affects even younger youths). Noting that the majority of people emigrated between the ages of sixteen and thirty-five, the author brought attention to the increasing numbers of migrants between the ages of twelve and fourteen and even ages seven and ten (Hernandez 2012). In the same year, Mexico's

Instituto Naciónal de Migración estimated that ten Poblano minors left the state every day (El Diario de Mexico–New York 2012). Likewise, the Mexican feminist news source *Cimacnoticias* noted similar increases in young girls and adolescents leaving Oaxaca for the United States (Lopez 2013). While these numbers include youths who were immigrating to reunite with parents no longer able to take part in circular migration due to heightened border militarization, when asked, youths gave additional reasons for both wishing to and actually immigrating that suggest that they were responding to economic effects attributed to NAFTA and related economic "reforms." For example, youths growing up in Cuautlancingo responded that they hoped to obtain better pay and improve their living conditions (Velazquez 2015).

Fourteen-year-old Genoveva could have easily been one of these surveyed youths wishing to emigrate for better pay and working conditions. During one of our talks in San Pedro, Genoveva, believing she had no other options but arduous labor in Mexico, seemed forced to think about immigration. After being told that she could not continue studying beyond secundaria, Genoveva compared her workplace options in Mexico versus the United States with only a secundaria degree in hand. She thought, "If I am not going to keep studying, well, maybe it's better [to immigrate], because I don't like to go to the fields, and I could go [to New York to] look for a good job because maybe with secundaria, I could get a good job, better than going to the fields."

As exemplified by Genoveva's statement, these NAFTA-affected contexts shape and conversely are being shaped by their inhabitants' orientations toward age, schooling, work, migration, and economic security. These orientations include responses to not only deepening poverty due to Mexico's neoliberal economic reforms but also the latest iterations of modernizing discourses and policies that have encouraged youths to extend their dependence on their parents and delay their transition to adulthood (Blum 2009). Unable to do either, instead, many left school before or immediately after mandated completion. Entering the labor market at first part time, then full time, and often in violation of Mexico's child labor laws, youths are faced with little choice: unable to conform to modernizing age discourses and policies, they instead work to meet their families' economic needs. Weighing economic and living conditions in Mexico with the promises that New York City wages offered, and assisted by family and friends, prospective independent Mexican teenage migrants found themselves preparing to abandon the "prospective" label so that they could complete one more marker of the transition to adulthood—leaving their households—to enter wholly new national and local contexts that would allow them to further uplift their families and themselves.

To do so, however, youths had to navigate immigration both as a process and, in terms of social reproduction, as a field. Before discussing just how Mexican youths do this, the following section introduces the idea of immigration as a field where entrance, capital acquisition for higher hierarchical positions, and "successful" transitions to immigrant status are not only aged but also not guaranteed.

MIGRATION AS A FIELD

While the act of migration is more popularly characterized as a process, it can also be understood as a field that reflects both local and global class relations and in which individuals "play." However, not everyone possesses doxa to this particular field or even the capital to enter it. Complicated by duration and maturity of migration flows and social networks, several scholars have discussed that the poorest individuals—or those without adequate cultural, economic, and/or social capital—are unable to immigrate (Cornelius 1976; Durand and Massey 1992). This was evident in the case of several San Pedro youths whom I met but was unable to interview. These youths were characterized as mischief makers, and several residents believed that they resented others because they did not have enough money to leave (Kandel and Massey 2002; Martinez 2016c; Zenteno et al. 2013). Those who can and do immigrate, as will be discussed later in this chapter, draw upon their networks to obtain and then exchange capital to move from prospective migrant to actual migrant status. Still others, including those receiving economic remittances from their parents and those who are able to pursue work or professional careers in Mexico, may opt not to try their luck at migration.

Spanning from independent Mexican teenage migrants' sending contexts in Mexico, to transit routes across Mexico and the United States, and finally to their receiving contexts in New York City, migration fields consist of a matrix of numerous positions that reflect varying amounts of accumulated capital and power dissimilarly held by an array of actors (Riaño-Alcalá and Villa-Martínez 2014: 95). For example, Sanchez (2014) describes in great detail how the act of migration has changed in recent years to include modifications in the *organization* of human smuggling. While this chapter focuses primarily on one set of actors and positions participating in the migration field—that is, independent Mexican teenage migrants who move from prospective to actual immigrant status—it is worth noting the larger array of positions that exist in and actors who engage with this field with whom the youths have contact, including coyotes, who upon receiving the youths' different forms of capital, facilitate their journeys to New York City. But ultimately, it is only independent Mexican teenage migrants themselves who can deem themselves "winners" in these fields after having successfully migrated to New York City without detection.

EXPERIENCING MIGRATION AS ACTIVE MEMBERS OF TRANSNATIONAL SOCIAL NETWORKS

First and foremost, it is the youths' membership in transnational social networks and their relationships with older adults in these networks that enable them to even imagine, much less undertake, entering the migration field. At the most credited with "participating" in family decisions to migrate and enter into these fields—while at the same time solely dependent on the information their parents use to make decisions for them—children and teenagers have primarily been characterized as passive tag-alongs without capital to contribute or exchange in the migration process (Boehm et al. 2011; Tyrell 2011).[3] Depicted as occupying "weaker position(s)" relative to adults and possessing little valuable social or economic capital in general, minors are not regarded as members of broader social networks of primary migrants who enact migration (Leonard 2005: 606). For independent Mexican teenage migrants, however, this depiction is inaccurate. These youths are in relationships with other adult kin and nonkin actors who are not their parents but provide both examples of and resources for migration and facilitate their movements into receiving communities.

OBSERVING MIGRATION: SEEING WHY ONE SHOULD EMIGRATE

As noted by Zenteno et al. (2013), Mexican youths born into and coming of age in communities and households with these adults have been developing doxa, or particular ideas about or orientations toward immigrating to the United States—including why individuals immigrate and its appropriateness for persons their ages—since birth. Youths observed that community members, neighbors, and even relatives immigrated to el norte as they approached their late teenage years, a process that accelerated by the time these individuals reached their midtwenties. As a result, youths also witnessed the absence, in many cases, of half their community members, most of whom were male (Kandel and Massey 2002). Only a small minority of male community members, Carolina said, "stayed in Mexico to take over their father's labors."

As if validating the rewards of migration, striking displays of material items were apparent in the homes of the missing young-adult men and, increasingly, women. Although direct contact with immigrants was limited to their infrequent return visits or phone calls, migrants could act, in a sense, as pedagogic agents and model in absentia the outcomes of their own migrations when family members converted the remittances they sent home into material evidence of what they were achieving through migration. Mexican youths observed the material benefits of their community members' remittances—the acquisitions and improvements—and, in Martín's words, became "motivated" to achieve as much for themselves and their families. As such, at early ages and independent of their parents, some Mexican children and teenagers began to develop "new imaginaries" and, as discussed in chapter 2, viewed migration as a strategy for fulfilling their obligations and improving their own and their families' futures (Bianet-Castellanos 2007; Malkin 2004; Zenteno et al. 2013).

The youths discussed not being able to help but covet, as early as ages seven and eight, their neighbors' and even family members' material successes facilitated by immigration. Unable to ignore the larger and sturdier concrete houses being built adjacent to or near their own mud and aluminum-roofed residences or, likewise, the nearby businesses set up with *dolares* and not pesos, it was not long before children began imagining earning money in el norte so they could do the same.

Subject to hardships, Rogelio had been thinking about immigrating since he was ten years of age, or since he was "very little": "I had this motive to come here because over there, life is very hard." When asked what gave him this idea at such a young age, Rogelio responded, "Because I saw many guys who came over here, [and] they made their houses, they put businesses there, [and] they began to produce more money. For example, I saw one of my neighbors who lived to the side of me, he was here fifteen years, [and] he made his house, bought his car, [started] his business, bought a taxi, and now the guy lives well."

The sight of late-model trucks at their neighbors' or relatives' homes or the new and more fashionable clothes of return migrants also prompted youths to think about migration. On their return trips to their hometowns in Mexico, well-dressed and accessorized adult and youth migrants would brag, offering mostly aggrandized stories about their lives in New York City. Martín's uncle was one of those adults who would exaggerate his wealth while hiding the conditions that he endured to amass it. On one of his returns, he said, "[My uncle] returned with a lot of money and, like, his personality was different. He arrived with gold chains and watches, and he had a new truck. So then I saw that and said, 'Oh, and what do they do over there to obtain that money?' And so then, yes, of course, [seeing] it influenced me, and since then my thoughts started to change, and I said, 'I think I want to go to the U.S.' But here, my uncle has a real life as a dishwasher."

Mexican youths knew few individuals who critically examined these stories. Teachers who knew about the realities of migration appeared to be the most vocal in challenging these images and would do so when former students would stop by during classes to bid them good-bye as they prepared to leave. Using these moments to influence the remaining youths' thoughts about migration, teachers attempted to counter the seductive images return migrants had planted in youths' heads. One of the teachers in San Pedro expressed significant concern about the effects that return migrants had on the town's youths: "Professor

Mendoza also talked about return migrants who come and regale the kids with stories about how they're the boss in restaurants, talk of wonders, with lots of gold chains around their necks, playing up their lives but not discussing the truth about the conditions in which they live. He seemed angry that they come in and create a false impression for the kids that only encouraged the youths' desires to migrate even more" (Martinez, June 27, 2006). Rodolfo was the only independent Mexican teenage migrant who spoke about his family's earnest discussions meant to dissuade his immigration. Emphasizing its dangers, Rodolfo's parents warned him and his siblings to not even consider immigrating:

> The truth was, my family was scared. Because on the news, you heard a lot that there were deaths, that they had encountered dead people in the desert, in the rivers, and more than anything, my family—like my papá and my mamá—were scared, and they never thought that we would immigrate because we knew of the danger. (So they spoke with you about the danger? Or how did you know that they had that fear?) By watching the news and, more than anything, when we were watching the news, my mamá and papá would talk to us about the idea, not to think about doing it because we already knew the danger.

Overall, independent Mexican teenage migrants discussed only knowing of the "positive" effects of immigration as young children, and as a result, they wished to immigrate for themselves. Observing the effects that immigration brought to neighbors and relatives at these tender ages, the youths wanted the same for their futures. However, with return migrants omitting details of the sacrifices they made and the indignities and conditions they endured to secure these material rewards, youths' impressions of immigration were incomplete. Few, it appears, shared negative details with the youths, leaving their ideas of easy success intact until the independent Mexican teenage migrants could experience the realities for themselves. Teachers like Professor Mendoza encouraged youths to stay and study and to become "something here, like a teacher, a doctor, a *licenciado*, or professional, and not have to return to carry heavy things or worry," while parents simply wanted them to avoid danger. Hard pressed to identify anyone else who dissuaded them from their departures, youths mostly continued to entertain untarnished dreams of immigration until they were able to leave.

"TO MAINTAIN ONE'S FAMILY . . ."

As discussed in chapter 2, youths' own humble goals of supporting their families were at the core of their desire to immigrate. Prospective independent Mexican teenage migrants learned, through observation as well as direct communication, the most about migration, especially its relation to familism, or "supporting their families," by witnessing firsthand the examples of migration undertaken by older kin, including older siblings, aunts, uncles, and cousins, as well as peers and other older nonkin friends—and less typically, parents, as cited by Dreby (2010: 123).

Independent Mexican teenage migrants said that they frequently observed and repeatedly benefitted from economic remittances sent by relatives to their households, which caused them to hold these relatives in high regard (Blum 2009; Bourdieu 1977b, 1990; Castañeda and Buck 2011; Malkin 2004). While growing up, Herminda and Martín were both beneficiaries of their uncles' migrations and, as exemplified by their remittances, their thoughtful and sustained natal household engagement *across borders*. In Herminda's case, her uncle's economic remittances actually prevented her from dropping out earlier when her mother (his sister) simply had no money. Herminda recalled, "Mamá doubted that I [would continue] in school, but my uncle, the man who constructed the house, who was here for seventeen years, working in the United States, he gave a little bit of support to my mamá and tried to convince her that education was important and that I [could] go with my cousin, because I practically did not go to school and it was him that [caused the] turning point, because my cousin had that privilege." Martín also recalled his uncles' generosity and sensitivity to his household's needs even from New York City: "Yes, my uncles always have been good people, and they are always conscious of the situation in Mexico, so then my uncles, when I was there [in Mexico], they always supported us emotionally and also economically. Yes, they supported us a lot. They sent us things like clothes, tennis shoes, and also money."

Lastly, friends, especially those who were already adults, provided critical examples of what they could achieve for their families through immigration. The youths recounted endless stories of friends who had immigrated and were able to provide their families with material comforts via their remittances. Antonio's economic remittances were the ones that made the greatest impact on Rodolfo. During one of Rodolfo's weekly stints selling fruits and vegetables in Antonio's hometown of Apalingo, Rodolfo learned that eighteen-year-old Antonio was sending approximately 4,000 pesos, or $400 USD, monthly to his mamá so that she could pay for household expenses and improve their home. After this fact was verified by his cousin's husband, Pedro (also a friend of Antonio's), Rodolfo began to think more earnestly about migration.

It is not surprising that youths began to develop ideas of accumulating wealth after years of observing how others' migrations impacted their surroundings, especially when they themselves were the beneficiaries of remittances. What was unexpected, however, were the young ages at which the youths began to understand the relationship between immigration and meeting a family's basic needs and plot their own journeys. Considered out of sync with the age norms touted by modern, globalizing discourses of adolescence, these youths challenge age expectations about household departure as they first think about, engage in, and then actually undertake consequential steps leading to migration (Arnett 2001; Hagestad and Neugarten 1985; Marini 1984a; Settersten 2003). The next section focuses on the arc of the youths' progress toward New York—from wishful contemplation, to active deliberation, and ultimately to immigration.

TIMING THOUGHTS OF EMIGRATION

As Martín suggested in the chapter opening, youths possess specific ideas about when, or at what ages, people should immigrate. While the youths' *actual* immigrations during their teenage years were usually timed around the end of their compulsory schooling, several youths had *toyed* with the idea of immigration many years before. Youths had already seen and experienced firsthand the material benefits of immigration. Other considerations prompting thoughts about leaving included financial difficulties that affected their school going and, as in Genoveva's and many other youths' cases, seeing no other future in their communities except for arduous labor in the fields. Aware even at these ages of their households' precarious financial situations and the difficulties associated with earning enough to remain in their hometowns, youths began to more seriously consider immigrating.

For most of the prospective independent Mexican teenage migrants, *further* deliberation about migration without parents coincided with dwindling finances that, among other things, ended youths' schooling. Even though academically gifted Manuel—who had been chosen to compete in regional academic competitions—had received a scholarship to extend his schooling beyond what was compulsory, such schooling would always be at the mercy of his household's precarious finances. Awarded only a partial scholarship to attend preparatoria, after only a couple of months, he found that he simply could not pay the remaining balance on his tuition. Even with a scholarship and *Oportunidades*, a government program that provided cash transfers to low-income households to offset the costs of schooling, the expense of attending the school had become too much to bear; by October of his first year, he was already considering dropping out. With no other recognizable pathways to social mobility, an idea that had been planted by his brother-in-law suddenly became more attractive:

> [Around the time when I couldn't continue my studies,] a brother-in-law came and told me [that] here to save 5,000 pesos you have to work a year, but there in the United States, [that's] what you earn in a month. If you work really hard [here], you can earn, like, 1,000 pesos in a month, and there, it's, like, 10,000 pesos

> if you work the entire year. It is like working ten years [here] as a farmer. If you are [there] over three or four years, you can earn 300,000 pesos, which here is like 30,000 dollars. And that is how I got the idea [to immigrate].

With this idea planted in his head, Manuel went to the fields to consider his options. He went to the fields to think, he said, because before his father died, he would always go to the fields to mull over important decisions. Weighed down by thoughts of his present and, most likely, future debts if he remained in school, Manuel yearned to have this burden lifted. By November, the month of his sixteenth birthday, Manuel would free himself from school debts by dropping out and making his way to New York City.

Other independent Mexican teenage migrants who had resisted the prospect of immigration were forced to consider it when faced with other types of crises, including financial and family conflicts. Long bouts of unemployment, parental death, and even family conflicts forced youths to consider what was previously inconceivable. Samuel was one of those youths who had not previously considered immigrating, but after voluntarily leaving school years before and after his father's death, now nineteen-year-old Samuel discussed how he had found moderate success supporting his mother and sister by migrating internally and "following [the] work." More than a thousand miles away from his home in Valle de Chalco in the state of Mexico, his last job in Mexico had taken him to Cancún, where he installed windows. These jobs, however, were temporary, and the company he had been working for informed him that he would not be needed again for at least three months. After three months had come and gone, he grew desperate for work, and his older friend's invitation to join him in Brooklyn appeared to be his only option. Although he had never considered it before, the long bout of unemployment made him feel like he "had to come here." Given two months to gather money for the journey, then seventeen-year-old Samuel decided to borrow from his friend and leave in January. Ironically, his mother would receive a call from his company only days later asking him to come for another job in Cancún.

Family discord could also *unexpectedly* prompt some youths' departures. Although his father's debts forced him to end his studies after secundaria, sixteen-year-old Carlos not only believed that he could eventually continue with his studies but also, as the youngest and only son who had not immigrated, felt he should support his mamá, both financially and emotionally, at home. With his brothers' return visit culminating in a particularly violent encounter with their father, he was forced to rethink his original plans and abruptly left "from one day to the next." Without much input from Carlos, his brothers simply told him that he was joining them. They made all the arrangements for him, giving Carlos little time to think about, much less process, this decision. Unable to imagine remaining in close proximity to his father after they had come to blows, he simply accompanied his brothers. Faced with these challenges as teenagers and believing immigration to be the only viable pathway to improve their situations, youths began to see leaving for el norte as an attractive—and oftentimes the only—alternative available to fulfill their aspirations and, in Carlos's case, tranquility.

When youths wished to immigrate at earlier ages, however, older relatives attempted to dissuade them by reminding them that they were too young to leave, much less enter the labor market in New York City. At age eleven or twelve, José Luis was told as much during one of his father's return visits home. As his father, uncle, and cousins prepared to depart again, he proposed leaving with them to work. Applying modernized discourses to these ages and perhaps drawing from what they observed in New York City, they all saw him as "a little boy" who "did not know how to work." Instead, he was encouraged to enter into and complete secundaria.

Suggesting something more than transient, immature thoughts about their futures, however, some youths were more cautious in determining their *own* age- and experience-related criteria about the timing of their immigrations. Concerned that they would be unsuccessful in entering into and participating in the New York City labor market in light of their lack of independent work experiences, they each had misgivings about immigrating at their young ages.

Although Antonio invited Rodolfo to join him in New York City when he was only fourteen, Rodolfo turned him down because—despite working for pay since he was seven (and working for his family long before that)—he had not consistently worked *away* from his family full time. Associating labor migration with independent, full-time work experience and the maturity that accompanied it, Rodolfo felt that he was not yet adequately prepared. Explaining why he did not jump at Antonio's invitation when he was fourteen, Rodolfo explained,

> [I] felt like even if they [had] offered me jobs [in New York], I [was] not going to do them well because I do not have experience. When one does not have experience, one is always like "How am I going to do this?" and "How are they going to show me?" or "[What] if I don't do it well?" That is what one suffers a lot when they do not have experience, but when one has experience, or they put me to do whatever they're going to put me to do, I know that I can do it even if it is difficult.

Rodolfo believed that it was at his last job, where he worked away from home, that he developed the skills and self-assurance that would ensure his successful immigration to and employment in the United States. Employed by a produce vendor who involved him in all aspects of the selling of fruits and vegetables, from negotiating with suppliers to selling to customers, Rodolfo felt that by performing these tasks over the course of the year, he had matured and significantly developed confidence: "The last job, yes, it gave me strength, more than anything, in myself—like self-esteem—to feel motivated. Like if I go to the United States and I go to work, . . . I am confident in what I am going to do."

Whether at ten or fifteen or sixteen, the ages at which independent teenage migrants even begin to consider migration without the security of their parents or guardians—much less embark for another country thousands of miles away—are generally considered "off-time," or premature, by Western norms. Reflecting this, most independent Mexican teenage migrants only possessed an awareness about migration and its effects after they reached adolescence. During their teenage years, their interest intensified after encountering family or financial hardships or realizing the scarcity of opportunities in their home communities. Oftentimes, even if the hardships were present their whole lives, it was only when they finally realized that the pathways for survival and social mobility were impeded at home that they seriously pursued emigration from Mexico.

This awareness and consideration of immigration occurred at ages that in "modern states" are not usually associated with living independently and away from one's parents. While many who began to consider immigration before the completion of secundaria suffered disapproval from their parents and other relatives, other youths self-regulated their own notions of the age-appropriateness of immigration until they believed there were no other options and/or were mature enough to take on the types of responsibilities associated with independent immigration and, more specifically, working. Regardless of the exact ages at which they began to notice and consider the effects of immigration, independent Mexican teenage migrants were persistent and pursued immigration until their thoughts become realities.

INDEPENDENTLY INQUIRING ABOUT IMMIGRATION

By their early teenage years, these independent Mexican teenage migrants began to inquire more earnestly about immigration, typically in the context of leaving to work and not leaving to reenter school. In these conversations, uncles, aunts, cousins, siblings, and even friends who resided in either Mexico or New York became resources who could provide the youths with information about immigration conditions and labor market characteristics that existed in New York City. Equipped with this information, youths were able to make more informed decisions, once and for all, about when and whether they would leave their homes to work in New York City.

The youths received this information about immigration and life in New York City in the form of social remittances, or "ideas, behaviors and social capital that flow from receiving to sending communities" when migrants return home for both short and indefinite stays and/or when they communicate by telephone (Levitt 1998: 926; Levitt 2001). In Alejandro's case, although he counted at least fifteen similarly aged or slightly older friends who had left for the United States in recent years, it was his friend Pablo who, during return visits and phone conversations, shared the most useful information with him. After being away for two years, Pablo had recently returned to San Valentín to stay for several months. During this visit, Pablo urged Alejandro as well as other friends to return with him, but he also cautioned that life was not easy in New York: "The lives for Mexicans who are there is very difficult, and . . . you cannot communicate over there with people in their language." He also advised them to "think about it [immigrating] seriously [because] it was difficult there, difficult to find work."

Other youths garnered information from phone calls that migrants initiated, on average, every eight to fifteen days. When older siblings, aunts and uncles, cousins, and friends called home, prospective independent Mexican teenage migrants took advantage of these opportunities to glean bits of information and overall impressions about immigration, the New York City labor market, and living there in general. By intercepting her aunt's calls home to her grandmother and parents, Genoveva was able to learn about working in New York City, especially with respect to the types of jobs that youths her age and with her level of education could hold and what would be expected of her on the job. In their monthly phone conversations, her aunt told her that "the work is easier," they had "secure work," and "they can earn well." Using herself as an example, her aunt also disclosed strategies to ensure employment. Describing how she obtained her job making and selling curios, her aunt shared that "when you work, they ask you if you have experience." Her aunt had lied and answered affirmatively when asked. In addition to the types of jobs that their relatives held, the youths learned more specific details about work in New York City. In particular, they began to compare the not-so-negligible hour and wage differentials that existed between the jobs they worked in Mexico and those that they hoped to obtain in New York—especially with respect to what relatives and friends told them about employment patterns and other histories. Considering all these conversations, Genoveva ultimately decided that if she immigrated, she would seek a job similar to the one her aunt held.

Like the aforementioned return migrants—wearing modern clothes and displaying new purchases—who only highlighted the positive material outcomes of living in New York City, return migrants were tight lipped about the true cost of these goods—namely, the exploitative conditions in which they worked. Instead, Saúl recalled hearing that "here [in New York City], all of the bosses are really good people, that here you work a few hours, and that the work is not hard and [is] well paid." Likewise, Rogelio remembered the stories of young men who returned and told him about how he could earn a lot of money; however, they omitted the downsides of the New York City labor market for undocumented, underage immigrants, including working conditions. Carlos surmised that return migrants left out negative aspects "because of shame or not wanting to say the truth about what happened here or simply that they had better luck or fortune here than there."

Only a handful of youths shared that they learned the contrary, mostly from relatives who spoke about the *downsides* of working in New York City—the poor treatment from bosses and the grueling schedules. Before he immigrated, Pedro's uncle had warned him that "it was very hard—no, ugly—that it was very hard, that they [bosses] scolded you a lot, that they [bosses] treated you very badly, and that you had to take it." Similarly, although Carlos's friends had told him more positive stories, his brothers had been more honest. Through them, he knew that he would be working up to sixteen hours a day and that the "work was more difficult than what we were accustomed to [in Mexico], [that] it was a big difference to work there than here [in New York]." The stories of exploitation, however, were largely ignored when considered alongside the overwhelmingly positive stories and material outcomes they heard and saw growing up—including the possibilities of helping their mamás or, more generally, alleviating their households' financial insecurities.

Besides learning about the labor market, the youths also learned about the logistics of immigration, including what they should acquire and do in preparation for it. Even in cases where relatives were arranging their migrations, youths recalled learning about which steps they needed to take to prepare for their own departures. Youths learned about "trustworthy" coyotes needed for crossing, how to identify them, and/or how to ask how much it would cost to cross the border (Spener 2009). Many of the youths already knew about the coyotes in their communities or were told which people could arrange for crossings as well as the costs: approximately two or three thousand dollars during the middle to late 2000s. They also discussed being told who could loan the money needed to pay for crossing.

Return migrants and immigrants communicating from the United States also shared that the crossing was difficult and imbued with significant risks ranging from apprehension to death. Youths such as Alejandro were told about the multiple dangers that immigrants encountered when crossing the increasingly militarized border of the mid-2000s with Operations Streamline and Jumpstart and immigration agents who abused sojourners (Martinez 2016b). Others were advised to take precautions against criminals who robbed immigrants of their possessions by leaving with only "the clothes on their backs." Ultimately, however, this did not protect them. On his own trek, then sixteen-year-old Ignacio learned that nothing was safe from criminals, as he and his fellow sojourners were robbed three times; he was forced to strip naked during his first assault, and his sweater and shoes were stolen. Females, including Carolina, Clementina, Herminda, and Izel, also learned from their older sisters and aunts about the risks of sexual assault. Lastly, the youths, including Rodolfo, shared that they knew of the widely documented unforgiving desert that could swallow them whole (Jimenez 2009; Urrea 2004).

Eventually, the prospective independent Mexican teenage migrants learned about living in isolation and fear in New York City. Adult relatives and friends shared cautionary stories about "the street" or complications they faced as foreigners (Malkin 2004), including difficulties communicating with others, racialized gang violence (as documented by De Genova and Ramos-Zayas 2003), and deportation (Dreby 2015). From friends such as Pablo, Alejandro and others learned to avoid African Americans and Puerto Ricans and to evade immigration officials by restricting their movements in public spaces or becoming "invisible." As a result, like the adults Malkin (2004: 79) discusses, youths' lives consisted of going "from their homes to their workplaces and from their workplaces home because if immigration grabs them, they will deport them." Mexican youths like Miguel discussed living enclosed, or *encerrados*, in their apartments. Underage and unable to drink and socialize in public out of fear of detection, "it was better to buy beers and drink them at home."

These adverse conditions and risks associated with migrating to and living in New York City were juxtaposed against the city's promises of modernity via beauty, wealth, and opportunity—all traits described to the youths since childhood and shown to them in photographs. Such images increasingly validated the plans they had already begun to concoct in their heads. When migrants sent photographs or shared pictures of their lives in New York City during their return trips to their hometowns, many contained the skyline, snow, or parks as a backdrop—symbols of difference and modernization absent from their towns in Mexico. Youths adopted this binary as prospective and actual independent Mexican teenage migrants and echoed the ways in which previous residents characterized their Mexican communities as "ugly" and "backward," or in terms that suggested an absence of modernity; the youths were told and believed that they would arrive in a modern city that was "better" and "prettier" than their own communities (Malkin 2004). They simply had to endure the "ugliness" of border crossing.

Conspicuously absent from most accounts, however, were two important and related details about settling in New York City: the difficulties associated with working and saving money and their living arrangements. Martín and Rogelio both felt "duped" by family and friends who had painted New York City as a "pretty" place where you could earn "lots of money." Laughing, perhaps at themselves and, in retrospect, their naivete at the time, the youths discussed how the city's "defects" and, as will be discussed in chapter 5, their undesirable jobs were often absent from conversations about New York City.

As a result, for several reasons, prospective independent Mexican teenage migrants appeared to possess doxa in the absence of an awareness of the costs—emotional, physical, and financial—associated with their newfound semiautonomous and autonomous statuses. First, to save face, relatives and friends were less than honest about their jobs. Emphasizing how pretty New York was, they failed to discuss their jobs or "all of the challenges that are in this country." As a result, youths knew little about the context they were preparing to enter and as such (even if it would not make much difference in their teenage decision-making) were unable to wholly weigh the costs and benefits of immigrating to New York City. As Martín stated, "So then I just came without knowing what I was going to encounter, because if I had known what I was going to encounter, I think that I would not have come over here."

Second, youths were privy to few discussions of the difficulties associated with living and saving money in New York City. When they observed people who returned to their hometowns with nothing to show, they attributed it to their weaknesses and wastefulness in New York—not to low wages and a high cost of living. It was an ill-kept secret that Martín's father, having immigrated and returned before Martín left, had nothing to show for his time in New York City because of his "vices" and his inability to "think": "When he came here, he just dedicated himself to drinking. And what my uncles tell me, because they lived with him, [was] that he was with women, and when he returned here—he did not know, you understand—because of that, he had to return with nothing." Few mentioned the costliness and low wages of New York and how that impacted their ability to save and send money home. Again blaming vices, Rodolfo's boss and role model, Jorge, who had immigrated to New York City at age seventeen and later returned to Mexico to open various businesses, buy a truck, and construct a home, advised him to always consider his reason for migration and actively resist expensive habits that would impede his ability to fulfill his dream of constructing a home and setting up a business back home.

Rodolfo shared that Jorge had advised him that

> if one day I would come to . . . work [I should take] all of the money that I earned [and] save it, to not waste it, because that is a sacrifice that one makes, to cross illegally, because one risks their life to cross illegally, because . . . more than anything, [one should] take advantage [of] what you are going to earn, [and] not spend it foolishly, because I know a lot of people who have gone over there, and they get lost there. . . . There they want to live the lives of rich people, and they

> pretend that they have everything, and the day that [they are] deported, they arrive [home] and they do not have anything.

However, Jorge left out the inevitable expenses Rodolfo would incur by living in New York City. The large sums the youths believed they would save and send home if they meticulously managed their money would be significantly reduced by the costs incurred as a result of their newfound independence in New York. When asked how much money they would really need to live in New York City, none of the prospective independent Mexican teenage migrants disclosed knowing that they would have to pay for utilities, transportation, or even cell phones aside from paying rent, nor could they approximate the costs. Although they dreamed of saving large sums in short periods of time, the youths soon found that these unforeseen expenses compromised their plans.

Lastly, other immigrants were also not entirely forthcoming about the new household configurations and living arrangements the youths would most likely encounter and be required to endure. While some knew that they would have to share rooms, several independent Mexican teenage migrants recalled that as they prepared to travel, they knew very little about where they would live and, more specifically, the crowded and cramped conditions that their relatives and friends endured. Prior to immigration, Rogelio recalled, "I thought that we were going to live in a big building. I thought that everything was going to be a wonder, everything of luxury. I imagined that."

With the social remittances shared through and across their social networks, which included return migrants as well as immigrants currently living in el norte, the youths began to create a picture, albeit incomplete, of immigration and the realities that awaited them in New York City. Absent, however, from all accounts, positive and negative, were discussions of just how independent they would be expected to become. Due to shortcomings in their inquiries and the selectivity of the information their contacts opted to share with them, the youths did not fully appreciate how immigration would require them to more fully adopt "adult" statuses. While discussions did tend to emphasize the primary activities the youths would be engaging in—that is, full-time work and earning wages—other adult expectations, such as supporting themselves, especially as undocumented immigrants, were not mentioned. Instead, most of those who prepared to enter the migration field viewed their imminent immigrations as extensions of their current lives, albeit on the northern side of the U.S.-Mexico border and with the ability to earn much more.

NEGOTIATING MIGRATION

Inevitably, learning about life in New York City from return migrants and individuals residing in New York City led to the question of the youths' own immigrations. With limited information but a strong desire to migrate to benefit their families and themselves, prospective independent teenage migrants broached the topic with members of their social networks and both elicited and solicited social remittances in the form of encouragement, invitations, and material offers of assistance to migrate.

Encouragement often came from relatives already in the United States. When fourteen-year-old Clementina spoke with her twenty-seven-year-old male cousin on the phone, he always prodded her and told her, "Let's go. I'll take you." Offering his assistance and also that of his sisters (her female cousins), who, he said, would help her, he was not only inviting her but *animandola*, or motivating her, to join them in the United States.

Other youths received invitations, but with conditions attached. Several described how their uncles and aunts were open to their arrivals in New York City and would let the youths reside with them, but only with the understanding that the youths would, reflecting adult-like independence, not become emotional or economic burdens. Perhaps aware of some of the troubles Mario was already facing in San Pedro, his aunt and uncle were clear that he could come but were also clear that they would not tolerate any behaviors that would cause them trouble or grief. He could come, but "with rules. You are not going to be able to drink, go out, none of that." Genoveva's rules included employment. Offering to help her pay for her passage, her aunts were very candid about why they would help her and what they expected from her when she arrived. They told her, in Genoveva's words, that "if I want to go, they can help me, but to go to work."

For other youths, getting relatives to support their wishes and assist them in making arrangements for migration was more of a negotiation. Both José Luis and Herminda had to convince their relatives to help with passage costs and provide housing once they were in New York. After obeying his father's wishes and completing secundaria, José Luis wanted to take advantage of his uncles' and cousins' imminent departure from San Pedro to New York City and accompany them on their trek north. His father, however, preferred that he remain at home with his mamá to continue his studies and accused him of knowing little about the realities of labor in New York City, as José Luis believed that work there was "easy." He remained unconvinced that José Luis should immigrate.

However, José Luis was undeterred and threatened to leave without his father's approval. He told his father, "If you don't give me permission to go with you, one day I am going to go [anyway]. I am not going to stay here." Preparing to return to el norte, his cousin Beto urged him to speak with his father once more and try to convince him that it would be best to emigrate with his cousin rather than going alone. After several back-and-forth conversations, José Luis's father finally relented and agreed to have his son join his uncles and cousins in New York City.

Herminda's negotiation took several years, even with her revelation that she was enduring sexual abuse in Mexico. Only fourteen, Herminda needed to convince her sisters that she would not become a *carga*, or economic burden, on them when she arrived. Although Herminda begged them to let her stay with them not long after her sexual abuse began, her sisters denied her requests. Two years later, they relented, and they, along with her uncle and aunt, agreed to help with arranging and paying for her trip to New York. When asked what had made the difference, Herminda pointed to her desperation, but she also suggested that being two years older lessened the perceived dependence on her sisters:

> I think that the reason was [because] she [my sister] could not take on that responsibility. She couldn't support me because she was already the mother of a child. So then I think that she was not in any condition, but when I was sixteen years old, I brought up the situation again, and the situation became more urgent, and I had to live there. I couldn't go on living there in Mexico with my mamá and that person, and that is when I decided to convince my sister, desperately, [of] what was happening here, and that is when she decided to help me with the money.

Confronted with relatives who resisted or outright refused to support their departures, some youths considered alternatives to ensure their migrations. Manuel devised a backup plan that involved calling on other relatives in case his brothers were unwilling to help him migrate to New York City: "At first, like, more than anyone, I spoke with my brother, and then I thought, if my brothers do not help me, my brothers-in-law are going to help me—no?—to get money, and I was sure that they were not going to let me go, since I am the youngest, and I commented to my mamá, 'They can't leave me like that, Mamá,' and then I told my brother-in-law, 'I do want to go, but I am embarrassed to ask to go with you,' and then if not, I have my brothers."

Instead of following the "luggage" model of parent-driven migration, some youths were forced to engage in "relay" migration to fulfill the wishes of older relatives or siblings, not parents, who spurred the youths to immigrate (Arizpe 1982; Wilson 1993). While Carlos was a last-minute addition, Miguel's departure had been planned by his brothers. Although he had not even considered leaving his mamá and Ciudad Nezahualcóyotl and he wished to continue with his studies after secundaria, his brothers decided that it was now his turn to immigrate and help support their family (Arizpe 1982; Wilson 1993). One brother was starting his own family, and he needed Miguel to join him and his other brothers so that some of the financial responsibilities could be shifted onto him. Emphasizing his sense of obligation while relating the sort of imposition his brother had placed on him, Miguel stated the following frankly: "Well, sometimes . . . it is not because one wants to come but because they do it to help their families so that they can improve things a little bit. Sometimes it is not because you want to, even if you have to do it so that the situation [at home] is a little better. Sometimes one has to do what they do not want to do, or you are indecisive, but the decision was already made."

Although contentious negotiations do occur, in most cases invitations to reside with relatives do not ring hollow even if they include conditions. Over periods of time—some shorter, some longer—prospective independent Mexican teenage migrants and relatives negotiated the youths' departures from their home communities to new host communities. Because these departures also usually entailed transfers from their own parent-led households to older-relative-led households in which the youths also had to become more independent, to varying degrees during negotiations, relatives relayed "rules" so the youths could become active contributors to the households rather than emotional and financial burdens. In these new environs, teenage youths were expected to move more quickly toward adulthood.

ARRANGING FOR CROSSINGS: CONFIANZA, COYOTES, AND CASH

As with adult immigrants, the social networks in which youths are located and the *confianza* (trust) and cash, or social and economic capital that flows through their relations in these networks, are critical to ensuring that prospective independent Mexican teenage migrants arrive in New York City.[4] Spanning across transnational spaces, the youths' networks are composed of trusted adult relatives and friends located in el norte who, in turn, contact reliable coyotes back in their hometowns. Youths depend on their older brothers, brothers-in-law, sisters, uncles, aunts, cousins, and sometimes even friends with whom they have remained in contact to act as trusted conduits who can, in turn, recruit and negotiate with coyotes, provide money, and even secure loans in preparation for immigration. The collective actions of this cast of actors, all embedded in transnational networks across the U.S.-Mexico border, guarantees that youths leave their hometowns, cross the U.S.-Mexico border, and arrive safely in New York City (Spener 2009).

However, as the U.S.-Mexico border has become increasingly militarized and the economic and legal costs of apprehension become more and more expensive for the youths, strategies for Mexican migration have shifted. The migrants' strategies include crossing in groups without guides (as my grandparents did at the turn of the twentieth century), using "freelancers" at the border, hiring trusted guides whose only business is human smuggling, or relying on more fragmented drug and human smuggling operations (Spener 2009: 158; see also Sanchez 2014; Andreas 2000). The independent Mexican teenage migrants with whom I spoke were fortunate, as they crossed no later than the mid-2000s with the help of individuals who had worked to earn the trust of their relatives, their friends, and themselves—whom O'Leary (2009a) calls "coyotes comunitarios"—as opposed to the operations of today's cartels (Corchado 2014; Dickson 2014; Sanchez 2014). When asked about whom they relied on to cross, both prospective and actual independent Mexican teenage migrants echoed Carolina's words: "Everyone knew of the coyotes; it was not a secret at all." The youths described human smugglers as individuals who had brought their relatives, their friends, or even their friends' relatives across the border. In Rodolfo's case, the man with whom he was negotiating, a recruiter for the local coyote, was the uncle of a good friend. At this point in time, coyotes were still trusted community members.[5]

Due to the personal nature of these relationships, coyotes also must trust the people they will cross (Sanchez 2014). Although youths or their surrogates can only offer partial payment, because they know the youths' family members and/or friends—some of whom they have crossed before—coyotes are confident that they will be paid in full and without hesitation. Thus they "put the youths' names on a list" and agree to take the minors with or without their older relatives. This was why relatives could arrange for the youths' migration from New York. From there, relatives made arrangements with coyotes who had brought them to the United States. When it came time for the youths to migrate, the coyote's previous transactions as well as conversations with the youths' relatives in New York City helped because the coyote had been assured that payment would soon follow.

Confident that the independent Mexican teenage migrants would work upon arrival and therefore be able to pay them back, relatives funded the youths' passages with or without previously established agreements about payback. Lazaro relied on his uncle and his uncle's friends in the United States for a loan to immigrate, but only under the condition that he would pay the money back. Beyond kin, youths looked to friends and even bosses to facilitate and finance their migrations. Samuel, Rodolfo, and Saúl all discussed nonkin who arranged their emigrations. In Rodolfo's and Saúl's cases, employers provided loans to cross over with the understanding that once in New York, the youths would pay off their debts. Although payback often took years, the youths discussed how they diligently kept their word.

Sharing confianza with those who lent the youths money proved to be essential to their departures. While Rodolfo was able to finance his journey half with his savings and half with money loaned to him by a close friend in Mexico, Saúl was asked for additional collateral before money exchanged hands. Nearly three years after he began searching for a way to finance his journey and after first asking a friend of his papá, by the time Saúl was seventeen, he found work through a man who engaged in annual circular migration among Tlapa, Guerrero, and New York City and was constructing a house in Guerrero. After developing a relationship with him through which he demonstrated his work ethic and trustworthiness, Saúl explained his situation and asked him for a loan: "Because I had worked with him, he [gladly] loaned me the money." Just in case, however, as a guarantee that the loan would be repaid, the man asked Saúl to surrender the deed to the land his father had left him.

Albeit to varying degrees, these negotiations with relatives and coyotes suggest one thing: these teenage minors are not idly and passively sitting by and allowing others to make decisions about their migrations. As with adult immigrants, relatives and friends assist with making preparations, but ultimately, the youths themselves exercise their agency as the ones who must execute all the steps to ensure that they will migrate. "Feeling big" and "gathering courage," as Fidencio stated, the youths make this life-altering decision. Perhaps it is Herminda's reflection on her decision to migrate that best sums up the youths' actions. After her sister sent her money and contacted the coyote, Herminda visited the coyote and asked about the dangers involved in crossing. Even after being told that "[she] could die there [in the desert]," Herminda said, "OK, I am going. I'm going because I don't want to be here, I want to start a new life, I want to work, [and] I want to take the reins of my life at sixteen years of age."

AGING MIGRATION

While the youths' seem to come to terms with making these momentous decisions at these ages, the coyotes are very sensitive to the vulnerabilities their clients' youthfulness and unaccompanied statuses may elicit at several junctures of their sojourns across Mexico, the U.S.-Mexico border, and the U.S. Southwest and finally to New York City. The youths' ages must be taken into consideration, as the coyotes and the youths make the final preparations for successful journeys. Before leaving, coyotes instruct the youths to employ several strategies to mask their young ages in case of detection. In short, these strategies figuratively turn the youths into adults.

The first strategy is to procure false papers that add years to their actual ages. Youths obtain birth certificates that cite birth dates several years earlier than their birth years. While some coyotes already possess altered birth certificates, others send the youths to other towns to obtain falsified documents, including birth certificates and identification cards. Airplane tickets are then purchased with these false papers. On paper, then, the youths are transformed into adults.

Youths are also coached to verbally falsify their ages. They are advised to state that they are at least eighteen, or no longer minors. This is especially important as they come into contact with officials who might challenge their documents as they travel. Airline attendants and security officers, they stated, scrutinized their documents and then their faces with skepticism. Both Manuel and Rodolfo recalled especially tense moments with airport security agents who viewed the ages listed on their IDs with disbelief. When Manuel was going through security at the Phoenix airport, well within the U.S. border, he and his friend were questioned. When he turned his falsified driver's license over to the Transportation Security Administration agent, the agent asked him how old he was, to which he replied, "Eighteen." Unconvinced by his response and his Mexican driver's license, the agent continued to ask him if he drove; Manuel lied and responded that he was actually a taxi driver in Guerrero. Satisfied with his response, the agent let him pass, and he entered his assigned concourse. After an agent grilled his friend, he too was allowed entrance, and once the excitement passed, the two purchased coffee with their remaining three dollars.

Rodolfo likewise drew the suspicion of airport agents on the first leg of his journey in Mexico. Already advised by his coyote to "not act like we knew each other so as to not elevate the suspicion [that they were migrants] on the plane," Rodolfo was stopped as he was making his way to his gate: "I got a little nervous, and the official asked me where I was going and who I was going with, because I looked underage. I told them that I was going with some of my uncles and that we were going to Hermosillo . . . to visit some of my aunts. He asked me where my uncle was, and I told [him,] 'All of that group over there,' and I told him that I went ahead, and he let me go."

Not simply considered akin to adult immigrants who are smuggled in, these independent Mexican teenage migrants are treated differently and are armed with different resources to assist their crossing. Coyotes take precautionary measures to ensure that despite their youthful appearances, the youths will not be apprehended. Coaching them to falsify their ages verbally and in documents in order to successfully arrive at their new households in New York City, the coyotes are effectively further clearing the path so that youths can transition to adulthood in New York City.

LEAVING PARENTS (AND DEPENDENCE) BEHIND

With their young ages obscured prior to emigrating, the last step they take definitively marks their continued and accelerated transitions to adulthood: their departure from their natal households. The process of leaving their families—and most importantly, their mamás—marks a significant shift in the youths' dependence and their relationships with their parents. A traumatic act, this separation also represents, as discussed in chapter 2, an abrupt shift in their parent-child relationships. With this one act, youths alter their relationships from children dependent on parents or even interdependence to parents dependent on children and children dependent on themselves (Macmillan and Copher 2005; Rossi and Rossi 1990; Schoeni and Ross 2005). Most of the youths' parents were opposed to this shift, resisting, both actively and passively, the youths' plans for departure. Most parents simply believed that at ages fourteen, fifteen, and sixteen, their children were too young to leave home.

As Luis outlined in the beginning of this chapter, the youths' preparations often occurred without their parents' knowledge. As their departures approached, youths asked for their parents' permission as the last necessary step in their preparation for immigration. In this case, however, the idea of "asking" is perhaps better understood as a combination of informing their parents of their decisions to leave and requesting their blessings as they embark on their journeys. This act, then, unambiguously signified the beginning of a period in their lives in which they would assert their own wishes and not necessarily those of their parents.

When I asked about their parents' reactions to the news of their leaving, dark clouds fell over the faces of most of the youths. All recalled strong reactions from their parents that ranged from denial to crying sorrowfully as they prepared to leave. When asked to recall his mamá's reaction to his departure at age sixteen, fat, juicy tears began to roll down Pedro's face, and we had to temporarily halt our interview.

By preserving the idea that their children were too young and incapable of making decisions leading to their independence, several parents, similar to Luis's father at this chapter's opening, remained in denial about their leaving and simply would not accept it. Similarly, Fidencio's parents deemed him, at age fifteen, "too young to go," yet he insisted and even cried to get his parents to cave in and consent to his departure. Fidencio stated, "They did not trust me. [They believed that] I was still [too] young to come."

Although Rodolfo had shared his plans with her six months before, his mamá pretended she did not hear him until faced with the day of his departure. After telling her that he had made arrangements to leave Mexico with his friend Pedro's uncle, she did not believe him; rather, she appeared patronizing, in disbelief that he, at such a young age, would actually plan such a significant event and consider leaving: "My mamá told me, 'Oh, but how are you going to go? It's dangerous; you should not go,' like [in a patronizing voice], 'Yes, of course [you are going]' and like that."

It was not until the day he was leaving that his mamá realized that he was determined to go to New York City. He arrived home late that evening, and when his mamá asked why, Rodolfo explained that he had been making last-minute arrangements for his trip. Then she realized that he was serious. She was unable to control her crying, so Rodolfo's uncle arrived and spoke with her to calm her down, and he convinced her that Rodolfo would be fine in spite of his young age: "So then my uncle spoke with her and told her, 'You know what? He is young, but he has matured, and I know that he is going to try hard.'" Emphasizing the inevitability of his departure as well as the importance for Rodolfo of receiving his mother's blessing, his uncle continued: "Then he advised my mamá, 'Let him go, and do not detain him, because if you detain him, he is still going to go, and [it's] better that you give him a blessing and that he goes well and that he communicates with you . . . than if he goes and does not communicate with you.'"

Interestingly enough, these preparations helped facilitate reunifications that were less discussed or examined: younger siblings with older siblings or, more generally, younger relatives with older relatives, some of whom behaved similarly with parents in Mexico when it was their time to migrate. When asked why they wished to leave for New York, some youths expressed the desire to be reunited with family members now in New York, whom they missed and to whom they had been close back in Mexico. In fact, Armando shared that he had missed his older sisters when he was in Puebla. He wanted to "come to be with them too. [He] wanted to see them."

Although more recent discussions of transitions to adulthood challenge the notions of five set markers—completing school; leaving home; finding productive, full-time employment; marrying; and having children—as indicators of becoming adults, in the cases of poor Mexican youths whose life courses are more standardized, one cannot minimize the impact that leaving one's home, one's parents, and more importantly, one's dependence behind in Mexico have on both the parents and the youths and their understandings of their ages (Arnett 2006; Shanahan et al. 2005). In this instant, the youths and parents renegotiated their understandings of the youths' ages, the appropriateness of independent migration at their ages, and of course, the continuum of dependence and independence. This was evident when parents challenged the youths' ability to plan and then embark on such a journey without parental assistance or presence. Tensions between parent and child with respect to the youths' ages and maturity came to a head as the youths, at their moment of departure, most explicitly asserted their own understandings of age and independence.

CROSSING THE U.S.-MEXICO BORDER

As the day of their departures approached, the youths discussed being not fearful but rather, as in Miguel's case, "a little sad because you know that you are leaving, [and] you do not know when you are going to return. Like they say, a million things cross through your head." When the day finally arrived, however, there was no time for sentimentality. With few belongings or, as in Mauricio's case, "two sets of clothes, food, and water," the youths set out on their life-altering journeys. While some youths went into great detail about whom they encountered on the trip and how they made their journey, others were more tightlipped, willing only to vaguely discuss preparations in Mexico, sites of crossings, and then arrivals in New York City.[6]

In all cases, however, two details were almost universally shared: the routes they followed to New York City and the modes of transportation they used. Most took buses from their hometowns to their state's capital and then another bus from there to Mexico City. From Mexico City, youths then took a plane to the state of Sonora. From there, by bus, van, or plane, youths arrived in Nogales, the border city from which they would depart by foot for its U.S. sister city: Nogales, Arizona.

As other scholars focusing on adult border crossing discuss, most youths either immigrated with older relatives or friends or quickly made friends, usually also with older adults, so as to take care of each other during the duration of the journey (O'Leary 2009a). While some youths, including Miguel, José Luis, and Rogelio, immigrated with their uncles and cousins, others crossed with older brothers who were leaving again after returning home. While Carlos immigrated with his brothers after their short return home, Lazaro's brother was finally returning to New York after eight months in his hometown and took Lazaro with him.

Both males and females who left without relatives discussed joining others and forming groups in order to survive their treks and arrivals. Some joined these groups to watch out for each other in case of assault, robbery, detection, or the risks they faced in an unforgiving desert; females clustered together in order to minimize the chances of sexual assault (O'Leary 2009b; Ruiz Marrujo 2009). Rodolfo recounted two thirty-something-year-old men from his hometown who acted as his protectors. As they crossed the Sonora desert and encountered immigration agents, he said, "[They] were taking care of me, they were calling me 'the little boy, the little boy,' and wherever I went, they followed me. Where I hid, they were going to hide too; since we were from the same town, we were always together." Female youths who feared sexual assault believed that there was safety in numbers. After arriving in Mexico City from

Puebla, Herminda and her friend met some other girls: "There, we started establishing a relationship to take care of ourselves, us, because the majority were men who we did not know, strangers, and we did not know what was going to happen."

Youths who do not have family or friends in New York City may also develop relationships with strangers with whom they are traveling. Then, upon arrival, they might have a place and people with whom to stay. Saúl discussed befriending a man on the journey who was headed to New York City because Saúl needed a place to stay upon arrival. Once in Arizona, his newly acquired friend called his friends in New York to see if they would let Saúl come and stay with them. Although his friends said no, his new friend opted to bring Saúl with him to the apartment in Queens so that they would not be able to turn him away.

With heavy border militarization causing an increase in the number of crossing attempts and longer durations for the crossings themselves, youths endured a passage through the Sonora desert that took anywhere from a handful of days to a month. In crossing, the youths faced the physical challenges of extreme heat during the day and extreme cold at night; the threat of *la migra*, or U.S. Customs and Border Patrol officers; and transnational criminal organizations that used the opportunity to transport humans and illicit substances or simply rob the immigrants. Masking the trauma of crossing and reinforcing his masculinity, Fidencio attempted to minimize the severity of the experience as he recounted an emotionally, if not physically, trying process. He described his crossing in terms of an absurd competition between the desert and himself. He shared that even when it got to the point that he had no water or food, it gave him *mas valor*, or more courage, and he became even more determined to make it across into the United States. Instead of thinking of the risks involved, he kept his thoughts positive, believing "I'll arrive to where I want to arrive." In his mind, it would be "counterproductive to be afraid or think of what could go wrong."

Others were more honest, speaking of the desperation they experienced in the desert. Ignacio discussed being robbed followed by dehydration and, after walking for hours, luckily finding a water source: "Since they had already taken everything away from us, we just decided to keep walking; with the heat, since the hills were dry like a desert, we got really thirsty, and we couldn't find any water. We came across a ravine with water, but up ahead from the ravine there were cattle that were drinking from the ravine. Since we were so thirsty, we just drank the same water the cattle were drinking from."

Few youths made it across on their days-long first attempts; others would try and try again, oftentimes taking up to a month to cross. While some youths were able to evade U.S. Customs and Border Patrol apprehension, others discussed multiple apprehensions. In most cases, both before and after the Trafficking

Victims Protection Reauthorization Act of 2008 (TVPRA), which requires U.S. Customs and Border Patrol agents to screen minors from contiguous countries for risks of exploitation or trafficking, independent Mexican teenage migrants were simply caught and released, free to attempt their crossings again and again until they were successful (Cavendish and Cortazar 2011).

Rodolfo breathlessly described the cat-and-mouse game he and the adults who accompanied him were forced to play with U.S. Customs and Border Patrol agents. Once they reached the U.S.-Mexico border, he and his group encountered immigration officials on quad-peds and in helicopters, and he discussed having to stop and wait numerous times for them to pass so his group could resume walking. After walking for two days and sleeping one miserable night in unforgivingly low desert temperatures dressed in pants, a sweatshirt, and a *gorra* (a sweater hat) and covered in a black plastic bag, Rodolfo was instructed by his guide to join the rest of the thirty-five border crossers in separating into twos and threes. They embarked across the desert in these groups, but soon, after being confronted with seven or eight immigration officials, they scattered.

At one point, an agent spotted him and was only two meters away when something that he could only describe as fate intervened. The official was called on the radio to assist with the capture of four of his fellow traveling companions: two brothers, a mother, and a daughter. That gave him time to run and hide. Thinking he was alone, he panicked, unsure of what to do next, but before long, the coyote came back around, repeating their safe word—*alacranes*, or scorpions. Rodolfo was soon reunited with the remaining fifteen people who had evaded the grasp of immigration agents. Their next attempt was more successful, and after hiding and then trying again at nine o'clock in the evening, by four in the morning, Rodolfo found himself on the U.S. side, awaiting a truck that would drive him to another van that would take them to a safe house. There they would "relax, call their loved ones to tell them that they were OK, bathe, wash their clothes, play cards, and watch television." Two days later, another van picked them up to drive them to New York City.

Likewise, Ignacio described an equally harrowing experience crossing the U.S.-Mexico border. After enduring several assaults by delinquents, his group was split into subgroups of four who were then summoned across a golf course by the coyote's whistles. Upon hearing the high-pitched signals, they needed to run as fast as they could to reach

> a car waiting for us on the other side. There were people playing on the course as well as immigration officers, but someone would distract them while we ran across. I was part of the second group to cross the golf course. My group consisted of my uncle, my friend, and I. When the coyote whistled for us to run, the Central Americans in our group pulled my uncle and my friend back so that they,

> the Central Americans, could cross the golf course first. My friend was able to quickly get up and continue running; my uncle, however, stayed behind.

He continued:

> When we got to the pickup truck, it was extremely crowded. Five people had to lie down and hide under the backseats. One person fainted in the car. We all wanted to cry because it was so hot. We were so thirsty, hungry, and since we had to hold up each other's weight, it was overwhelming. We told the chauffeur who was driving the truck, but he was stubborn and didn't understand what we were all feeling. All the chauffeur kept telling us was to wait, and he gave us a jug of water to pour on the woman who fainted. But since we were all on top of each other, someone poured the water on everyone.

After arriving at the town and then a safe house, then sixteen-year-old Ignacio and his fellow migrants were given food, but he was wracked with worry about his uncle and unsure about whether to wait for him. Regardless, he was told that he could not wait in the house and was forced to continue on. Separated from his uncle, he was moved to another city and then another safe house, where they were then grouped by destination cities and taken to bus terminals, where their tickets were purchased. Throughout this, however, he remained unsure about whether to continue without his uncle; ultimately, he decided that he had to go on. Recounting the crossing, he had no idea how he was able to arrive: "Between the fear and the nerves, I didn't know what to say. I bought the stuff I needed, but I am not sure how I did it."

Other youths found themselves on the brink of giving up after enduring failures in crossing or even serious danger. Then sixteen-year-old Mauricio found himself repeatedly apprehended and released by U.S. Customs and Border Patrol agents. After one apprehension, he was detained in a *hielera*, or a room that felt like a freezer, where they blasted the air conditioning for three nights before releasing him. The fourth time he and his group were caught, Mauricio called his mamá and told her that he did not know what he was going to do. Seemingly in the limbo that O'Leary (2009: 94) calls "an intersection," or the point where migrants are "temporarily unable to move forward in their migration journey and unable or unwilling to go back to their communities of origin," Mauricio had already spent all his money, and he thought he would have to just stay where he was and work to earn money to go back home. Finally, his guide tried to cross him and the others one last time. With helicopters flying overhead, the fifth time, it seemed, was a charm.

Herminda more vividly recalled being fearful of transnational criminal organizations during the journey. Describing it as a "terrifying experience," Herminda remembered crossing at a point where a shooting had occurred the previous day, and police were all around. She also noted, "Those who crossed us, they were taking drugs. They were taking advantage of the crossing to cross drugs." Sufficiently traumatized by the experience and fearful for her life, she began thinking that she could not continue on the journey, that she simply "cannot anymore."

SUCCESSFUL CROSSINGS

Unlike their less-fortunate counterparts, these independent Mexican teenage migrants were able to cross. When asked why they believed they had been triumphant, Martín, as mentioned in the opening of the chapter, attributed their success to their youthfulness, while others said that their embodied habitus—that is, their years of hard labor—prepared them for the precarious and arduous conditions they encountered on the journey. For instance, Fidencio compared the physical difficulties of crossing to being in *el campo*, or the fields, and he believed that "having performed hard work in the fields all of his life" had conditioned him to endure the challenges in the desert. Overall, demonstrating youthful bravado, the youths downplayed the difficulties of their journeys across Mexico and the U.S.-Mexico border as "not as bad as the experiences of other people." The demanding work they performed in their home communities since early childhood allowed them, in Fidencio's words, to "pass like nothing" and make it to New York City.

It is irrefutable that in their discussions of their migrations, these independent Mexican teenage migrants revealed significant courage, resourcefulness, determination and lastly, maturity. Unimaginable for many at these ages or older, these youths negotiated significant risks to their lives and well-being—without the protection of parents—to get one step closer to their dreams.

ARRIVING IN THE GRAN MANZANA

As "successful" crossers, these youths arrived in New York City, usually by plane, flying from Los Angeles, Phoenix, or Las Vegas into New York City's JFK airport. Here, the last stages of their transactions with coyotes transpired as they accompanied them either on the planes or in vans before they were taken to their new apartments in New York City. Prior to arrival, the youths unfolded their papers with carefully written phone numbers that they had protected throughout their trips, papers that were jammed deep in their pockets. They called their contacts, either friends of the coyotes or relatives in New York City, to meet them at the airport or arrange for taxis to bring them to their new homes. Within hours of arriving at their final destinations, youths ate, changed, or purchased clothes. More significantly, most were already on their way to find work.

CONCLUSION

Throughout their lives, from first thinking about immigration and its relationship to survival and social mobility to their arrival in New York City, these independent Mexican teenage migrants demonstrated significant planful competence, resourcefulness, determination, and courage seemingly unheard of at their young ages. However, they did not demonstrate or act upon these traits in isolation. Embedded in communities and families that more recently turned to immigration as a strategy for survival and social mobility, these independent Mexican teenage migrants grew up seeing its effects on other households and wished the same for their own. Uninterested in following in their parents' footsteps in agricultural work or even pursuing internal migration, they instead followed the lead of older relatives—uncles, aunts, cousins, siblings, and in very few cases, fathers—and friends who successfully crossed. Across a transnational space, these older kin and nonkin migrants shared social and financial remittances that prompted youths to first imagine, desire, research, and eventually plan their own migrations. These adult actors helped the youths acquire information about migration, assisted them in attaining funds, and finally aided them in finding, or even secured, residences for the youths after migration.

But does it matter that the youths are minors? When asked whether migration was an act for adolescents or adults, César contradicted Martín by saying that he believed that migration was not necessarily an aged act; rather, people of any age can migrate: "Children cross, women cross, elderly cross, young, all types of people—white, black, indigenous, educated people. It is an act—well, I am going to repeat it—of the experiences that life gives you."

In reality, however, certain age-related considerations must be taken into account when crossing the U.S.-Mexico border. Youths themselves, with and without the assistance of older adults, consider age when conceptualizing the appropriateness of their unaccompanied departures. Particular accommodations are made, both by human smugglers and by the youths themselves, to minimize age-based liabilities that could result in detection or violence during the journey. Coyotes instruct youths to change their ages, both verbally and on paper, while the youths mislead authorities about their adult statuses and seek protections to offset their age- and gender-based vulnerabilities.

Lastly, the youths' departures from their households bring attention to a less discussed form of family separation. While immigration literature has mostly defined family separation as the act of parents leaving their children behind, what may merit further attention is the act of children taking the lead and separating from their parents to reunite, in many cases, with other kin. Rooted in these youths' accelerated transitions to adulthood, there is evidence that this separation is traumatic for both children and parents. However, setting trauma aside and exhibiting significant emotional strength and maturity, independent Mexican teenage migrants make the difficult decision to leave their parents behind not only to assume independence but also to help ensure their parents' future financial well-being.

4 • PUSHED OR JUMPED?

School Going, School Leaving, and School Returning

> I didn't continue (beyond secundaria) because it was difficult to pay for the education. I realized how hard it was for my parents to pay for school, especially since my sister had started high school. I realized how expensive schooling was, and I did not want to give my parents another stressor.
>
> —Ignacio, age twenty-nine; arrived at age sixteen

Armando had worked hard to get expelled. Growing up in a rural, southern, semiurban town in Puebla, he observed his parents' hardships, and although he had sufficient access to school, he was uninterested in it, so he thought it was better if he worked. Both of his parents, who had only reached primaria, made it clear that they wanted him to continue his studies so that he could "become somebody." His father would draw comparisons between himself and his son: "[When he was my age,] he did not have the benefits that I had today. Like in the past, he had to leave his father, and he worked a lot, and how he did not have the privilege . . . I have [to go to school]."

Unfortunately, however, even though Armando wanted to please his parents and "realize that dream," at approximately age thirteen, he felt that he carried much of the burden of continuing his studies. Like many of the other independent Mexican teenage migrants whose families encouraged them to continue studying, Armando believed that his parents did not show him *how* he could continue studying, financially or otherwise: "[By secundaria,] I was already lost. I didn't [have] the motivation; I did not have it anymore. I just went out of obligation." Already helping his father and working after school, Armando noticed that his father appeared worn out and tired: "I would look at [my] father and how he was very jaded already, like already very beaten." Soon, Armando just wanted to drop out so he could help his papá.

The problem was, however, that even with his pleading, his papá was not going to let him leave school. Thwarted, he mulled it over for three months and came up with his own plan: "I [made] the decision myself, trying to get myself expelled." Unsure about how someone went about getting themselves expelled, I asked Armando to explain to me how he did it. He made it seem easy: "[I would] miss school, [or] go to school and . . . do things that I was not supposed to do. [I] lacked respect and all that, and I did it to be unbearable. The teacher talked with my dad, and they finally let me go. They looked at my work, and that is when I told them, when I was already doing poorly, that I did not want to study, that I wanted to help them, so that I could work, and I started to work. And that's how I made them . . . expel me."

While one could take what Armando said at face value, that he had gotten himself expelled, another interpretation is that the Mexican educational system, embedded in a transnational economic system, had failed him (Gonzalez 2001). Often thought of as great "equalizers," schools are actually one of the most effective "instruments" that contribute to social reproduction, and in the case of Mexico, schools promulgate U.S. economic hegemony (Bourdieu and Passeron 1990; Gonzalez 2001; MacLeod 1995: 11).

But how do education systems do this? When examined for their part in "legitimating of class differences," particularly in studies focusing on youths and social reproduction, schools are centralized as the fields across which struggles over capital, both its values and meanings, occur (Bourdieu and Passeron 1990: 164; Bowles and Gintis 1976; MacLeod 1995; Willis 1977). As citizens of a nation where schooling was only mandatory until grade nine and residing in communities where schooling was expensive, coverage was insufficient, and/or teachers were, at times, irresponsible, independent Mexican teenage migrants often found it difficult to remain in the field and exchange capital for higher positions. Setting aside the very idea of accumulating valuable human capital in itself—something that could be honored or recognized on the part of their teachers—most independent Mexican teenage migrants have simply not been allocated the economic capital to continue school beyond certain early grades. Once in the United States, the youths' previous experiences in Mexico continue to shape their doxa, or orientation toward the field. Because they believe they have already ended their educational careers, most do not engage in illusio, or invest to continue to "play" in the educational system. The few who obtain social and/or economic capital to invest in their educations can and do for both shorter and longer periods of time and obtain lower-value as well as higher-value positions.

This chapter argues that the educational system in which prospective and independent Mexican teenage migrants engage as they grow up helps create and reinforce their beliefs that their primary roles are as transnational workers and not school goers (Gonzalez 2001; MacLeod 1995; Willis 1977). Far too rarely considered, this chapter examines the youths' entire educational histories, including their scholastic antecedents prior to migration as well as how they might carry ideas from these experiences across borders to New York City, where they confront new contexts that include not only new responsibilities but also an educational system that reinforces the arguably purposeful marginalization of poor Mexican youths (Gonzalez 2001; Macias 1990). With respect to the levels of schooling deemed appropriate for themselves—in addition to beginning to understand the genesis of this range of ideas, expectations, and actions that causes independent Mexican teenage migrants to leave and remain out of formal education—the following section focuses on the youths' origins and their environments and contexts. For many of these independent Mexican teenage migrants, it is these past and current educational policies and trends in Mexico and within the youths' communities that begin to shape their orientations toward formal schooling.

DESCRIBING THE FIELD: MEXICO'S EDUCATIONAL SYSTEM

Since 1917 and up until 1993, obligatory education ended with primaria, or after six years of schooling (Gutek 2006). For many of the adults in the youths' communities, including the youths' grandparents and parents, if they had been able to attend primaria and had not dropped out prior to it, the end of primaria usually marked the end of their schooling. Attending secundaria, much less a preparatoria, or high school, was almost unheard of in their generations due to both costs of schooling and labor lost and also availability and proximity. Schools beyond primarias were not prevalent, and as such, beyond age twelve or so, many poor Mexican youths prior to 1993 were left free to engage in labor, unpaid or paid, to help the household.

According to Lazaro, though, "people now [attended] secundaria." Referring to his similarly aged peers, Lazaro believed that his own generation was attaining even higher levels of education, and he was right: although Mexican youths his age possessed on average 9.7 years of schooling, or nearly a year more than the national average for individuals his parents' ages (8.8 years), in the states the youths were from, the differences were less commendable (OCDE 2008). The average years of school completion in Puebla, Guerrero and Oaxaca were 8.5 years, 7.8 years, and 7.5 years, respectively. These generational increases could largely be attributed to changes made to federal educational laws and programs in the early 1990s. With globalization looming at the end of the twentieth century, Mexican officials believed that changes to their educational policies were critical to prepare youths for higher-skilled labor. Eager to abide by economic restructuring conditions and modernization opportunities, by the end of the 1980s, PRI President Salinas de Gortari (1988–1994) reorganized the educational field by enacting a new educational plan, *El Plan de Modernización Educativo,* or the Education Modernization Plan, which called for a commitment to several major educational reforms, including raising the general level of schooling for Mexicans and improving the quality of education.[1] This plan provided the blueprint for the first National Agreement on the Modernization of Basic Education of 1992 (ANMEB), which would later be inserted into the 1993 Ley General de Educación, or General Education Law.[2] Of most significance in this agreement-turned-law is its resolution regarding compulsory education. Extending schooling beyond the obligatory six years, the 1993 law mandated that the length of compulsory education be nine years, or until the completion of secundaria.[3]

The effects of these changes were reflected in the average levels of educational attainment of independent Mexican teenage migrants, which were still low compared to national averages and in relation to youths in the United States. Although nine youths attended high schools or GED programs in New York City, for the majority of the youths, departure from secundaria in Mexico marked the end of their academic careers.

Critics believed that these low levels of educational attainment could be explained by the shortcomings of the Ley General de Educación, especially in regards to its implementation and enforcement. Viewed as "symbolic" and designed to demonstrate little more than the country's commitment to modernization to the international community instead of expanding schooling to all, ANMEB reinforced educational disparities between urban and rural communities. While independent Mexican teenage migrants were still in Mexico, in the poorest Mexican communities, which were often located in rural areas, primarias were overcrowded and secundarias, much less preparatorias, did not exist. In communities that did possess these schools, many parents were unable to pay their high registration and maintenance fees (Levinson 2001; Sawyer 2013; Zapata 2013). With few resources earmarked to ensure compliance, it was no secret that school officials were unable to provide sufficient access to, much less enforce, mandatory attendance until the end of secundaria (Levinson 2001). For the most part, prospective and actual independent Mexican teenage migrants referred to all of these structural shortcomings to explain their short academic careers. The following section examines how these youths experienced Mexico's educational system and how it impacted their school attendance and ultimately their departures.

STRUCTURAL SHORTCOMINGS: MINEFIELDS IN MEXICO'S EDUCATIONAL FIELD

By the time Herminda was ready to enter secundaria in 2000, community members had joined together to turn the town's abandoned clinic into a school, effectively reintroducing telesecundaria studies, or teacher-led secundaria-level distance learning, into the community (Manjarrez Rosas 2008).[4] Prior to this, however, if students wanted to study beyond primaria, they were forced to leave the community and incur the costs associated with travel, food, and in some cases, even lodging. But this was a new day for San Pedro and a dream come true for Don Felipe, a primaria teacher who became the school's director. Although it was a small unincorporated school that would go unrecognized for years by the federal government, that first year the telesecundaria saw its first five students enrolled; six years later, when I arrived, the total school population was forty-three students: fifteen students in the first *generación*, sixteen in the second generación, and twelve in the third. On my first day in San Pedro, I saw the second generación painting a mural on their new building, located close to the highway.

Although the community continued without a preparatoria, the timing of the school's opening reflected the government's and the local community's commitment to expanding school coverage after the passage of the Ley General de Educación. Although Don Felipe and others spoke of how challenging it had been to open this particular telesecundaria, between 1990 and 2006, SEP officials embarked on a school construction campaign. At the primary level, most of the increases included the construction of comunitaria schools (multigrade schools found in mostly isolated regions characterized by extreme poverty) and indigenous schools (Parker et al. 2007). In the years immediately after the signing of the ANMEB, the total number of primarias increased by nearly 3 percent, with the availability of comunitaria schools increasing by 51.5 percent (Parker et al. 2007: 37).

The greatest construction boom, however, occurred among brick-and-mortar secundarias and specifically telesecundarias. The accelerated growth of these schools that utilized satellite-television-broadcast distance learning, especially in remote, impoverished areas with limited specialized teaching personnel, was the most economical vehicle for doubling secundaria coverage.[5] Telesecundarias would see their highest rates of expansion between 1994 and 1997, by 11.78 percent (1994), 8.95 percent (1995), 6.23 percent (1996), and 8.05 percent (1997) (Helper et al. 2006; Parker et al. 2007).

This increased availability of secundarias also translated into greater student enrollment at this level. Reflecting the expansion, in 1994, just after the signing of ANMEB, traditional secundarias saw a jump in student enrollment of 35.39 percent (Parker et al. 2007: 38). Likewise, student enrollment in telesecundarias also increased, first by 10.7 percent in 1994 and by 11.66 percent in 1995, and then after dipping to 8.0 percent in 1996, enrollment rose again to 11.8 percent in 1998. Studies examining the effects of regional residence on educational attainment demonstrate that the expansion of telesecundarias resulted in significant increases in educational attainment, specifically in rural areas (Parker et al. 2007).[6] Backed by a law and now infrastructure, youths, especially those living in regions most impacted by NAFTA, would now be obligated to attend and could spend longer periods of time in school and outside of paid or unpaid labor spheres.

A handful of youths, however, continued to grow up in communities without secundarias and, if they wished to continue their studies, they would be forced to wake up very early and travel long distances. Traveling to another town to attend school, however, cost money for transportation, food, and sometimes even lodging that many youths' families simply did not possess. Pedro, now working in a *taqueria* near Columbia University, was unable to continue his schooling because his town did not possess a secundaria. After completing the sixth grade in his hometown, he was faced with the decision to either continue his schooling far away from home or drop out. He decided that he would join many of the other youths in his community and not let his mother spend the money for him to continue studying: "Well, there, where I lived, there was a primaria, but the secundaria, there was not one. You had to go to [inaudible] because of that, so many people, many youth, did not want to study. It was far. [And how far was the secundaria from where you lived?] Well, walking, like, an hour and a half, one hour, maybe." Because of the distance of the secundaria from their home communities, as well as the costs associated with attending school, many youths did not want to continue studying beyond primaria. Even when youths opted to make the trek, Pedro said, schools were not sympathetic; often school officials would lock their doors and not allow tardy students to enter, no matter how far they lived from the school.

Attending preparatorias, however, was even more difficult. Many of the youths lived in communities that were still without preparatorias when they left in the mid-2000s. The absence could be partially explained by a lack of legal obligation and the tensions among federal, state, and local governments but also, according to Carlos, a lack of political will and, quite frankly, perceived utility by community members. When asked about the availability of a preparatoria in his town, Carlos shared that while he was still living there, one had never been approved:

> It [a proposal] was put forward, like a test to see, but the town always denied supporting the proposal to put a high school in the town. (Is there one now?) The last time that I heard, it was like six or seven years ago [2007]. They were going

> to [build] it, but it was the same as before—the town did not want to construct a school there. (And do you know why they denied putting the high school there?) Not exactly. The majority of the people who are there, I guess, are people without studies, and they think that it is a waste of time to construct it.

Not yet obligated by law and without examples of how high school studies could translate into employment opportunities, community members saw no need to invest in extended studies or create an opportunity that would not only continue to remove youths from labor but also demand money from local residents, both those with and without school-going children.

Like Pedro in relation to secundaria attendance, youths who lived in towns without preparatorias found that if they wished to continue their studies, they would have to spend a significant amount of money to travel, eat, and even reside in towns away from their homes. For Julio, the closest one was an hour and a half away. Because of this, he believed that if he continued school, he would have to pay and live away from home: "It was better to stay over there, close to the school, instead of traveling. (And was that very common, for those who went to preparatoria, to go there and stay alone, pay rent, and all that?) Yes." Unable to afford this, Julio, like Carlos, ended his educational career after completing secundaria.

When prospective and independent Mexican teenage migrants did possess schools in their hometowns, they often found that they were underresourced. Schools often lacked computers, libraries, and in secundaria and preparatoria, even laboratories, and when they did exist at the schools, oftentimes there were no teachers for instruction. When he entered secundaria, Diego found that his science teacher would ask the students to bring the materials that they needed for experiments, materials he and his family simply could not afford. Recalling the clinic they had converted into a secundaria, Herminda shared, "The first year was scary for me because the school did not have any resources. . . . Our classroom . . . was abandoned. We had to clean it, try to make it decent, because it was just about falling [apart]."

To overcome the schools' shortcomings, many Mexican youths found that they and their families were expected to pay fees associated with school going (Sawyer 2013). Most schools that the youths attended—especially those that were new, unrecognized, and as such, could not count as much on government funds—were forced to rely on fees that administrators charged families.[7] While federal programs such as *PROGRESA/Oportunidades* had been implemented to offset these fees as well as income and labor lost with the enrollment of youths in school, they fell short. Strict rules for eligibility and continued receipt prevented many families from receiving and retaining these funds. As a result, the majority of the prospective and actual independent Mexican teenage migrants discussed how they—if they had continued to preparatoria—and their families struggled to pay the totality of these fees.

But school going in Mexico was meant to be free without monetary costs. As legislated in the country's constitution, up until the end of secundaria, individuals were guaranteed a free basic education (Ley General de Educación 1993; Sawyer 2013: 191).[8] Mexican youths seconded this, but when I followed up and asked about specific fees, the amounts that their families had to pay for their continued school attendance started adding up. Mexican youths recalled fees for registration, *cooperaciones* (or fees related to the school infrastructure), uniforms, school supplies, resources, and services—and the fees were often higher in newer schools. They cited different amounts and frequencies for these costs, ranging from 300 to 750 pesos, or approximately $27 to $68 USD, for the once-a-year registration fee to the more frequent cooperaciones to cover costs associated with everything from ensuring that toilet paper was in bathrooms, to constructing sports fields, to cultural events.[9] Alejandro recalled that cooperaciones were not a set amount but flexible, subject to the decisions of school officials. For example, "If the school is in good condition . . . , [if] it lacks some benches or something like that, [then] you put [in] 150 or 200 pesos. . . . If a hallway is lacking or a classroom is already very ugly, they charge more—like they charged us 600 pesos." Esmeralda even recalled being solicited for funds to build a kitchen so that the school could serve hot breakfasts.

On average, youths believed that over the course of the year, their families were asked to pay approximately 1,500 pesos, or, at the time of their attendance, approximately $136 USD. Additionally, at the time when many of the youths would have been eligible for high school studies, Latapi Sarre (2005) put semester costs at well over 2,000 pesos a semester to attend preparatoria, including approximately 1,000 pesos in registration fees; 150 pesos a week for materials, computer costs, and other supplies; and transportation costs to travel to school from home.

Students could also be charged for curricular offerings. Although it was barely mentioned by other youths, Genoveva discussed how her school offered computer classes for a brief period, but they were not free. To take computer classes, students were asked to pay fifteen pesos a week toward the computer teacher's salary. Genoveva's family simply could not afford this additional cost, and her mamá went to ask for a discount on the fees: "Well, yes, my mother did not pay it, and then she went to speak with the director to see if he could give us a discount, because it was a lot, and he did give us a discount. Eight pesos was what I had to pay, but the rest said they were in agreement with the fifteen pesos. They continued to pay, but I just paid eight; each time that we entered, I paid eight pesos."

Students were also asked to purchase at least two uniforms—one for physical education and another for class—and especially as students reached the higher grades, they required funds for more expensive school supplies associated with higher-level coursework. On average, the youths reported that uniform costs totaled approximately six hundred pesos every two years. Some youths were unable to pay for more than one of each uniform and had to wash each one every day after school so that they could wear them the next day. Additionally, starting in primaria but accelerating in secundaria, school supply costs also began to mount, which was a source of anxiety for the youths who could not afford them. By secundaria, Diego was simply unable to purchase lab supplies for his science courses, and he began to skip classes to avoid embarrassment and penalties. Due to his poor attendance, his grades dropped, and he was told he would have to repeat the course the following school year: "When I arrived to secundaria, I put [in] two years there. I did not like it. They asked for supplies—bring this, pay for that—things that I could not get sometimes, and . . . I did not like to do it like that . . . I could not. [Like what types of things?] They asked . . . [for] things . . . to have a laboratory, to do that. . . . They asked you to bring that to do an experiment. Many things they asked [for], . . . really I could not get. . . . It was uncomfortable, because all my classmates got them, and for me it was very uncomfortable." Ultimately, the inability to purchase school supplies negatively impacted the youths' grades. Like Diego, Rodolfo recalled, "Many times . . . I went to school without turning in a project because we did not have money to buy the materials."

Undoubtedly, these fees caused significant hardships for the youths and their families, especially those with several children in school. Parents resorted to extreme measures to pay for their children's schooling, including seeking loans, working more hours, and selling or even pawning household objects when the school year approached. When she did not have money for Julio's schooling, and with livestock available to her, Julio's mamá would "sell an animal to pay for school . . . She had some animals that they gave her for Christmas, and she sold them." Martín recalled, "Some things that I asked for [for] school were very expensive. The books sometimes were expensive, or [there were] some expositions where we had to spend a lot of money. So then my mamá, then, I don't know if she borrowed money or sold personal things or pawned so that I could continue going to school."

When parents were unable to generate more money, students were forced to improvise and even miss school to avoid embarrassment. Carlos's father would complain every year about the fees that they had to pay and deny that he had the money. Sometimes, he simply did not have any money to give. In Carlos's words, "Each time he denied, he would simply say, 'I don't know why I have to pay. Why do they make us do this, and they know that we do not have money? I do not know why we have to cooperate for school things.' And always, it was the same, taking turns. There were days that we would not go to school because we had to give money and we did not have it to give."

Facing financial difficulties throughout their children's academic careers, by the end of obligatory schooling, some parents outright told their children that they could not or would not continue to pay for schooling. Reaching the end of secundaria and anticipating even higher costs at the high school level, their parents put the brakes on their continued studies. Both Clementina and Genoveva discussed how their grandparents and parents, respectively, had, in no uncertain terms, put an end to their academic dreams. Clementina's grandparents told her and her sister that they would not support more schooling. In Genoveva's case, she was informed even prior to the start of her third year of secundaria that she would not be able to continue her studies beyond that point. Expressing her desires to continue schooling beyond secundaria, she found, was a moot point. Her family simply could not afford it, and her mamá told her so: "I was telling her that I wanted to continue studying to be a [hair] stylist. And she told me no, that I was going to do nothing more than complete secundaria, that [they] would not be able to help to study more, and she told me . . . that I [should] forget about school."

Some Mexican youths who were determined to continue their studies in preparatoria took on the burden of these fees for themselves. Observing that his parents did not have enough money to pay for his schooling, Lazaro began to work to pay for "more things. It is more money in the prepa, you have to pay for your travel, and you have to pay all of your copies . . . and then the registration there, they charged you like 700 pesos, . . . so then it was already a lot of money for my papás." Eventually, however, the fees would be too much to bear, and upon finishing his first year of prepa, he had to leave his studies.

These difficulties occurred in spite of the government's promise that every Mexican child could obtain a free education up to the end of secundaria. To facilitate this, *Secretaria de Desarrollo Social* (SEDESOL) officials implemented what could be considered a "structural *curita*," or a Band-Aid, known first as PROGRESA. Renamed Oportunidades in 2002 and then, in 2012, under the Peña Nieto administration and in expanded form, *PROSPERA*, PROGRESA began as a conditional cash-transfer policy aimed at disrupting intergenerational poverty by ensuring school attendance for extremely poor Mexican youths between the grades of three and nine until 2001 and up to grade twelve thereafter (Behrman et al. 2011; Buenrostro 2011; Molyneux 2007; Parker et al. 2007). This conditional cash-transfer program is rooted in neoliberal antipoverty paradigms that assert that the poor can "grow out of poverty" if they change certain behaviors, including increasing their human capital and adjusting health and nutritional practices (Buenrostro 2011: 20). Placing emphasis on individual behaviors, this program minimized and continues to downplay the structural causes of chronic economic insecurity and inequality in Mexico, including those caused by NAFTA (Adato and Hoddinott 2007; Buenrostro 2011: 24).

More specifically, PROGRESA/Oportunidades was developed to overcome the opportunity costs associated with school attendance in extremely poor households and deter the participation of school-age minors in the labor market by providing cash to pay for school costs as well as compensating for wages associated with lost labor.[10] The receipt of the award was and continues to be conditional on school attendance (85 percent) and medical checkups for the family's children and pregnant or nursing mothers. Additional cash is awarded to improve nutrition (Behrman et al. 2011; Buenrostro 2011; SEDESOL 1998). Additionally, mothers are required to attend workshops, perform service work, and be available for home visits in return for their stipends. In many instances, the cash incentives could total up to 30 percent of a household's monthly income. Unfortunately, many poor families were excluded from PROGRESA/Oportunidades, and for those who did receive it, some believed that the payments were insufficient to offset schooling and opportunity costs.[11] By the mid-2000s, with 51.3 percent of the Mexican population in poverty, only one-quarter of the Mexican population received benefits, or slightly higher than the percentage of Mexicans deemed "extremely poor" (Rowe 2011).

Reflecting these findings, the majority of the independent Mexican teenage migrants with whom I spoke reported not receiving Oportunidades (the name of the program at the time most of the youths were in school). For one, the complicated process deterred application. Martín spoke of families having to undergo "profound" evaluations, and to his knowledge, his mother had never applied because of this one detail. Second, extremely poor Mexicans living in regions without the infrastructure (schools and clinics) to meet the conditions of Oportunidades and poor households located just above the income requirements were, and continue to be, excluded (Behrman et al. 2011; Buenrostro 2011). The latter appeared to affect many of the youths with whom I spoke. Poor, but not poor enough, they still struggled to meet the economic demands associated with school attendance in their communities, but they were ineligible for government funds.

Recipients of Oportunidades were also subject to strict guidelines, and funds could be temporarily or permanently terminated due to student behaviors and performance. Excessive absences and more than one course failure prohibited youths and families from receiving additional funds (Behrman et al. 2011). Gloria shared these guidelines with me while we were talking at her house with some of her classmates. After identifying Genoveva as a recipient of Oportunidades, Gloria continued, saying, "It [receipt of Oportunidades] depended on absences and that if you missed more than three days, they would not give you the funds the following three months" (Martinez, July 7, 2006). This had happened to Marco. When he missed two days of school, they did nothing. When he missed a week, however, payments stopped arriving. Gloria also added that students had to maintain average to high GPAs, or "between a 7 and an 8." With 12 percent of all primary-level students and 25 percent of all secundaria students failing to pass a grade or dropping out, poor Mexican students would be the most adversely affected by weak academic performance; they and their families would also experience a loss of income (Helper et al. 2006).

Others believed that the money was insufficient to cover school expenses. In their study, Latapi et al. (2005) found that these funds covered less than half of the lower secundaria costs and even less for preparatoria costs. This was echoed by several youths who were enrolled in Mexico: the money was simply not enough to pay for school attendance costs. Relying on these funds to attend school and support his household, Sebastian dropped out when he found that there was hardly any money left over for household expenses after paying for school fees. Calculating the costs of school compared to the amounts provided by PROGRESA, he demonstrated how it fell short: "(But how is PROGRESA? They send money, no?) Well, yes. . . . PROGRESA just gives enough . . . to pay supplies or registration fees, but until sixth [grade], it was 850 [pesos] . . . [And was that sufficient for all your expenses?] No, because then it would run out, and [with] the cooperaciones and the supplies . . . only about 150 stayed. (But if this money was all you needed for school, why did you need the 150?) To pay [for] the house [and] food, but it was not sufficient." Likewise, Manuel discussed how the scholarship only covered 80 percent of his costs; he had to work and save money in the summer to have enough one school year. Even with his contributions, though, he would sometimes see his mamá "crying, hiding from us, never in front of us," due to the school expenses that were not covered.

In Mexico, prospective and actual independent Mexican teenage migrants enter into and engage with an educational field that, although seemingly restructured at the end of the twentieth century to improve the lots of poor families, continues to be riddled with barriers that minimize the educational gains poor youths make. Against the backdrop of a lopsided dependence that has characterized labor relations between Mexico and the United States for nearly a century—a dependence that accelerated after the passage of free trade agreements and overall transnational labor restructuring—Mexico's educational field and its institutions continue to fail prospective and actual independent teenage migrants. With schooling also providing limited educational advantages in the Mexican and/or U.S. labor markets, youths are not-so-accidentally being primed to become transnational workers.

In spite of these structural impediments, when they are in school, Mexican youths generally enjoyed their experiences and performed well, at least until economic pressures, structural limitations, lack of interest, or in some cases, a combination of all the above ended their academic careers. The following section traces the educational trajectories of prospective and actual independent Mexican teenage migrants until they reach the point where they are "pushed" or "jump" from Mexico's educational field.

COOLING OUT

Mexican youths' stories about their academic careers mostly started similarly. The majority had enjoyed their years in primaria, with some even boasting exemplary academic achievements. Even though they stopped attending school after completing primaria, many, including Fidencio, began strongly in school, earning 8.5s or 9s (the U.S. equivalent of As and Bs) and were even called on to carry the flags during morning formation exercises as a reward.

Luis and Manuel, however, were standouts among the youths. Both had been among the highest-performing students in their classes and were even invited to compete in academic competitions outside of their hometowns. By his sixth year, Luis was already experiencing the "disappointment" that came with being only the fourth best student in his region:

> [I was] the best student of everyone in that classroom. We went to a competition in another city, close to there. It was the best, and we joined ten other small cities, . . . and I had a lot of confidence there. . . . I was the best [in my school], but . . . there, I only got to fourth place. But it was good. That was the day that I put everything [I had into it], no, like I achieved what my parents did not expect. (But it was still an honor, no?) Yes, it was an honor to me, because I put [in] all that I could, but for them to be there . . . and not be able to get what they wanted . . . (But you were still the best student, no?) In primaria, I was.

Likewise, due to his performance in mathematics and oration, Manuel believed that he was the third best out of seventy students in his grade level.

After completing primaria, however, these prospective and actual independent Mexican teenage migrants began to take divergent pathways. Some youths, including Pedro, Fidencio, Concepción, and Mateo, left schooling at this point. Others attended secundarias *técnicas* that focused on trades such as electricity, refrigeration, secretarial work, or even accounting, while the majority enrolled in telesecundarias. Here, although youths planned to or did complete secundaria studies, many were limping along. Like Armando, some simply began to lose focus and/or motivation and began to experience dips in their grades and even failed courses. José Luis and Samuel started to goof off during secundaria and saw their grades fall. Although José Luis left primaria with an average between 8 and 8.5, by the time he arrived in secundaria, he found himself repeatedly failing subjects:

> In secundaria, I always had to . . . repeat subjects. . . . In the first year that I was there, in secundaria, I had to repeat two subjects, . . . Spanish and mathematics. In the second year, I had to take the exam so that I could pass those subjects during vacation. I only passed Spanish and mathematics. I continued going, and in the second year, I had to repeat four subjects, and I said that I was going to repeat them, but I did not pass a single subject, only mathematics. But the same, in the third year, I failed seven subjects, and that is why I [asked], "Why am I going to continue if they are not going to give me the degree?" That is why I left school two months before ending.

Similarly, Samuel began to skip classes with his friends during secundaria. After enrolling in a técnica where he was studying refrigeration, he said, "[I began to have] friends who would always tell me, 'No, don't go. Let's go here,' and I was like, well, 'Yes, let's go,' and that is when my studies started going down. Getting together with some friends is where I started failing, because until there, I was doing well." After his parents learned that he would not pass his courses because of his excessive absences and missed exams and assignments, they pulled Samuel and his sister from the school to attend a school that was closer (and cheaper). Samuel did not want to attend this school and also felt that the coursework there lacked rigor. When he went to the new school, he said, "I had already learned what they were showing, like, half a year before. That was the difference—they taught more in the técnica than the new school." Bored and already disengaged, Samuel asked his papá to let him leave school to work.

Secundarias *abiertas* (or "open," second-chance schools) were available to youths over the age of fifteen who had experienced disruptions or otherwise not completed their primaria and/or secundaria studies (INEA 2010), but they too were quite limited in resources and not easily accessible. Invited by a friend, Concepción was relieved to be able to enroll in secundaria studies even though she was already seventeen. Though the school possessed minimal resources (a blackboard, chairs, and a table) and only met on Sundays from eight o'clock in the morning to noon, she was glad to be earning credits toward a secundaria certificate with twenty other teenagers and adults. However, it was difficult to access, and without buses or car services that ran early, she had not been able to attend school there until recently. Rodolfo likewise enrolled in a secundaria abierta, but only after remaining out of school for a couple of years and working.

Around his fourteenth birthday, a local teacher began to recruit students who had been out of school for years, and eventually ten students, including Rodolfo, would enroll for two hundred pesos for registration. Paid for by his older brother, the expenses would eventually become too prohibitive, and Rodolfo had to leave schooling after one year.

Overall, however, the majority of prospective and independent Mexican teenage migrants were either on schedule to complete or actually completed secundaria studies. Deferring to the laws, many parents and youths believed that because it marked the end of compulsory education, their schooling was completed. For the few youths who did pursue preparatoria studies, their entries and continued studies were usually fraught with difficulties and were temporary and tenuous. Without parental support, Mexican youths had to figure out their own way to pay for these studies that were not only more expensive but outside of their communities. Most had to pay for travel, higher registration fees, and at this level, even higher fees for materials.

After his secundaria director told him that he could continue to be enrolled in Oportunidades and receive another scholarship that he held in secundaria, Manuel made plans to attend preparatoria. Although he could have attended less expensive schools, instead he chose a school known for its rigor. Interested in becoming a lawyer or a teacher, Manuel believed that this school would provide him with the foundation to continue studying human rights or political science. Unfortunately, Manuel had no idea that by continuing, "he was going to spend so much." After paying fifty pesos for an entrance exam and then registration, he also had to spend forty pesos a day to travel to and from school on the bus. He also discovered that the high school asked for more things. For one, you could no longer calculate in pencil; you needed a calculator. Second, assignments could no longer be handwritten or hand-drawn; teachers were asking for computer printouts. Unable to afford the fifteen to twenty pesos internet cafes charged to surf the web and print images, Manuel borrowed a friend's typewriter and glued in pictures he found in magazines. In his chemistry class, he was asked to bring his own thermometer; for art, he was required to bring his own paints and paper; and across all classes, he had to pay for his own books. On top of all this, he was asked to pay 150 pesos every six months for cooperaciones. After a while, he felt like all these expenses were accumulating and closing in on him. Already overwhelmed, the last straw was in October, when he was told that a mistake had been made and he would not be granted the two scholarships. Although he was earning 9s in his courses, he had to leave because he simply saw no way to continue paying the associated expenses.

TEACHERS

Countering these realities were teachers who motivated them to continue with their studies. Reflecting recent social reproduction literature that identifies teachers as playing a significant role in encouraging students to continue or discontinue their studies, youths echoed Santibanez et al.'s (2005) findings about education in Mexico, suggesting that teachers did not motivate them. Individually, however, there were specific teachers who cared for them and did everything they could to not only encourage their continued studies but also, as discussed in chapter 3, discourage their migration.

Schools and, more specifically, teachers possess various tools of symbolic (and actual) violence that direct poor Mexican youths away from school achievements and aspirations of higher positions in the educational field. One such tool, corporal punishment, was omnipresent and widely accepted during these youths' academic careers. Over and over again, youths named at least one teacher in their academic careers who had been strict and in some cases engaged in physical violence with students. Fidencio, who ended his academic career after primaria, vividly recalled how in the second grade, he had "really bad, mean teachers" who "would grab students by the skin on his cheek [or] by his ear if he did something poorly." After enduring this violence, Fidencio began to fail. Rather than register again for the second grade, where he would have the same teacher, his parents let him stay out of school for two years while they worked in Morelos. This would ultimately create a situation in which he was over-age and undercredited, which made him very uncomfortable and ultimately led to his departure from school. Teachers who disciplined through violence had also taught Pedro. He recalled being afraid of a mathematics teacher who would grab students by the hair or by the ears and hit them with a ruler. Unsurprisingly, Pedro too ended his studies after completing primaria.

Other youths recalled teachers who simply were not interested in their learning. Both Solomon and Carolina recounted how some teachers would arrive late to class and then, after entering and leaving students with work, would "escape." After abandoning their students for the entirety of the class, they would return at the end to dismiss them and let them go their ways; others simply did not return. Clementina even recalled "one male teacher who never taught us" and the school administration that permitted his behavior. According to her, the secundaria director knew but would not say anything when he saw her teacher leave the class alone and spend the period eating and socializing with other teachers by the food stand. At the prepa level, Manuel also believed that this neglect was due to class differences between the teachers and the students. Manual expressed a problem he experienced with teachers who were not from his hometown: "There are already different teachers . . . who are not [there] anymore. They just care about themselves, and they do not care about your family, because you already know what you are doing. . . . [They want] you [to] leave your problems outside [because] you are just here to study. Family problems, whatever, [leave] over there, over there." In his mind, at this school away from his hometown, he believed that the teachers were not personally invested in him; he felt unimportant—and the school charged high fees.

Countering these negative experiences, however, were a few teachers who genuinely seemed to care for the youths' well-being and future. Herminda named several teachers, including a teacher who taught her during her last year in primaria whom she believed had been critical for her continued studies. This teacher had a "grand impact" on her life because she was the one who told her, "Herminda, yes you can. . . . Yes, we see a great future for you." Herminda attributed much of her academic persistence, even in New York, to this teacher, who remained understanding even during a time when her continued schooling was in question and intervened to convince her mamá that her continued schooling was in her best interests.

Even though he would ultimately leave his high school studies, Manuel believed that the secundaria director offered to go above and beyond in supporting his dreams. Although the information he gave Manuel regarding his scholarships proved to be erroneous, in Manuel's words, the director always strove to "awaken him" and had encouraged him to continue with his studies to become someone.

Unlike the teachers encountered by MacLeod's Lads and the Hallway Hangers (found in his seminal work *Ain't No Makin' It: Aspirations and Attainment in a Low-Income Neighborhood*), prospective and independent Mexican teenage migrants did not necessarily view their teachers as "agents of repression"; rather, they saw them as individuals who, although they may have cared about them, had little to do with their futures and social mobility. Harkening back to the overall community belief that schooling was not that important to obtain future employment and embedded in the larger structural inequalities that appeared to have a greater impact on the youths' school completion, as in Manuel's case, it seemed that youths did not place too much importance on teachers in regards to their futures. Some were good, and others were bad; that was just the way it was.

PUSHED OR JUMPED? MEXICAN YOUTHS BECOME SCHOOL DROPOUTS

Prospective and actual independent Mexican teenage migrants who ended their studies in Mexico believed that they had done so forever. Although poverty is often cited as the catchall reason for this, in the cases of these youths, explanations of their departures were often significantly more complicated and mindful

(Lukes 2015). Taken in toto, these explanations reflected the intersections of a variety of structural and individual forces, including household poverty, but also insufficient school accessibility and excessive school costs. Impaired motivation at the following key junctures often drove students from their schoolhouses: after completing primaria, during or after completing secundaria, or before the completion of preparatoria.[12] Regardless of the moment, however, youths also cited reasons that ignored structural inequalities in favor of "personal responsibility," or their and their families' inability to continue to pay for schooling. In reality, however, the youths' school departures were results of the incongruence between the structural "panaceas" and modernization attempts that the government required and what the families could afford. It is this incongruence that created and maintained low levels of educational attainment among the youths.

As discussed previously, for some youths, the actual decision to end their schooling was not theirs. These prospective and actual independent Mexican teenage migrants were simply told by their parents that unless they themselves paid for their own expenses, their schooling would be over. While Clementina and Genoveva were told this as they approached the end of their secundaria studies, Felipe was told after completing primaria: "My papá did not have the money to help me study—that is why I left. I wanted to study, but she [my mamá], she told me no, that they did not have money, [and] they did not know where they were going to get money, because they did not have work."

More striking, however, were youths who stated that it was their choice to end their schooling. As in their decisions to emigrate, these Mexican youths believed they were exercising agency and *planful competence* as they contemplated leaving and ultimately did leave school (Clausen 1991, 1986). The youths did not make the decision impulsively; after much observation and consideration of their contexts and what was possible for them, they make the decision to leave school.

Like Armando, who had been contemplating leaving for three months prior to his expulsion, Alejandro had also considered dropping out, but even earlier—*in the fifth grade*. The eldest in a family of six, Alejandro, as an eleven-year-old, was already wracked with guilt associated with the financial pressures his mamá experienced. He noticed the fees she was asked to pay as a result of his and his siblings' schooling:

> I [first] got the idea [of dropping out] because one of my brothers was in kinder[garten]. My two sisters were in the first. My little brother had not yet entered into school, [and my] other brother was in the second or third year of primaria when I got to secundaria. (But when did you begin to think about dropping out?) When I was in the fifth year, when [we] went to my registration, I remembered that it would be 200 pesos, or in the primaria, she was going to

> pay 400 [pesos]. Since then, I [thought] that my mamá did not have a good job where they paid her sufficiently, and that was [where I got] the idea that maybe I was not going to continue studying.

As discussed in chapter 2, Alejandro, as well as other youths who had younger siblings, discussed making these observations and decisions on their own so that their younger brothers and sisters could advance in their studies. Honoring their obligations to their families, these youths would drop out.

Lastly, although the specter of migration was not mentioned as influencing their decisions to leave school, various scholars point to its role in incomplete schooling (Fry 2002; Oropesa and Landale 2009; Zenteno et al. 2013). This was noted by one of the secundaria teachers in San Pedro when I was giving a presentation to the students:

> After responding to Profe Tamez's question about whether or not I would recommend migrating or staying there in school, Señor Flores and the teachers agreed, saying that people who migrate to the United States do not enter into the school system there and even dropout here because they see that someone with a primary education and a college degree from Mexico may end up working in the same job, so why invest in education in Mexico? They may both end up washing dishes, one having invested much more money and time in their education than the other. (Martinez, June 27, 2006)

For youths who did not continue their schooling, their justifications were not so much about migration as they were about their understandings of the differences between opportunity structures in their home contexts and the United States. Studies have cited a lack of field correspondence attesting to the reasons people migrate, including a lack of labor opportunities, perceived and real, for poor people in Mexico. Sebastian, who had left schooling after primaria, knew that one did not need high levels of education to obtain work in New York—he had heard how his father had secured employment at a pizza parlor in New York City with little education. But when asked to explain why he dropped out so soon, instead he explained it in terms of the futility of pursuing education in Mexico: "Why am I going to study if I am not going to become a doctor, I am not going to be anything, [and] studies are not going to help me? I just want to leave already—leave to do this or the other. I have a cousin who one time, they told him, 'Why are you going to continue studying if you are not going to be a *licenciado*?'" Echoing community members who did not support the construction of schools in their towns because they did not put stock in the value of higher levels of schooling, poor rural and urban youths believed that even if they continued their schooling, they would not have access to professional careers.

Without professionals in their communities, a tangible, visible correspondence between schooling and professional careers was absent. In the absence of these examples, schooling, they felt, was a waste of time; they would be leaving anyway.

In spite of the pressures and, ultimately, realities of leaving school, youths shared that family members had encouraged them to continue studying throughout their academic careers. The problem was, however, that even with encouragement, the adults in the youths' lives could not provide the material support they needed to continue their studies. Rather, as Julio eloquently captured,

> My mamá would tell me to study, my grandmother would tell me to study, and everyone told me to study, and I did not want to study because they told me to study, but they did not tell me, "See, we have to help you however we can." They just told me to study, study, and they did not tell me that they are going to help me with what they can; they just told me to study. No, I did not see where I was going to get the money from to pay rent [and] all of that.

And the youths knew this. They knew that in addition to words, material support to remain in school was needed. They knew that youths whose parents could afford to financially back them had continued their schooling.

Dropping out after only one year of bachiller, Rogelio believed, "[It is] those who can count on resources who can continue studying. For example, store owners, the people who make *tabique* [concrete], et cetera, their children have opportunities to continue studying. Or also people who have their mamás and papás here [in the United States], and they support them to continue studying. I don't know. Business owners have their children, and they send them to other states and the sons and daughters of teachers too." Rogelio's theory was illustrated in San Valentín, the town where I recruited high school students to interview. Even there, aspirations were tenuous. As Rogelio said, most of the youths enrolled had parents who were business owners or were already in the United States. There were only a few—Alejandro himself was struggling to stay in school—who remained. One such youth was Esteban, whose mamá was in Los Angeles and who had his eye on becoming an engineer. His backup plan was to immigrate to the United States and become a cook like his uncle.

For prospective and actual Mexican independent teenage migrants, the premature ending of their studies before completing high school—now the Western norm—demonstrates the structural shortcomings inherent in Mexico's educational system. Advanced levels of schooling inadequately subsidized by the national or federal government, in tandem with students unable to meet these demands/obligations/laws, jeopardize poor Mexican youths, setting them up for failure and, ultimately, migration.

WHEN KNOWLEDGE SHAPES ASPIRATIONS: SCHOOLING IN NEW YORK CITY

Similar to the knowledge that they possessed about the housing and labor markets that awaited them in New York City, prior to migration, they knew little about the educational field and its positions, especially about how they would enter it and which types of schooling were available to them. Already planning to work and not enter into schooling, youths asked their adult relatives and friends very little about it prior to leaving. Like Armando, who shared that schooling "did not interest [him]," other youths such as Luis had not thought about studying or reentering schooling at all. Rather, they believed that their experience in the educational field was over—one more marker of the transition to adulthood completed.

Those who did know about schooling in the United States knew of two dimensions: (a) those experienced by younger relatives, usually the U.S.-born children of their aunts, uncles, and siblings who had immigrated before them and were now sharing social and economic capital with them, and (b) English classes. From the former, youths were able to secure limited information. For one, they understood that in NYC, unlike in Mexico, the government supported the schools, making them free, and on top of that, they gave students food to eat, like pizza. Aside from that, however, they knew very little about the type of schooling in the United States that was considered most appropriate for youths their ages: a continuation and/or extension of their studies in Mexico, K–12 studies. Alluding to their lack of particular types of capital that they believed were necessary to participate in the educational field in the United States, including citizenship and language, they did not know whether "they were capable of studying there" or if they were even allowed to enroll in these schools. When asked about the schools themselves, youths were unaware about differences between Mexican and U.S. schools, including the grade levels, with a few believing that teachers in the United States were "better prepared." In most cases, however, it did not matter. The youths were not interested in enrolling in "regular" schools.

Youths knew much more about English classes. With access only to "aged" social capital, or social capital shaped by the ages of those who possessed and shared it, by virtue of who they were communicating with the most—adult relatives and friends—the youths only knew about schooling available to adults (McDonald and Mair 2010). Youths knew that English schools existed as well as the types and value of capital that could be obtained by assuming these particular positions in New York City's educational field. Concepción had the idea that knowing English "helped more" and that it was "the best" in terms of helping immigrants communicate with people and settle into the city, or integrating. More precisely, some youths knew from friends and relatives that learning English was directly tied to both retention and promotion in employment or in the labor market field, which Alejandro believed would "help [his] family . . . in Mexico." In Genoveva's case, she knew that her father's cousin took an English course after his boss told him to take one if he wanted to continue working. Employed in a restaurant, he "had to take the English course so that he could wait on people who went and could not speak Spanish well but also so he could understand better what people were saying." But knowing English was not only tied to job retention; it also led to job promotion and/or upward mobility. Prior to leaving Mexico, José Luis's cousin had already informed him that knowing English could also assist in job mobility. After taking classes at age fifteen, "he began to tell me that now . . . at work, he rose a little." All in all, Mexican youths were well aware that learning English was valuable for obtaining access to higher positions in New York City's labor market, something that, in turn, would help them achieve the goals they hoped to fulfill when they decided to emigrate.

Considering the short lengths of time that prospective and actual independent Mexican teenage migrants wished to spend in New York City as well as their fiscal goals, which were linked to these lengths of time, it was no surprise that the majority of these youths immigrated with the desire to remain out of school. However, when equipped with this knowledge about learning English, as well as the relationship between obtaining this linguistic capital and earned economic capital, some Mexican youths changed their tunes. Whether they would enter into English courses and how they did so is discussed in the following section.

WALLS AND WELCOMES: NEW YORK CITY'S EDUCATIONAL FIELD

Upon arrival in New York City, independent Mexican teenage migrants unknowingly entered into a context in which K–12 schooling, by virtue of their ages, was not only available and accessible but also compulsory. Unbeknownst to the youths, U.S. schools, by law, not only accept undocumented students but, in the case of New York City, legally require individuals living within the district limits to attend school until age seventeen, although they are actually eligible for educational services until age twenty-one (New York City Department of Education 2017; Plyler v. Doe 1982).

Independent Mexican teenage migrants enter into New York City wholly unaware of these laws and largely remain outside of New York City schools. As recently as 2010, approximately five thousand Mexican foreign-born teenage minors between the ages of fifteen and seventeen in the New York–northeastern New Jersey metro area were not in school (Fry 2012, 2005). However, because dropout counts are based on numbers of students who leave after attending

New York City schools, not only are independent Mexican teenage migrants not included in counts of minors with incomplete schooling; they are literally outside New York Board of Education statistics. All in all, these youths are invisible. *But shouldn't they be in school?*

Riding the subway home after a long night of researching and writing in the university library, I asked myself this question after noticing a peach-fuzzed-face male whom I guessed to be Mexican who was also on the train. I wondered why this "kid," appearing exhausted and with no parent in sight, was on the subway so late at night. Shouldn't he be at home, sleeping or finishing his homework? Instead of working, shouldn't he be in school? In the youths' minds, I found, the answer was no; they arrived in New York City to work. As will be further discussed in chapter 5, within hours or sometimes days of arriving, youths set out and successfully found work so that they could pay off their debts, support themselves, and fulfill their goals in New York City. To do this, they, like their undocumented adult counterparts, immediately undertook, on average, seventy-two-hour weeks of work characterized by irregular schedules. As a result, even if they wished to, youths found that they simply did not possess the time to commit to any type of schooling, either English or traditional classes.

This is their main consideration when deciding whether to enroll in any sort of coursework: Will school attendance interfere with earning wages? Arriving with timed plans to work, earn, and save specific sums of money that they soon find are difficult to amass quickly due to low wages, high expenses for rent, and loans related to their immigration and other costs, most youths decide to "never enroll" or forego schooling (Oropesa and Landale 2009: 240). This was Pedro's reasoning at first. Although he eventually entered into English classes after being convinced by Columbia University students who frequented his taqueria, Pedro admitted that he had initially thought that attending classes "would not be useful": "We want to return quickly for a year and a half and that's it, but I've already stayed four years. So then I thought, 'Why am I going to enter into an English class and then go?'" Ignacio provided me with further details as to why many youths opted to forego any sort of schooling in New York City. Working excessive hours to pay off his debts and support himself and his family, Ignacio, even though he wished to, did not even try to enroll in English classes when he arrived: "When I arrived here, the first thing I had to do was pay off my debt. I had to pay back my uncles for financing my trip to get here, so I focused on finding a job and work only. I had the illusion of going to school, but between tiredness and laziness, I didn't go."

Aside from sheer financial need, independent Mexican teenage migrants also continue to possess limited ideas about schooling by virtue of their membership in the same social networks in which they were embedded prior to migration. Although they do meet other individuals after migration, independent Mexican teenage migrants primarily associate with adult men who are too old for traditional schooling. Consigned to these networks, even after spending several years in New York City, youths remain unaware of pathways that could lead to traditional school enrollment. In addition to not possessing an interest in schooling immediately after arrival, Pedro added that in spite of arriving three years prior and working blocks away from one of the most prestigious universities in the world, he had only recently been informed that he was eligible to take courses in the city: "You do not know anything about . . . [the] laws of the schools [or] about . . . the programs that are, so then . . . some people are afraid of asking. One feels like, well, I do not have rights here, and you're afraid that the police [are] going to get you." As a result, most youths remained in the dark about resuming classes in the Big Apple—whether they could enroll, the requirements for enrollment, or whether courses were easy or difficult.

Also, similar to what they learn premigration, when independent Mexican teenage migrants do obtain information about entering the education field, that information is biased toward particular field positions most associated with adult immigrants. Learning about this particular educational niche reflects the youths' social networks as well as the ages and legal statuses of those who engage with them. For instance, now nineteen-year-old Samuel knew about English classes from his friends who were "all older than him." From them, he learned about the schedule of classes and even about fees. Alternatively, like the majority of independent Mexican teenage migrants, he knew nothing about "schools like that." Rather, he knew about schools that were more accessible to immigrant workers because their courses fit their schedules.

When youths did know about more traditional schools, they mostly knew about the incongruence between their labor demands and the schools' schedules. Because the majority of New York City schools are designed for youths who are dependents able to attend without full-time work, independent Mexican teenage migrants are simply shut out of attending school during the peak hours of 8 a.m. to 3 p.m. in light of their work commitments. Julio explained it more clearly, exhibiting his belief that for youths like him, participation in the education field and the labor market were incompatible. When I asked why he had not resumed his studies, Julio responded, "I work twelve hours a day. And it is difficult to find a job that gives you eight hours to attend school. . . . Here too, it is a little difficult because there are only schedules in the morning and in the afternoon, and they don't leave me time. I do not see how I can attend school."

But even adult education courses designed for adults with full-time work schedules seemed out of reach for some youths. For one, the minimum age requirement for enrollment was eighteen, and in the case of City College—a venue that was geographically convenient for Fidencio—the age was nineteen.[13]

Most youths, however, were unaware of this, nor was the rule enforced. Instead, when asked why, in spite of the availability of adult classes that were less demanding in terms of commitment, they had not enrolled in these courses, they continued to point not to age but to the dissonance between the timing of these classes and their work. This was exacerbated in the case of undocumented immigrants who were working excessive hours with little schedule flexibility. When asked about this, Fidencio simply said that it was difficult to find classes that fit his work schedule. After he unsuccessfully looked for some courses near his residence and place of employment in Washington Heights, I offered him information about Community League of the Heights (CLOTH) classes held from 10 a.m. to 1 p.m. He maintained that he could not enroll because he had to work at 1 p.m. Youths who had been at their jobs for shorter periods of time especially felt that they had little bargaining power to change their schedules.

Fidencio was not alone in his inability to access English-language classes that fit his needs. In New York City, the demand for English-language classes to accommodate immigrant New Yorkers far exceeds the supply. According to a report published by the Center for an Urban Future and the Center for Popular Democracy, at a time when more than 1.7 million adult New Yorkers were categorized as "limited English proficient," state funding for ESL classes was declining. For example, between 2005 and 2013, the number of state-funded seats declined by 395 to a low of 28,862 (Hamaji and González-Rivera 2016; Hilliard 2012). In the entire state, only one in every thirty-nine adults with limited English proficiency had access to courses (Giles and Wijering 2015).

Although independent Mexican teenage migrants arrive in New York City with the idea of earning money to send back home, they are entering into contexts characterized by Western age norms that legally oblige them to continue their schooling in New York City. While many are unaware of these laws or even how to access schooling in New York City—not to mention possessing wholly different ideas about their priorities at their ages—many do learn, at least generally, about educational possibilities in their midst. Unfortunately, given the need to support themselves and their families, they believe that such education is simply unattainable. Some youths, however, do not. The following section discusses the conditions and factors that enable the enrollment of *some* independent Mexican teenage migrants into New York City's educational system as well as the fragile circumstances of their school attendance that result, for many, in temporary tenures.

DROPPING INTO AND OUT OF NEW YORK CITY SCHOOLS: ENGLISH CLASSES

While Pedro arrived in New York City "without the illusion of going to school," after much introspection and contemplation, as well as encouragement from adults, he decided, like the majority of the independent Mexican teenage migrants who ended up returning to school, to drop into the more flexible "adult" English courses rather than traditional classes. In his case, it was the encouragement of adult clients at his worksite that finally motivated him to seek out and attend classes. For others, however, adult relatives obliged their attendance. In these cases, the youths' relatives were concerned about age norms, and by default, even if they were unaware of compulsory education laws in New York City, they believed that the youths could be apprehended if found not in school on the streets during the daytime. As noted in chapter 2, in addition to fears about detection, these concerns and subsequent negotiations around school attendance reflect deeper struggles around age and autonomy playing out between youths and their adult relatives. For both reasons, adults were critical in nudging and sometimes forcing youths back into schools.

For Pedro, the proximity of his place of employment and its popularity with young college students—some in possession of social consciousness—were factors in his enrollment in English classes: "Some[one] from Columbia, since many go there to eat, . . . told me that there was an English school . . . [sponsored] by the university, and then I told him that I was going to go look, and already I am in my second semester. And like that I went, we went—he accompanied me, [but] I don't remember his name." Although I also accompanied Manuel and helped him negotiate enrollment in English classes at one of the CUNY Xpress Immigration Centers years later, he also discussed first receiving encouragement and information about English classes from a customer who frequented the Washington Heights store where he worked. Unlike Pedro, although the classes were being taught at a nearby library, Manuel simply did not have the time. It is important to note, however, that enrollment began after they had become legal adults and after they had been in New York City for at least three years. As mentioned earlier in Pedro's case, although initially believing that they would only be in New York City for a few years, the youths found themselves staying for longer periods of time than anticipated and began to engage in activities, such as taking English classes, that are the first steps toward obtaining skills that suggest more permanent stays.

Fear of detection also stirred adult relatives with whom the youths were living to insist on the youths' enrollment in school. Worried that law enforcement officials would notice the youths during school hours as they traveled to or from work, they required them to enroll in English courses during the day. Although the youths arrived ready to work, their adult siblings, uncles, aunts, or parents (in José Luis's case, his papá) wanted them to enroll in English classes in the morning or the afternoon so that they would not be on the streets during peak school hours. Then, if they were detected, they could show proof of school attendance. In these cases, family members with whom they were staying had themselves taken English courses and/or researched and paid for the classes. Arriving at age seventeen, Narciso's brother had taken English classes at one of the city's Zoni Language Centers. In Narciso's words, "My brother told me, he made me take [classes, so] . . . I went to study." Likewise, Carlos's brothers sent him to English classes while he waited to enroll in traditional high school.

For others, enrollment in English classes proved to be a test of their perceived autonomy in New York City. When José Luis arrived in New York City, his father continued to encourage him to enroll in high school: "[For] my papá, the idea was that I was going to enter to study in high school, and I was going to wait . . . some months until classes started in September, . . . but I told him no, that I just wanted to study a little English and enter to work; that's why I came. If I was going to continue studying, better that I would have stayed in Mexico." Although initially defiant, after rounds of negotiations, José Luis compromised and did enroll in English classes.

After youths decided to attend English classes, they followed two routes: approximately half sought classes at more expensive, private, for-profit schools in New York City, including American Language Communication Center, New York Language Center, or Zoni Language Center, and the other half pursued lower-cost and sometimes less-resourced classes offered at colleges, nonprofit organizations, and public libraries. Independent Mexican teenage migrants discussed learning about this spectrum of schooling from adult relatives and friends, both those who asked around for them and some who had been students there themselves. Other sources of information included advertisements on the subway, sources found at Mexican street festivals, or in Rodolfo's case, word from a court social worker who negotiated a deal for him to complete six months of classes in exchange for the court's expunging of prior juvenile delinquency charges. With registration costs, on average, between $120 and $170 a month, as well as additional costs for books, attending these schools was not cheap.[14] Regardless of whether the school was for-profit or nonprofit, youths reported irregular educational experiences and classes that varied in teacher quality, class availability, and organization. These factors—in addition to the sheer realities of the youths' excessive and unconventional (for youths) work schedules, course costs, and overall diminishing interest in learning English—impacted whether the youths continued studying.

For the most part, youths discussed mixed experiences with teachers who ranged from "very good" to outright awful. On average, youths believed that their teachers were "just giving their classes" and "did not get close to [them]." Carlos (Zoni Language Center) and José Maria (New York Public Library) were the only youths who discussed being taught by good, patient teachers, one who was a retired English teacher and, in José Maria's case, one who was "very loved" and "wanted to know that her students were learning." Other students, however, were much more critical of their teachers and their teaching. José Luis had completed the first two levels of English classes without a problem, but one-quarter of the way through the third level, he became disillusioned. Although it was his father who was paying more than $200 per level at the for-profit American Language Communication Center, José Luis described feeling cheated by his teacher, who "would arrive tardy sometimes, like twenty minutes," and "did not give them a complete class." Carlos described a bleaker situation when he took courses at the Our Lady of Guadalupe community center. At age twenty-four, he decided to return to English classes after a five-year hiatus because he was thinking more seriously about his future. With classes held at night, he asked to leave his job in Queens an hour earlier so that he could make it down to Lower Manhattan for the 7 p.m. class. Imagine his disappointment when he found a class that was rarely taught by its assigned teacher: "The teacher was never there. He arrived to give us something to do, he left, he did not return, [and then] the next day when we would return to classes, he would not even go over a grade [that] he gave us the day before. [He] put [out] new assignments, but he did not even have the last ones revised." The last straw came when the teacher "left sometimes and would leave a student who had been in the class longer to teach the class." Manuel experienced a similar situation after he convinced the coordinators to let him into English classes without the requisite Social Security card. This had been useless, Manuel shared, as he only attended the classes a couple of times because "the teacher never came." The youths considered these classes, with their poor instruction or outright absence of teachers, as Carolina succinctly put it, a "waste of time" in which they learned "nothing" and soon left.

Other youths cited the disorganization of the schools as the reason they lost interest and gave up on taking English classes. Prior to attending classes at Our Lady of Guadalupe, Carlos attended Zoni Language Center, where his classes were not much better. Dissatisfied with his new teacher, Carlos tried to switch into other classes that were just starting. After being promised a seat in a new class at his skill level, when Carlos actually went to the class on the start date, he found it was canceled for lack of student enrollment. This happened on and off for two months until he finally decided to give up and leave his classes for good. Youths found the opposite in nonprofit organizations, where the demand for classes was too high and the supply was too low. Casualties of insufficient funding to meet the language needs of New York City's immigrants, youths such as Manuel and Fidencio were placed on waiting lists that never seemed to move.

In several cases, I attempted to intervene to get youths enrolled or taken off the waitlist with varying degrees of success. A year after I helped him register, Fidencio was still not in English classes.

In the end, these challenges, in addition to the lack of favorable work and school schedules, led to the youths' final departures from English classes after only three months on average. Although they initially tried to balance their schedules to include morning or afternoon classes along with their long work days, with growing frustration and boredom exacerbated by poor teaching, the youths soon gave up trying to juggle both; it was simply too taxing without a sufficient payoff. José Luis shared,

> It was possible to [attend school and work], but it is very difficult. You can, but it gets very difficult . . . because if I want[ed] to continue studying, I would have to wake up at seven in the morning to enter school at eight, leave at ten, go to work, and well, it seems like a short amount of time for me, plus sleeping. I get home at one in the morning, and then after I take a bath and everything, I go to bed like at two or three. To get up at seven would be too little time for me.

Exhausted from intense work schedules and without supportive teachers who taught well, youths simply started to give in to "laziness" and then, like Miguel, began missing classes, always saying, "Tomorrow, I'll go; tomorrow I'll go."

Although he characterized it as "laziness," a better word to describe why Miguel and others stopped attending English classes is probably *surrender*—surrender to exhaustion but, more specifically, surrender to a system not sufficiently designed to educate undocumented immigrant workers, adult or otherwise. Instead, the youths experienced firsthand a system that had little serious concern for the education and upward mobility of immigrants or their achievement of the American Dream via education. As discussed earlier, these youths enrolled in English-as-a-second-language programs that were woefully underfunded and run by poorly trained staff. As such, the youths left long before course completion or English-language mastery.

But what about the youths who made it into educational programs, both traditional and nontraditional, that resulted in high school diplomas or the equivalent? The following section turns to the nine independent Mexican teenage migrants who did manage to find themselves in schools and programs that, upon completion, would secure a highly valued credential that could be converted into, at the very least, admission into college. Three of the youths were enrolled in college at the time of their interviews, with one completing college afterward. These youths provide some hope for the educational credentials independent Mexican teenage migrants can attain after arriving in New York City with low levels of education.

BECOMING NEW YORK CITY HIGH SCHOOL STUDENTS

Scholars have already noted the relationship between the ages at which immigrant students arrived and the decreased likelihood of dropping in at older ages (Fry 2003; Hirschman 2001; Oropesa and Landale 2009). Partially explained by the youths' educational experiences prior to migration, the educational field that they encounter is also important to consider. In New York City and elsewhere, few educational programs exist that address the needs of minors, especially non-English-speaking immigrant minors who, at these young ages, are unable to financially depend on adults and possess profound economic obligations (New York City Department of Education 2010). In spite of the scarcity of such programs, nine independent Mexican teenage migrants found themselves pursuing high school credentials—either traditional or alternative—in one of three types of educational programs in the city. The majority of the youths found themselves in the expanding Internationals Network for Public Schools that, at least in text, adhered to Western notions of the life course and assumed the presence of parents nearby. However, a couple of other youths found themselves in programs that were more explicitly designed for adults, including the Manhattan Comprehensive Night and Day High School (MCNDHS), one of the New York City Department of Education's schools for older, overcredited youths and adults and GED (now TASC) programs. Although they described different experiences when pursuing their high school or equivalency studies, all expressed a sense of pride and accomplishment that they were continuing their educations after hiatuses and now, having caught the education bug, wished to continue onto postsecondary studies.

DROPPING INTO HIGH SCHOOL

Unlike the case of English classes, where, in at least some instances, adult relatives demanded that the youths return to school, in all the cases where youths returned to more traditional schooling, the youths themselves—three of whom were already young adults—had made the decision. Although all but two of them had arrived *without* the idea to resume their studies, after living in New York and both realizing and becoming dissatisfied with the type of work and/or wages they would be subject to without more advanced studies—as well as, more generally, wishing to learn more—the youths began to inquire about the possibility of taking high school courses. Supporting Lukes's 2015 findings that immigrant youths enrolled in ESL (English as a second language) classes aspired to continue their studies beyond their current levels, for five of the youths, or 56 percent, this occurred after previously completing English classes for varying lengths of time.

After initially being offered the opportunity to enroll in high school and first turning it down, Rodolfo began to think about returning to school more and more. After completing his court-mandated English courses at the nonprofit The Door, the program's executive director asked him to consider transitioning into high school. Uninterested and more concerned with earning money, Rodolfo left to accept work with his friend at an upstate New York supermarket. After working there several weeks, Rodolfo observed how other workers who performed less work earned $3 more an hour simply because they knew more English. He wondered, "Why is it possible that they can do it [speak English] and not me?" Disturbed by this inequality, Rodolfo began to have anxiety dreams about returning to school: "In the time that I lived [in Monticello], everything was like the same as school, like I was getting to school late. I had dreams [that] my sister returned to my house, and my sister would tell me to call The Door, and . . . ask why [I had not] gone if they were going to fix my schooling and my papers. . . . I would always wake up with that idea, that I had to return to The Door. And then I went to The Door and I spoke with the director that I wanted to enter into high school."

Compared to the other youths, Martín arrived with more of the mind-set of a "transfer" student rather than someone who had experienced a serious disruption of his schooling. Leaving Mexico just one month shy of his high school graduation, sixteen-year-old Martín still possessed a strong desire to enter high school, but he found that his uncle and aunt, with whom he would be staying, just thought he "was going to have the routine of everyone else: arrive, work. Just arrive and work, truthfully." While he did work initially, the deep desire to finish his studies—a desire that was stoked when he saw children going to school every day—led him to "take the initiative" and convince his uncle to accompany him as he asked about studying in New York City. His uncle, who held the same notion as many of the Mexican youth interviewees—that only children born in the United States could attend school—attempted to dissuade him from going to ask about school. Determined to at least get an answer, Martín coaxed his uncle to go along with him to confirm one way or another. "We won't lose anything," Martín said. And they didn't. Although they initially encountered resistance—"a lot of buts, buts, buts"—in the first educational office they visited, Martín insisted that they go elsewhere, and the representative with whom they eventually spoke proved his uncle, and their first interlocutor, wrong. There, they spoke with a *hispana* who challenged the ideas and information they had been given at the previous high school. Instead, she told them, "How is it that you cannot go to school? Of course you can go to school!" She told him "not to think because you do not have documents or you do not speak the language you cannot go to school. Of course you can go to school; you can educate yourself here very well."

Mostly encountering helpful institutional agents who directed them to appropriate offices and educational programs, this handful of independent Mexican teenage migrants began the process of enrolling in schools deemed appropriate for them. In addition to being limited by the usual zoning restrictions around enrollment in New York City high schools, independent Mexican teenage migrants found that additional factors, such as age, language, and nativity, shaped their enrollment. The following section focuses on the three main types of schools independent Mexican teenage migrants would eventually enroll in and attend—newcomer schools, second-chance schools, and adult education programs—and the structural features of the schools that would provide clues as to the youths' schooling experiences.

THE SCHOOLS INDEPENDENT MEXICAN TEENAGE MIGRANTS DROP INTO

Although these independent Mexican teenage migrants decided to search for information about school enrollment, whether they wound up in particular schools often depended on the institutional agents with whom they spoke, including staff from New York City's Department of Education and nonprofits. These individuals provided them with information regarding specific schools where they could and should enroll based on their ages, residences, language, and, although unstated, foreign-born statuses. In a context with few options and given little choice, the youths were guided toward particular schools that staff believed would best serve them.

Like most of the Mexican youths who would pursue some sort of high school studies, Rodolfo was guided to one of the city high schools specifically designed to meet the needs of recently arrived immigrant youths and/or students who still required ELL services. After he returned from Monticello at the end of August, one of the first things he did was speak with the executive director at The Door, who had offered to help Rodolfo enroll in high school before. When Rodolfo returned, he walked him over to the office of the director of education, who told him, "'You know what? Your best option is Liberty [High School Academy for Newcomers] . . . for two reasons. Because you live in Brooklyn, and this is closer.' And he told me that [I] don't speak much English, and you need one where they also teach in Spanish, and it was the best option." After being told this and which documents he would need to register, Rodolfo called his mamá to get his birth certificate and his primaria diploma. One year after arriving in New York City, Rodolfo took these documents and became a new student at Liberty High School Academy for Newcomers.

Similar to the other high schools that the youths attended, Liberty High School was designed as a bilingual/English-as-a-second-language transfer school, meaning that officials expected to receive youths who had not necessarily disrupted their educations, as was the case for most of the independent Mexican teenage migrants. Rather, Liberty High School served youths who had left their schools in their home countries and were immediately enrolling in ones in New York City. With a more traditional schedule characterized by full-time programming, classes ran from 8 a.m. to 2:20 p.m., but this seemingly early dismissal did leave time for full-time employment, which at first Martín engaged in.

Designed for youths whose ages were better aligned with those of conventional high school students, Liberty did not admit students younger than 14.5 or older than age 18 and expected students to graduate in four to five years. Additionally, extending traditional norms of high school age, the school's website explicitly stated the city's policy of guaranteeing an education until age 21. Because migration knows no schedule, the school accepted students year round as long as they provided the requisite documents, immunization records, birth certificates, and so on and, reflecting the school's orientation toward dependent youths, were accompanied by a parent or guardian upon registration. Across their website, youths were de-aged, as they were referred to only as "students," but the school further emphasized the presence of parents and dependence by providing a parent coordinator and hosting a parent-teacher association separate from students (New York City Department of Education 2014). To register and attend several parent meetings, Rodolfo brought his older brother, but after he transitioned into foster care, no one accompanied him. Lastly, as one of the campuses located in New York City's District 79 for alternative high schools, in 2016, Liberty High School reported a 59 percent graduation rate, while 16 percent completed college and career preparation courses and exams. Fifty-two percent of the graduates enrolled in college or other postsecondary programs within six months.[15]

Other students attended schools included in the lauded Internationals Network for Public Schools, including Flushing International High and Manhattan International High School, noncharter high schools with curricula that emphasized native-language and English-language development and project-based learning geared toward immigrant students who lived in the United States for fewer than four years (INPS 2017; Lukes 2015). At Flushing International High School, for example, students followed a traditional bell schedule from 8 a.m. to 3:30 p.m. and also counted on parent coordinators and support (New York City Department of Education 2016b). In 2016, Flushing International boasted a 72 percent four-year graduation rate, with 36 percent of the students successfully completing college or career preparation coursework and 48 percent of the graduating students enrolled in college or other postsecondary programs within six months.[16]

Herminda eventually enrolled in Manhattan Comprehensive Night and Day High School (MCNDHS), a school initially designed for older youths with adult responsibilities but whose mission seemed to recently shift more explicitly to include new immigrants (New York City Department of Education 2017). Although she wanted to pursue high school studies, Herminda did not know the difference between GED programs and regular high school, but after being pushed out of two GED programs—one that ran out of funding and another that would not admit her without a Social Security card—she was directed to the New York City Department of Education Family Welcome Center in Queens Plaza. There, age determined her fate. Already approaching twenty and having never enrolled or earned credits in New York City high schools, she was told about MCNDHS, which accepted students ages 17.5 to 21. Approaching the school's maximum age, she was told that she would have to complete four years of material in only one and a half years (New York City Department of Education 2017).

When Herminda described the school in 2009, she referred to three shifts: one during the day, one midafternoon to early evening, and one from early evening to late evening. However, with the motto of "serving students around the clock," in 2016, the school only held classes in the morning and evening, from 8:00 a.m. to 9:31 p.m. This schedule reflected the school's commitment to, in Herminda's words, "young adults" who possessed significant adult responsibilities, including children. The text on their website somewhat reiterated this by referring to students in a variety of ways, including as "young people with adult responsibilities," "non-traditional," "older," and "adults." Conversely, the school also possessed a parent coordinator and included information about ways that parents could be involved in their children's education. Slightly above the city's average for comparable students, in 2016, the school's graduation rate was 53 percent, with 21 percent successfully completing college-ready or career-preparation courses or exams. Thirty-six percent of the graduates enrolled in college or other postsecondary programs within six months (New York City Department of Education 2016b).[17]

Only one youth, José Maria, was enrolled in GED classes at the time of the interview, at Borough of Manhattan Community College. With the New York City Department of Education placing age limits at age twenty-one, twenty-two-year-old José Maria had already unwittingly surpassed the age limits of both the International High Schools and New York City's alternative high schools, including MCNDHS. Instead, she simultaneously took courses to prepare for the high school equivalency exam at Borough of Manhattan Community College (BMCC) as well as English-language courses at a library after realizing that she did not want to be "working in the same [jobs], that she wanted something better." Because she attended classes on Saturdays, José Maria's course costs did not include lost labor; instead, she provided the expensive payments.

She calculated that in the year she had been taking classes at BMCC, she had already spent $3,000 on the course, books, and other incidentals.

In spite of the high costs, José Maria might be considered fortunate to have registered in these courses. Hilliard and Dann-Messier (2015) argue that stagnant funding since 1995 has impeded expansion of free and low-cost high school equivalency courses, even as more than 1.6 million New York adults lack a high school diploma or its equivalency. A review of New York City's 2017–2018 Office of Adult and Continuing Education (OACE) course directory revealed that across the city, the New York City Department of Education sponsored only thirty-six high school equivalency (HSE) preparation courses, twenty-seven of which were in Spanish. These courses were eclipsed by dramatically higher numbers of English-as-a-second-language and adult basic education courses, or courses that focus on "primary adult literacy skills, educational goals and personal interests" and can lead up to entry into HSE courses (New York City Department of Education 2017). These trends imply (a) that as Hilliard and Dann-Messier (2015) suggest, that the city is simply unable to meet the demand for this sort of schooling, leaving thousands of New Yorkers without pathways to postsecondary opportunities, and/or (b) that immigrant adults are gravitating toward courses that focus more on skills rather than credentials, with limited transition into high school studies. This may be due to the limited value of a GED (now TASC in New York State) for undocumented immigrants, especially those without English proficiency and legal status. Participating in labor market niches and segments that are predicated more on language, young adults who take the TASC in Spanish without improving their English-language skills and/or making plans and obtaining transitional support to enter into postsecondary schooling may be obtaining "little more than a piece of paper" (Lukes 2015). Time would tell for José Maria, who, in addition to her plans to become a beauty stylist, was also thinking about attending college.

BECOMING "TRADITIONAL" STUDENTS . . . AGAIN

Of the independent Mexican teenage migrants who returned to full-time schooling, all but one described returns that, although stressful at times, were welcomed and full of learning, support, and leadership development. Youths spoke of engaging curricula, supportive teachers and administrators, and opportunities for leadership development. Unsurprisingly, all three factors contributed to their academic and interpersonal growth.

Although students' recollections of their academic development during high school centered on their language acquisition, they also spoke of being awakened by taking "'normal' classes, like [in] a common school." Rodolfo also went into great detail to describe each of the English classes he took, ESL levels 1 through 8, each one corresponding to a semester during which he learned English at varying speeds—slow one semester, faster another. He remembered his favorite semester, where he felt his writing improved because he had to read in English and then write up analyses in English. His new passion, though, was history, especially global history; in that class, where his teacher would also speak in Spanish, he excelled. Even after initially falling behind when he was assigned a stricter teacher for U.S. history, he worked hard to catch up; his grades in history were high, never falling below an 85.

Youths also developed their interpersonal skills in these high schools. Applauding the Internationals Network for Public Schools project-based approach to learning, Martín also described how the curriculum helped him socially. At first he and the other students who had arrived were timid and afraid, but after working "more in groups," he said, "You think more about relating more with other people, and you start to have more confidence. . . . When you speak with another person, you are also improving your writing, your language."

Youths also talked about the emotional support they received during moments of doubt and despair. Especially interested in whether the youths would be sufficiently motivated to resume full-time schooling after the disruptions they had experienced and the time spent out of school, I asked them whether their returns had been difficult and, if so, how they had managed to persist during difficult times. As discussed by Lukes (2015), the youths encountered teachers at the schools who were particularly sensitive to the needs of immigrant youths, especially those who missed their homelands and, in the case of independent Mexican teenage migrants, their families. Martín described teachers who held him up when he began to feel "bad": "[They] continued pushing me so that I would continue ahead, . . . and they, of course, motivated me to continue to college." He described them as "worrying a lot" about him. Administrators also took notice of them. Remembering back to when he first arrived at the school, Rodolfo recalled how, noting his limited English skills, the principal made it a point to talk with him and introduce him to other Mexican students who could take him under their wings. Once he became more proficient in English and advanced through grade levels, the principal asked him to return the favor to other recently arrived Mexican students. He believed that this was because the principal watched out for him to make him feel like he was part of the school. Not only well liked by administrators and teachers, Rodolfo found that he was also popular with students. Elected to the school's student council during his last year, Rodolfo became involved with decision-making on the campus and soon found himself making presentations to his classmates as well as the principal about changes the students wished to make to the school. Little did the youths know, however, that as they were suggesting changes to their schools, they themselves were changing. The following section discusses these shifts in their educational and life trajectories as well as who helped and how these shifts were facilitated.

FROM CAMPOS TO COLLEGE: WHEN HABITUS SHIFT

> Manhattan Comprehensive Night and Day High School specializes in providing older students, like you, a second chance to earn a high school diploma. We offer older students a second chance but we are in no way second best.
>
> —MCNDHS website, 2017

> It does not matter when or how you got to the finish line; it only matters that you finished with pride.
>
> —Liberty High School website, 2017

Recalling her tenure at MCNDHS, Herminda let out a long "Whoooo!" and described it as "precious." Possessing fond memories, Herminda recounted attending a school that not only was flexible in schedule but also provided her with high-quality academic skills and content. Additionally, she marveled, the school was true to its name—comprehensive—and was committed to seeing its students succeed. From administration to teachers, Herminda believed that the school addressed the little things that impacted learning, such as providing students with papers and pencils if they did not bring them as well as food and Metro cards. With the Comprehensive Development Initiatives (CDI) on campus as a partner organization, students also received extra support in the form of legal, medical and housing assistance, case management, intensive tutoring, and other services. In addition, the organization provided college and career counseling (MCNDHS 2018).

It was this curriculum and counseling during their high school careers, coupled with overall support and motivation from their teachers, counselors, and even principals, that appeared to influence the youths' significant changes in future plans that no longer drew them to return to Mexico. Similar to Lukes's findings about young adults who were enrolled in adult education classes, the youths who had made it this far only wanted to continue to advance in their studies (Lukes 2015: 78–79). Successful in school and exposed to the possibilities of college, youths began to imagine different lives and expressed interest and in three cases pursued four-year college degrees. One youth wished to obtain a PhD.

These were significant changes from the ideas they possessed in Mexico or even those they held upon arriving in New York City. When in Mexico, Rodolfo said he had only envisioned his life as existing in Mexico, in his hometown and in the surrounding towns. There, no one needed a diploma to be successful; rather, the only thing they needed was "to work hard and save money so that you could have something in your future," and that was all that Rodolfo had in his mind.

Somewhat accounted for by Bourdieu as he discusses the fine-tuning of primary habitus, Rodolfo arguably was doing more than "fine-tuning" since arriving in New York City. Introduced to alternative possibilities in the eleventh grade when he participated in a college preparation program, College Bound, at St. John's College, it appeared as if his first thoughts about continuing his studies beyond high school were further crystallizing. At College Bound, Rodolfo began to hear about college and its benefits as well as its costs and length of time. This caused him to "start to orient [himself] and think . . . , 'If I can invest four years in high school, why can't I invest another four years and do what I have to do?" This sort of thinking appeared to impact his immigrant classmates as well, as witnessed by a quick look at the Liberty High School website, which lists their students' college admissions, ranging from Borough of Manhattan Community College to University of San Francisco. Rodolfo ticked off the list of colleges in which his classmates were enrolled: SUNY and in CUNY, Brooklyn College, Queens College, and York College. Only one other person he knew was enrolled at John Jay, and just the other day he had run into her at the computer lab.

Others credited their high school counselors with motivating them to enroll in college. In Martín's case, he went back to his high school counselor after seeing information about CUNY Start, a remedial program that helped students improve their mathematics, reading, and writing skills so that they could pass the assessment exams needed to enter into a four-year CUNY campus. After returning to his counselor to talk it over, Martín believed that she had motivated him to enroll in this program. Now attending part time, Martín believed that he was drastically increasing his vocabulary and could now better structure an essay. This would assist him in fulfilling his dream of becoming an attorney.

The youths' resumed and continued schooling and gradual shifts in life-course trajectories, however, would not come without significant renegotiations of their relationships and participation in other fields. The following section discusses how the resumption of school attendance shaped these renegotiations in both the labor market and household fields and how they impacted not only the youths but also their families' daily lives.

ECONOMIC CONSIDERATIONS: MODIFYING PARTICIPATION IN THE LABOR MARKET AND HOUSEHOLDS

The independent Mexican teenage migrants found that their decisions to pursue advanced positions in education had significant consequences for their movement and positions in corresponding fields—namely, the labor market and their households, both in New York City and in Mexico. Youths who enrolled in more traditional high school programs found that they had to renegotiate their labor schedules and the financial arrangements they made with both their relatives in New York City and their parents in Mexico. Unable to work as many hours as they did before they were enrolled in school, the youths were also unable to pay as much rent and/or send as much money back home as they had previously. Overall, relatives in both New York City and Mexico were understanding and supportive of the hard work the youths had decided to undertake.

The first thing independent Mexican teenage migrants had to do was recalibrate their work schedules. Although some of the youths first attempted to fulfill both full-time work and school schedules, they soon found it too difficult and stressful to continue to do so. Arturo attempted to do this when he first enrolled at Liberty. At first, he kept his job as a dishwasher, working from 3 p.m. to 12 a.m., but he soon found himself sleeping in class, and his grades suffered. After seeing his friend do the same and then finally leave school, Arturo decided that he did not want the same to happen to him, and he opted to reduce his work schedule. He had concluded, "One kills oneself doing that [going to school and work at the same time]—exhaustion, stress, and all of that."

But a reduced work schedule translated into less money to pay for expenses, including rent as well as money they could send home. With less money, the youths needed to renegotiate the monetary agreements they held with their relatives and/or other individuals who depended on them for payment. Martín described an aunt and an uncle who were very understanding and supportive of his studies allowing him to reduce the amount that he paid for rent from $500 to approximately $300 a month. He described his uncle as "a little more conscious" than when he first had to convince him to ask about high schools, and he felt that because his uncle saw him "putting [in] more effort" and "taking his education seriously," they were helping him pay his part of the rent. Notably, however, Martín's return to school put a strain on his aunt and uncle's budgets as well.

Returning to school affected more than their living expenses in New York City; it also impacted their ability to send remittances home. When Rodolfo first arrived, he was sending his mamá between $350 and $400 a week to build her fence, add two rooms to their home, and cover her and his little brother's expenses. When he entered into high school—and, not so coincidentally, into foster care—his employment and the remittances he sent to his mother ceased. As discussed more extensively in chapter 2, Rodolfo's mamá did not shame him or become angry when the remittances ceased; rather, she demonstrated maternal understanding by telling him "not to worry. If you do not have money, do not send. I will see how I can manage and to eat." In spite of her assurances, Rodolfo resumed working two years later, as he entered the eleventh grade, because he realized that his mamá was not living well in Mexico. According to Rodolfo, she "depended on him, so he had to work hard to send money to her and his little brother, who was still going to school." Rodolfo began sending a lowered amount, or roughly $200 a month, but his grades started to suffer. Whereas his average had been a 90, after he started working and was unable to "concentrate totally in school," his average lowered to an 80. This was simply the sacrifice he would have to make to attend school and support his family.

Quite different from what they imagined when they arrived, these were the experiences and challenges that independent Mexican teenage migrants encountered when they pursued a high school diploma and, with dedicated work, college. Youths such as Rodolfo and Herminda now believed that a high school diploma, and then a college degree, in New York best defined their accomplishments in New York City. As Rodolfo shared, "My dream is to graduate and have a diploma that says that I graduated from New York, [to have] something that was worth the effort, like if I left [New York] and I did not build a house [in Mexico] or have money, I can show my diploma that showed that I studied." With a desire to join the Drug Enforcement Agency as a John Jay College of Criminal Justice graduate, Rodolfo was in a better position to pursue this dream with his degree and recently obtained legal status. He could see himself achieving his new goal after fulfilling the U.S. citizenship requirement mandated by the DEA and now with a college degree in hand.

Herminda, however, had a wholly dissimilar experience. After successfully applying, being admitted to, and then enrolling into Queens College as an economics major, she earned high enough grades to transfer to one of CUNY's most selective four-year campuses, Baruch College, where she would continue her degree and work on her plans to found a nonprofit organization to support low-income individuals pursuing higher education. However, a disturbing turn of events drove her to leave for Italy, marry, and then divorce. There, she took language classes and is now an airline attendant. She wished to enroll in and major in a tourism program, but to date, she has not yet completed a college degree, though she still dreams of doing so.

CONCLUSION

Across Mexico and New York City, independent Mexican teenage migrants encounter an educational system that is structured to marginalize poor Mexican youths. In Mexico, these youths attend schools in a context that, by law, mandates limited school attendance but in practice is costly, uneven, and insufficient. With messages conveyed through the schooling's accessibility and costs, as well as by teachers' behaviors, prospective and actual independent Mexican teenage migrants learn, at early ages, that schooling is not constructed to ensure their attendance and social mobility; rather, for poor youths, it is the opposite. Compounded by the absence of professionals in their communities who have completed high levels of schooling, these youths learn that as engaging as their courses may be, they are not meant for them, especially if they cannot afford them.

In New York, youths experience much the same. They encounter an educational field that while permitting access, does not necessarily accommodate individuals such as themselves—independent Mexican teenage migrants who work excessive hours and are self-reliant. With the original plan of working only to save and send money home, some become attracted to the idea of enrolling in English classes at the least so that their newfound English fluency can translate into greater economic capital. However, conflicting work and school schedules in New York, as well as inconsistent organization and instruction, much as in Mexico, impact the youths' ability to enroll and remain in adult education courses.

Only a handful of independent Mexican teenage migrants, however, enter into traditional schooling. These youths encounter adults who encourage, support, and provide information about more traditional schooling leading to high school diplomas and their equivalencies. Provided with important support from both the adult relatives they live with in New York City and their parents back home, these few youths acquire higher positions in the educational field and begin to experience a shift in their habitus. Reconfiguring their goals and their lives, these youths are no longer guided by the prospect of a future return to Mexico; instead, they begin to imagine professional lives in the United States made possible by degrees in high school and then college.

5 • FROM CAMPOS TO KITCHENS

Becoming Immigrant Workers

> One becomes accustomed [to] working all of their lives in Mexico. One is never waiting for someone to come help, . . . since [in] Mexico, they program them that they have to work all of their lives.
>
> —Rogelio, age twenty-four; arrived at age sixteen

As NAFTA was taking effect, Carolina was a toddler and no bigger than a lump. At this age and size, she was already being directed to perform simple chores such as going to "cut little plants, go cut these herbs, [and] begin to take out some corn kernels from the cobs." By the time she was four or five years of age, she was caring for her younger siblings while her mamá worked in the fields. Ten years later, she was folding and inspecting hundreds of shirts a day in one of the several *maquiladoras* that had recently opened in San Benito de los Lagos, which imported goods from the United States for assembly and export across the world.

Carolina and other Mexican youths did not realize it, but they were coming of age not only in the era of NAFTA but also amid extensive, century-long global debates about whether, under what conditions, and at what ages children and adolescents should begin to labor. Although typically children's rights advocates argued against the early performance of labor—much like the situation of Carolina and the other youths in this book—for the most part, these debates frame child labor as an aspect of one's early life that, if it does occur, should not begin until adolescence. For those who must labor at these ages, accommodations to avoid interference with primary tasks of school and leisure should be made (Mortimer et al. 2003; Zelizer 1994; Hall 1904).

For millions of Mexican minors, however, including countless prospective independent Mexican teenage migrants, these resolutions are largely irrelevant (Orraca 2014). Significant numbers of poor Mexican youths begin their careers of lifelong manual labor, both paid and unpaid, during early and middle childhood (Blum 2011; Cisneros 1997; Edmonds and Pavcnik 2005; Leira and Mortimer et al. 2003; Saraceno 2008; Tuttle 2006; UCW 2012). As discussed in chapter 2, the youths provide considerable amounts of labor to their households via chores and then waged work, often as early as they can walk. By participating in family enterprises that produce primary products for use in the household and sale and then engaging in waged labor, the youths become economically active at early ages to help support their families.

Although early and uninterrupted work are not new phenomena for poor Mexican children and teenagers, what are new are the conditions of and destinations where this labor is being performed (Aitken et al. 2006; Bey 2003; Bianet-Castellanos 2007; Giorguli Saucedo 2005; Jennings et al. 2006; Sosenski Correa 2010; Tuttle 2006). No longer limited to reproductive economies in Mexico, poor Mexican youths increasingly find themselves working outside of their homes in the waged economy and learning skills that "actually help broader political-economic processes in unintended ways"—namely, reproducing labor flows from Mexico to the United States (Magazine and Ramirez Sanchez 2007: 53). This chapter argues that poor Mexican youths are, from early ages, prepared to continue and/or complete one of the markers of the transition to adulthood, full-time work, as independent Mexican teenage migrants in New York City. Despite rigorous global debates about the rights of children, global and local socioeconomic forces in combination with family expectations still compel poor Mexican youths to enter into a labor field and provide copious amounts of labor to their households in the form of chores and then waged work. The introduction and/or expansion of modernizing institutions such as schools, instead of enabling full-time devotion to studies, compels children and teenagers living amid unrelenting poverty to balance traditional and modern age-graded expectations or work with schooling. Finding this balance untenable, youths drop out to work full time either in Mexico or, in the cases of this book's independent Mexican teenage migrants, outside of their communities and Mexico, in New York City.

With attention to their ages, time, and space, this chapter demonstrates how prospective and then actual independent Mexican teenage migrants, as Rogelio stated in the chapter's opening, "become accustomed to working all of their lives." By providing a comprehensive look at how these youths learn and integrate these understandings and orientations toward manual labor into their habitus and then act upon them, first in their Mexican households and labor markets and then in New York City, we begin to understand how these youths become underage, undocumented workers.

NOT JUST ECONOMIC: HOW HOUSEHOLD LABOR SHAPES UNDERSTANDINGS ABOUT WORK

As discussed in chapter 2, most independent Mexican teenage migrants learn to understand their labor as possessing social, in addition to economic, value in the household (Bourdieu 1984). Reinforced by institutionalized laws and customs, Mexican parents are expected to teach their children doxa, or an orientation toward the household field that is undergirded by the idea that household membership and identities are shaped by and intergenerational family expectations and reciprocities are met through their household labors (Blum 2011). Bound by these laws and customs, parents, then, are the pedagogic authorities (PAu) who "teach and model" the manual labor that will be performed early and often as well as their meanings in their households (Bourdieu and Passeron 1990). These pedagogic actions (PAs) become the foundations for the youths' primary habitus that include specific orientations toward manual work and the fields in which it can be practiced (Bourdieu and Passeron 1990).

LESSONS LEARNED: ENDURANCE, RESPONSIBILITY, AND TIME MANAGEMENT

The labor that Mexican youths engage in prompts particular types of skills and trait development, such as endurance, responsibility, and self-reliance, that result in the creation of their *embodied habitus*, or "trained bodily movements of habitus" that are not only preferred and essential in ensuring their households' reproduction but also deemed valuable by employers to obtain and also retain paid work (Swartz 1997: 114; see also Donato and Bankston 2008; Tuttle 2006). Youths strongly believed that their household labors facilitated their development of the embodied habitus that manifested in their endurance, tolerance, responsibility, and self-reliance in performing long, difficult, monotonous labor.

Much like the ten-year-olds of Magazine's and Ramirez Sanchez's 2007 research who had internalized the pace of twelve-hour-a-day work schedules in San Pedro Tlalcuapan, prospective independent Mexican teenage migrants as young as six years of age could be found working alongside family members in excess of eight hours a day and honing physical abilities that would serve them well upon employment in Mexico and then New York City (Magazine and Ramirez Sanchez 2007; Tuttle 2006). Especially in the cases of rural youths, learning how to *aguantar*, or endure, harsh, repetitive conditions for long hours for the sake of household reproduction would translate into success in their jobs as they aged. Often fulfilled under severe conditions—such as, in Marco Antonio's case, excessive heat that made his nose bleed—their labors were highly scheduled and regimented and included not only traveling to the fields after school, on weekends, and during the summer months and performing the strenuous and monotonous work of stooping, cutting, picking, pulling, and gathering different crops to be used for consumption and sale but also small, one-step tasks that were repeated hour after hour, day after day, month after month *since childhood*.

In New York City, these preparations paid off. Rodolfo attributed his employability in New York City to the rigorous *ritmo de trabajo*, or rhythm of work, that he had developed by assisting with his father's contract work, carrying heavy rocks from structures his father was paid to break up in Mexico. Rodolfo shared, "Construction . . . helped me a lot because when I arrived here, I found a demolition job, and for that, you have to lift a lot of heavy things, and when I worked with my father, I had to carry many heavy things and work was really hard, and when I arrived here, there were people older than me—like twenty or thirty years old—who could not endure the work that I was doing [here] at age fifteen." Despite being conditioned to endure hard labor and follow particular rhythms of work, youths repeatedly stated in interviews that unlike their parents, they did not want to perform endless, harsh work for the rest of their lives.

Responsibility

In addition to developing the physical ability to perform rigorous and repetitive manual labor, prospective independent Mexican teenage migrants also learned the soft skills, or the "skills, abilities and traits that are related to personality, attitude and behavior rather than formal or technical knowledge," that are highly coveted among employers, especially those hiring in nonsupervisory jobs (Holzer 1996: 60; see also Handel 2003; Moss and Tilly 1996, 2001). When asked to name the most valuable skill for obtaining work in New York City that they had learned while performing household labor in Mexico, most of the youths identified responsibility as a trait that, first learned in relation to their families, they integrated into their habitus until it became internalized and automatic (Bowles and Gintis 1976; Willis 1977). Carolina believed she learned responsibility when she was no older than seven or eight. At these ages, she was expected to awaken before dawn, take corn kernels to be ground, and quickly return so that the *masa*, or dough, could be transformed into the morning's batch of tortillas that would feed the entire family for the day. Cognizant that her timing would affect her household's schedule, not to mention make her late for school, Carolina had no time for "goofing off" on her way to and from the mill. Although barely awake, she followed this same routine every morning as a child and then as a teenager.

For others, responsibility was learned under the threat of punishment. Samuel's exaggerated face and hand gestures revealed his mother's wrath, in absentia, as he explained the consequences of not fulfilling the chores his mother asked of him. He believed that these fears of punishment were converted into internal motivations and self-control that enabled him to work diligently in New York City. By the time Samuel and other youths arrived in New York City without their parents, this internalized responsibility learned in Mexico, now second nature, revealed itself to be essential to their integration into the secondary labor market (Handel 2003).

Time Management

In addition to learning skills and traits by performing labors for their families, youths were compelled to develop additional work (and life)-related skills due to competing state-sanctioned obligations in both rural and urban Mexico. As discussed in chapter 4, educational reforms created demands that encroached upon the youths' time to perform household chores (Bey 2003; Jennings et al. 2006; Magazine and Ramirez Sanchez 2007; Ruddick 2003). In response, rather than decrease their household obligations, prospective independent Mexican teenage migrants had to learn to balance potentially conflicting responsibilities. Because of this, youths believed that they experienced smoother transitions to demanding employment schedules and task regimens in New York City because they had already learned to follow regimented lives and had mastered time management by being able to complete all assigned tasks in a timely fashion, no matter how "monotonous," in Mexico.

Like Carolina, Manuel became quite accustomed to waking up early to satisfy a responsibility-heavy schedule lasting from morning until night. By age five or six, his mother would wake him up close to six in the morning to leave grain for their livestock, including pigs and chickens, and after completion, he would return to eat breakfast: "At 8:15, I was ready. I would clear the table [and] go to school, and by 8:20 we had to enter [into school] because the entrance was large, and at 8:30 they closed the door and we could not enter anymore, so then we had to go running, leaving my nephew first . . . in preschool first, rapidly, and from there, . . . we got out [of school] at 2:30 and then at 3 on the dot we were there [at home], always a half hour." By age eight, Manuel would add on a job feeding their neighbor's goats in the mornings and after school, finally arriving home at seven in the evening or even later.

Most youths followed similar schedules prior to and after school. By juggling household chores, school, and paid work, they learned how important it was to time activities to ensure their completion. Abiding by regimented schedules, they learned how to meet numerous responsibilities within certain time frames. As a result, the youths had developed strong organizational and time management skills that were rewarded first in Mexico and then in the New York City labor market. The next section introduces the extent to which youths participated in these fields.

THE CHANGING NATURE OF MEXICAN YOUTHS' WORK: ENTERING INTO THE LABOR MARKET

Child labor in Mexico—that is, illusio, or investment in the Mexican labor market as minors—has long been considered an integral part of the nation's sociocultural traditions, especially among poorer youths (Aguila and Torres B. 2009; Cos Montiel 2000). Throughout the twentieth century, the Mexican State expanded several labor laws to, at least on paper, minimize and regulate child labor, particularly among younger minors (Aguila and Torres B. 2009; Cos Montiel 2000).[1] By the twenty-first century, however, these policies, meant to highly discourage or outright prohibit early entry into the labor market, demonstrated mixed results.

Although the World Bank (2013) estimates that 40 percent fewer minors between the ages of twelve and fourteen were actively employed in 2010 compared to 2000, an estimated three million, or 12.5 percent, of Mexican youths aged five to seventeen were employed, with nearly a million, or 30 percent, aged thirteen or younger working illegally (Negrete Prieto and Leyva Parra 2013; Orraca 2014; UNICEF 2010; World Bank 2013).[2] Most are employed in agricultural work (48 percent), followed by artisanal employment (20 percent), informal commercial services (14 percent), and then domestic work (4 percent; Muñoz Rios 2005). In 2010, UNICEF projected that youths under the age of seventeen made up as much as 29 percent of the agricultural workforce.[3]

It is unsurprising that the birth states of the majority of the youths with whom I spoke demonstrate the highest rates of youth labor—approximately double the national average. Seven out of every ten workers between the ages of five and seventeen reside in the southern states of Chiapas, Puebla, Guerrero, and Veracruz (all with significant indigenous populations), which possess the highest rates of youth employment between the ages of six to fourteen years. Across them, 22.4 to 29 percent of the youths are employed, including many who work full time (UNICEF 2010).

These large numbers of minors, albeit declining in recent years, participate in a waged labor market that reflects the NAFTA-related social and economic transformations of other fields—namely, the economy, their households, and schools (Aitken et al. 2006; Bey 2003; Bianet-Castellanos 2007; Jennings et al. 2006). Today, past and current intersections of poverty, inconsistent school attendance due to coverage and cost, and lax labor enforcement have significantly restructured how, where, when, and under what conditions child labor is performed in Mexico. Rising economic insecurity, as well as increasing numbers of adult migrants, have driven youths not only from household-related labor but also into widely available, unregulated, informal and formal waged labor (Aitken et al. 2006; Garabito Ballasteros 2012; Jennings et al. 2006; Tuttle 2006).

The following section discusses the prospective independent Mexican teenage migrants' entry into this particular field and position, the Mexican labor market, first part time and then, for some, full time. Moving from considering "investment" in the labor market to the youths' actual participation in it, this chapter highlights the purposefulness behind the timing of youths' entries as well as the means they use to enter it. Relying on their social networks as well as their youthful attitudes and bodies, prospective independent teenage migrants seek employment in particular niches of the Mexican labor market that welcome and, whether consciously or not, prepare youths to become workers in New York City.

MOTIVATIONS FOR WAGED WORK

Manuel believed that he had to earn money after seeing the economic and emotional toll his and his younger siblings' school expenses were taking on his mother. Having lost his father when he was not yet two years old, he was already accustomed to performing a variety of household chores from dawn to dusk. One night, not long after his eighth birthday, Manuel recalled spying on his mother and seeing her distress over her inability to pay all the household expenses: "She always, well, sometimes I would see her like that, like crying, like crying, hiding from us, never in front of us. I just saw her like two times, that I saw that she was crying." In addition to his household chores, he began looking after and feeding his neighbor's goats before and after school, and although it did not pay much, it was "something" that could help his mamá.

Manuel was not unlike the majority of working youths in Mexico. With 68.4 percent of working Mexican youths surveyed in the 2007 Mexican National Survey on Occupation and Employment citing the need to contribute monetarily to their households as the primary reason for their employment, prospective independent Mexican teenage migrants who had employment experience responded similarly (UNICEF 2010). Like Manuel, they entered into the Mexican labor market not to become independent but rather to help relieve financial worries in their households. Oftentimes the result of the death, abandonment, or recklessness of one or both parents, youths needed to work to help their families survive (Giorguli Saucedo 2005).

Carlos began working after their father's irresponsibility with money had taken an emotional toll on his mother. Carlos's father, although present, was a "drunk, a womanizer, and simply a bad businessman." His irresponsibility had pushed his household so deeply into debt that he was selling off his properties, one by one, to simply pay off small percentages of what he owed his debtors. On some days, Carlos recalled, "two or three people arrived to collect their money, and my papá was never at home, so my mamá had to be in charge [and face them]."

At first, though, Carlos remained out of the labor market. His two older brothers had immigrated to New York City when they were sixteen to remit money home to pay off his father's accounts. Unfortunately, Carlos's father would pocket the money instead of paying his debts. Carlos recalled, "There were days when we did not have enough to eat because all the money that my brothers sent, he would keep."

Finally, after witnessing his mother's embarrassment and worry about feeding him and his younger siblings, Carlos "felt the necessity [to work], to help support [his] family, because his papá was not." Making the decision to support his mamá and siblings, fourteen-year-old Carlos, in addition to working with his father, began to work clandestinely for a local vendor who sold balls of string. He would wind string into balls and sell them to the vendor. He covertly turned over every peso he earned to his mother: "If my papá had found out that I was giving money to her, he would have automatically said that the money was his."

As discussed in chapter 2, other youths entered the labor market after their parent(s) experienced difficulties in paying for their and their siblings' school expenses. Aware of the burden that schooling fees placed on their households, children began working part time as early as age seven to pay for their own and even their younger siblings' schooling. As youths entered into secundaria and even preparatoria or bachiller, where school costs multiplied, the youths' labor market participation changed. First working part time, youths often dropped out of school when their households could no longer afford the exorbitant fees. Their school departures in turn triggered their transitions to full-time workers, a transition that occurred in both Mexico and New York.

With the seed of working planted in his head by his mamá, ten-year-old Julio got a job working in the fields during his summer vacation to pay for his upcoming school year's expenses. His mother would save everything he earned and use these savings to pay first for his registration fees and uniforms and then for school supplies as needed. Other prospective independent Mexican teenage migrants began their part-time work similarly after their schools demanded additional fees. Required to bring costlier school supplies to her secundaria class, thirteen-year-old Hilaria began working on weekends *a escondidas*, or in secret, at a plant nursery and chicken farm just outside of San Benito de los Lagos. She did not want her mother to scramble and scrape together more money to meet what she viewed as *her* school obligations.

While Alejandro contemplated entering into preparatoria, he felt a responsibility to minimize the financial burdens shouldered by his mother. Struggling to pay the schooling expenses of his four younger siblings, who were enrolled in primaria and secundaria, his mother would not be able to undertake the expenses associated with continuing his studies. After completing secundaria, he sought higher-paying work in the plant nurseries that surrounded San Valentín and worked there full time until he saved enough money for his first year of high school. Although this delayed his entry into the town's preparatoria until October, a month after school began, at least he did so, he said, "without a cent from his mother."

Lazaro similarly dreamed of continuing his studies so that he could become a medical doctor. Although his parents had not told him outright, he knew that the fees required by the preparatoria he wished to attend would further exacerbate their household economic pressures. When he entered secundaria, his father took on more work hours just to pay for the additional fees, and now he knew that his parents would be unable to afford the doubled registration fees and extra expenses, including supplies, copies, books, and money to travel between preparatoria and his house. Sixteen-year-old Lazaro decided to "take on a little of the responsibilities himself—no, the same—to help them" and stop asking his parents for money related to his schooling. Instead, he devised a plan to work without telling his parents, and he began to spend every Saturday and Sunday of his first year of high school working as a street performer, or a clown, in one of the plazas located on the outskirts of Mexico City, in Valle de Chalco. He thought he had earned enough to pay for nearly all his schooling expenses, but unfortunately, his calculations were incorrect. Before the end of his first year, he was forced to drop out because he simply could not pay the fees. Within weeks of leaving school, Lazaro stopped working as a clown and transitioned into full-time employment at a construction site, where he remained until he left for New York.

PURPOSEFUL ENTRIES INTO THE LABOR MARKET

Although economic insecurity either pushed the youths into market participation or intensified it, they were purposeful in timing their entries and controlling the conditions under which they would enter the labor market. The youths considered household needs and balanced their assessments with understandings about their physical abilities and ages to time their labor market entry and participation (Clausen 1991; Dinovitzer et al. 2003; Shanahan 2000). Whereas employers appeared to care little about the youths' ages at hiring, the youths, as they considered when to emigrate, possessed ideas about being too old or, in many more cases, too young for *particular* jobs and conditions.

With little mention of compulsory education and/or labor laws, the youths discussed avoiding full-time work until during or after secundaria completion, an act that coincides with adolescence. Youths based their decisions on their own interpretations of biological time, or their matching of their physiological, cognitive, and/or socioemotional development with age-graded social roles (Pallas 1993). Understanding the physiological limitations of their statures and endurance at these ages, most youths remained in school after the completion of primaria and if they needed to work, they did so part time. If their part-time work had been extended to full-time hours, several independent Mexican teenage migrants recalled, they would have been unable to withstand it. Quite simply, at their young ages, they would have been unable to endure long hours of work.

This was the reason that Manuel, Alejandro, and Julio offered to explain why they had been uninterested in pursuing full-time work immediately after primaria. Although they were already working part time, they believed that they were "too small [in size]" and that the work would be "too hard and heavy" for them to endure for long periods of time. By age eighteen, they believed that "you can resist more," and by that time, "you can do [work in] whatever you want." Other youths even explained their continued secundaria studies as a result of their physical inability to engage in full-time work. Expressing a desire to work, Genoveva continued her secundaria studies, she said, "because my father told me that to work, I was still very young, and I would not be able to work, and better that I went to school to learn things." In her case, her father's understanding of her biological time dictated her labor market absence.

Youths who were less able to delay full-time labor market participation suffered the consequences of their off-time entries. Unable to afford the school fees and the costs related to daily bus trips he would have to take in order to attend the nearest secundaria and supposedly uninterested in continuing his studies, slight, eleven-year-old Pedro secured full-time employment in a candy store in Tlapa, Guerrero, after graduating from primaria. His boss's harsh treatment and the tasks assigned to him, including receiving, carrying, unpacking, and stocking heavy boxes of candies and other items, made the job extremely difficult for him. After struggling for a year, Pedro quit and found work at a hardware store, where the owner asked him to perform tasks that he believed were more appropriate for someone his age and size. Several years later, when Pedro returned to work at the candy store, he explained that he was more successful because he was "older, more mature, and able to endure more physical labor."

Corresponding closely to the minimum age requirements designated by child labor laws as well as when they exited secundaria, prospective independent

Mexican teenage migrants usually delayed full-time work closer to age fifteen, after they either dropped out of or completed secundaria studies. Supporting the employment of youths who completed their compulsory studies, signs soliciting the applications of individuals who could demonstrate secundaria completion filled the windows of businesses such as *zapaterias* (shoe stores), clothing stores, and so on in San Benito de los Lagos as well as several other Puebla towns I visited. With baby-faced sales clerks tending to customers, it appeared as if at least in Puebla, fifteen was the acceptable age for being a full-time worker.

ENTERING THE LABOR MARKET: RELYING ON SOCIAL CAPITAL

But just how did these Mexican youths actually enter into and then move within the Mexican labor market? Possessing low levels of human capital, youths spoke of relying on two sets of resources to acquire work: social capital and agency. In the former, youths' memberships in social and interpersonal networks afforded them valuable resources, including information about jobs and credibility with employers (Aguilera 2003; Binder and Scrogin 1999; Coleman 1990; Portes 1995: 12; Ramirez and Hondagneu-Sotelo 2009). Within these networks and webs of relationships, these essential resources facilitated the youths' entries into and effective participation within labor market niches that included jobs as laborers' helpers and assistants (Portes 1995: 12; Stanton-Salazar 2001: 20). Once in the labor market, however, youths more actively and independently sought and obtained subsequent jobs *by themselves*. By "exerting some control over the conditions of [their] existence"—namely, their labor—after obtaining first jobs, Mexican youths independently asserted their individual agency within the sets of opportunities and constraints that surrounded them as laborers to obtain their second, third, and even fourth jobs (Gomberg-Muñoz 2010: 9; see also Boehm et al. 2011; Giddens 1993; Rosenblatt 2004).

As children, many prospective independent Mexican teenage migrants drew on social capital rooted in their relationships with adult kin, including their parents (family-based social capital), and similarly aged friends in their social networks for work (Furstenberg and Hughes 1995; Furstenberg and Kaplan 2004). Notably, these individuals held disparate degrees of obligation to the youths. In the case of family-based social capital, stronger family ties existed, and family members sometimes not only offered social capital but also doubled as pedagogic agents in the workplace. After recommending them for work with the same employers, family members kept them under their watchful eyes and trained them to perform labor.

At ages ten and twelve, respectively, Alejandro and Marco Antonio began paid, part-time work as assistants in their uncles' workplaces—an auto repair shop and a construction site. In Alejandro's case, his uncle taught him to perform small tasks such as washing car windows and checking the air in tires. Alternatively, Marco Antonio learned the trade of bricklaying. "Little by little," his uncle taught him how to lay bricks and mix the cement that went between them. While earning modest wages under these circumstances, they also gained valuable experiences and skills that they eventually took to other jobs in Mexico and New York City with nonkin employers.

In some instances, weaker, nonkin ties provided the youths entrée into the waged labor market. It was Lazaro's friend who negotiated his work as a clown. Loosely employed by a company that managed street performers, his friend asked his employer about work for Lazaro, and the following Saturday, Lazaro began working on weekends in plazas across Valle de Chalco, first near his friend but then, after observing and learning from him, by himself.

FINDING WORK ON THEIR OWN

After obtaining first (and sometimes second and third) jobs through kin and friends and building confidence and skills under their tutelage, many prospective independent Mexican teenage migrants next sought employment by themselves. Navigating the constraints and opportunities of their local labor markets, many youths exercised their agency and procured better pay and conditions away from relatives and kin. By simply visiting different work sites and inquiring about work, they were able to negotiate their own contracts and work independently of relatives and other sponsors.

Fourteen-year-old Rodolfo decided to leave his cousin's husband, Pedro, to work with another fruit and vegetable vendor, Jorge, after learning that Jorge was interested in hiring him. With Pedro's and Jorge's fruit and vegetable stands located in close proximity in the *mercado,* or open-air market, Jorge witnessed firsthand Rodolfo's work ethic and skills, and he was duly impressed. On the outs with Pedro and encouraged by an aunt who had previously disclosed Rodolfo's availability to Jorge, Rodolfo decided to visit Jorge at his fruit and vegetable stand. Within minutes of talking, he began to negotiate his own hiring. He was able to reach a deal that included better pay and more responsibilities that he felt would allow him to learn and develop more skills.

At the start of their work careers, these independent Mexican teenage migrants were anything but aimless, thoughtless, or inert. They strategically planned their entries into the labor market, considering factors such as economic need, their ages and physical abilities, and who could assist them in obtaining first and subsequent employment. At first depending on older, trustworthy kin and nonkin who could help orient and train them to work, the youths became increasingly self-assured and began to seek out improved work conditions without the security of kin and friends. Since young ages, these youths were not only becoming oriented toward waged work but also developed the knowledge, confidence, and skills, both manual and interpersonal, needed to obtain work in both Mexico and New York City.

ACCOMMODATING LOCAL LABOR MARKETS

Mexican youths would not be able to move from household labor to waged work if an accommodating labor market did not exist (Bey 2003; Jennings et al. 2006; Magazine and Ramirez Sanchez 2007). Over the last thirty years, particular conditions—including the expansion of specific transnational industries, a scarcity of adult laborers in towns characterized by high levels of out-migration, and the influx of economic remittances into communities—have translated into waged job prospects for minors. Varying by region and gender, youths found in rural areas would be unlawfully absorbed into agricultural and construction sectors, while urban youths were mostly found in construction and commercial sectors. Female prospective independent Mexican teenage migrants also discussed being hired for factory work or domestic services, including working in private homes as maids or nannies (Tuttle 2006; UCW 2012). Without sufficient adult labor and obliged by little to no regulation, employers eagerly contracted minors because they would work for relatively low wages. In addition, employers believed that these minors were obedient and rarely complained and were willing to perform repetitive, monotonous tasks in accordance with their small statures (Tuttle 2006: 148–150; UCW 2012).

Most rural, prospective independent Mexican teenage migrants found strenuous, poorly compensated, and exploitative work—sometimes with other family members, sometimes not—on small or medium-size farm plots owned by their own families or nonkin owners. Youths, including Saúl, recalled the nearly unbearable, hot, brutal, physically demanding conditions that characterized agricultural work. In Saúl's case, most days his family arrived at the farms by seven o' clock in the morning, and he had to trudge through mud that sometimes reached his knees: "One had to enter into that mud whether they wanted to or not to pull the weeds, like that, with their hands, with thorns. . . . The owner did not care how you pulled them, but the important thing was that you finished the work of clearing the land." Because pickers were charged for gloves, Saúl and his family went without them, and after several hours of picking tomatoes, Saúl remembered that his hands were green from the leaves and red from blood oozing out of wounds caused by thorn pricks. Also recalling working in the fields, Alejandro and Marco Antonio shuddered at the thought of resuming agricultural work that was "hard because of the sun."

In addition to being strenuous, agricultural work is notorious for its poor compensation and long hours. Youths, both females and males, recalled being paid, on average, from fourteen pesos a day (or slightly more than one U.S. dollar) for two hours of work after school to seventy pesos (or fewer than seven U.S. dollars) for a full eight-hour day of stooping, pulling, and picking in the scorching sun. As the only youth who had been employed by larger, transnational agricultural firms since he was twelve, Saúl earned an average of three hundred pesos a week after laboring nine hours a day, six days a week, on five different farms across central Mexico. This added up to fewer than fifty cents an hour.

Male youths also found employment in the construction industry (Tuttle 2006). Paying more than agricultural work, construction projects were ongoing in many of the youths' hometowns and in Mexico City's exurbs. Fueled by remittances, the construction of immigrants' homes in their hometowns as well as in areas such as Valle de Chalco, Iztapalapa, and Ciudad Neza ensured desirable employment for prospective independent Mexican teenage migrants prior to migration (Magazine and Ramirez Sanchez 2007). Hired without proof that they (a) were at least age sixteen, (b) had completed secundaria, and (c) had obtained parental permission—each a legal requirement for employment—the youths handily found employment performing arduous and not-so-arduous tasks for wages they believed were adequate.

At age fourteen, Julio found full-time employment at a construction site in Cuatlacco, Guerrero. In spite of lacking the required paperwork and having no experience working in construction, Julio was hired after simply walking up and asking for work. Possessing strength and vigor as physical attributes as well as soft skills such as a positive disposition toward hard work, he was deemed eligible and desirable for employment. At his job, he learned essential skills for construction work, including mixing cement, creating bricks, breaking up rocks, putting up walls, installing windows, painting, and so on. For forty hours of work, he earned between 500 and 1,000 pesos, or between 48 and 95 U.S. dollars—amounts that far exceeded the wages he earned in the fields. Additionally, he said, he learned to build homes, a trade that could serve him anywhere, in Mexico or the United States.

Mercados were also sites for informal youth employment. Working alongside parents as well as nonkin vendors, prospective Mexican teenage migrants learned and/or continued to develop valuable skills, including calculating prices and negotiating with customers (Bey 2003; Ramirez and Hondagneu-Sotelo 2009). At the age of five, Samuel was already mimicking his father's salesman techniques. He persuaded his father to let him help him sell items and keep half of the money he earned. After a string of successful sales and seeing the pesos in his pocket add up, Samuel's motivation to remain a seller grew because "the more that we have, the more that we want, no?"

Underage Mexican youths were able to find employment due to a pervasive unstated "don't ask, don't tell" policy in regards to age. Farm owners appeared to be the most dismissive of child labor laws, with several youths discussing how they continued their hiring practices in spite of knowing that underage workers were among their employees. Subject to the grueling work described earlier, after admitting to one of the farm managers that he was younger than the mandated age of fourteen, Saúl was simply begged off and paid his wages for the week's harvest. Although this instance occurred on a larger farm, other youths confirmed the same circumstances on small and medium-sized farms as well as in rural areas where farms harvest crops not for cross-border trade, as in Saúl's case, but for local sale.

Even employment sites seemingly subject to stricter regulations knowingly violated child labor laws (Bey 2003; Edmonds and Pavcnik 2005). "Indoors" and clean, even "regulated" maquiladoras are notorious for hiring underage workers (Nathan 1997; Pacheco 2013; Tuttle 2006). This information, that rules are lax and that proof of age and educational credentials are unnecessary, is shared among underage children and teenagers looking for work. These rumors encouraged Lalo to seek employment at a car factory in Mexico City performing tasks that depended on his small, nimble, fifteen-year-old fingers. In spite of being in violation of labor laws, the factory in which he was employed soldering iron onto car parts and putting tubes into car engines clearly benefitted from his size. However, not only was he too young to be working in a factory; he was also being exposed to hazardous conditions and tasks prohibited by Mexico's federal child labor laws.[4]

LOOKING FOR BETTER WORK: LEARNING JOB TURNOVER

Although prospective independent Mexican teenage migrants are able to find employment, albeit under harsh conditions, given their reasons for work, as well as their ages, it should come as no surprise that in these typically low-paying and difficult work conditions, these Mexican youths are frequently moving in search of better pay and work conditions (Blumen et al. 1955; Munasinghe and Sigman 2003). Seeking "upgrades," prospective independent Mexican teenage migrants develop "hobo syndrome," or repeated movement between jobs (Ghiselli 1974; Munasinghe and Sigman 2003). Moving across a labor market and employers who themselves are in constant search of cheaper labor, minors find work relatively easily, although not in positions that are desirable enough for them to remain for long periods of time.

Between the ages of fourteen and seventeen, Samuel held more than five jobs across central and southeast Mexico, constantly leaving positions that were dissatisfying to take others that he believed would provide better conditions and pay. In Mexico City, he worked in construction, as a taxi driver, and as a bus driver before finally landing in Cancún, where he installed glass windows until three months before he left for *el norte*. Dependent on relatives to help him obtain these jobs, he had no need for specialized skills. Instead, his social capital enabled him to effortlessly change jobs across sectors, moving from, for example, agriculture to construction and back again with little difficulty. While he was moving across these positions, Samuel gained myriad experiences and soon grew accustomed to participating in a flexible labor market characterized by limited upward mobility. Before long, Samuel learned that high job turnover was simply a "normal" strategy to improve his pay and conditions.

At young ages, prospective independent Mexican teenage migrants begin to learn about the features of specific niches of the Mexican labor market. They learn that in spite of federal laws that prohibit their employment, first before age fourteen for part-time work and then at sixteen for full-time work (and other particular types of work), particular labor market sectors—namely, agriculture, construction, and commercial—are accessible to them regardless of their ages. In these sectors, the youths are subject to harsh and harmful conditions that are difficult even for some adults to endure, so they move from job to job. Unbeknownst to them, however, this participation enables their familiarity and ease with labor market conditions and practices that are similar to those they will encounter in New York City. At these young ages, prospective independent Mexican teenage migrants are developing an understanding of not only the types of jobs that are appropriate for them but, overall, their relationship to the labor market.

LEARNING TRANSFERABLE ATTITUDES AND SKILLS

Although prospective independent Mexican teenage migrants move around a bit from job to job, they manage to reinforce and extend the learning that began in their households. Working in Mexican labor sectors that depend on and cultivate particular manual aptitudes, youths expand on skills and traits previously acquired through household labor and learn new ones that will be desirable to New York City employers. As in their households back home, young Mexican minors are further prepared for the work that awaits them in New York City in specific labor market niches.

First and foremost, youths build upon "being responsible." Believed to separate the employed from the unemployed in New York City, this attribute, further developed on the job in Mexico, was, according to independent Mexican teenage migrants, beneficial for their work in New York. Similar to the examples provided when discussing household labor, the teenagers developed this trait as they fulfilled their work obligations. Comparing his success in finding work with the failures of his university-educated cousin, in our talk, Rodolfo thanked his father and then Jorge for providing him with labor opportunities that helped him learn this trait; because of this, he believed, he was gainfully employed in New York City.

Well documented in child labor literature, youths' efficiency and speed—two traits that, in addition to the endurance and tolerance developed through their household labors, were also further developed and integrated into the youths' embodied habitus,—also make them attractive candidates for employment (Cox 1999; Tuttle 2006). Tasked with performing repetitive manual labor, these prospective independent Mexican teenage migrants believed that rote duties in Mexico—such as picking fruits or laying bricks, for example—had prepared them for future work.

Saúl learned efficiency through his previous agricultural work. Although he was working indoors at the time of his interview, Saúl believed that picking tomatoes and cucumbers in Sinaloa helped him fulfill his current responsibilities as a food server at a New York university. Because his wages in Mexico were dependent upon the number of baskets that he filled with vegetables and fruits, Saúl learned to pick rapidly. Working in the fields, Saúl would race to fill his buckets and then run to the manager so that she could mark another line in the column by his name. Seeing the lines add up was, in Saúl's words, "his motivation," as the counter would also tell him, "If you hurry, they are going to pay more."

Although there were no bushels at the university's cafeteria, Saúl worked rapidly or else he would be reprimanded. While other workers moved at slower paces, one of his bosses would scold him if he did not complete tasks in a timely fashion. In New York City, working quickly and competently was an issue not of more pay but of job retention. Barely paid above the $7.50-an-hour minimum wage for seventy hours of work a week, Saúl was constantly threatened with firing if he did not work swiftly. The efficiency he mastered as a child laborer in Mexico became the difference between his employment and unemployment.

Lastly, developing effective interpersonal skills was also deemed important to the youths' future labor successes. Those with experience working in markets had especially been afforded opportunities to improve their communication skills and overcome their shyness. During their phone conversations, Esmeralda's aunts shared that this skill was important in New York, especially during the initial period of searching for work. Esmeralda thought that her time spent selling her family's crops in the market had helped her overcome her shyness by "los[ing] fear with people and [learning] how to express [her]self with other people." In New York, she believed that possessing this skill would work to her advantage.

Rodolfo also learned about just how important it was to acquire and hone this skill from his boss, Jorge. Himself a former undocumented immigrant in New York, Jorge understood that knowing how to interact with a wide array of people would be important for Rodolfo's future employment in New York. To prepare him, Jorge went out of his way to introduce Rodolfo to various actors who were essential to the success of his fruit and vegetable businesses, including distributors, vendors, and customers. In this way, Rodolfo learned to *convivir*, or get along with, other people, a skill that would assist him once he began to seek work in the Big Apple.

Youths also learned more specific skills that would be suitable for employment in certain trades, including the seemingly robust construction industry (Fuchs et al. 2014; Gomberg-Muñoz 2010; New York Building Congress 2010). Lalo, Samuel, and Lazaro all discussed learning specific skills—such as how to put up walls, lay bricks, make and install glass windows, and paint—from "professionals" in Mexico. Upon arrival in New York, they believed that mastering these skills provided them with advantages, and they purposefully sought work, both successfully and unsuccessfully, in the higher-paying construction industry.

Thousands of miles apart, in Mexico, youths appear to be employed in contexts and jobs that seem wholly unrelated to the postindustrial New York City labor market. Working in labor niches where they develop soft skills—including responsibility, efficiency, and sociability, as well as more specific trade aptitudes—the youths are actually learning and developing competencies that will be transferable to New York City's secondary labor market (Donato and Bankston 2008; Gomberg-Muñoz 2010: 298). For this reason, most independent Mexican teenage migrants do not arrive in New York City unskilled; instead, they possess exchangeable skills that are desired by employers and will ensure their employment (Donato and Bankston 2008; Gomberg-Muñoz 2010).

IMAGINING PATHWAYS TO SOCIAL MOBILITY

As I sat outside in San Valentín with sixteen-year-old Esteban, it immediately became clear that he was a thoughtful teenager who spent much time on his studies. He had been able to complete secundaria with his mother's remittances and now, in his second year of preparatoria, was a mathematics standout. With encouragement from his teacher, Esteban dreamed of becoming a mechanical engineer, but he knew that fulfilling this dream would require costlier university studies. Discouraged by this, he had recently turned his gaze northward. His male cousins began speaking to him about immigrating to New York City, and with this, his occupational aspirations shifted. In the Big Apple, he envisioned himself not as a mechanical engineer but rather working like his cousins in a restaurant kitchen.

Like Esteban, some prospective independent teenage migrants, especially those who are still in school or have plans to return to it, develop dual plans about work early on. One plan reflects the possibility of remaining in Mexico. Even if material conditions obstruct their ability to do so, these youths believe that if they remain in Mexico, they will pursue the middle-class professions they learn about in school. They may become future teachers, hair stylists, architects, business owners, or lawyers—professions mostly associated with continued schooling either through *carerras cortes* (trade careers) or university studies.

As growing economic insecurity jeopardizes these dreams and the possibility of migration becomes more certain, the youths' ideas about their futures expand to include occupations they could secure in New York City. These occupations, which they learn about through conversations with members of their transnational social networks by phone and after return trips, are wholly different but, according to their contacts, desirable. The youths learn about higher wages, tasks that are less "heavy" or less "hard" than those found in Mexico, and, of course, the relative ease with which jobs are found, even without educational credentials. Genoveva, who wished to become a hair stylist, was imagining these dual pathways while still in San Pedro. Her family's economic situation vetoed the possibility of her continuing her studies to earn a trade certificate, and she feared that instead, she would be stuck working in the fields. With an invitation from her aunt to work in New York City, she began to imagine working amid skyscrapers instead of the stalks and thorns that scratched her outside: "If I am not going to continue studying, well, maybe it's better, because I do not like to go to the fields, to work in the fields, and, well, I could look for a good job, because maybe with secundaria, I could get a good job [in New York], better than going to the fields." Her plan? To immigrate and seek a job where she could put her interpersonal skills to work selling curios in a store, just like her aunt.

As discussed in chapter 3, only a handful of independent Mexican teenage migrants knew the truth about the hardships of work in New York City prior to leaving due to the information shared by older, closer relatives and friends. Judith's sister tried to dissuade her from emigrating by disclosing how difficult the work was: "She had to do many things—well, clean all the house. Since the house was very big, . . . she would get tired a lot." Judith demonstrated that she understood the exaggerations fed to youths considering immigration: "Many say that . . . over there you are going to earn more, and over there . . . is a lot of work, . . . but they do not pay a lot." In spite of these understandings, however, Judith was undeterred; she still dreamed of immigrating and working alongside her older sisters.

For many Mexican emigrants, this steadfastness may be a product of their confidence that their time in New York will be a short-term "means to an end." Unfazed by sober counternarratives, they instead believe that they are simply temporarily switching labor markets in order to return to higher positions in their Mexican communities, households, labor markets, and for some, schools. Rather, they believe that their time in New York City will be brief and last only long enough to earn the money necessary to finance their dreams—dreams that include returning to Mexico and embarking on careers there.

With this strategy in mind, youths spend the months and days leading up to their departures preoccupied with conversion formulas that exchange dollars into pesos and years into accomplishments. Calculating the amount of pesos needed to construct houses and businesses and the number of years it will take to accomplish personal and professional goals situated in Mexico, the youths are interested in U.S. dollars, not U.S. careers. Instead, they wish to work in "whatever [job] hires me" so that they can begin earning and converting dollars as soon as possible.

In the months leading up to his departure, Rodolfo lay awake in bed every night to figure out how much economic capital he would need to set up businesses and a home like his boss, Jorge, had done. With phone updates from his friend Antonio coupled with firsthand sightings of the improvements and additions at Antonio's mother's home, Rodolfo knew not only how much Antonio was earning and sending home but also the purchasing power of those earnings in his hometown. Rodolfo could not fall asleep without doing these mathematical exercises: "Before going to sleep, when I was with my pillow, I would start thinking, if I could save 20,000 pesos a month, with those, I need, like, 250 pesos for the (fruit and vegetable) stands; I need, like, 150 pesos for the truck; and I need about 100,000 pesos for the house; and for example, I would bring, like, 200,000 pesos to invest. And I calculated how much this would be a year, saving from $350,000 to $300,000 [pesos]—like 30,000 [dollars]."

Other youths saw leaping into the New York City labor market as a way to revive their professional dreams in Mexico. They planned on using savings earned in New York to resume their schooling and obtain the requisite credentials to become professionals. Samuel was one of the few youths who had emigrated with the specific idea to use his earnings to return and continue his schooling in Mexico. Unable to afford to attend the police academy while living in Mexico, he left, he said, so that he could earn and save enough money to return and enroll. Before leaving Mexico at age seventeen, he thought, "Better that I go over there to New York [to] work [and] gather my money, and already, when I am about twenty or twenty-one years, I [can] return to Mexico and enroll in the academy when I already have my money to pay for my studies. That is what I thought, no?" Once in New York, however, he found that saving money was difficult, and his plan of leaving sooner rather than later seemed to be slipping away.

For better or for worse, these are the notions that prospective independent Mexican teenage migrants possess when they bid their families and friends farewell and head to New York. Shaped by their relatives and friends, the information they receive about jobs leads to the creation of dual frames of reference: they compare their present severe working conditions and the probability of attaining a professional job in Mexico to the promise of New York jobs and the pay and working conditions of jobs that their New York social contacts hold (Suárez-Orozco and Suárez-Orozco 1995). Even if they are aware of dehumanizing and difficult work conditions in New York, they "go to get ahead," rationalizing these more severe conditions by imagining the accelerated pace with which they will be able to construct homes and, in addition, establish businesses and pay for continued schooling by their middle to late twenties back in Mexico (Malkin 2004). Believing that their professional and personal dreams cannot come true if they remain in Mexico, independent Mexican teenage migrants imagine and increasingly become oriented toward immigration and entry into the New York City labor market.

EFFORTLESS ENTRIES? LEAPING INTO THE NEW YORK LABOR MARKET

> Although [illegal immigrants] broke the law by illegally crossing our borders or over-staying their visas and our businesses broke the law by employing them, our city's economy would be a shell of itself had they not, and it would collapse if they were deported.
>
> —Former New York City Mayor
> Michael Bloomberg, Fox News, September 9, 2010

Just as Mexico's labor market has been undergoing a transformation ushered in by neoliberal economic policies, New York City has also found itself developing an economy that, for young, unauthorized Mexican immigrants, is simultaneously rewarding, challenging, and exploitative. While New York City can and does absorb undocumented, unskilled immigrants, its economy has dramatically shifted away from sectors that once promised upward mobility to these workers. Since the 1960s, the manufacturing jobs that provided moderate social mobility for other immigrant and ethnic groups have disappeared, leaving in their place service jobs characterized by high turnover and no opportunities for entry into the middle class (Kallick 2013; Kasinitz et al. 2004, 2008; Mollenkopf and Castells 1992; Waldinger 1996). Today, the city's economy reflects a narrowing "hourglass," with jobs concentrated at both the high-paying "top," increasingly reserved for high-skilled financial and increasingly technology sectors, and a low-paying "bottom" of service jobs, including restaurant workers, child care providers, and so on to serve the wealthiest New Yorkers (Kasinitz et al. 2008; Portes and Zhou 1993; Waldinger and Perlmann 1998). Between 2000 and 2006, unauthorized immigrants were vigorously overrepresented in particular sectors at the "bottom" of the hourglass—namely, "back of the house" positions in food services, including dishwashing, cooking, and food preparation. In these sectors, over 30 percent of workers in New York City were unauthorized; nationally, less than 20 percent were (Bernhardt et al. 2007; Fiscal Policy Institute 2007; Passel and Cohn 2015).[5]

Underage, undocumented workers found themselves in these sectors as well. Similar to the lax enforcement of labor laws in Mexico, in New York City, underage, undocumented youths find a labor context that, in spite of child labor laws written to restrict their employment, is willing to overlook not only their lack of legal status but also their young ages.[6] Valued for their youthful, strong bodies, reputed to possess strong commitments to work, and understood to ignore and be unaware of workplace abuses and labor law violations due to fears related to deportation, independent Mexican teenage migrants, like undocumented adults, quickly find that employers are willing to overlook their ages, legal statuses, and low levels of human capital (Cornelius 1998; Saucedo 2006; Semple 2010). As a result, in many instances, independent Mexican teenage migrants find themselves quickly hired to perform undesirable work in the city's secondary labor market, usually within hours of their arrival in New York City (Bernhardt et al. 2007; Cornelius 1998; Kim 1999; Saucedo 2006; Treschan and Mehrotra 2013).

Arriving at dawn, Pedro literally appeared at his cousin's friend's apartment, cleaned up, and turned around to seek work downtown. His cousin's friend provided him with instructions about the subway system and oriented him toward a "good" area for work: Greenwich Village. Within a few hours of going from business to business, he was hired to stock items in a deli six days a week for twelve hours a day: "That same day, I started to work, on West Fourth Street, downtown, and Sixth Avenue. I did not even rest; arriving at six in the morning, by the afternoon, I went to work, and there I worked." Although he was fired within two weeks for his unfamiliarity with this type of job, he found his next post within hours the same way: by simply asking.

A few independent Mexican teenage migrants delay their entries into the New York City labor market, both voluntarily and involuntarily, for several weeks. For these youths, arduous journeys and overprotective relatives postpone their waged work. Relying on the conditional family safety nets discussed in chapter 2, some youths, such as sixteen-year-old Rogelio, are able to take time to regain their vigor. Exhausted and weak, for approximately fifteen days, Rogelio recuperated from his journey. During those days, his father supported him, but after he found work, he had to "become independent and pay for his rent, his clothes, his food, and everything."

Others have relatives who *involuntarily* keep them from seeking employment, at least for a while. These family members fear that if these minors are seen during school hours, police will deem them truants and detain them. To offset this threat, relatives attempt, often unsuccessfully, to first enroll the youths in schools. Marco's older brother tried this. Arriving at age fourteen, Marco wished to begin work immediately, but his older brother would not permit it. Instead, for the next twenty days after his arrival, his brother pleaded with him to enter school, going as far as to identify and bring home a flyer about the school. Each day, Marco vehemently refused, and as a result, he was forbidden to leave the apartment until after three o'clock in the afternoon, or when other similarly aged youths were dismissed from school. Tired of being stuck inside and watching television all day, Marco's obstinacy finally wore his brother down, and he allowed him to work. On his twentieth day in New York, Marco accompanied his brother to the pizzeria where he was employed and started working fifty-hour weeks as a pizza packer.

Like Pedro, once he was "allowed to," Marco quite easily entered into the labor market. This is due, in large part, to both employer preferences and lax enforcement of federal and state labor laws in New York City (Bernhardt et al. 2007; Foster and Kramer 1997). Although obligated by law to ask for and receive proof of age and work eligibility, employers overlook these requirements. Rather, most employers operate with a de facto "don't ask, don't tell" policy and simply hire these baby-faced Mexican teenagers without the required proof of age, academic credentials, or parental permission.

Only three employers raised questions about the youths' ages when they were minors, but even after asking, employers were willing to ignore suspicions about their ages. In Julio's case, his employer believed he must be older because he simply worked "too well." Seeking someone to arrange the store's inventory, including clothes, shoes, luggage, and other goods, the Chinese storeowner outright asked fifteen-year-old Julio about his age when he asked for work at the Washington Heights variety store. Like most of the other youths, Julio lied about his age and was hired. A few days later, his employer grew more doubtful about his age, and he was questioned again: "They asked me if I was nineteen, and I told them yes to get the job, and then after, some days later, they found out that I was not nineteen, that I was a minor, and he wanted to fire me, but he told me that he was not going to fire me because I worked fast, I knew how to do things quickly, and he did not fire me, and after that . . . I worked there, where I was."

Marco nearly averted dismissal from the pizzeria where his brother worked, but the steady patronage of law enforcement officers raised his manager's anxiety about his age. After discovering that Marco was only fourteen, his manager feared that Marco's youthfulness would attract the attention of two police officers who regularly ordered pizza during their beats. At first, his manager counseled him to keep quiet, not wanting "him to say that he was a minor." Eventually, however, the threat of discovery and accompanying violations drove the manager to let him go. Several hours later and a few street blocks away, Marco was able to procure work as a delivery person.

In spite of laws upholding the contrary, independent Mexican teenage migrants encounter a labor market that is quite accessible. These youths find that employers disregard not only their legal statuses but also their ages. Instead, for these sectors of the low-wage labor market, employers see their legal statuses and ages as assets: youths can endure much and are vulnerable, and as such, they are obedient and quiet (Saucedo 2006). Considered alongside their national origin, the youths find that these traits are "rewarded" in the New York City labor market. The unpleasant truth is that the national and New York City labor markets are constructed in ways that encourage the participation of undocumented Mexican minors in certain sectors in which employees remain invisible: the restaurant industry, construction and retail sectors, and for females, domestic services.[7] Regardless of the sectors in which the youths were found, because of their vulnerabilities, they were expected to work in violation of labor laws in several ways: by working for less than the minimum wage, in excess of the hours set by child and even adult labor laws, in hazardous conditions, and without benefits.

As the largest employer of undocumented immigrants in New York City, the restaurant industry employed independent Mexican teenage migrants at the lowest rung of intermediate culinary sectors, or restaurants whose services were between fast food and full service (Bailey 1985; Fiscal Policy Institute 2007). Although limited by their lack of food preparation skills as well as English-language proficiency, youths possess skills honed in Mexico—endurance and responsibility—that are desirable for these positions that require minimal training. Like their undocumented adult counterparts and in violation of labor laws, the youths earn less than minimum wage and are obligated to work beyond forty hours without overtime pay, all in the "back of the house" or on the streets, only entering into dining rooms to bus tables (Fuentes-Mayorga 2011; Waldinger 1992).

After a brief stint in retail at age fifteen, Fidencio became a delivery person. On six days and nights a week, from 12 p.m. to 12 a.m., one could see him flying through Upper Manhattan on his bicycle, rushing to make deliveries. In rain or snow, Fidencio showed up, often within an hour, with food in hand. On particularly inclement evenings, Fidencio appeared at one's door, always prompt and courteous but with his straight, jet-black hair soaking wet. After nearly six years of working twelve- and thirteen-hour days, first at La Luna and then at Las

Cazuelas, he was finally earning $350 a week, which usually totaled about $6.25 an hour, a dollar below the federal minimum wage of $7.25, two dollars below New York State's minimum wage of $8.75 in 2015, and even less than the median wage of the lowest-paid occupations in food services, $6.89 an hour (McGeehan 2016; Restaurant Opportunities Centers 2005; U.S. Department of Labor 2016). When asked why he didn't pursue higher-paying construction work, Fidencio shared that he preferred consistent, "secure" work to seasonal, weather-dependent construction work. Plus, he preferred working later hours.

Other independent Mexican teenage migrants found work in the third largest industry in which unauthorized immigrants in New York City are located—retail, including, for several of the youths, florist shops. At these shops, located primarily in Spanish-speaking ethnic enclaves, including Washington Heights and East Harlem, youths were hired to perform tasks that required little interpersonal interaction. They stood around all day long, cleaning, sweeping, arranging, and watching customers and the merchandise to prevent theft. The work was "boring," with "many hours passing doing nothing, seated." Subject to poor treatment, Julio recalled being forced to stand in freezing temperatures to make sure that no one walked up and took merchandise displayed outside. During the winter months, he was even prohibited from drinking coffee to keep warm while he stood watching the merchandise.

Although the work was seasonal, higher wages and better hours moved a few youths to seek construction work, the second largest industry that employs unauthorized workers in New York City and New York State (Fiscal Policy Institute 2007; Passel and Cohn 2015). Independent Mexican teenage migrants knew that in construction, they could earn more than double than what they earned in restaurant jobs in half the time (Repak 1994). Several youths, including some who had prior experience with construction work in Mexico, held these seasonal jobs and, in spite of enduring periods of unemployment, were satisfied with the wages they earned. Some would even turn down available albeit lower-paying work to remain free for the sporadic, better-paying construction assignments. When I met Armando in April, this was the reason he gave for his unemployment. Broke and in debt, seventeen-year-old Armando had worked on and off for the past two winter months in construction because, in his experience, he could earn more money working a few days than if he worked a full week as a dishwasher. In spite of his underemployment, Armando remained hopeful that the weather would soon be warm enough for work, and he awaited his foreman's call.

Employment Strategies

Although independent Mexican teenage migrants appear to randomly seek out and obtain these jobs, they actually strategize to secure and then retain employment. Drawing on similar strategies that were successful in Mexico for obtaining employment, youths utilize social capital and their own agency to find work in New York City. Additionally, some youths are introduced to and come to rely on a new resource they find in the city that specifically caters to immigrant laborers: employment agencies. By drawing on all their resources, independent Mexican teenage migrants are quite successful in securing employment.[8]

As in Mexico and similar to their adult counterparts, youths find that drawing on social networks and the social capital found in them is the most effective strategy to secure their employment, especially first jobs (Aguilera 2003; Fernandez-Kelly 1995; Massey and Espinosa 1997). The youths call on adult kin as well as friends, both their own and those of family members, for job recommendations and information about possible employment opportunities. Similar to Mexico, older relatives including uncles and brothers as well as other friends vouch for the youths at their own jobs, and in many cases, they are automatically hired—sometimes within days, other times within hours of their arrivals (Bailey and Waldinger 1991; Kim 1999). To ensure that the youths will perform well and not damage the relationships they share with their employers, these relatives and friends again become pedagogic agents, agreeing to a "contract" where they will train the youths on the job sometimes before and other times while the youths earn wages.

Two days after Miguel arrived, he accompanied his brother to the restaurant where he was employed. To become an *ensaladero*, or a salad preparer, his brother would spend the month teaching him to identify different vegetables and the knives that would cut them and how to assemble different salads: "My brother would take me with him in the mornings and show me [so I] had enough time to learn." Reflecting on his fifteen years in New York since then, Miguel knew that the skills his brother taught him had helped him obtain and retain the following five restaurant jobs he had held.

Those who cannot rely on adult relatives or friends and/or wish to be more self-sufficient strike out on their own to find work. Like in Mexico and similar to Kim's (1999) findings in her study of Mexican and Ecuadoran adult immigrants, independent Mexican teenage migrants find that canvassing is critical to job hunting in New York, and they learn to rely on not only their youthful brown bodies but also verbal assurances that they can perform difficult work as they go from storefront to storefront. Associating their youthfulness and Mexican origins with their ability and willingness to work more and their legal statuses with compliance, employers hire the youths on the spot with little to no proof of experience (Gleeson 2010; Gomberg-Muñoz 2010; Semple 2010; Smith 2006).

After lasting only one week in his first job as a dishwasher that he found with the help of Antonio's friend, fifteen-year-old Rodolfo found his second job about a week later in Harlem, on the corner of 121st and Lenox Avenue. Although he had assistance finding his first job, after Rodolfo was fired, Antonio was unable to help him further because he was never home due to long work days. Unwilling to wait for his help, Rodolfo started to canvass near the apartment where he was staying. He was sure to remain close, first canvassing within one block from the apartment, then two blocks, then three blocks.

Several days later, Rodolfo was on the edge of a demolition site, where he "stayed watching, thinking whether or not [he] should ask if they would give [him] work." Catching the eye of the foreman, he was called over. He was asked if he wanted to work, and Rodolfo responded affirmatively. Asked to return the next day by 8 a.m., Rodolfo arrived at 7:30 a.m. ready to assume his responsibilities. He was paid $90 a day to fill metal baskets with waste from the demolition, sticks, boards, dirt, concrete blocks, and so on. He would work there five days a week until January, or when the weather made it impossible to work.

Newer to these youths are institutionalized forms of job searching found in New York City. Often criticized for their predatory practices, employment agencies, some licensed and others unlicensed, offer additional, oftentimes unscrupulous channels for minors to procure work (Bernhardt et al. 2007; Hamaji and González-Rivera 2016; Kim 1999; Nee et al. 1994; Pearson 2014; Turkewitz 2013; Valenzuela 2003). Notorious for unethical practices, including asking clients for money before finding them work and taking exorbitant amounts of money out of their paychecks for "finder's fees," employment agencies also overwhelmingly sent youths to undesirable jobs that were short lived or paid worse than nonagency jobs, all less than the minimum wage (Bernhardt et al. 2007; Hamaji and González-Rivera 2016). Turning to an employment agency to find work opportunities, Samuel complained that he had only been sent to jobs that were "poorly paid" or to work on temporary, low-paying jobs where "you work three days and then the job ends." When they did send him for longer, more permanent jobs, the conditions were either different from what he had been told or outright awful. In one instance, Samuel had been sent by the agency to a job where he understood that he would deliver baked goods. Instead, he was immediately handed steel scrubbing brushes to clean out their ovens, a task that he had not agreed to perform. After arguing with the employer over this discrepancy, Samuel left without completing the task; he simply would not be paid enough. In other sites, he was asked to work "six days a week, twelve hours a day, for $300. Some do not even pay $300; they pay $250." After a string of abysmal agency jobs and hopeful that he could find work that paid more, Samuel began to lie when the agency called, telling them that he already had work when he was simply looking for work on his own.

Limited Occupational Mobility

Armed with these resources and strategies, the independent Mexican teenage migrants did manage to get one foot on the bottom rung in New York City's secondary labor market and, with no intention of remaining on that rung, believed that they could successfully engage in occupational mobility. In their minds, occupational mobility meant acquiring better pay and better work conditions and even climbing the job ladder, or gaining higher status positions at their jobs or other work sites. They viewed their jobs as "temporary," and their plans were to stay in them only "a while" until they found better jobs. While waiting for these better jobs, the youths absorbed whatever skills they could so that they, as Felipe said, "could go higher, learn more things, and have a better work position."

In the restaurant industry, youths found that like their adult counterparts, they could "climb" the occupational ladder, but only "backstage," or in the back of the house (Bernhardt et al. 2007; Smith 2006: 27). First hired as dishwashers, delivery boys, or busboys, as time passed, some were granted more responsibilities in the kitchen. They were "promoted" to preparing food, such as cutting vegetables or being a cook's assistant, to eventually, as Pedro had done, becoming a grill cook. In recounting how he had obtained his current position, Pedro expressed pride that he had managed to "move up" in a job he had almost declined. When a *compadre* from his hometown told him about the job at the Upper West Side *taqueria*, he hesitated, accepting it only because it was located near the apartment he shared with other Mexican immigrants. But he "went over there to make deliveries, and one year later, they passed [him] to cook, and now, he has been there three years, making tacos two years but one year making deliveries."

Marco also discussed how, at a juice bar in Inwood, at his fourth job within six months of arrival, he had been able to expand his pay and scope of responsibilities significantly. His delight was evident as he shared that at age fifteen, he was already supervising other employees. Retaining his original responsibility of making deliveries, he also worked assisting the head chef, cutting vegetables for salads, and bussing tables in the front of the house. However, it was his boss's *confianza* in him that made him beam the most. She had recently asked him to perform management duties to make sure that her other employees remained on task.

In order to climb the job ladder, youths generally expressed that they believed that the skills most needed for employment in New York City were not those garnered from formal education but rather appropriate attitudes and orientations toward work (Handel 2003; Moss and Tilly 2001). Recalling their labor experiences in Mexico, these were the same attitudes and orientations that they had learned throughout their short lives, first in their households, then in Mexican worksites, and now in New York City. They believed that they could offset their low levels of formal education with basic levels of acumen and, in light of a positive disposition toward learning new things, a willingness to admit when they did not know how to perform tasks. As Marco explained, "Formal education is not as important as the intelligence that one has and the efforts that you put in your job, . . . because if . . . I go to work and they ask me, 'Do you know how to do this?' and I say no, but then . . . you just tell me how to do it, you do it and then I do it, [or] show me, and I'll do it."

Some independent Mexican teenage migrants who interacted more regularly with English-speaking coworkers or customers believed that increasing their human—namely, linguistic—capital could improve their chances for mobility. More specifically, these youths believed that it was in their best interests to learn English to better perform their jobs. Suggestive of the gendered characteristics of occupational niches, two female independent Mexican teenage migrants were most vocal in discussing their need to learn English to fulfill their work obligations. For example, Hilaria, a member of a late-night cleaning crew, and Herminda, a youth who had worked as both a maid and a nanny, both believed that they needed to attend at the very least English classes to better communicate with their bosses and, in Hilaria's case, colleagues. Without English, they would not be able to obtain occupational mobility.

Arriving in New York City, independent Mexican teenage migrants mostly rely on strategies that they honed in Mexico to obtain employment in New York City—namely, social capital, agency, and the newly encountered employment agencies. Regardless of which they employ, however, there are only a limited number of labor sectors and positions where they can find work. Like their adult undocumented counterparts, most independent Mexican teenage migrants were employed in New York City's restaurant industry, followed mostly by brief stints in the retail and construction industries. Entering on the lowest rungs and relegated to "backstage" positions, their efforts and positive attitudes were enough to get them ahead in their jobs, and via their own mobility, they had proven this, at least within parameters. However, this mobility is extremely limited and, as will be discussed in the following section, often accompanied by a variety of labor law violations and abuses.

LABOR VIOLATIONS

Regardless of the sectors where they work and the rungs they reach, independent Mexican teenage migrants face significant exploitation in these jobs that include wage theft, excessive hours, and hazardous conditions (Cornelius 1998; Foo 1994; Kim 1999). First, the youths were mostly paid less than the minimum wage for a greater number of hours than permitted by law, not only for minors, but also for adults. At ages fourteen and fifteen and then sixteen and seventeen, the youths averaged nearly seventy-two hours a week, or six days a week for twelve hours a day—hours that fell outside the number of permitted working hours for minors in New York State—and earned approximately less than $5 an hour for strenuous work, far below the minimum wages set by state and federal laws. Exceeding the maximum number of hours that New York State allows by nearly fifty-five and forty-five hours, respectively, the youths earned lows of $200 a week when first entering into the labor market and highs of $450 after repeatedly exchanging lower-paying jobs for higher-paying ones (New York State Department of Labor 2015). Additionally, like many undocumented adults, youths were not granted overtime pay when they worked in excess of their permitted hours a day, even when, as in the case of Rogelio, they worked double shifts, or sixteen-hour days.

Describing the conditions at his first job in New York, Rogelio lamented that he was treated unlawfully, but he explained that he had based his ideas about work on what he had endured in Mexico and had not known his rights:

> It was bad. More than anything, I felt defenseless. I did not know what happened to me. I didn't know what my rights were. I felt like in Mexico, that [when] they yelled at me, that it was part of the work . . . if they scolded you. They made you do work that was not part of my work, and I would do it. I did not know that it was required to give you a half hour or an hour for break. I would leave without having eaten anything all day, not even water. The truth is that they were exploiting me there, and I did not know how to say anything—I couldn't say anything. I did not know anything about this country. I did not know the laws, nothing. I was lost.

Other youths were denied wages owed to them. After working for more than a month at a party supply store to which his employment agency had referred him, Samuel walked off the job because the manager threatened to withhold his wages. Hired only to assist in filling out orders, his employer added extra responsibilities, including managing other workers and remaining late when he was away from the business. While demanding more, Samuel said, "He [his employer] was only paying me the minimum of what I was doing, and I was working more." Samuel demanded more pay, stating, "You are leaving me in charge here. You have to pay me more. You cannot just pay me this." After his employer blamed him for a mistake made by two other workers, Samuel told him, "I do not want to work like this. If you are leaving me to be in charge here, that I do this and I do that, well, you have to pay me more. You cannot pay me the same that you pay him, a helper, that you pay me." After recouping a portion of the wages owed to him, Samuel left, vowing never to accept employment from the agency that had procured this work.

As is widely documented in studies of female immigrant labor, female independent Mexican teenage migrants also discussed being subject to sexual harassment at the hands of their employers (Gleeson 2010; Romero 1992; Vellos 1996). Unlike most male independent Mexican teenage migrants, their frequent job turnover was due not solely to searching for higher wages and better conditions but also to abuse. In two different sites, as a waitress in a Mexican restaurant and later as a cashier, Herminda had been subject to sexual innuendo and outright advances. At each worksite, after the incessant harassment grew increasingly uncomfortable, Herminda felt she had no other choice but to quit.

Employers of independent Mexican teenage migrants were also in violation of various aspects of New York State child labor protections. Barring special exceptions, in New York State, all youths under the age of eighteen must present working papers to their employers demonstrating their age-based work eligibility. Distributed by guidance counselors, applications for the working papers require parent signatures; youths who are out of school must still submit an application at their local high school (New York State Department of Labor 2017). In terms of work hours, youths younger than age sixteen are prohibited from working during school hours in excess of three hours or eighteen hours weekly after school and after 7 p.m. (New York State Department of Labor 2013). After age sixteen, youths who were not in school were prohibited from working past midnight and more than forty-eight hours a week.

In spite of these laws, the youths reported egregious violations. None of them were ever required to provide proof of age, much less working papers. Additionally, the youths reported working excessively during school hours and late into the evenings. For example, not only had Fidencio exceeded the number of hours a day he was permitted to work ever since, at age fifteen, he began working as a delivery boy, but his hours were always from noon until midnight, way past the seven o'clock evening curfew set by the New York State Department of Labor. Mauricio also exceeded the number of hours permitted to work, as well as the times to work, when, following his sixteenth birthday, he took on ten-hour shifts as a dishwasher at a twenty-four-hour diner. His shifts began at nine o'clock at night and ended at seven o'clock in the morning. Lastly, youths such as Rodolfo were also in violation of New York State labor laws by working during school hours.

In light of these violations, however, most youths expressed ambivalence about their jobs. Like Rogelio, many were critical of the jobs they held in New York City, but the youths also employed a dual frame of reference and voiced relief that they were not working in the jobs they left behind in Mexico

(Gleeson 2010; Piore 1979). Especially for youths who had worked in the agricultural industry in Mexico, they believed work in the restaurant, retail, and construction industries in New York City was less taxing and a vast improvement in terms of pay, which allowed them to support themselves and send money home. Sebastian echoed this sentiment when he explained that he viewed his new employment as a significant improvement from his jobs in Mexico because he was "not in the sun's rays."

Other youths who had worked in Mexico—both those who had worked in agriculture and those who had worked in other sectors of the Mexican labor market, including retail, food services, and manufacturing—pointed to one considerable variance between their work in Mexico and that in New York City: it seemed endless north of the border. As Lazaro shared, "Here it is to work, work, work." In Mexico, one could work one day and not work the next or rest one week and work the next, but in New York City, there was pressure to work every day, all day. On his days off in New York, he had no choice but to rest and do minor household chores in order to recuperate.

Several independent Mexican teenage migrants believed that their work schedules came at significant costs to their physical and/or mental health. In Pedro's case, it was not as if he was unfamiliar with hard work; he had been working since he was eleven. Instead, he found the *incessant* work, which was accompanied by constantly thinking about work—something that seemed to characterize labor in neoliberal New York City—especially demanding, and it affected his mental health. Always worrying about being punctual and fulfilling seventy-two hours of work a week, he would often awaken in the middle of the night, afraid that he would sleep through the start of work—something that would result in either a loss of his wages or, worse, his firing. Of course, this also impacted his ability to send money home: "What happens is that there is a lot of pressure—well, maybe it is the same—but they pressure you a lot, and you have to arrive on time, and if not, they get mad. (Is there a clock to punch into?) Yes, and they fire you. . . . There is a lot of pressure, . . . and . . . I don't know, the worries that you are just always thinking about work, the hour you are going to enter, that you don't oversleep."

CONCLUSION

These are the "rules" that shape the labor experiences of independent Mexican teenage migrants in Mexico and New York City. From early ages, youths, especially those growing up in economically insecure households, learn particular types of work for the survival of their families, an association that will influence their decisions to immigrate to New York City for work. Growing up in these households and contexts in which adult workers are already in New York City, prospective independent Mexican teenage migrants develop habitus that orient them toward el norte and particular fields and positions.

Reacting to growing economic needs in their households, youths eventually leave or balance their household work with waged work, first successfully entering Mexico's informal labor market and then entering New York City's secondary labor market with the help of others and/or of their own accord. Aware that the informal labor market in Mexico overlooks Mexican child labor laws, prospective independent Mexican teenage migrants become accustomed to working at ages and under conditions that are not sanctioned, a custom they carry to New York. Over time and in contact with migrants living in New York City, youths begin to learn about and, after immigrating, invoke the resources that they obtained in Mexico as well as the ones that they have access to in New York City to successfully secure work. Employing social capital, agency, and even formal institutions to procure work, independent Mexican teenage migrants find that employers desire employees who are young, Mexican, undocumented, and as such, vulnerable. In spite of their low levels of human capital, they find that these aforementioned traits make them successful in finding work, albeit low wage and exploitative.

Once in these jobs, the youths experience multiple abuses. In addition to enduring labor violations enacted against undocumented adults, youths find that employers are also in flagrant violation of child labor laws by scheduling them to work excessive hours beyond the total number of hours per week permitted by law. In fact, independent Mexican teenage migrant workers find themselves disproportionately subjugated in New York City due to not only their legal status but also their ages. Oftentimes, at these young ages, they experience significant stress.

In spite of their treatment in the New York City labor market, independent Mexican teenage migrants employ dual frames of reference and believe that these temporary work experiences are bearable if not better than those in Mexico. Because they have prepared for this work their entire lives across borders, in their minds, the work in New York City is significantly less difficult and is seen as a means to an end. Wages from these jobs will facilitate the fulfillment of their household obligations and afford them the opportunity to disrupt social reproduction back home by occupying better occupations and statuses than if they had remained in Mexico.

6 • BETWEEN BECOMING AND BEING ADULTS

In Martín's mind, youths who grew up in the United States had "everything." After living in New York City for four years, he believed he understood the differences between his upbringing and that of youths born in the United States: youths born in the United States were able to enjoy lives with protracted lengths of time without responsibilities, being cared for and dependent on family members, whereas the Mexican youths he knew had grown up poorer and were forced to live with fewer protections. While the youths he had met in the United States could expect "breakfasts made by their mothers upon waking, spending time with their families, and passing time on Facebook, playing video games, or even being spectators to hockey and American football," Mexican youths with whom he grew up "[did] not have that life"; rather, they went without shoes and were forced to work away from their families. That was, in Martín's words, "the reality" as he grew up.

According to Martín, as well as most of the youths with whom I spoke, lacking "everything" meant that economic necessity had shaped their lives. Growing up in communities whose social age systems were molded by material necessity in dialogue with sociohistorical conditions, Martín and other independent Mexican teenage migrants were subject to fewer protections at earlier ages and early engagement with the activities previously discussed: financial contributions to their households at a young age, premature departures from both school and home in the pursuit of work, and excessive participation in domestic and waged labor (Nurmi 1993; Zenteno et al. 2013). Added together, these actions propelled youths ever closer to adulthood at early ages and further and further away from the dependence and leisure broadly attributed to youths, especially those living in the United States.

This chapter summarizes these activities to better discuss how the youths have understood these steps toward independence and how their experiences and understandings of their own life courses and transitions to adulthood were shaped. Focusing primarily on the ways the youths defined, understood, and lived their life-course stages, completed or did not complete markers of transitions to adulthood, and lastly, subjectively understood their statuses—as teenage minors, adolescents, or adults across various fields and locales—this chapter demonstrates how, while under the age of eighteen, these youths lived lives of limited dependence that included early transitions to adulthood that were simultaneously standardized and accelerated, only to then be delayed (Bruckner and Mayer 2005; Burton et al. 1996; Macmillan and Copher 2005). Complicating common ideas about the "American Dream," this chapter instead argues that for independent Mexican teenage migrants, the concept is not only age graded but also understood as being fulfilled in Mexico, where they may assume roles as self-sufficient individuals. At a time when deportations are becoming more aggressive and net adult Mexican migration is below zero in large part due to return migrations, it is necessary to take these youths' understandings and predictions of their adulthoods into account (Gonzalez-Barrera 2015).

CONTEXTUALIZING "GROWING UP"

The social and cultural contexts that individuals find themselves born into and raised with shape how they come of age, their experiences as they do so, and their understandings of these experiences (Arnett and Taber 1994; Elder 1999; Shanahan et al. 2005). Across contexts, material disparities inform dialogues between social institutions such as the family, schools, and the labor market; the agents that make up these institutions; and the youths. Agents who are deemed pedagogic authorities help socialize youths to understand how these institutions that are available to them within their communities fit together and can inform their pathways to adulthood, including the opportunity structures, or pathways to success (Arnett 2004; Bourdieu and Passeron 1990; Kanaiaupuni 2000; Shanahan et al. 2005; Swartz 1997).

Complementing Bourdieu, Arnett and Taber (1994) believe that this socialization, or at least the probable pathways and opportunity structures that youths are introduced to as they grow up, differs due to the characteristics of the disparately developed communities in which they are found as well as the historical times in which they exist (Shanahan et al. 1997). For example, youths located in preindustrial communities may receive narrow socialization in which youths' behaviors and activities are tightly coupled with their families' and communities' expectations and needs. In communities emphasizing familism and labor, youths who are narrowly socialized are encouraged to follow only a few pathways to adulthood. Alternatively, youth in industrialized societies are broadly socialized and encouraged to value independence, individuality, and self-expression. Ultimately, they are presented with wider options and numerous opportunity structures—that is, fields of the possibilities and positions—in their pathways to adulthood (Bourdieu 1983; Shanahan et al. 2005; Swartz 1997).

For countries such as Mexico that are heterogeneously developed and disparately impacted by migration, even within regions and communities, this binary depiction of socialization is too tidy. Mexican intellectual Enrique Krauze (2006) may be more accurate in describing a Mexico that is "at once premodern, modern, antimodern, and postmodern," suggesting the presence of multiple stages of development in the country. Realistically, evidence of heterogeneous development in Mexico exists even within the towns that I spent time in. In the case of San Pedro, poorer shanties inhabited by indigenous Mexicans who do not speak Spanish surround the remittance-driven town center and the houses there (Martinez 2006). Without Spanish-language ability and less social and economic capital, the surrounding households may count on fewer opportunity structures to lead them out of poverty. Here and in similar communities, households that contain immigrants and/or receive remittances not only are dissimilarly developed, but its members are more likely to consider migration as an opportunity structure or strategy for mobility relative to households without immigrants. Lastly, schools in these same towns teach Western curricula more appropriate for urban centers than rural areas and as such promote pathways to adulthood and success that could be misaligned with their local realities.[1]

In addition to overlooking uneven development *within* contexts, Arnett and Taber (1994) ignore context shifts, or moving from contexts characterized by narrow socialization to those characterized by broad socialization, or vice versa, and the changes that may result. Without discussing migration outright, Bourdieu (2002, 1990: 110) does accommodate possible changes in socialization—that is, the encounter of differently structured fields due to "collective or individual events," such as wars or crises, which may even result in "shifts in trajectories." For instance, as discussed in chapter 4, youths may experience alterations or, in Bourdieu's understanding, "fine-tuning" to their primary habitus, which in turn may lead them to be exposed to and consider different pathways, ways of field participation, or the field of the possibilities, such as higher education (Bourdieu 1983; Swartz 1997). As such, when considering independent Mexican teenage migrants' lives in New York City, we must acknowledge that while the past is still very much present in their self-identification and the youths continue to draw from their premigration contexts in their decision-making, their postmigration contexts may also shape their thoughts and actions about their lives and futures (Bourdieu and Passeron 1990; Shanahan et al. 2005).

How the youths in Mexico and New York City understood growing up in disparately structured contexts became evident even as I began to ask them to describe the life courses, both generally and in their own lives, from birth to death as well as the ages that defined the beginnings and ends of those life courses (Alwin 2012; Belli et al. 2009).[2] Already a tricky methodological task, asking the youths to draw and describe their understandings of life-course stages elicited images and responses that reflected the paradoxes inherent in where the youths dwelled. All the youths and young adults with whom I spoke struggled with the exercise, but when speaking generally, they adhered to linear, Western ideas about which life stages existed, at what ages they began and ended, and what occurred during these stages, including which fields the youths would engage in and how they would engage in them (Bourdieu 1977b, 1990; Levinson 1999; Swartz 1997). These characterizations, however—arguably learned about in school—differed from their own lived experiences. Growing up in poverty simply had not permitted them to wholly enjoy these stages that were more suited to youths living in a culture that Arnett and Taber (1994: 517) refer to as the "contemporary West" (Belloni and Carriero 2008; Katz 2004).

Generally speaking (and in accordance with the conventional wisdom of most life-course scholars), prospective and actual independent Mexican teenage migrants named childhood, adolescence, young adulthood, adulthood, and old age as stages of the life course. These youths mostly placed childhood as ending around age ten; adolescence ending at age eighteen; *juventud*, which could be translated as "young adulthood," lasting until one's midtwenties; and adulthood, which many youths considered as overlapping with young adulthood, starting at age eighteen and lasting until age forty or so. After adulthood, people would be elderly.

When asked how they learned to construct the life course and define its stages in such ways, the majority pointed to their teachers as their main pedagogic authorities (PAu), especially in defining childhood and adolescence (Bourdieu and Passeron 1990). Similar to Levinson's (1999: 15) discussion of how teachers in Mexican secundarias described adolescence to their students, youths' conceptualizations of childhood and adolescence were attributed to schools that were simply following centralized, Western-influenced SEP curricula. Pedro shared that these discussions began as early as primaria, where "they more or less explain when you are going to pass to secundaria. They explain, and that is when they say how many years to be an adolescent." Echoing developmental psychologists, teachers regarded adolescence as the life-course stage during which students would experience the most "change," physically, emotionally, and behaviorally, and thus distinguishing it from childhood.

Interestingly enough, however, the youths' general definitions of life-course stages did not wholly reflect their own lived experiences of those same stages. In the case of childhood, youths generally described it as a life-course stage dominated by play, the presence of parents, school attendance, and an overall absence of responsibilities. Youths most named play, a "voluntary activity with no extrinsic goals," as integral to childhood, but they considered it to be brief and impermanent (Punch 2003: 278). Even though Manuel himself had begun laboring at age six or seven and had little time for play, he defined childhood in this way, as the life-course stage "when you start playing with cars. From there is where your childhood begins to wake up. . . . You start to play . . . with cars, . . . [play] basketball, run a lot. That is childhood."

School attendance and academic achievement were other activities that the youths attached to childhood. Hilaria associated age-graded primaria with childhood, declaring that this was a time when "you learn more things." Reflecting the truncated schedule for compulsory education, youths also suggested that childhood was a time during which familism was still partially fulfilled by academic performance (Valenzuela and Dornbusch 1994; Rumbaut and Komaie 2010; Suárez-Orozco and Suárez-Orozco 1995). Reflecting this, José Luis described childhood as a time "where the important thing there is to try hard in school." These beliefs could arguably help explain youths' reported higher performances in primaria (childhood) and then lowered performances in secundaria, at the time the youths entered adolescence.

Even though the tenability of adolescence has been questioned in economically marginalized contexts, prospective and independent Mexican teenage migrants all named adolescence as the life-course stage following childhood (Burton et al. 1995, 1996; Bush and Simmons 1987; Dehne and Riedner 2001). While adolescence has largely (erroneously) been characterized as a time of "storm and stress," the youths with whom I spoke believed that adolescence was a life-course stage marked by significant planfulness and thoughtfulness (Hall 1904: xiii–xiv; see also Arnett 1999; Clausen 1991, 1986). Lazaro broadly illustrated this transition, demonstrated by youthful "self-confidence, intellectual investment, and dependability," as one in which youths begin "adopting goal-directed actions": "With adolescence, you are getting things. You have to start thinking, more or less, . . . about what you want to do and not do. You are planning your life" (Dinovitzer et al. 2003; Shanahan and Flaherty 2001). Arguably the opposite of the experimentation often associated with adolescence, Samuel believed that avoiding vices was related to "thinking things through," while several youths, including César, believed that adolescence was linked to the development of a consciousness about one's material realities. César discussed adolescence as a time when one began to understand ones' households' economic needs and act on them. Whereas as "a child, you have everything," as an adolescent, "you realize that you want to help your parents, but you cannot. And that is when you take on the burden of your family, and you see the necessity."

For others, adolescence was marked by changes in individuals' bodies, or puberty. However, the youths tied these changes not to, as is normally expected at these ages, ideas about romantic partnerships but to greater engagement in the labor field or greater exertions of labor (Dornbusch 1989; Martin and Steinbeck 2017). The onset of puberty ensured that both males and females developed greater strength, and according to Jorge, they were thus required to work more hours and perform more strenuous tasks in their households and/or the labor market. As Carolina discussed, "The majority of the boys, their bodies undergo some changes. They begin the chores that are more laborious, like cut[ting] wood, that require more strength. You have to do it with the ax or machete.... And the girls also start to do harder work—carry[ing] water, for example. You have to go even to the waterfalls if there isn't any potable water and tie up your pails and walk carrying [them] so that you can have water in the home."

Lastly, in qualitative research, omissions can hold as much importance as confessions (Kawabata and Gastaldo 2015). After the inclusion of school attendance as a major component of childhood and, by default, participation in the educational field, its exclusion in discussions of adolescence only seemed more obvious. Aside from the aforementioned discussion of how youths' learned about life-course stages, its omission was surprising in light of the historical association between secundaria and adolescence that began at the turn of the twentieth century. Integrated into the national discourse about adolescence, by the 1960s, educators had constructed secundaria curriculum to facilitate the "integral" formation of adolescents (Meneses Morales 1988). An analysis of discourse surrounding the secundaria and its curricula today continues to suggest that the Western concept of adolescence and particular meanings and practices associated with this stage are still deeply intertwined with the ideology and practices of secundaria education. However, as discussed in chapter 4, irregular secundaria coverage and completion could explain both its omission and the youths' ambivalence about it. This is of particular importance, as compulsory education has often been viewed as establishing unequivocal divisions between life-course stages (primaria and childhood, secundaria and adolescence) and is required to assist youths in planning their future (Arnett 1997).

Although youths often discussed juventud in terms of ages and as separate yet overlapping with both adolescence and adulthood, this life-course stage—largely considered as one that follows adolescence—is defined by Mexican scholars as a "transitory period" lasting until one's early twenties and includes those markers that define the transition to adulthood (Esteinou 2005; Tanguenco Belmonte 2009). In the words of prospective and independent Mexican teenage migrants, juventud marked a stage where individuals' thinking became "clearer" and "better," especially in relation to their commitment to individual fields and whether they would advance themselves and their families in those fields (Arnett 2000,

2001, 2004; Mortimer et al. 2005). However, it appeared that during this stage, a long-term commitment to particular fields and roles was still not guaranteed. Samuel and Manuel both subscribed to this idea that juventud represented further development but not total achievement of maturity. Continuing his thinking about vices and expanding on other youths' ideas about adolescence, Samuel believed that juventud was the life-course stage during which individuals were more aware of the consequences of their actions: "[It is] where one says, 'If I do this, why am I going to continue doing it? That does not give me anything good.'" He continued to make a distinction between when one is in Mexico and preoccupied with the future and later when one is on his or her own in New York City: "You are using your head [and thinking], 'Well, I have to be doing something for me, because if not, who will?'" Continuing to consider consequences that accompany people's decisions, Manuel believed that this life-course stage, ending around age twenty-three, marked the time when "you already have to know what you are doing . . . [and] see if there are any consequences."

Even as conceptions of marriage and parenthood have become more and more uncoupled from the actual attainment of adulthood among individuals who grew up in the United States, independent Mexican teenage migrants have steadfastly held on to the belief that adulthood is achieved after finding a romantic partner and having children (Vespa 2017). In their communities, however, this often occurs before the youths turn eighteen, or when the youths approximated the start of adulthood. As if adjusting for this misalignment, youths added that it was not simply the achievement of these statuses that would make them adults. Equating not only family formation but also social mobility with adulthood, for those youths with whom I spoke, becoming adults meant not only forming and supporting conjugal families but also possessing the means to provide their partners and children with lives that were "better" than the ones they themselves had experienced. This would mean that their children would have a level of financial security that they had not known as teenage minors. By adulthood, Manuel shared, "you are already formed to be prepared for that [having a family]. (And what do you do to be prepared for this?) How can I tell you? It is the responsibility of having a child, encountering . . . society. Like, I take them to school, prepare them, like that, [so] that he does not have to live *what I am living*. He lives a different life, like in a tranquil school, without worrying that he has to work."

After adulthood ended, in the youths' words, between ages forty and fifty, individuals would be elderly. The youths with whom I spoke were uncertain about this stage, and only a few included it and described it as the final category in their admittedly truncated view of the life course. People who reached this age, in Felipe's words, "already do not think, you cannot do anything, you cannot shout at the grandchildren anymore because they are big, you have to be in the house because they cannot walk, they are old." As this topic was not discussed in school and because the youths reported that family formation began in their communities, on average, at age fifteen, their reporting suggests that at this point, their general ideas about life were blurring with their actual lived experiences.

CONSTRUCTING THEIR OWN LIFE COURSES

When asked to describe their *own* life courses and their categories, however, the youths' conceptions diverged from the characterizations they had previously offered, especially for childhood and adolescence, and instead, they described life-course stages that were stunted by economic insecurity. Different from even the lives of their friends, many of whom had remained in Mexico, prospective and independent Mexican teenage migrants such as Juanita and Pedro underlined their households' financial instability. Juanita simply noted that her childhood was different from that of her friends "because, well, my friends had a little more than I did . . . money." Likewise, Pedro related that the absence of his father and, by default, the absence of an additional source of income made for an adolescence that was, unlike that of his peers, without leisure and far from carefree: "I think that they [my friends in Mexico] have had more of an adolescence because they had their parents and, well, some did work during the day, but they paid them, and they went out to have fun, and I did not."

Illustrating Fussell's (2004a) declaration that in Mexico, there is "no time for youth," prospective and actual independent Mexican teenage migrants discussed enduring "shortened" childhoods and adolescences that contained "limited" amounts of play in terms of either at what ages play would ultimately come to a close or simply the number of hours they could devote to this activity daily, especially compared to their peers. By age six or seven, much as Manuel and Carolina had discussed previously, Rogelio was forced to limit his play and commit himself to working. Rogelio described when these changes occurred in his childhood, recalling an end to his carefree days: "Before age seven, play. My grandparents lived there, and on one side of my house, my uncle and aunts lived. We played, we would get together to climb up the hill, fly kites with my cousins, play tricks, hide-and-go-seek—all of those games. But after six or seven years old, I started helping in the house, sweeping, [and] my mamá would send me to buy things."

Echoing Rogelio as well as the majority of independent Mexican teenage migrants, Martín illustrated how balancing involvement in two institutions, his home and school, left little time for anything else in his childhood: "[During] childhood there, I did not have time to play or watch television. It was just do your chores, go to school, return to do your homework, and continue doing your chores. You never have time for yourself, to distract yourself a little, watch the television. There is always something to do." Noting variation within communities, Armando said, "[My] childhood was very different from my friends'. Sometimes I played; sometimes I worked. The majority of the time was helping my parents. . . . Maybe once a week I played. The [other children] would always come over to tell me, 'Come play with us,' and I would tell them I had homework, but instead, I had to help my father. They did not have to work; they wanted to play and have fun."

Financial obligations to their families, much like Armando's to his, affected not only the ways that the youths experienced childhood, including their time use, but also the timing of their transitions to adolescence. Saddled with their households' economic insecurities, youths appeared not only to experience childhoods in which responsibilities to family and school trumped amusement, but relative to their friends, they also embarked earlier on their transitions to adolescence. Again using the activity of play as a reference, Genoveva not only associated the end of play with adolescence, as discussed earlier, but when asked about whether she had transitioned to adolescence at the same time as her friends, she explained the time of her earlier transition by contrasting her female classmates' continued association with dolls with her leave-taking from such acts. When asked if she believed that she had passed from childhood to adolescence at the same time as her friends, she replied, "Well, no, because I have some friends, classmates, girls in my class who [are] already like, 'Oh, my child!' and . . . they still carry around their dolls."

By adolescence, however, other elements were under consideration that would lay the foundation for the youths' transitions to adulthood and future independence from their parents. Against a backdrop of greater amounts of work, prospective and independent Mexican teenage migrants described engaging in actions commonly associated with teenagers, such as beginning romantic relationships and spending more time with peers, but also some associated with transitions to adulthood, including resolving problems without their parents, both in Mexico and in New York City. With these actions compounded by work, youths believed that their ability to engage in leisure during this time period—and as such, their adolescences—was constrained and even nonexistent. For example, when asked about whether she believed she had experienced adolescence or was an adolescent herself, sixteen-year-old Judith emphasized the prolonged periods of labor required of her (but not her friends) since she was a child to explain her self-identification with adulthood. This was at the expense of focusing on a romantic relationship, a topic more typical for a young woman her age, that she had already embarked on with an independent Mexican teenage migrant who was going back and forth between San Valentín and New Jersey. She related, "Well, my parents got us accustomed to that, to work. We were always there, since we were little, and well, because [of that], . . . I feel a little more like an adult, because I am working, and then they [my friends] do not do anything. They are only in the streets, or like that, without doing anything."

Additionally, youths were beginning to resolve problems by themselves. Whereas numerous youths discussed deciding to leave school without their parents' input by ages as young as twelve or thirteen, other youths, such as José Luis, discussed getting out of trouble without alerting their parents by age fourteen. He confided, "Well, in Mexico, it was a little more serious, we could say, because there I was in the streets, and I would get into problems that were sometimes big, and I wouldn't tell my parents anymore that I got into problems. Because I was already growing, I had to get out of those problems however I could."

By the time youths arrive in New York City, there is no question that they believe that they are moving toward or are already entering adulthood. However, back in Mexico and already beginning to imagine themselves as adults, youths who will eventually become independent Mexican teenage migrants begin or continue their transitions to adulthood as they work to immigrate to New York City. There, they perform their objective role transitions, or they subjectively self-critique and evaluate these transitions. The following section draws from academic literature studying the transition to adulthood as an opportunity to examine their objective marker completions and delays as well as their personal evaluations as to whether, as minors, they had come into adulthood.

OBJECTIVE, SUBJECTIVE, ACCELERATED, COMPRESSED, REVERSED, AND DELAYED: TRANSITIONS TO ADULTHOOD IN THE LIVES OF MEXICAN YOUTHS

More recent discussions of the transition to adulthood have vacillated between emphasizing "Big Five" markers—leaving school, leaving home, full-time entry into the labor market, marriage, and childbearing—and more subjective analyses based on youths' reported cognitive, emotional, and behavioral transitions to adulthood (Arnett 1999, 2006; Pallas 2007; Rumbaut and Komaie 2010; Schulenberg and Schoon 2012: 164; Settersten 2005; Shanahan et al. 2005). Reflecting both this debate and the unique conditions in which independent Mexican teenage migrants find themselves as they traverse heterogeneous contexts composed of disparately structured fields (i.e. crossing the border), this section explores that phenomenon: the multiple ways that the youths' describe and understand their role and stage transitions as they pursue social mobility as teenagers. While it is not my intention to definitively conclude whether the youths are adolescents or adults, I do attempt to emphasize the futility in assigning static, universal labels to youths caught between contradictory contexts and life-stage transitions.

TRADITIONAL TRANSITIONS TO ADULTHOOD

In spite of increasing variability in young adults' transitions to adulthood, many life-course scholars adhere to the "Big Five" markers of this experience, or five "interrelated events that represent movement from economic independence and participation in the family of origin to economic independence and concurrent families of procreation": these events include school leaving, full-time entry into the labor market, home leaving, marriage, and rearing children (Marini 1984b: 63; see also Arnett 1999, 2006; Mortimer et al. 2005; Rumbaut and Komaie 2010; Schulenberg and Schoon 2012). Meanwhile, as the life courses of individuals living in the United States and Europe have increasingly become destandardized, less predictable, and more varied, on the other hand, by the time independent Mexican teenage migrants turned eighteen, they had followed, for the most part, the first half of this model in the outlined order (Bruckner and Mayer 2005; Furstenberg et al. 2003; Giorguli Saucedo 2006; Zenteno et al. 2013). Albeit accelerated, tightly coupled, ordered, and compressed, youths completed the first three markers, experiencing variance only in the timing and locations of full-time entry into the labor market; while some youths entered before immigration, others entered after.

Echoing Pallas's (2007: 173) assertion that social scientists do not sufficiently understand the meanings that individuals assign to role transitions that compose the transition to adulthood, the following section attempts to discover (a) whether independent Mexican teenage migrants believed themselves to be adults because of these singular role transitions and (b) what it was about the role transitions that caused them to believe or not believe that they were adults while they were indeed still legally minors. By drawing from Arnett's methods by listing particular acts commonly associated with adulthood and asking respondents to evaluate them in relation to life-course stage and status issues and by following through and inquiring into their encounters within these particular domains, a better understanding emerges as to how independent Mexican teenage migrants experience these transitions to adulthood (Arnett 1999).

LEAVING SCHOOL

As discussed in chapter 4, the ages at which independent Mexican teenage migrants completed the first marker of leaving school tended to reflect both the failures of NAFTA to "lift all boats" and the Mexican State's educational expansion efforts to ensure that all school-age youths could attend school without hardships. The costs of these expansions and upgrades, passed along to Mexican families, have been prohibitive and uneven, especially in families with multiple children or in communities where secundarias remained elusive. As a result, while youths had secured higher levels of education than their parents and earlier generations, after completing primaria, educational gains, nonetheless, had diminished (Fussell 2005; Giorguli Saucedo 2005). Rather, independent Mexican teenage migrants were particularly susceptible to these shortcomings, with most leaving schooling at the end of secundaria and only a handful able to complete, at most, two years of high school.

Reflecting Pallas's (2007) findings in his study of mid-Michigan adults who were out of school—that there is little correlation between the ages when individuals left school and the ages when they claimed to become adults—I found that of the five markers, the youths least associated leaving school with adulthood. When asked about the relationship between leaving school and adulthood, youths shared that in spite of relief from costs that occurred after leaving school—something that *could* be considered a proxy for movement toward economic (and socioemotional) independence, as I discussed in chapter 2—they did not associate school departures with age or moving toward adulthood.

For this youth population, this was not surprising. Growing up in communities where, in some cases, schools were not available beyond grade six, youths such as Pedro and Erik left school at ages as young as twelve. Generally, independent Mexican teenage migrants reported that the average grade of educational attainment in their communities was secundaria completion, and the average age of school leaving was approximately age fifteen. Overlooking connections between leaving school and other markers of the transition to adulthood, including full-time work, and also compelled to leave school long before even approaching the role transitions they more strongly associated with adulthood—that is, family formation—the youths declined to associate school leaving with adulthood.

But there were a handful of youths who believed that the circumstances surrounding their leaving school in Mexico—or their own decision-making to leave school—*had* made them *feel like* adults. For example, Samuel and Manuel, both of whom had decided on their own when to leave school, associated school leaving with adulthood. Telling their parents that they were leaving school rather than asking for permission to do so had made both youths feel like adults. Ascribing it to economic independence (as well as challenging his father's authority), at age fourteen, Samuel believed that the act of departing from a school—to which his father had transferred both him and his sister without their consent—actually reduced his dependence on his father. After being expelled from one school and faced with resuming his education in a new school, Samuel told him, "Papá, no, I don't want to go to that school. How am I going to go to that school? Better if I go to work." He continued, "Know what, Papá? Why are you spending our money? Better that I start working and [that] I do my own [thing]. And he told me yes." Manuel, however, associated leaving school with an irreversibility more often associated with adulthood. After a period of attending school for two months that only added to his financial difficulties, Manuel made the decision to leave his high school. He believed that this decision was permanent, that "you cannot regret it and return the next week." In New York City, however, an urban context replete with numerous second-chance programs, Manuel's assessment would be erroneous; leaving school, although difficult, could be reversed. In Guerrero, however, access to a preparatoria was already tenuous, and second-chance programs were rare; as such, with limited knowledge of actual escuelas abiertas, or schools where individuals over the age of fifteen could complete primaria and/or secundaria, for example, he believed his departure to be permanent.

Ironically, independent Mexican teenage migrants who were able to reverse these decisions in New York City, as discussed in chapter 4, by attending either adult education courses such as English-as-a-second-language or GED/TASC courses or more traditional schooling such as newcomer or night high schools dissimilarly discussed how their school attendance affected their identification with life-course stages. Those who enrolled in adult education courses overwhelmingly believed that it was here in these spaces—as the youngest students in a room otherwise full of adults—where they were treated as adults and, as a result, felt like adults. Additionally, with courses costing up to and more than a hundred dollars and with no grades or other punitive measures, the youths were held responsible for their learning, an act that was, in large part, dependent on their attendance and participation and their completion of the assignments. José Luis, Lorenzo, and others believed that they were treated like adults because their teachers "just taught their classes" and were not "telling you that you have to do the work, that if you do not do the work, you are going to fail." Rather, "because you are paying, they cannot tell you anything."

Alternatively, youths who enrolled in more traditional public newcomer and alternative high schools after being out of school (in most cases, for years) experienced an iteration of what Galli (2017) describes as a "rite of reverse passage." In these spaces, youths believed that their newly acquired adult statuses were repealed. As a student at Liberty High School Academy for Newcomers, where the school day followed a full-day schedule that took for granted ongoing student dependence on adults while excluding the attendance of full-time workers, Martín enjoyed the protective approaches teachers took toward him, maintaining that his teachers treated him "like a person, like a child, like an adolescent. They worry about you and they tell you, 'Oh you have to do this, you have to do the other,' you understand?" Unlike his middle school experience, where teachers had punished him by hitting him, at his new school, they demonstrated care and provided direction and supervision—acts he did not associate with adulthood.

ENTERING THE LABOR MARKET

Independent Mexican teenage migrants were more apt to assign the second marker of the transition to adulthood—entering the labor market full time and making money in both Mexico and New York City—to adulthood alone for several reasons. For one, the age-graded characteristics of the labor market field as well as positions in the field—that is, at what ages individuals could participate in the labor market and hold particular positions—are attested to by both legislation and social time. In the cases of the youths, both contributed to their feelings of adulthood. Second, independent Mexican teenage migrants believed that adults usually performed the tasks they were assigned. And lastly, the youths' earnings provided them with a level of financial independence that they associated with adulthood.

In the first case, despite being the youngest workers at their worksites, independent Mexican teenage migrants overwhelmingly worked alongside adults and in the same conditions in both Mexico and New York City. As youths such as Marco further developed adult peer networks by virtue of working alongside them and fulfilling similar work responsibilities, they began to feel "like them," like adults, at least in the workplace. Working alongside adults also allowed them to be privy to "adult" conversations, just as Martín recalled taking part in conversations with his adult colleagues when he was working as a painter's assistant in Mexico. Such conversations were different from those he had with his teenage friends, instead focusing on topics attributed to older people, such as "responsibilities and family." As a result, he noticed that his "mentality start[ed] to change, to be a little more open, a little more mature." Once they transitioned into the New York City labor market, all the youths continued to work primarily with other adults and, as such, sustained associations with them. As discussed in chapter 5, youths' access to social capital, which, in turn, allowed them to advance their mobility in the labor market, was embedded in these interactions and conversations with adults.

By joining other adults in their workplaces and being considered capable of the same activities as adults, the youths' minor statuses were overlooked and blurred. In fact, they were asked to perform mental and physical tasks similar to those performed by their older counterparts. In general, youths felt like Martín, who, at age fifteen, was treated like an older person when he was working at Boston Market. Drawing on his understanding of biological or chronological time, or the ages that corresponded with particular tasks, he believed that he was asked to "do the work of a person who was thirty years old, and like that, he was treated the same" as a thirty-year-old person. In many cases, this meant strenuous, physical work. Youths such as Julio had been expected to perform physical tasks that they believed betrayed their biological or chronological times—tasks that were demanding and in some cases more suitable for older, stronger individuals. Charged with lifting heavy boxes at his first job, Julio believed that he had been treated like someone whose physical maturity was much greater than that usually associated with his age of sixteen.

Other youths discussed how being entrusted with supervisory roles (after they had long been supervised earlier in their tenures) contributed to their feelings of adulthood even though they were minors in the workplace. Working in a flower shop and juice bar, sixteen-year-old Manuel and fifteen-year-old Marco, respectively, were placed in roles where, after quickly developing relationships of trust and respect with their bosses, they oversaw the work of other employees. Trusted to act without immediate supervision and doing work they associated with older people, the youths began to feel "like adults."

Manuel began to feel older after he was afforded the significant responsibility of managing sales money at the Washington Heights flower shop where he was employed. When asked if working in New York City made him feel like an adult, Manuel considered how his boss would leave, place him in charge of money, and trust him not to steal it—even though he had the opportunity to do so. That trust, he shared, had made him feel like an adult.

Similarly, Marco's boss, the owner of a successful juice bar in upper Manhattan, placed him in charge of supervising several of the business's operations and employees. In his words, "[I do] things like an adult at work because I am in charge of everything. [I make sure] that everything is OK, everything is clean, that my coworkers do their jobs well. I am in charge of the kitchen, I have to tell them what is missing in front, [and] I do things when my coworkers do not want to do them. . . . She [my employer] always tells me that I have to correct them so that they do things well."

Youths also related earning and managing their economic capital in Mexico and then in New York City with adulthood. More than earning money, however, it appeared to be the responsibility for oneself and others as well as financial autonomy sparked by either wage earning or remittances sent back home that instilled these feelings of adulthood. Fortunate enough to live with his papá and uncles in New York, José Luis would single out other persons' shortcomings with respect to financial responsibility and accountability—a trait he saw as the opposite of adulthood. Narciso affirmed this trait, characterizing it as a defect when others were unable to monitor and control personal spending; that, combined with the license to use their earnings however they wanted (even after, of course, paying their rent and other expenses and then sending money to family members in Mexico), enhanced youths' feelings of economic independence and, consequentially, adulthood.

LEAVING HOME

Characterized as a "rite of passage" for independent Mexican teenage migrants, the third marker—leaving home and, most importantly, supporting oneself—was most strongly associated with adulthood (Furstenberg et al. 2003; Marini 1985).[3] Recalling Rumbaut and Komaie's observation that for immigrants "who were the protagonists of their decision to migrate . . . , immigration itself is a definitive adult transition," leaving home is arguably more momentous for independent Mexican teenage migrants than for the youths most often discussed in life-course literature (Rumbaut and Komaie 2010). In discussing American youths and young adults, life-course literature has primarily focused on individuals who (a) are most likely to set up independent households within the same nation-state boundaries as their parents, (b) continue to receive assistance in the form of cash (as well as time) from parents until their late twenties, and (c) enjoy a greater length of downtime before being required to provide money to their parents (Arnett 2004; Goldscheider and Goldscheider 1993; Schoeni and Ross 2005; Wong 2008; for exceptions, see Rumbaut and Komaie 2010 and Furstenberg et al. 2003, who focus on or include immigrants and children of immigrants). This is different for independent Mexican teenage migrants. For them, leaving home entails entering into and negotiating their participation in another country as well as in other households located across nation-state borders (as discussed in chapter 2) and organized quite differently from their natal households or even the so-called independent households that more readily come to mind. Rather than establishing or becoming the heads of their own households, they are joining others who are sometimes older relatives, friends, or strangers maintaining semi- to wholly independent lives. In addition, youths are largely unable to rely *on* their parents for continued support; instead, they report increasing financial support *to* their parents within months of their home departures.

But how do independent Mexican teenage migrants understand their departures from home as "adult" behavior? Unlike prior discussions of the transitions to adulthood and the relationship between leaving home and settling within U.S. nation-state boundaries, any understandings of the actual dangerous physical barriers that one needs to cross or overcome—that is, the hardships of the crossing—simply do not exist. (For mention of migration as a rite of passage, see Kandel and Massey 2002.) As discussed in chapter 3, in the cases of independent Mexican teenage migrants, they believe that successfully crossing the U.S.-Mexico border marks their "rite of passage" and transition to adulthood. At this physical-turned-metaphorical space, they were alone, passing into another country where they were neither native nor protected. Here Manuel realized that by crossing, he would have to "take care of [him]self, not do bad things": "That is where I felt like an adult, because now you are no longer with your mamá, who is going to take care of you. You have to think about what you are doing."

For the majority of the youths, however, the stage that followed the journey to New York elicited their strongest associations with adulthood: financially supporting themselves. Different from earning their own money and no longer being accountable to others as discussed earlier, it was paying their own way—for rent and their own bills—that independent Mexican teenage migrants most cited when defining their associations with adulthood. As Armando stated, it was this new act of depending on oneself that made him feel like an adult. He believed that he had been an adult since he arrived in the United States: "No one helped me. I have to pay for my own things here, no? I have to buy my own clothes, my rent, the light bill, food, all of the things that I did not have to do in Mexico." In addition to finances, youths were forced to become independent in other ways. Harkening back to Mario's efforts to learn how to wash, iron, and cook in preparation for migration, youths such as Lazaro cited their newfound self-reliance and domestic independence as invoking associations with adulthood. Living with his older brother in New York, he explained, "I started to cook. I started to be responsible. I cook, I wash my clothes, I have to go to work."

Even though they were supporting themselves in ways that affirmed their independence, independent Mexican teenage migrants were still split in their evaluations of how they were viewed and being treated in their new households. Outside traditional models of taking leave from home and other pathways to independent living, when the youths left their natal homes to join older relatives (including uncles, siblings, and in three cases, fathers), they found themselves in more interdependent settings, where they were treated simultaneously as both adolescents and adults—minors who needed to be protected as well as equal, independent partners (Goldscheider and DaVanzo 1985). As discussed in chapter 3, in their New York City households, older relatives gave the youths advice, successfully and unsuccessfully set rules, and oftentimes waited up for them when the youths were returning late at night. Miguel recounted how his older brothers treated him, in his eyes, like an adolescent, counseling him and then physically intervening when they were concerned about the company he was keeping. As such, these behaviors accounted for beliefs that minors still warrant supervision and guidance. Miguel recalled,

> [My brothers] sometimes corrected me for being a minor and taking care of me. (And how did they take care of you?) You know, like when one is young, sometimes one wants to go toward other pathways . . . , you understand? (Can you give me an example?) So, for example, I would get home from work at night, like eleven o'clock at night, [and] there were . . . some guys who would gather around there [downstairs], but they were in a gang. So then my older brother would

> come down, and he would tell me to go up already. He tried to. Sometimes one sees it as bad, like they take a lot of care of you, but at the same time, when you are a minor, they are in charge of you. They are responsible for you. That's why he told me to go home or not to get together [with them].

Similarly, Rogelio's father would worry about his safety when he was out late at night. For years after turning age sixteen, Rogelio's father directed him to come straight home from work. On nights when he had gone out, he said, "[My father] was there waiting for me until I arrived, with worry. . . . [He would] call me, [asking,] Where are you, what time are you going to arrive? Like worrying that [some]thing was going to happen to me." His father even instructed him, "If you arrive really late at night and you are afraid, call me; I can come meet you at the train." By the time Rogelio was nineteen or twenty, though, "he did not worry anymore."

At the same time they were being treated as "minors," independent Mexican teenage migrants felt like adults because they were being included in household decision-making, such as how bills would be divided, chore assignments, and even who would be allowed in their households to share rent. Martín and Miguel both recalled, on the one hand, being treated as minors but, on the other hand, in Martín's words, being considered "as an adult person who can make decisions and who can also give ideas." When asked if he was included in the decision-making that occurred in his household, Martín responded that he was: "We all have to be in agreement with the decisions. And if someone does not agree, we do not do it." Miguel further explained that some of these decisions included deciding on accepting or not accepting adult roommates. Always consulted, even when he had just arrived at age sixteen, Miguel felt as if his opinion had always been taken into account.

AN ADDITIONAL MARKER OF THE TRANSITION TO ADULTHOOD? REMITTING MONEY TO NATAL HOMES

In mainstream life-course literature, teenage minors and even those who are older receive significant support and cash assistance from their parents (Rumbaut and Komaie 2010; Schoeni and Ross 2005). Life-course scholars who focus on immigrants and children of immigrants and their transitions to adulthood, however, have noted that for first-generation immigrants, or those who immigrated after the age of thirteen, the flow of money is reversed. As highlighted in chapter 2, independent Mexican teenage migrants discussed contributing to their natal households via remittances.[4] The youths believed that sending hundreds of dollars home a month reflected not only economic independence but also a reversal of the direction of dependence that made them feel *most* like adults. Whereas between the ages of eighteen and thirty-four, U.S. adult children received approximately $38,340 a year in financial assistance from their parents, as discussed in chapter 3, independent Mexican teenage migrants at approximately the same ages reported sending several thousands of dollars home each year to their adult parents (Hartnett et al. 2013; Rumbaut and Komaie 2010; Schoeni and Ross 2005).[5]

Both age seventeen at the time of their interviews, Arturo and Armando felt that fulfilling these responsibilities to their parents further identified them with adulthood even though they were still minors. Arturo considered himself an adult because he had "responsibilities to maintain [his] family, [his] mamá and papá," and Armando discussed supporting himself to explain his adult status in spite of the chronological "mismatch." Although he had provided cash assistance to his parents before he left Puebla, this practice accelerated in New York City and led to a change in how he identified himself. Armando shared, "I felt like a child over there. And here, I don't because the responsibility is on me. I have to watch out for myself and also for my parents." Furthermore, he added, "I have to help my parents and all of that. I already consider myself an adult even if I do not have the years." Leaving little doubt that it was the reversal of dependence that stirred feelings of adulthood, Samuel explained why sending money home to his mamá and sister made him feel like an adult. The direction of the money flow was most important: "I always liked to give them money not that they gave me." This giving so that neither one of them would have to work, he said, "makes me feel like an adult, a responsible person."

DELAYED TRANSITIONS TO ADULTHOOD: FAMILY FORMATION

In spite of the seemingly early, compressed, and accelerated completion of the first three markers of the transition to adulthood, independent Mexican teenage migrants appeared to approach family formation more slowly (Arnett 2004; Fussell 2005; Mortimer et al. 2005; Shanahan et al. 2005). Although they hailed from communities where age norms for the completion of the last two markers in individuals' transitions to adulthood—*juntando*, or getting together, as in living together or marrying and having children, began prior to age eighteen—these actions were delayed in New York City. Here, independent Mexican teenage migrants were waiting longer to commit to partners and have children.

In their opinion, in the communities they left behind, including among their own friends, getting together and having children was occurring early and quickly. When asked about the average ages that people in their communities began forming their families, the majority of the youths cited a minimum age of fourteen and a maximum age of eighteen, with parenthood first occurring just slightly after juntando. Evaluating these ages as "very young," Martín recounted the story of his cousin: "She was fourteen, and she got together with a boy who was sixteen years old, and now they live together. That just happened, and I think now they are going to have a baby. Now she is fifteen and he is seventeen. . . . The family begins very young." Martín's response reaffirmed what I had observed and had been told by youths one day as I was *hechando relajo*, or goofing off, with a group of girls from San Pedro's secundaria who had identified themselves as thinking about migration:

> While the girls and I were talking about what they were going to pursue as careers, they jokingly pointed to one another, saying that they were studying to be "madres." I jokingly asked whether or not they meant nuns or mothers of children. Genoveva said she wanted to be a nun so that everyone would kiss her hand, to which Jessica replied that she would never become Mother Superior. When I asked if lots of girls wanted to become mothers, fourteen-year-old Genoveva offered that lots of girls their ages were already mothers. I asked why they didn't want to be mothers yet, to which Milagros answered no, that she could not stand when babies cry. There did not appear to be much interest in motherhood right now, but they said maybe later. (Martinez, July 7, 2006)

Independent Mexican teenage migrants do understand that they are out of sync in relation to the ages at which family formation begins in their home communities. None of the youths with whom I spoke reported living with someone or having children prior to turning eighteen in Mexico or New York City. Of the youths and young who had immigrated as independent Mexican teenage migrants but were older than eighteen when we met, thirty-three-year-old Miguel had completed both markers at the earliest age, age nineteen, while the majority of the remaining individuals discussed being in their twenties when these life events occurred. When asked about the ages at which youths from his hometown of Chachihuapa began marrying and having children, Carlos remarked on the irony of how "off-time" he was by marrying at age twenty-eight and still being childless: "I had classmates who started the secundaria and they, one of my female classmates, she was twelve years old and she was already pregnant, and she thought about marrying at twelve years of age, but of my friends, I was the last one to get married [*laughs*]. The majority of my friends already have children who are twelve or fourteen, some over there, some over here."

Independent Mexican teenage migrants such as Carlos appeared to be consciously delaying family formation. Referring back to general definitions of adulthood and associating social mobility with delays in family formation, he discussed wishing to complete college before starting a family. Twenty-year-old Martín thought similarly. Attending a CUNY Start program at the time of the interview, he explained his thoughtfulness in considering his second-chance school completion as well as family formation:

> I think that for me, to have a wife, I do not like to talk about ages. I talk more about achievements. I want to have a family when I have something better to offer them, when I have my house, when I have enough money, when I am really happy. Because . . . I want to offer all of that to my family. I do not want to get together and take the woman who I am with to rent and then have children and see ourselves in bad situations. I think that first I want an education, have a house and like that, offer something to them so that like that, we can have a better life and we can both be happy with my family.

After completing three out of the Big Five markers of transitions to adulthood across nation-state borders, these independent Mexican teenage migrants discussed alternately being treated as, and feeling like, adolescents and adults. By far, youths most associated their feelings of adulthood with leaving home and, more specifically, crossing the U.S.-Mexico border, becoming financially independent, and as a proposed additional marker, supporting their families back home. In the cases of leaving school and entering the labor market, those who believed they had independently made decisions about completing these markers rather than being forced to complete them were able to claim stronger associations with adulthood. In particular, youths who joined other adults in English-language classes and those who participated in the labor market full time, either "voluntarily" or involuntarily, discussed feeling like adults. Often the youngest in both situations but treated much like their adult classmates and coworkers, they simply blended in with their disparately aged colleagues.

Relative to their home communities, however, independent Mexican teenage migrants were delaying completion of the last two markers of the transition to adulthood that compose family formation. Youths extended the same ideas that compelled them to leave their communities and households—to improve their lives and the lives of their parents—to their future conjugal families. Because of their low statuses in the U.S. labor market, including undocumented status, low levels of education, and absence of English-language skills, they simply needed more time to improve their lives and reach positions in which they could provide better situations for their partners and children than those they had encountered to date. Failure to complete these markers most influenced the identifications of those who did not yet consider themselves adults.

STILL ADOLESCENTS? ALREADY ADULTS? SUBJECTIVE EVALUATIONS OF ADOLESCENCE AND ADULTHOOD

In spite of having completed three of the conventional markers of the "transitions to adulthood" and an implied additional one, these independent Mexican teenage migrants were decidedly ambivalent when asked how they identified themselves while they were still minors in New York City. Citing their lack of experiences and self-assuredness, general immaturity in making some decisions, and finally, the absence of responsibilities in relation to conjugal families, approximately half of the youths believed themselves to be adolescents, even up to age nineteen. Seventeen-year-old José Luis talked about *hechando relajo* (goofing off), which he liked to do with his friends on the weekends. He was, in his words, an adolescent because he still "liked to go there a little . . . a little like a slacker, you could say." Although his priority, "what is first," was work, where he acted responsibly, he defined himself by his behavior in the streets, where he would still goof off.

In spite of living and working in New York City for several years, seventeen-year-old Marco, who had been a supervisor, believed that the experiences that could have provided him with more confidence and self-assuredness still eluded him and, as a result, stalled his identification with adulthood. Pedro shared that although he had initially identified himself as an adolescent, the "harsh experiences" he had in New York City, in the labor market as well as living alone, had made him "feel stronger" and had propelled him into feeling like an adult.

Supporting Arnett and Taber's writings about narrow socialization and family formation as one of the few pathways to adulthood available to youths growing up in rural areas, many of the youths who identified themselves as adolescents either at the time of the interviews and/or when they arrived in New York City attributed their still-unfulfilled family formation as the reason why they did not yet identify themselves as adults. In spite of supporting himself and his mamá each month, with no romantic partner in sight and, as such, without the added responsibilities associated with conjugal family formation, eighteen-year-old Manuel explained, "I still consider myself an adolescent because I am not like an adult to take on major responsibilities, because, like I said, I still have not formed a family. . . . I am not prepared for that, [and] because of that, I consider myself an adolescent."

Narciso went further, stating that he was not ready to be an adult and was consciously delaying completing these last markers of the transition to adulthood: "I still do not think about getting together with someone. I just think about working. I do not want to have responsibilities."

Independent Mexican teenage migrants who had been able to reverse at least one marker of the transition to adulthood—school attendance—also discussed continuing to identify as adolescents, but in their cases, they made a distinction between the ways that they experienced adolescence prior to and after the marker reversal. Suggesting, in some ways, that they had been able to return to and recover integral components of adolescence that they had previously been unable to enjoy, youths, including Martín, discussed how after migration, their adolescences had improved. As a result of his enrollment in high school, Martín said, "I met people from a lot of other countries, people who have helped me, who have made me feel good."

Other youths bucked the conventional family formation norms they had previously cited as necessary to become adults and again supported the idea that independent decision-making followed by action enabled their transitions to adulthood. Peppered throughout this chapter, decisions ranged from "choosing" to leave school in Mexico, to immigrating, to reentering school in New York City, and to saving money for their futures. As discussed previously, most independent Mexican teenage migrants staunchly believed that the by-products of their independent migrations—processes initiated in Mexico but finalized with their arrivals in New York City without their parents—had cemented their adult statuses. Echoing peers such as Carolina and Martín, Ignacio believed he had become an adult when he resolved to shed his dependence by leaving Mexico at age sixteen. From his point of view, he identified as an adult: "I had to learn how to mature at a young age. This maturing began since I decided not to depend on my parents and when I decided to cross the border and live in the United States. I would say that I truly became an adult when I decided to cross, because in Mexico, I still had my parents to support me, to watch me, and to back me up whenever I needed help. But when I crossed, I was alone and did not have my parents' support anymore. I was sixteen."

Complementing previous discussions about adult treatment in adult education courses, others further situated their transitions to adulthood at the time when they decided to engage in activities that would secure better futures than those available in their communities. Arriving at age seventeen and almost immediately seeking English classes in which she could enroll, José Maria believed that she was apart from others her age who preferred to go to clubs to dance and spend their money. Unlike these teenagers, José Maria identified herself as an adult because she wanted to "save, work, and study." Attributing this orientation to her economic need, she believed that she had become an adult when she decided to immigrate but that this adult status was compounded when she sought and enrolled in English and then GED classes. She felt that committing oneself to improving one's future, whether via immigration or continued schooling—along with saving money—exemplified adulthood.

IMAGINING AND TIMING FUTURE FIELDS

Regardless of the heterogeneity of opinions about their age statuses after arriving in New York City, youths were certain that by twenty years after our interviews, they would have completed all five markers of the transition to adulthood and be adults themselves. When asked how they envisioned themselves then, all the youths and young adults discussed working and having families. What varied, however, was *where* they would complete their transitions to adulthood—in Mexico or in New York City. While approximately two-thirds of the youths discussed wanting to spend their adult lives, at least part time, in Mexico, either engaging in circular migration or permanently settling down, one-third, acknowledging the difficulties that they left behind and that had continued or, in some cases, had worsened, discussed wishing to remain in New York City.

It is a common sojourner story: individuals plan to leave their home countries for specific short amounts of time so that they can later return home to secure better social and economic positions (Chavez 1988). For independent Mexican teenage migrants, this was no different. Youths had left Mexico with ideas of grandeur that included rapid accumulation of money so that they would return socially mobile to their home communities. As such, they alternatively laughed and showed discomfort when asked about their original plans that projected they would stay in New York City for only a few years and then return to Mexico. Because they had not accounted for both what they did not know, including the time needed to pay back debts related to their crossings, and the effects of their legal status that hindered their earnings, as well as unforeseeable events, such as injuries or illnesses, they had not understood that achieving their goals would take longer than they had anticipated.

Rogelio had planned on being in New York for only ten years, or until he reached his midtwenties. His plan had been to "gather money, go to Mexico, [start] a business, and stay in Mexico . . . but that is my objective, to be here ten years, working, gathering money, and returning to Mexico and [start]ing a business." Arriving at age sixteen and already eight years into his plan, Rogelio was facing the reality that he needed to extend his stay in New York City by at least three years if he did not want to return to Mexico and work in the fields. Planning on becoming a taxi driver, he had been unable to save enough money to purchase a taxi and construct his home. He reasoned that to avoid fieldwork and live "comfortably" in Guerrero, he simply had to gather just a bit more money.

The individuals who had emigrated as independent Mexican teenage migrants—now living in New York City for more than a decade—were amused when I shared the stories of youths who were still teenagers. Like them, they too had initially planned on remaining there only a few years. Approaching his fifteenth year in New York, Carlos admitted that when he arrived that April, he thought he would stay only one year, during which time he would work part time and attend a traditional school. But after his mother fell ill and the money needed for her treatment cut into his savings, he could not leave. Carlos shared, "When that time came [one year], I did not have enough money. I cannot go. . . . There were other problems, and that's how time passed. Time passed, and it passed very quickly."

Extended plans to accumulate capital and begin family formation did not discourage some of the youths, now adults, from deliberating and building on their original plans, now with modifications. Youths such as Manuel, Armando, and Ignacio still dreamed of returning home, citing their communities' positive attributes—namely, tranquility, peacefulness, and safety—as desirable for future family formation. Ignacio, in particular, missed the freedoms he enjoyed in his hometown and wanted his future children to experience the same. Thinking about forming a conjugal family, Ignacio said, "In reality, in New York, you feel trapped. You don't have the same liberty as you do in Mexico. In Mexico, you have the whole town, and you can walk around the town without fear, and you know everyone." Anticipating a future with a wife and children, Ignacio believed that in New York, "there is more danger here in the city for my family compared to *el pueblo*."

Other youths who wished to return to Mexico highlighted the differences in the labor market fields in their former and current contexts. Although they had been able to earn more pay in New York City, in the future, they could secure more lucrative positions in Mexico. Using their savings, youths would be able to establish their own businesses and be employers, not employees. Already tired of working for others who determined their work conditions, tasks, and pay, independent Mexican teenage migrants such as Narciso saw themselves establishing their own businesses so that they would not be "bossed around." Instead, Narciso said, "I will boss around." Other youths expressed more specific business plans that would draw on the skills that they had acquired working for others in New York City so that they could open their own businesses. Having spent more than five years working in restaurants as a delivery person and more recently as a cook, Fidencio believed that he could use the money he had saved and the skills that he had learned working as a cook at La Mexicana, a Washington Heights *taqueria,* to open a restaurant in his hometown in Guerrero. Thinking about his mamá, who was a gifted cook, especially when it came to making *guisados* (stews), he believed that he could open up a restaurant there and employ his parents. The locations of these dreams were in no small part due to the great expense and difficulties associated with becoming business owners in New York City. When asked why he wished to establish a business in Mexico rather than in New York City, Saúl cited the costs of renting space in New York City: "A business here is very expensive, the rent is very expensive, . . . [so] you cannot pay rent, . . . [and] there, you can construct the same business and not pay rent."

Aware of the expenses incurred after family formation, those with children or who were cynical about their abilities to economically thrive in their hometowns were more apt to discuss circular migration. Expressing hopefulness about future immigration policies, two former independent Mexican teenage migrants who were now fathers, Miguel and Saúl, cautiously expressed that they wished to spend several months in Mexico and then return to the United States. As thirty-year-old parents, Miguel and Saúl anticipated that by then (in twenty years), perhaps they would have their papers. If that occurred and his children already had careers, Miguel said he could "go and come back." If they were still unable to obtain legal status, however, their return to Mexico would be more permanent. Both discussed setting up their own businesses—in Saúl's case, a bodega. Even without plans for children, Felipe, now eighteen, could not envision remaining in Mexico for more than four months at a time. Describing his hometown in Guerrero as "sad" and having grown accustomed to New York City, he simply could not envision a permanent future back in Mexico.

Others, however, had completely shifted their focus toward their present situations. More than Bourdieu's "fine-tuning," it appeared as if some youths had experienced turning points, or "new situations that 'knife off' the person's past from the present and serve as catalysts for long-term behavioral change by restructuring routine activities and life-course pathways, enabling identity transformations and setting into motion processes of cumulative advantages and disadvantages" (Rumbaut 2005: 1043). These youths had changed their original plans to earn money and return home, planning to remain in New York City instead. Entering into schools in New York City, marrying, and having children all appeared to have impacted the former independent Mexican teenage migrants' trajectories.

Whereas Rodolfo and Martín's original plans had been to come to New York City, earn money, and then return to establish businesses, they said life got in the way. Before arriving in New York City, Rodolfo had meticulously mapped out the course of the five years that he would spend there. In year one, he would save enough money for his home. In years two and three, he would save enough money for the business that he planned to set up. In year four, he would save to buy his trucks, and in the last year, he would earn enough money to invest. If he stuck to his plan, he would achieve what he set out to do in five years. But as Rodolfo said, "If one does not have the perfect plan, it is not going to come out right." What transpired for Rodolfo was less about perfect plans and more about status upon arrival as an undocumented, unaccompanied minor—as well as what is incalculable from afar. Ultimately, Rodolfo significantly deviated from his plan and instead planted roots in New York City. Seven arrests brought him into contact with The Door, a social service organization that provides legal assistance to undocumented youths. After enduring a near-death experience while working in upstate New York, Rodolfo soon dreamed about attending school, and after speaking with the director of education at The Door, he finally enrolled in high school. Along the way, he met his son's mother, was granted Special Immigrant Juvenile Status, and completed his studies at John Jay College of Criminal Justice. With legal status, a diploma, and now a beautiful toddler son, his roots were being more firmly established in the Lower East Side.

Martín had also dreamed of arriving in New York City and remaining for only three years. During these three years, he planned to make and save money and to construct or buy a home for his mamá. However, after seeing children and teenagers on the bus reading, he wished to return to school. After being discouraged from enrolling into traditional high school, he obtained his high school diploma from Flushing International High School. After graduating, Martín enrolled in CUNY Start at Queensborough Community College. Designed to support and provide intensive preparation for students who had not passed one or more sections of the CUNY assessment test and who needed significant remedial support, CUNY Start was his gateway to community college studies. No longer interested in returning to Mexico, Martín saw himself becoming a professional, perhaps an immigration attorney who, following in the footsteps of Martin Luther King Jr. and Malcolm X, would argue for the rights of his people. His only worry was that his undocumented status would thwart his plans.

Manuel was different from Rodolfo and Martín, however. Four years after his initial interview and six years after he had arrived, Manuel had not really experienced what is traditionally considered a "turning point." He had not returned to English classes after complications during his first attempt at enrollment. In addition, he did not have a partner or child, and he was still employed in the same flower shop as when he was first interviewed. His pay, work schedule, and amount of responsibilities had all improved, and he was still sending hundreds of dollars back home a month—$600 to be exact—to pay off the piece of land he had bought.

Lately, however, he had been rethinking his initial plans to return to Mexico. Ironically, it was information shared by return migrants—the same migrants who had returned to Mexico and regaled youths with stories about New York City—that had changed his mind. When he and other prospective independent Mexican migrants were minors, return migrants enticed the youths with stories about the Big Apple and the social mobility they were able to enjoy in their hometowns thanks to remittances; now, however, return migrants were advising them to remain in New York City.

Manuel shared, "They told me stories about the limits that their money had back home." Planning on returning home to stay, a friend who had gone back home had returned. After his friend moved back to his *campo*, he went with his father into the city to buy some personal effects: "After buying a hair gel, a cheap toothbrush, and toothpaste, his money was gone." Furthermore, Manuel's initial plans to return to school were simply no longer viable. He had spoken to his older sister, who told him that at his age, twenty-three, it would be difficult to reenter into the *Colegio de Bachiller* he had left prior to emigrating; they were only allowed to enter until age twenty. His dreams and his initial goal of returning to school, at least in Mexico, were dashed.

When asked if he would have made the same decision to leave if he could go back in time, Manuel said no. He lamented that if he had remained in Mexico, maybe he could have found a way to go to school, and by now, he would be finished. But instead, when he was told that he could not go to school anymore in Guerrero, right away he made the decision to come to the United States without thinking. He said that he had done it because of his age (sixteen years old) and that he had not thought it through. Now, rather than making rash decisions, he was thinking about his future and how he wanted to be. When asked about settling down with his girlfriend and starting a family, he, like many of the other youths, said that first he wanted to become financially stable.

To become financially stable, there were several steps he was going to take. First, he wanted to go to school even if *se desvele* (he became exhausted) attending after work, studying, going home to sleep, and then working again. This was part of a larger project, he said, "to demonstrate my stability here": that is, he wanted to go to school while he could still do "something." If he waited much longer, it would not matter if he had a degree; he would not be able to obtain employment. Second, he was rethinking sending money home and instead had begun to save it in a bank account in New York City. By doing this, he believed, it would be easier to demonstrate that he was established and assimilating into U.S. society.

It was no accident that this conversation occurred in the midst of the early implementation of Deferred Action for Childhood Arrivals (DACA), something that, at the time, was dominating the Spanish-language news media. Although he had always planned to return to Mexico and reenroll in school, his age and the limited educational pathways back home, as well as the political context in which he presently found himself were compelling him to more seriously consider becoming a "good" immigrant in New York City.

CONCLUSION

Across their lives, independent Mexican teenage migrants construct ideas about which fields they should and will participate in as well as when and how. Sometimes at odds with more conventional ideas about appropriate behaviors and activities at particular life-course stages, these ideas are shaped by myriad actors, including parents, teachers, relatives, and even return migrants who—socializing the youths toward particular timed considerations and then commitment to and/or retreat from particular fields, as well as ways of interacting in them—contribute to the reproduction of class relations that have long characterized their communities and households. Influenced by economic precariousness in Mexico, as children and adolescents, youths who consider and do become independent Mexican teenage migrants—again, relative to conventional timelines—perform actions that are considered off time and markers of early transitions to adulthood. Standardized, or occurring mostly in order and in a compressed fashion, while still children and adolescents, independent Mexican teenage migrants enter the labor market early, leave school early, and—perhaps most relevant to their age identities—leave home early.

Completing these three events across nation-state borders suggests early transitions to adulthood. Ironically, however, immigrating to New York City appears to delay the completion of the last two markers relative to the youths' peers back home. The completion of markers associated with family formation, marriage, and childbearing decelerates among independent Mexican teenage migrants, who instead put off marriage and childbearing until at least their mid- and late twenties. Rather, their delays are driven by a failure to obtain social mobility, or to be able to provide "better" lives for their spouses and children than the ones they possessed back home and within the time frames that they had originally imagined. Absent these achievements, youths maintain that supporting their natal families, not conjugal families, is critical to their identifications as adults.

In light of partially completing the Big Five markers associated with transitions to adulthoods as well as considering more subjective evaluations about the achievement of these milestones—along with the material and emotional realities of New York City—the independent Mexican teenage migrants in this study were ambivalent about whether they identified themselves as adolescents or adults. Affiliating their life-course stages with the fields in which they engaged, their positions in these fields (and their experiences in them), and the ways they arrived at them, youths identified themselves as either adolescents or adults. Whether they had formed their own conjugal families overwhelmingly dictated youths' explanations about identifying as one or the other. Because some youths believed they were still immature and not yet ready financially or otherwise to be responsible for others, they avoided adulthood affiliations. Alternatively, even without conjugal families, other youths who interpreted their actions as purposeful and independent of their parents—that is, choosing to leave school, migrate, reenter school, and so on—believed themselves to be adults.

Looking ahead to when they would be adults, at least in terms of social time, youths predicted their future field engagements and, just as importantly, their geographic locations in Mexico or the United States. It is important to note that none of the youths—neither those who expressed interest in coming to New York City nor those who had arrived and even settled here—intended to remain indefinitely. Rather, they arrived with plans to remain and work in New York City for brief periods of time, or just long enough to achieve their monetary goals, and return. Once here, however, their plans changed. Not one of the youths had remained true to their original plans of immigration from Mexico; younger youths who were approaching the ends of their originally anticipated stays in New York City imagined a few more years before they would return, and older youths and young adults, with timelines long surpassed, anticipated more indefinite stays. Unsurprisingly, those youths whose habitus had been the most "finely tuned" via entry into New York City schools or by having children reported the greatest commitment to New York City as a place to live. Somewhat worried, but not overly so, with respect to the feasibility of their plans given their legal statuses, the youths and young adults appeared flexible about their futures. They imagined returning to Mexico to establish their own businesses or perhaps remaining in New York City and working, as long as their lives and those of their family members would be improved.

7 • CONCLUSION

> Immigrants wept, pleaded for water and pounded on the truck before ten died.
>
> —Bajack and Merchant 2017

In the early morning hours of Sunday, July 23, 2017, news broke that yet another human smuggling operation had gone tragically awry in South Texas. After a "disoriented man emerged from a tractor trailer parked in the parking lot of a San Antonio Wal-Mart," an employee found an all-too-common horrific scene unfolding (Jarvie 2017). Thirty-nine immigrants were discovered fighting for their lives. Of the thirty-nine, eight were immediately pronounced dead; two more died in a local San Antonio hospital.

Twenty-five Mexicans would be among those who were found living. They came from all over the Republic of Mexico: Veracruz, Zacatecas, Oaxaca, Michoacán, San Luis Potosi, Jalisco, Nayarit, Coahuila, Estado de Mexico, Nuevo Leon, Coahuila, and Ciudad Mexico. Twenty-one were taken to the hospital, among them, two fifteen-year-olds.

Those words—*among them, two fifteen-year-olds*—would play over and over in my mind in the days after as I closely followed this news story to find any further information about these youths. Similar to previous accounts of migration and in accordance with my arguments in this book, details were hard to secure: the Mexican youths' stories, in the name of protecting the identities of victims who were minors, were simply unavailable and invisible.

What could be gathered from news reports in English and in Spanish, from the United States and Mexico, was that these two fifteen-year-olds had traveled from Nuevo Laredo to San Antonio in the middle of a Texas summer with temperatures that reached 101 degrees Fahrenheit in a trailer without air conditioning or refrigeration, without food or water. The only ventilation, survivors recalled, was a small hole in the trailer wall. They would take turns breathing hot air from the hole. The youths saw and heard people dying around them in this *trailer del muerte*, or death trailer that some described as turning into a "mobile oven." More likely, people died on top of them.

By the time the youths were finally assisted, they required immediate medical attention and were transported to one of the local hospitals by the authorities. The San Antonio fire chief stated that they, as well as the adult survivors, would likely have irreversible brain damage (Karimi et al. 2017). In the days after the discovery, one fifteen-year-old would be released to the Office of Refugee Resettlement, the agency charged with caring for unaccompanied minors. The other would remain hospitalized. Talks of U-Visas—or visas granted to victims of crimes, including human smuggling—were bandied around, but as seen in other high-profile human trafficking cases, there was no guarantee that justice would be at all served. In fact, by the first days of August, preparations for deportation were already underway for seventeen-year-old Luis Angel, an independent Mexican teenager migrating from a small town in Zacatecas, Mexico, who had also been discovered in the trailer. He had been friends with one of the dead men, twenty-four-year-old Richard Martinez, and most likely witnessed his death (Mejia 2017). While it is highly possible that the youths were en route to reunite with their parents, with few details released about the identities of the fifteen-year-olds, one can only speculate that they, like Luis Angel, were among the most recent independent Mexican teenage migrant arrivals.

This tragedy in San Antonio, Texas, is simply the latest evidence that the fundamental problems that push Mexican teenagers to leave their hometowns continue unresolved. Without meaningful structural changes in their home contexts to address persistent poverty and now unparalleled violence, there is little reason to believe that they will simply stay put. While revived tough talk of a wall may cool their migration aspirations, they will not completely thwart them and may only redirect them internally and/or internationally. What is more likely is a decline in the number of their border crossings (as is already occurring overall), but for those who continue to have no other recourse, more expensive and more dangerous treks loom ahead in the near and possibly longer-term future.

If migration is unlikely to stop, it is essential that we examine and understand the reasons independent Mexican teenage migrants, past and present, leave their families and home communities and immigrate to the United States. In this book, I have considered these reasons as they were foregrounded on either side of the twenty-first-century mark. Such reasons were due, in part, to the economic and social impacts of NAFTA as well as by weak institutional commitments in Mexico and the United States toward both a protracted and protected childhood for poor Mexican youths—all in the context of competing notions of age and social mobility in poor rural and urban Mexican communities. By focusing on independent Mexican teenage migrants—a largely invisible group of youths who exist in the shadows of not only adult immigrants but, more recently, Dreamers and unaccompanied Central American minors—a better understanding emerges of the heterogeneity that exists among immigrant youths and the particular nuances of this group's age-graded migrations. It is also an opportunity to design possible remedies to better support them in their home communities and in New York City.

Lumped into a category and propagandized as "criminals and rapists" by current U.S. president Donald Trump, if truth be told, these youths, like my grandmother before them, are not malefactors but instead possess an immense readiness to better U.S. society when they transition to adulthood. This is in contrast to their present situation of being heaped into suffocating trailers, living fearfully in strangers' apartments, being subject to inadequate teaching, and being exploited and sexually harassed in workplaces as opposed to dwelling in safe, secure, and empowering environments. Rather, policymakers and practitioners must adopt more intentional rights-based approaches to supporting the well-being of poor Mexican youths. The following section posits whether this is likely to occur in Mexico or in the United States. For those who arrive in the United States, I argue for policies and programs that can better facilitate their transitions to adulthood so that they are in a position to secure their rights and fulfill their personal potential.

WILL INDEPENDENT MEXICAN TEENAGE MIGRATION CEASE?

Given the recent trends that demonstrate declines in overall Mexican migration numbers as well as efforts to further mandate protective stages beyond childhood to the end of adolescence, the most probable scenario is that Mexican teenage departures for the United States may slow to a trickle if not be delayed. Given the increasing poverty and violence plaguing Mexico, however, as well as the context of overall unprecedented global migration, one could also argue that youths may continue to undertake risky, oftentimes deadly, journeys. With this in mind, the following section discusses, generally, the forces that continue to influence independent Mexican teenage migration.

"EN MEXICO, CADA VEZ HAY MÁS POBRES EDUCADOS"

> In Mexico, the political economy is not to help the poor, but rather the rich because it favors those who have more, which has generated more inequality and poverty.
>
> —Dr. Miguel Reyes Hernández, June 21, 2017

> The poorest is rich in the United States.
>
> —Manuel, age twenty-two; arrived at age sixteen

In theorizing a culture of migration, Kandel and Massey (2002: 983) discuss how individuals still in Mexico who "aspire" to migration due to their understandings of its benefits—relayed by both return migrants and those who have stayed in the United States—may "psychologically invest less" in their potential success in Mexico. This, however, is not necessarily the most complete characterization of the youths with whom I spoke. While most had been influenced by the changes they observed in their communities and homes due to American dollars invested there, many, regardless of their aspirations, began to "psychologically" disinvest in school only after being penalized for their poverty and an inability to finance their schooling. Many in fact, had wished to continue their studies and had not even considered migration so early, but due to economic necessity, they felt they had few other choices. Unable to afford the costs associated with obtaining academic credentials, they began to "disinvest" and finally leave.

Paradoxically, in spite of increasing educational levels, poverty levels may continue to increase. Between 2006 and 2014, the percentage of Mexicans in poverty increased from 42.6 percent to 46.2 percent, or by two million people (CONEVAL 2006, 2014; Rama and Yukhananov 2015). This is especially true in the southern states, from which the majority of the youths hailed. While Guerrero and Oaxaca were the two poorest states in the republic, at 65.2 and 66.8 percent, respectively, Puebla's poverty rate was just slightly lower at 64.5 percent (CONEVAL 2014).

Although lauded as a solution, high school completion has not wholly translated into protection against poverty. With only 65 percent of fifteen- to seventeen-year-olds in school, of the 49 percent who *completed* preparatoria, approximately 54 percent live in poverty (INEE 2011; Rios 2017). Rather, demographers have found that in Mexico, higher levels of education did not necessarily translate into better wages and/or employment opportunities (OECD 2014). With universal high school attendance set for achievement by 2022, it is wholly plausible that prospective independent Mexican teenage migrants who can barely afford continued schooling and who observe high school graduates in poverty may continue to skip high school altogether or continue to leave early (OECD 2014).

FLEEING VIOLENCE

In addition to persistent poverty, Mexican youths are increasingly subject to conditions that Central American youths face—namely, violence and abandonment (UNHCR 2014). Both urban *and* rural areas of Mexico are now dominated by cartels, a situation different from the contexts I encountered in 2006 (Reed 2015). In fact, on a recent return visit to the capital of Puebla, when I suggested I would return to the sites where I conducted my fieldwork, several scholars shared that those communities had fallen into the hands of criminal organizations, the highways had become violent, and fieldwork had all but ceased in those areas. The last two times I was in Mexico, in 2016 and 2018, I was unable to return these villages.

This growing violence is yet another reason Mexican youths are migrating north. In their 2014 study of Mexican and Central American youths being held by U.S. Customs and Border Patrol, UNHCR found that approximately one-third of the Mexican youths interviewed cited violence as the reason they were fleeing their communities. By 2016, drug-related homicides reached peak levels seen at the height of former president Calderon's bloody crackdown on criminal organizations: approximately twenty-three thousand in a single year. One year later, 2017 was declared the country's most violent since the country began keeping records in 1997.

Young people are especially vulnerable to violence. The World Bank (2013) estimates that approximately 38 percent of the homicide victims in Mexico between 2000 and 2010 were youths, with rates tripling between 2008 and 2010. Mexico's War on Drugs specifically can also be considered a "War on Youth," as youth disappearances and murders have experienced a significant uptick, with impunity, since Calderon's proclaimed attack on drugs (Carlsen 2014). In addition, schools located in areas controlled by criminal organizations are frequently subject to closures: in 2017, more than six hundred schools remained closed in Guerrero due to a wave of violence in the region (de Dios Palma 2017). Subject to threats, extortion, and kidnapping, teachers have also protested or outright left their positions out of fear (Paley 2014; Partlow 2017; Proceso La Redacción 2017).[1]

This increased violence has translated into spikes in asylum applications from Mexico. In spite of overall declines in migration during the same time period, between 2009 and 2011, asylum applications from Mexico tripled to 2,422, and by 2015, 9,000 applications for affirmative asylum had been submitted from individuals of Mexican origin. Notoriously difficult to obtain, in 2015, only 870 Mexican cases, both affirmative and defensive, were granted (Blake 2012; Zong et al. 2017). Of these, 29 percent of all affirmative asylum cases granted were for minors under the age of seventeen (Zong and Batalova 2017).

Even given the increase in violence against youths, U.S. Customs and Border Patrol practices toward Mexican youths have not changed. Under the 2008 William Wilberforce Trafficking Victims Protection Reauthorization Act, Mexican youths continue to be treated dissimilarly from Central American youths. Central American youths are apprehended, screened, and placed into the custody of the Department of Health and Human Services' Office of Refugee Resettlement within seventy-two hours of apprehension. However, because of Mexico's shared border with the United States, Mexican youths, although required to be screened to determine if they are trafficking victims, are often simply "voluntarily deported" to Mexico within hours regardless of whether or not they fear return (Cavendish and Cortazar 2011; Pizzey et al. 2015).

These statistics all imply that independent Mexican teenage migration may continue, but for reasons more varied than the economic insecurities suffered by the youths with whom I originally spoke. This suggests that Mexican youths should, under law, be considered not solely as economic migrants but also as refugees.[2] However, with asylum notoriously difficult to secure, a fact that has only been exacerbated by a current presidential administration that is slashing refugee admissions by more than half from the previous administration, asylum seekers have increasingly and illegally been turned away (Executive Office of the President 2017). In a report produced by Human Rights First, a nonpartisan international human rights nonprofit based out of Washington, D.C., numerous incidents of U.S. Customs and Border Patrol agents stating, "Trump said we do not have to let you in," were reported (Human Rights First 2017). Unable to wait, Mexican youths may be mirroring the movements of other groups who have rerouted; in fact, countries such as Canada have received increasing numbers of asylum applications from Mexico since December 2016.

If the reasons for independent Mexican teenage migration change, then the orientations to and participation in all the aforementioned "fields" may also change: family, the labor market, and schools. Regardless of the orientations of the youths, social institutions that can best serve these independent youths wherever they arrive must be allowed to exist. In other words, if independent Mexican teenage migration continues—with youths such as Rodolfo, Martín, and Herminda crossing the border—mechanisms to disrupt their almost certain poverty must be in place that service both their agency and their vulnerability. As we endure a period, not unlike previous periods in U.S. history, of xenophobia and misguided immigration and refugee policies, we can consider, however, three general policies that will impact youths' transitions to adulthood upon arrival in the United States: immigration policies, educational and labor policies, and housing policies.

ESTABLISHING PATHWAYS TO CITIZENSHIP

Over the last two decades, two separate yet simultaneous discussions about immigrant youths and their eligibility for legal relief have dominated discourse about immigrant youths. One discussion has emphasized Dreamers, or "good" immigrant youths who, free of serious criminal records, have been largely perceived as arriving as children and being enrolled in school, enlisted in the military, and/or working. Arguments around the citizenship of these mostly

Mexican immigrants have centered on how and why they arrived in the United States and their behaviors since their arrival (Krogstad 2017). Brought here by their parents with the implicit understanding that it was "no fault of their own" and enrolled in school as soon as it was possible, these youths are characterized by their lack of agency at the time of arrival and their engagement in activities deemed age appropriate in relation to the Western life course. They arrived not to assist their parents in surviving or to pursue social mobility; rather, they were brought here under the assumption that both dependency on parents and school attendance would resume. These details were and continue to be used to justify then-president Obama's 2012 Executive Action Deferred Action for Childhood Arrivals (DACA), which shielded many of these youths from deportation and provided them with work permits.[3] This stopgap to compensate for Congress's inability to pass a DREAM Act would provide temporary legal status for nearly a million youths and young adults, effectively preventing their detention and/or deportation and permitting their lawful employment—actions that translate into the sort of higher-paying, white-collar jobs that better enable professional careers here. For example, the United States currently relies on almost nine thousand teachers and fourteen thousand health care practitioners who are protected under DACA (Capps et al. 2017; Sanchez 2018). This administrative relief enabled their greater integration into the U.S. economy, including the labor market, as well as into higher educational systems—not to mention permitting better mental health outcomes (Gonzales 2016; Gonzales and Rendon-Garcia 2016). Recent attacks on this program by the current presidential administration has provoked lawsuits and, at the state level for some, assurances of greater commitments to this group of youths (for an exception, see Arizona). At the federal level, more comprehensive legislation modeled after previous DREAM Acts has been envisioned. However, with a strong nativist sentiment and a White House that demands that funding for a border wall with Mexico be in place before offering any legal remedy for DACA youths—and after several failures by Congress to include remedies in spending packages—there has been limited hope for a resolution to DACA "limbo" in Washington, D.C.

Legal advocates have also more recently focused energies on the unaccompanied Northern Triangle (Honduras, Guatemala, and El Salvador) minors who captured the nation's attention in the summer of 2014. Fleeing violence much like that plaguing Mexico, these youths arrived either on their own or to reunite with parents and have sought legal reliefs such as asylum and Special Immigrant Juvenile Status (SIJS). According to Terrio (2015: 181), however, proving "well-founded fear" as a basis of asylum claims is extremely difficult when dealing with children. While many legal scholars and advocates have argued that the targeting of children and teenagers by governments and criminal organization is grounds for their consideration as a protected social group under asylum law, as it exists currently, U.S. asylum law does not recognize children as a group that is persecuted and should be granted asylum (Bien 2004; Terrio 2015).

Introduced in the 1990 Immigration and Nationality Act and reconfigured with the 2008 TVPRA, Special Immigrant Juvenile Status (SIJS) was created to provide pathways to citizenship for a particular population of vulnerable immigrant youths. In general, this status allows unmarried immigrant youths who are younger than twenty-one and who have been abandoned, abused, or neglected by at least one parent the ability to obtain a Green Card, or lawful permanent resident status, with the potential for citizenship (Terrio 2015; Thomas and Benson 2016).[4] Enlisting both state juvenile or family courts and the Department of Homeland Security's United States Citizenship and Immigration Services (USCIS), in the first phase, a state court must approve a special findings order that determines that it is not in the youths' best interests to return to their home countries and identifies and approves guardianship and/or custody under the auspices of either a state agency or an individual. Only after approval may youths be deemed eligible to apply for SIJS through USCIS. Of particular significance to this discussion is the fact that in claiming abandonment, abuse, or neglect, youths who obtain SIJS cannot sponsor any parent for lawful permanent residency nor sponsor their reunification in the United States. Estimates from UNHCR (2014) suggested that during that year, up to 58 percent of the youths who have arrived from Central America possessed legitimate claims for remaining in the United States, including not only asylum and SIJ but also U-Visas and other categories (Chen 2014).

Situated between these two groups of youths—Dreamers and unaccompanied minors—independent Mexican teenage migrants cannot be considered Dreamers in the conventional sense, although they do in fact possess their own dreams for themselves and their families—usually in Mexico. Although of similar ages as Dreamers, because some do not arrive before their sixteenth birthdays and, more importantly, do not embrace traditional Western models of adolescence and young adulthood—which, for the most part, include school attendance with the premise that one or both parents are here—independent Mexican teenage migrants have been left out of almost all legislation aimed at providing a pathway to legal citizenship. Only Congressman Luis V. Gutierrez's American Hope Act of 2017 includes independent Mexican teenage migrants who arrived prior to December 31, 2016. By raising the required age at arrival to eighteen and including all undocumented youths regardless of educational level, work history, or military service, the American Hope Act of 2017 provides a pathway to citizenship for immigrant youths who arrived as dependents as well as those whose objectives were to raise their families out of poverty back home

(HR 3591).[5] However, with little likelihood of this legislation passing, some critics believe it only raises false hope.

Rather, the most likely legal remedy for independent Mexican teenage migrants is closer to that pursued for unaccompanied minors and is what Rodolfo eventually obtained—Special Immigrant Juvenile Status. In the case of the independent Mexican teenage migrants whom I met, most if not all might have qualified for this particular form of legal relief before the age of twenty-one at the time of their arrivals—now, however, they are too old. If they had applied with appropriate legal counsel, they likely would have been approved, although since 2010, SIJ approvals and denials appear to be equal. However, with legal representation, unaccompanied minors experience much higher success rates in immigration court: 73 percent (American Bar Association 2016).[6] Like Rodolfo, these youths came forth or were detected—that is, they became visible. As noted in chapter 6, undetected at these youthful ages, most of the independent Mexican teenage migrants did not regard seeking pathways to legal status as necessary, as they simply did not anticipate long-term stays in the United States.

As violence escalates back home, programs such as these—as well as others, such as asylum—can and should be made accessible from the youths' homes in Mexico. Largely described as ineffective, the recently ended Central American Minors (CAM) parole program, which allowed Central American minors to be screened at face value in their own countries, appeared to be a step in the right direction. Introduced to prevent immigrant youths from making dangerous treks across Mexico and the United States, its strict requirements—including at least one parent lawfully living in the United States as well as traditional "credible fear" category evaluations—led to few approvals for youths. One year after its announcement in 2014, out of 5,400 applications, only 90 youths had been interviewed, and only 85 were recommended for either asylum or humanitarian parole (Nakumara 2017; Shear 2015; Thomas and Benson 2016). Not to throw the baby out with the bathwater, similarly modeled but more efficient processing centers in Mexico could be established to allow Mexican youths to be screened as they apply for various sorts of legal statuses, including asylum.

Of course, however, these recommendations toward immigration based on humanitarian outcomes are in conflict with the current direction of immigration policies claiming to redirect U.S. policies toward "high-skilled" immigrants. As discussed in chapter 4, nothing suggests, however, that these youths could not become highly skilled college graduates if provided the conditions to access, enroll in, and complete affordable, high-quality schooling. The following section considers education and workforce development policies that can improve the skill levels and life-course outcomes of independent Mexican teenage migrants as they transition to adulthood.

ESTABLISHING EDUCATIONAL *CAMINOS*

In addition to embarking on pathways to citizenship, youths should be able to access flexible school programs that combine more traditional discipline-based education with skill building and that can lead them to careers that they are interested in and, of course, higher salaries. Long a city of immigrants, New York City is uniquely positioned to provide schooling that in conjunction with pathways to citizenship, can lead independent Mexican teenage migrants out of low-wage and exploitative occupational niches and into more fulfilling work and careers. Echoing Lukes's (2015: 154) call for educational programs that take "developmental approaches" and consider both the youths' agency and "adult" responsibilities and their continued need for understanding and both career and life advice, I discuss several existing programs that range in levels of "comprehensiveness" and the inclusion of more thoughtful pedagogies that take into account the youths' ages. I also discuss several individual programs that merit attention as well as a more integrative model to support independent youths' transitions into adulthood.

Expanding English-as-a-Second-Language Curricula

As discussed in chapter 4, independent Mexican teenage migrants arrive in New York City with little interest in returning to school. They do, however, possess interest in English-language acquisition: the one skill that they believe will most result in higher wages and, as such, a more rapid achievement of their objectives of saving and sending money back home. However, for the few who were able to drop into them, most found that the scheduling of the classes and the quality of the classes themselves were undesirable and not worth the sacrifices they made or would have to make in order to continue as students. As such, to better serve youths who are working long hours, it will be necessary to change the availability of and/or expand class offerings and improve the training for teachers of both English-as-a-second-language classes as well as other subject classes. Additionally, it would be remiss not to note that for those few students who successfully enrolled in English classes, these may have been a gateway to more traditional, credit-bearing courses. This detail should be examined more closely as we consider educational opportunities for immigrant youths.

In terms of scheduling, a cursory review of the English classes sponsored by New York City's Office of Adult and Continuing Education shows that classes were offered at inopportune and lengthy blocks of time that made attending virtually impossible for youths working more than seventy hours a week. For example, in the Bronx, classes were held in three-hour blocks several times a week, from 8:30 a.m. to 11:30 a.m., 12 p.m. to 3 p.m., or 5:40–9 p.m., or on Saturdays from 9 a.m. to 2 p.m. For most youths, these blocks were simply too long and/or interfered with work schedules that only allowed interruptions of one to two hours at most. Additionally, youths who worked six days a week would most often be exhausted and unable to undertake a five-hour school schedule on Saturdays. For most, Saturdays were days of rest as well as time set aside for laundry and other household chores, and youths were generally not interested in sitting through five-hour classes.

This predicament was only compounded by poor instruction. Reporting highly varied experiences, most youths discussed being dissatisfied with the instruction they received at least once during their tenure in English classes. Relying on under- and untrained interns and volunteers, programs providing English-as-a-second-language courses (offered especially but not exclusively by nonprofits) suffer from uneven-quality instruction and in some cases are unable to provide basic training for their teachers.[7]

To better serve independent Mexican teenage migrants, several changes must be made. For one, more-flexible scheduling must be offered in more-convenient locations. This includes not just shortening the blocks of time but expanding the time spent teaching each level and providing instruction in nontraditional sites and in proximity to both immigrant workplaces and immigrant-dense communities. Additionally, to address variations in instruction, I argue that funding for English-as-a-second-language courses should be tied to mandated teacher training, evaluation, and proof of student achievement.

Lastly, several youths mentioned being "shut out" due to their youthful ages as well as their legal status requirements (Lukes 2015: 115). These should be promoted in the former case and lowered and relaxed in the latter case in order to more fully serve New York City residents who need and/or desire English-language instruction. In the matter of age, high-school-age youths should be allowed to enroll in these courses; in the matter of legal status, no requirements should exist. Following these suggestions will only better prepare them for the New York City workforce.

Developing On-Ramps to Bridge Programs

In recent years, New York City's focus on workforce development has shifted away from simply "job attachment" toward programs that "prepare individuals with low educational attainment and limited skills for entry into a higher educational level, occupational skills training or 'career-track' jobs." This shift has included an emphasis on "skill-building" as well as "career progression" over the life course (González-Rivera 2016: 5). This entails much more comprehensive instruction and support to youths that include not only English-language courses and job training and certification opportunities but also support, such as holistic, age- and situation-appropriate career counseling essential for "getting onto the on-ramps" toward careers. Additionally, when considering the youths' life-course stages, these curricula should link this career exploration and development to overall life skills. At ages just prior to marriage and starting families, youths must be shown how all these pieces fit together.

One example draws from many of the youths' experiences in the food industry. As mentioned in chapter 4, a recent review of one of CUNY's Continuing Studies websites revealed courses in food preparation, an occupational niche of the New York City service industry that could offer an accessible pathway to business ownership and perhaps—as in the case of one of Houston's former Mexican teenage migrants, Hugo Ortega, who also completed culinary courses at Houston Community College—a James Beard Award (Nofz and Stevenson 2017). Although fees are relatively low, these classes possess educational prerequisites that may be out of reach for the youths, including English proficiency and high-school-level math skills, not to mention legal status requirements. Providing instruction to obtain necessary certificates needed to work in food preparation, however, courses such as these are also necessary for undocumented entrepreneurs to get "onto ramps."

LaGuardia Community College's New York City Welcome Back Center also provides a positive example of how a comprehensive bridge program may work, especially in relation to a particular employment sector (LaGuardia Community College 2016). In this case, highly skilled immigrants who were previously trained in the health care industry in their countries of origin are provided with coursework toward licensure as well as counseling to enter into the U.S. health care sector. What is also promising is its holistic approach. Students in the program are provided with "case management and support services as well as referrals to education, community or professional programs and organizations, as needed" (LaGuardia Community College 2016). However, Lukes (2015) warns against establishing programs that are only for high-skilled immigrants while neglecting those who may possess lower levels of educational attainment, literacy, English-language fluency, and/or numeracy. Instead, these sorts of programs must assist young people at all stages in exploring and identifying career options, developing skills—however low or high—and drawing from counseling and support services as well, lifting students onto the ramps and into career pathways.

Unfortunately, however, in the cases of adult education and workforce development training that are designed for "adults," these programs exclude undocumented immigrants by requiring proof of legal status. In these aforementioned cases, programs required participants to possess work authorization. As such, state and city governments must not only include undocumented immigrants in larger workforce development plans but also develop funding streams that can specifically support undocumented immigrants pursuing workforce development, training, and/or certification (Center for an Urban Future 2016).

Expanding High School Programming for Recently Arrived Immigrant Youths

As discussed in chapter 4, some independent Mexican teenage migrants made it into and thrived in immigrant student and English language learner–centered newcomer high schools and alternative education programs. Variations existed across newcomer schools, them, with some of them operating on traditional school schedules and others less so. New York City–based newcomer schools in the Internationals Network for Public Schools outperformed city schools in graduation rates as well as in postsecondary attendance rates of recently arrived immigrant youths (Lukes 2015; New York City Department of Education 2016). Based on best practices, the school curricula prioritized project-based learning while, in the name of development and support, providing instruction in the students' native language as well as in the introduction to the English language and discipline-specific content (Lukes 2015: 160). These schools, however, were ideal for youths who were able to resume some semblance of dependence while cutting back on employment commitments.

Although less intentionally designed with the needs of newcomer students and English language learners in mind, alternative education high schools such as Manhattan Comprehensive or even adult education programs do permit the flexibility that independent Mexican teenage migrants desire so as to continue to work while also attending school. Varied in levels of social support, these programs at least can provide independent Mexican teenage migrants with the coursework they need to resume their studies and obtain credentials to be eligible for postsecondary schooling. As a variety of educational options are designed for independent Mexican teenage migrants who possess diverse economic situations and obligations, special consideration of these youths' need to work, often full-time, is critical to making a return to educational settings more feasible and attractive.

PROVIDING SAFE HOUSING

When Rodolfo decided to enroll in Liberty High School Academy for Newcomers, his reversal of the previously completed marker of school completion was accompanied by his return to a state of financial dependence, albeit at the expense of New York State, and, arguably, marked an abrupt deceleration of behavioral autonomy as he entered into the foster care system. Portraying this as a largely unpleasant period in his life, Rodolfo discussed living in no fewer than four foster homes and experiencing great discomfort throughout the three and a half years he was in the system. From being subject to romantic overtures in one home to not being given enough to eat in another home, to being abandoned without money for two months while the foster parent was on vacation to being repeatedly yelled at and insulted, Rodolfo had his fill of the foster care system. In his case, his fourth foster home was the charm, and he remained there while he was enrolled at John Jay College of Criminal Justice. Although all his foster parents received payments that were to be used to pay for his expenses, Rodolfo saw little of this money and was subject to several rules: he had to clean, he could not bring friends home, and he had a midnight curfew.

This is not the housing situation that I would suggest for independent Mexican teenage migrants. In the case of those who are able to reunite with family members, a better option would be to support the youths' family reunification with financial support such as that given to strangers—that is, foster care parents. In order to honor the youths' autonomy and agency, these stipends could be granted to youths and used to pay for their personal and family expenses, such as rent and food. Through trusted organizations, social workers could also be assigned to assisting them in securing necessary social and economic supports while also facilitating this family reunification and overseeing tensions that may arise as teenagers who have developed high levels of independence join adult relatives who still view them as children.

Another model could draw from the foster care system but specifically place newcomer youths with individuals who are carefully screened and sensitive to their needs. Although not part of the foster care system, a positive model of how we may better support independent Mexican teenage migrants is provided by Father Arias at the Church of Sion in New York City (de Moya et al. 2017). A member of the New Sanctuary Movement in New York City, between 2007 and 2017, Father Arias became the legal guardian of twenty-seven independent Latin American child and teenage migrants who qualified or will qualify for SIJS. In order to preserve the youths' autonomy, Father Arias allows youths to approach him and seek guardianship but also rent a room, work, and continue to send money home. He requires the youths to resume or continue school and attend and be active participants in his church. In the current climate, advocates are needed who will boldly step forth and honor the autonomy and agency that the youths have spent years cultivating, become their sponsors as they seek legal status, and also act as guides as youths transition to adulthood in the United States.

Again, however, much of this is based on the youths'—and frankly, the youths' families (uncles, aunts, brothers, sisters, etc.)—willingness to come out of the shadows to receive these benefits and seek a more permanent legal status. In this current political climate, however, the costs are often considered too high; a denial of legal status such as asylum or SIJ, for instance, quickly turns into detention and immediate deportation (Thomas, in conversation, 2018).

CONCLUDING THOUGHTS

This book introduces readers to prospective and independent Mexican teenage migrants whose entire lives are being shaped and fulfilled by transnational flows across borders: of capital, of people, and of ideas. Subject to competing forces—economic forces that push their families and communities into poverty and keep them there as well as modernizing ideas and policies that aim to draw youths into stages of protracted dependence—the youths find themselves caught somewhere in the middle, forced to take part in institutions that espouse these ideologies but, compelled to work and finding themselves struggling financially, unable to enjoy more modern characterizations of childhood and adolescence. In the short spans of their lives, these youths absorb the world around them, observing older adults, including relatives and neighbors, who leave for *el norte* so as to improve the lives of their families left behind. With little knowledge about the realities that await them but wishing to act similarly, youths leave their schools, their families, and their communities behind to pull their families and themselves ahead. With timed expectations for their returns, they find the difficulties of saving money and the absence of labor opportunities once they return to Mexico compelling enough to keep them in their *jaulas de oro*, or gold cages, in New York City (Los Tigres del Norte 1984). As the youths turn into legal adults, they find their planned returns home even less a sure thing.

At the center of this maelstrom, however, is the question of the "age" of the youths and how to best consider this so-called age to better ensure their survival and social mobility. Are they children in Mexico? Are they adults in New York? Are they somewhere in between? As we consider these youths and the international effort to support their "best interests," it is important that policies and programs fall somewhere in the middle and that they both "protect" these teenage migrants and also honor their autonomy and agency here and there (Bhabha and Young 1999; United Nations General Assembly 1989). This means providing more economic and social supports for families in Mexico and the United States so that they can ensure the positive development of their children as well as centering the youths' voices in all types of policymaking and programming to best meet their needs.

Additionally, it is time to broaden international protections and advocacy to include not only economic immigrants in general but also minors in particular. As discussions of how to best provide legal support to immigrants typically privilege adult refugees, a whole group of immigrants is marginalized and left unable to fully realize their basic human rights due to economic deprivation. Not only adults are impacted here, but minors are often subject to greater consequences. Excluded because these independent-acting youths are often considered "unchildlike child[ren]"—an issue that, according to McLaughlin (2017), is oftentimes raced and classed—it is undeniable that without adequate education, food, housing, and so on, they are more vulnerable to forms of violence and persecution currently considered in asylum cases—for example, human trafficking and recruitment into criminal organizations or militaries (Aitken 2001).

These considerations are more important than ever as the numbers of immigrant youths under the age of nineteen are steadily rising—from thirty million in 1990 to thirty-six million in 2017 (UNDESA 2017). With approximately a third considered refugees, the vast majority remain unprotected by international and national laws (UNICEF 2016). Instead, national concerns in the name of security have been granted predominance over the fundamental welfare concerns of immigrant minors, especially teenagers whose "vulnerability" is often instead characterized as criminality. We see this in the United States, as we are currently living at a time when, against the best interests of children and expert opinions, youths are being separated from their parents both inside the country and at the border (American Medical Association 2017). We see this as the Department of Homeland Security directs USCIS and U.S. Customs and Border Patrol to classify fewer minors as "unaccompanied alien children," effectively clearing a pathway for children of all ages to be subject to expedited removal, or deportation without a hearing before an immigration judge—an act that for some guarantees a return to dangerous and unsustainable conditions that may end in death (Immigrant Legal Resource Center 2017). And lastly, we see this as young, Latin American, teenage males are being rounded up and wrongfully labeled as gang members to be deported (Gonzalez 2017).

In the United States as well as all over the world, these increasingly aggressive neoliberal acts have only made the fates of young people with little hope for survival or social mobility in their home contexts more uncertain, both here and there. Our collective goal should be to eradicate youths' ideas that survival and social mobility are only achieved by leaving one's family, as they face the very real possibility of harm or even death when doing so. In its part as a member of a global society and as the "winner" in U.S.-Mexico relations, it is imperative in the United States that we challenge these predicaments and instead honor our unspoken and spoken commitments to young people by continuing to seek and enact means to provide them with opportunities to transition to adulthood as safely and securely as possible.

APPENDIX
Considerations When Researching with Unauthorized and Independent Minors

There are numerous ethical issues related to interviewing not only unauthorized individuals but specifically independent teenage migrants.[1] Whereas many of these ethical issues are covered through Institutional Review Board (IRB) approval, I was also required to obtain a Certificate of Confidentiality from what is currently named the Eunice Kennedy Shriver National Institute of Child Health and Human Development (NIH 2015). This certificate provided certain protections: it protected my data from involuntary disclosure; also, under no circumstances would I be compelled to reveal the identity of my participants. In light of the intensification of deportation practices during the time period associated with data collection, and already distrustful of so-called institutional protections, I took additional measures. I decided not to record the true identities of my participants, and after interviews, I would destroy any information documented to arrange our meetings, including telephone numbers or addresses (Cornelius 1982). Having done this, follow-up with participants ranged from challenging to impossible, but I believed this was the only way to truly protect the youths' identities and whereabouts.

Although I was interested in interviewing unauthorized youths, due to difficulties associated with developing trust with vulnerable populations, I opted to indirectly rather than directly inquire about the youths' legal statuses (O'Leary et al. 2013). This seemed particularly critical at the outset of the study, as I was a relative stranger, and it is generally acknowledged unwise to presume trust (or lack thereof) between participant and interviewer (Cornelius 1982). Instead of assuming that the youths were undocumented until proven otherwise, the youths' legal statuses would emerge when they discussed how they arrived in New York City and what their labor conditions, including their wages and schedules, were (Cornelius 1982: 397). Some participants were more comfortable in our conversations than others, and they elaborated on the issue of border crossings, but I never asked specifically about being unauthorized in New York City. I remain conflicted about this decision for both theoretical and methodological reasons. For one, not asking about legal status limits my analyses. Any analysis related to legal status depends on proxies—that is, modes of arrival or labor conditions unless they stated otherwise. Second, I fear that by not asking outright, I am somehow complicit in perpetuating the notion that unauthorized status is "criminal" and should be hidden. However, given the timeline of this study, which corresponded with President George W. Bush's and, subsequently, President Obama's deportation regimes and politically driven subpoenas of data at the University of Virginia and the University of Arizona, I opted, even with a Certificate of Confidentiality, to neither document nor store any information that would outright reveal the undocumented statuses and identities or whereabouts of my participants (Biemiller 2010; Ewing 2014; Jaschik 2010).

RECRUITING AND INTERVIEWING "HARD-TO-REACH" POPULATIONS

In Puebla and in New York City, I utilized two different approaches to recruiting and interviewing youths. In Puebla, I relied on my relationship with a professor and her graduate student who conducted fieldwork in two Puebla communities with high levels of out-migration to New York City. Once introduced to the communities and its leaders and teachers, I was, in turn, welcomed into their classrooms to recruit possible participants. During the last days of the school year, I presented my project to students in several classrooms in one telesecundaria and one preparatoria. Not all the youths who signed up during my school presentations would later agree to be interviewed, and as I spoke with community adults and youths, I asked them to identify other youths in the community who would be eligible for the study, both those who were still in school and those who had incomplete schooling. I purposefully included youths who had incomplete schooling (by either Mexican or U.S. standards) so as to ensure that a specific population—youths who may have thought themselves done with schooling—would be included in my study and would be able to indicate whether they would remain dropouts or return to school. Through these two methods, I created a sample that, by identifying and including youths who were both in and out of school, was more reflective of the varying educational levels of teenagers who immigrate to the United States.

The recruitment of out-of-school Mexican teenage migrants who worked in New York proved to be quite difficult; in light of their ages and legal and independent statuses, they are a clandestine, hidden, and "unfindable" population (Chavez 1992; Cornelius 1982; Heckathorn 1997; Watters and Biernacki 1989). With "public acknowledgement of membership in the population(s) potentially threatening"—that is, unauthorized as well as independent and out of school—these youths were not interested in being identified or detected (Heckathorn 1997: 174). Additionally, because of the demands on their time, they are largely absent from social institutions such as churches or even immigrant rights organizations. As a result, I relied on purposive sampling and variations of snowball sampling with a methodology that required several steps (Cornelius 1982; Heckathorn 1997; Patton 1990; Watters and Biernacki 1989). I recruited participants through community contacts and immigrant rights workers and activists from around the city who allowed me to present my research project at their community-based organizations. In many cases, immigrant adults who observed my presentations were either sharing residences with, related to, or working with youths who were eligible for the study, and they put me in contact with them. Additionally, I spoke to youths at soccer fields and at their work sites, and once interviewed, they referred me to friends or relatives. This "snowball sampling," however, rarely yielded more than two referrals; as such, the study population hardly contains any "snowballs" but rather "snowflakes."

In spite of community or personal introductions, I encountered significant difficulties recruiting, building trust, and then interviewing youths, especially during the first stages (Cornelius 1982).[2] Most youths were reticent when approached or contacted and agreed to interviews only after numerous encounters, after thorough explanations of my motives, and after I had received the full blessing of friends or relatives. I quickly found that both in Puebla and in New York City, research methods sanctioned by the academy, as well as written protections such as consent forms and IRBs, are not culturally relevant for poor, unauthorized Mexican youths who possess low levels of literacy. In their minds, the youths only had my word that they would not be harmed if interviewed. Rightfully so, youths who were less sure of who I was were significantly more reserved in their answers, as they were still not fully convinced of my reasons for sitting and talking with them for an hour or so. Over time, however, I found that becoming more familiar with Mexican immigrant rights organizations and their leaders and members—and more importantly, becoming better informed about programs and information that could be useful to the youths and sharing this information with them—made recruiting and interviewing them much less challenging (Cornelius 1982).

Research experience and maturity made the last stage of this study easier to conduct than the beginning. Over the years, I continued to be involved with the immigrant rights organizations that initially assisted me, and I have maintained friendships with both original study participants and their relatives and friends and have also made it a point to disseminate important information to Mexicans in my own and other communities. In several instances, I became known as *la señora de educación,* or the education lady, due to the enrollment and scholarship information I distributed. Possessing this reputation also improved the ease with which I recruited and interviewed, as community members recognized me as someone who was interested in supporting, not harming, the Mexican community.

There are several challenges when interviewing unauthorized, underage, independent teenage migrant workers. First, one's sample will be nonrandom and small. Because the youths are hiding not only one but several atypical, illicit statuses that, if discovered, could lead to negative consequences, identifying the youths is difficult and time consuming. As a result, I engaged in purposive sampling that allowed me to identify Mexican youths who, for the first two stages of the study, either planned to immigrate or had immigrated as teenage minors and had either (a) planned to drop in or had dropped into school or (b) stayed out of school and, for the final stage of the study, had immigrated as independent teenage minors to work instead of enrolling in traditional schooling. Although perhaps not generalizable, the findings from this study are rich and advance understanding of this particular underexamined immigrant youth population (LeCompte and Goetz 1982). Second, individuals may be less than truthful in answers to questions both in closed communities such as those in Puebla, where there is fear of public disclosure, and in New York City, where there is fear of deportation (Cornelius 1982). In spite of both considerations, I worked to ensure validity of the results in several ways. Primarily, I triangulated across data sources, or different groups of Mexican minors and adults whom I interviewed, including triangulation by location and by statuses, such as in school versus out of school and so on (Denzin 1978; LeCompte and Schensul 1999: 131). I also compared participant observation notes in Puebla with the interviews. Lastly, in the final stage of the study, I enacted member checking. Using a convenience sample, I distributed transcripts and book chapters to several study participants who were in or whose spouses were in college. Their feedback is incorporated throughout the manuscript (LeCompte and Schensul 1999; Lincoln and Guba 1985: 314).

BEING A U.S. LATINA RESEARCHER

While there are many discussions of researcher positionality from the perspective of white researchers entering into and interviewing in spaces that are "minoritized," few accounts exist from the perspective of Latina researchers. As such, as a Latina female graduate student in a predominantly white academic institution, prior to beginning my fieldwork, I had few examples, and as such, I did not sufficiently consider how my statuses (gender, legal, national, ethnic) would have been considered in traditional Mexican rural contexts experiencing high levels of out-migration. Like many other Latina researchers who are insider-outsiders in the academy, qualitative methods courses provided neither the proper time nor space to interrogate identities other than those that are dominant in the academy: white and male. As such, I naively developed my own understanding of my research position that was based more on my shared Mexican ancestry with my study participants and less on my gender, nativity, generation, or citizenship (Beoku-Betts 1994; Martinez 2016c; Zavella 1993). Not unlike Zavella (1993: 53), my "understanding of the nuances of ethnic identity were hindered," and in focusing on my grandparents' histories of immigration rather than my own history of assimilation, I was trying to establish a shared cultural identity that glossed over the changes brought by immigration and assimilation that had transpired over time and space. In reality, I could have well been a female visitor from the future to the Mexican families with whom I would be visiting and interviewing, as Mexican New York was barely entering into its third generation (Martinez 2016c).

Rather, as the adult grandchild of immigrants, my statuses of nativity, generation, and citizenship also intersected to create something that has not yet emerged in the spaces where I conducted fieldwork. A third-generation Mexican American from Texas who was born to the U.S.-born children of Mexican *campesinos* from Guanajuato, I was, first and at best, a distant relative to my participants and community members. In a diverse city such as New York that fancies itself as a place whose denizens lack easily categorized identities, this may have been less of an issue, but in rural Puebla, where their New York–based second-generation offspring are barely entering young adulthood, being a third-generation Americana made my kinship meaningless at best and questionable at worst.

In addition, I insufficiently considered the gender hierarchies that existed in the contexts that I would enter. Although I believed myself to be adequately sensitive to the complex relationships of gender in Mexico, these notions were limited and based on my own experiences as a third-generation Mexican American woman whose gender, ethnic, and national identities had been shaped by second-generation, Mexican American, Catholic parents and, at the time of the study, through my experiences as the romantic partner of someone born in Mexico and residing in the northern, urban capital city of Chihuahua. At the time, I believed that these experiences, in addition to my academic training, had fully prepared me to understand gender hierarchies in my field sites.

Lastly, I had not sufficiently considered how my statuses would be interpreted during a time and across spaces in which several outcomes of globalization were particularly salient. Who I was as a nonkin, U.S.-born female poking around and asking questions about youth emigration would be interpreted diversely by community members just as flows of migration from these Mexican communities to New York were cresting and other complications, such as border militarization and the institutionalization of human and drug trafficking, were emerging. To some, I was innocuous, a teacher genuinely interested in improving schooling for Mexican youth in New York. To others, I was a possible coyote, able to accompany youths to New York. To a few, I posed a more threatening risk: I was there to identify and convince Mexican youths to return to New York with me, taking them away from their families. Additionally, males who were not able to migrate and who were either embarrassed, ashamed, or ridiculed would arguably not take too fondly to my emphasis on this topic (Kandel and Massey 2002; Zenteno et al. 2013). Prior to entering the field, I had not counted on these interpretations of my statuses, some of which would prove to be more harmful than others. As such, I experienced sexual and, more generally, gendered harassment in the field (Martinez 2016c). During the duration of my data collection for my dissertation, I employed higher levels of precaution both in Mexico and in New York City.

ACKNOWLEDGMENTS

This book is the culmination of the generosity of many individuals who, in ways large and small, made sure that the stories of these youths were told. I appreciated every inquiry into the book's progress, every kernel of animó to get it done, and of course, every reminder that these youths' stories needed to join their rightful place in the United States' larger immigrant narrative.

In Mexico, Gloria Marroni, Josefa Manjarrez Rosas, and César Cantú Jácquez helped me conceptualize and begin this project while folks in Puebla, including Blas Parada and his family, watched over me as I learned how to conduct fieldwork and strike up conversations with teenagers. They were all generous, kind, and concerned, and I will always be indebted to them.

In New York, countless individuals and nonprofit organizations helped me meet and interview Mexican youths, including Rafael Samanez and Vamos Unidos; Don Leonardo and his wife, Trinidad; Andrés Muro and Asociación Tepeyac; Carolina Gonzalez, Leticia Alanis, and La Unión; Brett Tolley; AB, Felipe; Anthony Albertorio; Karla Sevilla; Gabriel Martinez; Julio Olmedo; Luciano Perez; Margarita Ramirez; Nathaly Ramirez; and Teresa Xelhua.

Several grant-making entities also provided much-needed financial and other support to bring this project to fruition, including the Office of Diversity and Community and the office of the dean at Teachers College, the Spencer Foundation, the Society for the Study of Social Problems, the Consortium for Faculty Diversity, the CUNY Faculty Fellowship Publication Program (FFPP), and the Woodrow Wilson National Fellowship Foundation.

I have been blessed to be in the company of many wonderful scholars who read drafts, filled in gaps, and encouraged me along the way from dissertation to manuscript, including Aaron M. Pallas, Rubén G. Rumbaut, Lenni Benson, José Luis Morín, Lisandro O. Perez, Anna Neumann, Patricia Sánchez, Cinthia Salinas, Maria Franquiz, Ruben Donato, Carmen Mercado, Margaret LeCompte, Antonio "Jay" Pastrana, Irma V. Montelongo, Nicholas D. Natividad, José Aranda, Janice S. Robinson, Virginia Sanchez Korrol, Angela Valenzuela, Dennis Bixler-Marquez, Lenni Benson, Claire Thomas, Marie Miville, Nicole P. Marwell, Alyshia Galvez, Stella M. Flores, Francisco X. Gaytan, Adrian Bordoni, John Gutierrez, Brian Montes, Jodie G. Roure, Nilda Gonzalez, Pamela Quiroz, and the CUNY FFPP working group.

My students' constant declarations that they couldn't wait to read the book kept my fingers typing. Many thanks to Daynia Vasquez, Maria Xique Ramirez,

Maria Munive, Marilyn Alvarado, Danyeli Rodriguez, Gladys Rivera-Martínez, Julio Olmedo, Nathaly Ramirez, Mirka Tejada, Myriam Santamaria, Arlienny Hernandez, Rosa Calosso, Roswell Ramos, Diana Chacón, Eduardo Garcia, Magdalena Oropeza, Michelle Sención, Tomás Guzmán, Ismary Calderón, Yessenia Moreno, Angy Rivera, Laura Alvarado, Lizzette Rincon, Patricia Padrinao, Claudia Holguin, Maria José Delgado, Pablo Perez, Lesley Fernandez, Maria Negrete, Yujerly Paulino, Katherine Lopez, Michelle Lopez, Celines Rodriguez, Yajaira Cabrera, Jesus Lopez, Karina Davila, Colleen James, Sharna Mckenzie, Nanci Avalos Omaña, Celines Rodriguez, Dillon Epperson, Yemelissa Rosario, Lisa Cho, and the countless other students who always inspire me.

Many loved ones made this journey less lonely. Special thanks go to Nancy Yang, Aurora Añaya-Cerda, Laura K. McKenzie, James Alford III, Rachel Pierre, Manuel Huerta, Christopher Aviles, Jackie Nieves, Rosa Poncé, Orlando Plaza, Martique A. Lozada, and my furry research assistant, Murray.

One could not ask for better editors: Leslie Mitchener was kind and encouraging from the start, and Nicole Solano and Jasper Chang made the transition seamless.

My angels in life and in the book are Angel D. Nieves, PhD, and Paul Richard Foote. Their ruthlessness in ink and most of all their love throughout the years have provided me with honesty and strength when I needed it most.

This book was born a century ago with the brave journey of my grandmother. While my Tio Felipe Salazar II's meticulous documentation of her arrival in South Texas inspired me to tell the contemporary story of independent Mexican teenage migrants, my Tia Ana Maria Salazar's stories about her and my dad would ensure that their spirits remained close to me in my storytelling.

Ever since I was born, my father, Ramiro S. Martinez; my mother, Belia Martinez; and my brother, Ramiro Martinez II have always sustained me in mind, heart, stomach, and soul and in my commitment to social justice. I never could have written these stories without their unconditional love.

And because you cannot spell "book" without "boo," I thank my love, Angelo Lozada, for always believing that this book would see the light. Te amo.

Lastly, I thank all the Mexican youths who entrusted me with their stories as well as the countless others who became adults long before the age of eighteen. After reading the draft three times, Rodolfo shared, "[I hope] many people who would read your book [will] know and learn from our experiences to become better human beings [and] never give up on [their] purposes." This book is for these young people.

NOTES

CHAPTER 1 IN THE SHADOWS OF SKYSCRAPERS AND IVORY TOWERS

1. Marroni (2009) notes that this flow of Mexican migration is the second one in contemporary times, the first occurring between the 1980s and 1994 and then the second between 1994, or the signing of NAFTA, and 2008, the start of the United States' most recent recession.
2. Per 6 U.S.C. 279 (g) (2), to be considered unaccompanied, four criteria must be met. The individual in question must (a) be under the age of eighteen, (b) lack unlawful immigration status in the United States, and (c) satisfy one of the following two conditions: (1) have no parent or legal guardian in the United States or (2) have no parent or legal guardian in the United States who is available to provide care and/or physical custody. In a call to reduce the backlog of cases of unaccompanied minors and essentially treat minors as adults who can be placed in expedited removal proceedings, Secretary of Homeland Security Kelly estimated that approximately 60 percent of minors initially deemed unaccompanied alien children were, because they were reunited with parents residing in the United States, not technically "unaccompanied" but continued to be treated as, and protected under law, as such (Kelly 2017: 10). Reflecting this trend, scholars, attorneys, and practitioners alike have used this term as a catchall phrase that has included youths who meet the first two criteria but have traveled alone to reunite with parents in the United States.
3. In spite of the youths' legal ability to work in New York City after age fourteen, a number of restrictions are placed on the amount and types of work that they may do. For that reason, I refer to them as underage or younger than the age at which they are eligible to perform the amounts and types of work they do in New York City.
4. In *American Apartheid*, Massey and Denton (1993) define an *underclass* as a group characterized by distinguishability, segregation, and poverty passed through more than one generation. Drawing from these criteria, Massey and Pren (2012) and Massey (2007) argue that Latina/os have surpassed African Americans in occupying the lowest strata of the U.S. class hierarchy. After occupying a middle position between whites and blacks, by 1994, Latina/o poverty rates first matched those of African Americans and then in 2000 surpassed them. Additionally, Latina/os now demonstrate higher rates of spatial isolation than African Americans. Enacted and exacerbated by a punitive immigration system, the exploitation and exclusion of Latinos, mostly Mexicans, has reached new extremes so that they are a "better" underclass. By "better," Massey suggests that Latina/os, especially those who are undocumented, suffer greater vulnerability and are at higher risks of exploitation and exclusion, with the greatest risk being deportation (Massey 2007: 156–157; Massey and Pren 2012). Without legal protections, their precarious conditions in the United States are compounded, and even legal immigrants remain at risk for deportation under the current immigration regime.
5. Under current Department of Health and Human Services policies, unaccompanied minors who have been apprehended and detained must be released to their parent or guardian after they are deemed able to provide safe and secure environments. In order to do this, youths must identify their parent and/or guardian, who then comes forth and submits to a whole host of screenings to ensure the safety and security of the child postrelease. Current Department of Homeland Security memos, however, threaten to criminalize parents who

have "facilitated the smuggling or trafficking of alien children" into the United States (Kelly 2017: 10). New York Law School professor Lenni Benson believes that this will only place children further at risk in evading their own detection and/or in parents paying and entrusting their children with smugglers for longer and costlier periods of time (Gonzalez 2017).

6. More prevalent among youths in removal proceedings and/or applying for legal status, these two categories point to adults, regardless of legal status, who are willing to come forth and formally "claim" them. In the former, sponsors are adults to whom youths being held in Office of Refugee Resettlement (ORR) custody can be released after undergoing rigorous screenings to ensure the youths' care and attendance of immigration court hearings. Sponsors include (a) parents or legal guardians, (b) adult relatives, (c) individuals designated by the parent or legal guardian, and lastly, (d) licensed programs or adults approved by the ORR (Terrio 2015; Thomas 2016). Legal guardians become significant for immigrant youths applying for Special Immigrant Juvenile Status (SIJS), a legal remedy most of the youths qualified for. In order to qualify for this legal status, youths under the age of twenty-one must enter first into a state juvenile or family court and demonstrate abandonment by one or both parents but possess an adult caretaker who, along with any other adults living in the dwelling, has undergone a criminal background check and fingerprinting. In a climate of fear and anxiety in regard to detention and deportation, these policies have deterred undocumented adult guardians from coming forward (Mendelson et al. 2017).

7. In their 2013 policy brief "Young Mexican-Americans in New York City: Working More, Learning and Earning Less," Treschan and Mehrotra report that in New York City, 36 percent of Mexican youths ages sixteen to twenty-four lived in households where they were either a sibling/sibling-in-law, other relative, or simply a roommate in relation to the household head.

8. In 2009, the official number of Mexican minors who were "encountered" totaled 16,114. At this time, they made up between 82 and 75 percent of the apprehended unaccompanied minor population, a number that dropped, although similar in total numbers, to approximately 28 percent by 2015. These youths were predominantly male and between the ages of fifteen and seventeen (Chishti and Hipsman 2014; Kandel 2017; U.S. Customs and Border Patrol 2015a).

9. In 2013, Laura Carlsen, the director of the Americas program at the Center for International Policy, estimated that immediately after the implementation of NAFTA, half a million Mexicans immigrated each year.

10. Former president Carlos Salinas de Gortari is credited for negotiating much of Mexico's role in the North American Free Trade Agreement. A staunch supporter of neoliberal policies, President Salinas de Gortari and his administration strongly supported economic globalization, privatization, and modernization. To support Mexico's transition to a globalized nation, Salinas de Gortari also supported educational reforms that are strongly associated with neoliberal economic policies, including increased school privatization, as well as other modernization initiatives, including expansion of secundarias in rural areas (Gutek 2006).

11. Nearly twenty years after the completion of junior high school was made compulsory, in 2012, high school completion was mandated. By amending article 3 of the General Education Law once again, Mexican officials indirectly lengthened some sort of teenage dependence at least three years more, or until approximately age seventeen (Zapata 2013).

12. In 2014 and 2015, Mexico's Congress and Senate increased the minimum age of labor market eligibility to age fifteen for most; however, all other conditions for work remained similar. This law went into effect in June 2015 (Melendez 2015).

13. Although wealth transfer and economic interdependence is discussed in life course studies, it has traditionally been characterized as a unidirectional process that occurs from parent

to child long into the child's adulthood, or until, on average, their early thirties (Schoeni and Ross 2005; Swartz and O'Brien 2009).

14. In 2000, Martinez-Leon and Smith (2003) placed out-migration from Valle de San Benito de los Lagos and her surrounding communities at two hundred thousand, compared to a million residents from the state overall.

15. By the start of the twenty-first century, high levels of poverty and accelerated migration characterized San Luis Tlalapa and Coyopec, the two municipalities in which the two communities, San Pedro and San Valentín, are located (CONAPO 2005; Marroni 2003; SEDESOL 2010). By 2010, more than 80.6 percent of the population residing in San Luis Tlalapa lived in either moderate or extreme poverty, and 58.2 percent of the Coyopec population was similarly poor. Among 217 municipalities in Puebla, San Luis Tlalapa ranked sixth in rates of migration, resulting in a scoring of *alta*, or "high," in terms of intensity of migration, while Coyopec ranked fifty-ninth of all Poblano municipalities and possessed "moderate" migration intensity (COTEIGEP 2010b).

16. In 2000, approximately 34 percent of the homes in San Pedro possessed two or fewer rooms. For cooking, 52 percent of all households used wood, while 45 percent used gas. Approximately 55 percent of the homes possessed full plumbing. In San Valentín, approximately 12 percent of the homes possessed only one room. For cooking, 52 percent used materials other than gas, including wood. A total of 58 percent of all households had plumbing, drainage, and electricity (INEGI 2000).

17. Across age ranges, the numbers of males in these communities decline dramatically. In 2011 alone, in San Luis Tlalapa, the number of males drops first by 23 percent between the zero-to-fourteen and fifteen-to-twenty-nine age ranges and then by 45 percent between the ages of fifteen and twenty-nine and thirty and forty-four. In Coyopec, these numbers are similarly high, between the age ranges of zero to fourteen and fifteen to twenty-nine, or 26 percent, and then by 39 percent between the ages of fifteen to twenty and thirty to forty-four.

18. In Puebla, I spent significant amounts of time with the youths as they went about their daily lives. This proved to be more difficult in New York City given the organization of the youths' lives and my concern with getting the youths in trouble with their employers. Sensitive to my intrusion, as well as the dangers associated with being a female researcher in predominantly male settings (see the appendix), I opted not to extend participant observations in New York City.

CHAPTER 2 "GIVING MY FAMILY A BETTER FUTURE"

1. Bourdieu (2002) argues that individuals' primary habitus cannot be destroyed but rather only slightly adjusted in extreme circumstances. Arguably, migration is one of those "extreme circumstances."

2. Atkinson (2016: 52) makes a distinction between households and families, opting to focus on families, as they are more tightly "united" across generations and distance by understandings of kinship. In the former, cohabitees may not be subject to such consequential field-specific doxa that affect engagement across other fields. I opt to use households instead of family and then identify their members due to the varying compositions across borders.

3. Reflecting the methodological issues associated with self-reporting, especially in relation to remittances, Fidencio's and Martin's reports of sending monies home and already acquiring and constructing properties and multiple homes in short time periods may have been inaccurate (Brown et al. 2014: 1266). In Lopez's (2010: 33) discussions of "remittance houses," or houses built with "money earned by a Mexican migrant in the United States who sends dollars—remits—to Mexico for the construction of his/her dream house," she notes that their construction occurs slowly over many years or, according to Sandoval-Cervantes (2017), in phases. This reality casts doubt on the youths' self-reporting and may instead reflect their aspirations and/or eventual achievement.

CHAPTER 3 "WE ALL COME YOUNG"

1. Basing their opinion on findings from various reports and surveys completed and published by UNICEF, CEPAL, INEGI, and other organizations, authors of an editorial published by *La Jornada* on the Day of the Child (April 30, 2017) found little to celebrate. With 21 million Mexican minors in poverty, of which 4.6 million are in extreme poverty, and Mexican children and adolescents facing challenges since birth, including malnutrition, deprivation, violence with impunity, educational failure, labor and sexual exploitation, and so on, the authors predicted a "dark shadow" over the years to come.
2. This figure actually reflects the aspirations of similarly aged youths in other regions who desire immigration to the United States. A 2013 survey of youths in Huimilpan, Queretaro, revealed that 50 percent, or five in every ten, youths in secundaria also wished to immigrate to the United States. As in other studies, these youths wished to seek better employment and income opportunities (El Universal 2013).
3. Since the 2014 Central American refugee crisis, increasing attention has been paid to unapproved departures of unaccompanied minors in search of family reunification. Perhaps one of the most oft-discussed is Enrique, a seventeen-year-old "unaccompanied" minor from Honduras whose life was documented by *Los Angeles Times* Pulitzer Prize–winner Sonia Nazario.
4. In her important work on human smuggling, Sanchez (2015) purposefully calls coyotes "facilitators" who, in the eyes of individuals who use them, provide a particular altruistic service in the current political and legal context. Given the increasingly oppressive and punitive legal limitations for immigration, migrants often view facilitators as helping them improve their lives amid a set of global and local constraints. Within the recent economic and legal constraints, emigrating with the help of smugglers has emerged as "one of the least stigmatized" and risky strategies for economic uplift. This is in direct contrast to the hypercriminalized depictions given by law enforcement officials and the U.S. president Donald Trump. This is not to say that some coyotes have not enacted horrendous acts against migrants, but especially before the mid-2000s, these tended to be the exception and not the rule; it is exceptions that are most often used as examples to advance harmful policies.
5. Much has been written about changes in the human smuggling enterprise in the past decade. While previously, human smuggling and drug cartels coexisted side by side, in recent years, drug cartels have integrated human smuggling operations into their financial endeavors and now dominate this industry in Mexico. According to U.S. intelligence officials, for at least the Gulf and Zeta cartels, human smuggling has become a more lucrative industry than drug trafficking (Corchado 2014; Izcara-Palacios 2012; Sanchez 2014; Spener 2009).
6. As a novice researcher, I had not adequately established trust prior to the interviews with many of my early participants, so I refrained from asking them the details of their actual crossings across the Sonora-Arizona desert. Many did, however, share minimal details of their treks across the desert, including crossing points. Later, as a much more seasoned researcher, participants with whom I had longer relationships provided greater details about their crossings.

CHAPTER 4 PUSHED OR JUMPED?

1. In fact, by the 1990s, primaria school enrollment reached rates of approximately 90 percent (INEGI 2000).
2. To support Mexico's transition to a globalized nation, former president Carlos Salinas de Gortari also supported educational reforms that are strongly associated with neoliberal

economic policies, including increased school privatization as well as other modernization initiatives, including expansion of secundarias in rural areas (Gutek 2006).

3. According to Levinson (2001), secundaria attendance was long considered a stepping-stone only for students, usually urban, who were interested in pursuing professional studies at urban preparatorias.

4. Manjarrez Rosas (2008) states that San Pedro possessed a secundaria since 1987, but according to youths with whom I spoke, they did not know of one before the clinic was transformed into one.

5. Still in widespread existence, in telesecundarias, instruction is transmitted through a classroom television by subject, and instructors are available to facilitate exercises and answer student questions (Ulloa and Potter 2008). Students received nationally broadcast lessons through the classroom television for approximately twenty minutes, after which the students completed subject lessons. Rather than teach the materials, instructors were responsible for assisting the students with their lessons, acting more as support to the national lessons than as main teachers. Upon completion of telesecundaria, students received a regular secundaria certificate (Levinson 2001: 36).

6. Escobar Latapi (2005), however, found that in some communities, school construction and infrastructure are insufficient to meet increased educational expectations.

7. Professor Mendoza would share with me that because the town secundaria was new, some parents may have thought that they were going to be asked for more things, including money, to help expand the school (Field Notes, 2006).

8. By law, tuition for public primaria and secundaria, otherwise known as *educación básica,* is free.

9. To convert Mexican pesos to U.S. dollars, I used Banco Mexico's conversion rate on July 16, 2006, on which day I was conducting fieldwork in San Pedro. The conversion rate on that day was 10.9 pesos to every U.S. dollar, which I rounded up to 11.

10. Households are eligible to receive PROGRESA/Oportunidades payments beginning the third year of primaria. In addition to monthly payments, households receive 175 pesos at the beginning of every school year for school supplies for students grades three to six in primaria and 90 pesos at the start of the second semester of the school year and 330 pesos per household for each student in secundaria (SEDESOL 2008). In preparatoria, payments for school supplies occur only once at the beginning of the school year and total 330 pesos.

11. For the 2008–2009 school year, primaria students enrolled in their third year received 130 pesos a month, reaching double, or 265 pesos a month, during grade six. At the level of secundaria, a student's gender was taken into account when determining the amount of payment. Due to the higher dropout rates of females than males, females received incrementally greater amounts of scholarship money than did males. In the first year of secundaria, households received 385 pesos for every male enrolled versus 405 pesos for every female enrolled. By the third year of secundaria, these amounts reached 430 pesos and 495 pesos, respectively. At the high school level, scholarship payments increased once more. During the first year of preparatoria, males received 645 pesos a month, while females received 745 pesos a month. By the third (last) year of preparatoria, males received 735 pesos a month, while females received 840 pesos a month (Behrman et al. 2011; Buenrostro 2011; SEDESOL 1998).

12. The Economic Commission for Latin America and the Caribbean (ECLAC) asserts that there are four points in the dropout pipeline: during primaria, at the end of primaria, during secundaria, and at the end of secundaria or above. Because different reasons characterized the youths' exits from the educational field at the end of secundaria and during high school, I distinguish between these two points.

13. City College, Continuing and Professional Studies, English as a Second Language, https://www.ccny.cuny.edu/cps/esl.

14. Only one youth discussed classes being free. In New York City, ESOL classes held at more than forty New York Public Library branches are advertised as free on their website: https://www.nypl.org/events/classes/english.

15. This is compared with 40 percent, 10 percent, and 21 percent of comparison groups in New York City public high schools. The New York City Department of Education defines a comparison group as "students from other schools across the city who were most similar to students in this school according to incoming test scores, disability statuses, economic need, and overage status. The comparison group percentage is an estimate of how the students at this school would have performed if they attended other schools throughout the city" (New York City Department of Education 2016b).

16. In 2016, comparison groups were 77 percent, 49 percent, and 57 percent, respectively (New York City Department of Education 2016a).

17. In 2016, comparison groups were 47 percent 19 percent and 34 percent, respectively (New York City Department of Education 2016b).

CHAPTER 5 FROM CAMPOS TO KITCHENS

1. For the youths who were under the age of fourteen, their entry into the labor market violated long-standing labor laws. Preceded by individual state laws, Article 123 of the Constitution of 1917 had, by the first half of the twentieth century, placed the minimum age for employment at twelve years of age, with dangerous work prohibited for youths under the age of sixteen. By 1962, federal labor law reforms increased the minimum age for work to the age of fourteen, with youth workers between the ages of fourteen and sixteen subject to special vigilance, including periodic medical checkups. In addition, youths under the age of sixteen were not allowed to work in establishments that sold alcohol on site for immediate consumption or that could negatively influence the youths' morality. Reinforcing prior legislation, the reforms of 1962 also prohibited employment in dangerous conditions, including underwater or in underground occupations such as mining, and in other employment that could stunt the youths' normal physical, mental, or emotional development. Total daily and weekly work hours were also reregulated, with youth under the age of sixteen prohibited from working (a) more than six hours a day (which included one hour of rest), (b) on Sundays, and (c) overtime (de Buen 1980). Perhaps most reflective of the minor status attributed to youths, especially those under the age of sixteen, the reforms also required that these youths obtain the written permission of their parents or legal guardians to work. Lax enforcement of these labor laws ensured that youth labor under the ages of twelve would continue; however, now it would be unofficial, unregulated, and without contracts. These regulations would remain law for an additional fifty years. Although occurring after the migration of the youths found in this book, it is imperative to note that Mexico's child labor laws were reformed in 2014, and the minimum age of employment was once again raised. Amendments to the Federal Work Law (Ley Federal de Trabajo) raised the age at which youths could begin to work legally from age fourteen to fifteen, with special restrictions prohibiting employment for most youths until age eighteen (Flores 2014; Martinez 2016a). The 2012 changes to educational laws raised the level of compulsory education to high school completion. One of the restrictions to legal employment of minors, the completion of basic education, effectively marginalizes the minimum age of fifteen and, in actuality, determines the age at which individuals without secundaria completion can begin work: age eighteen. In other words, although youths younger than age eighteen who did not complete secundaria may obtain special authorization from their parents or the *Junta de Conciliación y Arbitraje* (Secretariat of Labor and Social Welfare) to work, for most who cannot obtain these permissions, work should begin at completion of high school, or approximately age eighteen (Martinez 2016; Secretaria de Trabajo y Prevision Social 2015).

2. These figures, however, may underestimate the levels of child labor in Mexico. For one, Mexico's National Survey on Occupation and Employment only includes waged labor and not the more informal labor that many poor youths engage in, such as cleaning car windshields in the streets, performing in public spaces, or watching cars, all for tips. Additionally, companies such as Wal-Mart, *Gigante*, and *Comercial Mexicana* exploit a legal loophole in Mexican labor laws that allow youths to "volunteer" their labor for tips. While these companies "hire" minors for a variety of services, including bagging groceries, they do not provide them salaries or benefits; they only allow them to collect "gratuities," which in some cases can total more than twice the minimum wage (Aitken et al. 2006: 366; Contreras 2007). In 2007, approximately nineteen thousand youths ages fourteen to sixteen worked at Wal-Mart in this capacity, with many forced to work double shifts and without adequate training. As "volunteers," however, little could be done to sanction their North American employer (Contreras 2007).

3. With special attention to the years during which independent Mexican teenage migrants were coming of age, Cos Montiel (2000) points to globalization and its effects on Mexican agriculture as being one of the main reasons that youth labor plagues Mexico. Between 1980 and 1997, agricultural exports tripled, and with it, so did a demand for cheap, plentiful labor. As these agricultural exports have increased, several consequences surfaced. For one, the agricultural market transformed to meet export demands, thus requiring a larger (exploitative) labor pool. Second, in rural areas where families had previously relied on subsistence farming, poverty has increased and a greater demand for outside sources of income has also increased.

Lastly, more and more of the country's social services have become privatized, requiring individuals to shoulder more and more of the costs of basic services such as health and education, creating a further strain on poor families (Cos Montiel 2000). Despite a decline in numbers, at the turn of the twenty-first century, SEDESOL still estimated that just under a million youths were working in export farms, some of them as young as four years of age (Cos Montiel 2000; Marosi 2014; SEDESOL 1999). In 1999, approximately 374,000 youths between the ages of six and fourteen and 526,000 youths between the ages of fifteen and seventeen were working on farms. By 2014, 100,000 youths under the age of fourteen were illegally toiling in small and midsize farms, picking crops that, after a long series of transfers across distributors in Mexico and the United States, make it into U.S. kitchens (Marosi 2014; SEDESOL 1999). Woefully undereducated, these youths suffered from both illiteracy and low levels of schooling. Whereas 64 percent of the youths over the age of twelve had not completed primaria, 40 percent of those between the ages of six and fourteen did not know how to read or write (SEDESOL 1999). Considered in combination with high levels of malnutrition, chronic exposure to agrochemicals, and physical labors incommensurate with their abilities, these youths' low levels of education are setting them up for a lifetime of marginalization (Marosi 2014).

4. After several high-profile exposés of child labor, however, multinational companies such as Wal-Mart and Whole Foods, as well as the Mexican government, have made highly publicized announcements and joined the calls to end child labor, including *Tod@s contra trabajo infantil*, launched in 2016. Time will tell if these efforts, without addressing the root causes of child labor, will be successful.

5. New York City's economy is highly dependent on unauthorized workers. By 2006, approximately 374,000 undocumented people were employed by individuals and firms found in New York City. Mirroring national trends in types of employment, New York City's service industries employed the highest percentage of undocumented immigrants, with specific occupations filled by, in some cases, more than 50 percent undocumented workers. In 2007, for example, the restaurant industry hired more than 36 percent of all of the city's undocumented workers, with 54 percent of all dishwashers, 33 percent of all cooks, and 32 percent of all food preparation workers lacking legal status (Fiscal Policy Institute 2007). Without these workers, as former mayor Bloomberg stated, New York City's economy would simply collapse.

6. Federal and state laws shape the performance of child labor in the United States. Since 1938, the Federal Fair Labor Standards Act (FLSA) and, more recently, laws specific to New York State have regulated child labor performed in New York City (Levine 2003; New York State Department of Labor 2016; U.S. Government Accountability Office 2002). Establishing minimum child labor guidelines, the FLSA strictly limited the employment of youth under the age of eighteen from excessive work and labor in hazardous conditions, including construction, mining, and the operation of motor vehicles, and set minimum age requirements for work, with few exceptions, at age fourteen (Zelizer 1985). During the Reagan administration, the enforcement of the FLSA was weakened, funds for worksite inspectors were slashed, and particular restrictions on youth labor, including the assignment of housework, were repealed. These changes set the stage for the contemporary lax enforcement of federal child labor laws. New York State possesses more stringent regulations. Under the age of eighteen, employment that prevents or interferes with K–12 school attendance (occurring during school hours or after certain hours) is prohibited as well as work performed under hazardous physical and emotional conditions. Between the ages of fourteen and fifteen, minors cannot work more than eighteen hours a week during the school year and forty hours a week in the summer months. For youths ages sixteen and seventeen, the rules become more lax. During the school year, minors may work no more than twenty-eight hours a week, and if working between 6 a.m. and 10 p.m. or until midnight, they must produce both parental permission and certificates of good academic standing. During the summer months, only parental permission is needed. Lastly, seventeen occupations are deemed too dangerous for minors under the age of eighteen. Youths under the age of sixteen are prohibited from working in factories and/or in businesses where processing, such as dry cleaning, is done. Under eighteen years of age, youths cannot perform dangerous work, including construction work (New York State Department of Labor 2016). Independent Mexican teenage migrants were hired and required to work in violation of many of these laws, including the number of hours worked, work conditions, and so on.

7. Trends for unauthorized immigrants in New York City differ from national and other regional trends in terms of employment. At the national level, in 2014, the agricultural industry possessed the highest percentage of unauthorized immigrants, with 26 percent of farming occupations held by unauthorized immigrants (Passel and Cohn 2015).

8. Mirroring their adult counterparts, among Latina/o youths in New York City, Mexican youths exhibit the lowest rates of unemployment (Treschan and Mehotra 2013). Overall, Mexicans possess the highest rates of employment not only in the city but also in the country, surpassing employment rates for native-born New Yorkers and ten additional immigrant groups as well as national rates. In fact, in 2010, 97 percent of the working-age Mexican male population in New York City was employed (Semple 2010).

CHAPTER 6 BETWEEN BECOMING AND BEING ADULTS

1. "Borrowed from the United States," the introduction of secundaria would import northern educational philosophies into the Mexican educational system and introduce and/or intensify a particular Western "age" ideology in Mexico that, at the secundaria level, emphasized adolescence as a difficult stage with youths demonstrating increased independence and individualism (Levinson 2001; Mabry 1985).

2. Mayer (2003) distinguishes the life course from the life span. Whereas life course theory seeks to understand lives as a series of age-graded roles, opportunities, constraints, and events marked by the outcomes of "social structural forces and institutional regulation," life span theory frames lives as developing from birth to death due to genetic and behavioral adaptations over a period of time.

3. As discussed in chapter 2, it is the act of not only leaving one's home but also severing financial dependence on one's parents that separates independent Mexican teenage migrants from other groups, including "Americans" surveyed by Schoeni and Ross (2005). While youths in the United States may leave their parents homes, approximately 40 percent of all young adults continued to receive support for, among other items, living expenses into their late twenties, which is unheard of among these youths as teenage minors as well as many immigrant youths and young adults (Furstenberg et al. 2003; Rumbaut and Komaie 2010).

4. Several studies discuss a reversed flow of financial support from adult children of immigrants to their parents. Fuligni and Pedersen (2002) studied family obligation among twelfth graders in San Francisco and found that East Asian and Latin American youths, the majority of whom were first and second generation, did report living at home and providing financial assistance to their parents at higher percentages than other race/ethnicity youths. In addition, Borgen and Rumbaut (2011) found that San Diego participants from their CILS study who were already in their twenties and thirties also provided significant amounts of financial assistance to their parents. However, neither the amounts of assistance nor the youths' evaluations of this act as a marker of the transition to adulthood were discussed.

5. Rumbaut and Komaie (2010) note that Schoeni and Ross's (2005) findings may be largely based on a population that is predominantly of native parentage.

CHAPTER 7 CONCLUSION

1. It is important to note that this area is responsible for much of the United States' heroin supply. Half of Mexico's opium poppies, which provides 90 percent of the United States' heroin supply, originates in Guerrero (Partlow 2017).

2. Asylum is granted by proving that you possess a well-founded fear of persecution based on race, religion, nationality, political opinion, or membership in a visible social group. Youths or minors are not considered a particular "social group." As such, minors must meet the same requirements as adults petitioning for asylum. However, the application of refugee status must take age and gender into consideration and must consider the ways in which persecution could be experienced by minors (CGRS 2015).

3. DACA recipients met the following criteria: (a) must have arrived before the age of sixteen and be no older than thirty-one at the inception of the Executive Action (August 15, 2012); (b) must have lived in the United States continuously for the previous five years; (c) must attend high school or a GED program and/or possess a high school diploma or equivalency or be honorably discharged from the Coast Guard or armed services; (d) have not been convicted of a felony offense, a significant misdemeanor or three misdemeanors; and

(e) do not pose a threat to national security or public safety (Gonzales et al. 2014; National Immigration Law Center 2012).

4. Due to differences in state rules for juvenile court jurisdiction, youths may be deemed ineligible for the special findings order that is the necessary prerequisite to apply for SIJS. For example, in New York State, juvenile jurisdiction ends at age twenty-one; in Texas, it ends at age eighteen.

5. The American Hope Act of 2017 creates a three-step path to citizenship to the individuals who (a) entered the United States before the age of eighteen, (b) have been continuously present (have departed for more than 90 continuous or 180 cumulative days) since December 31, 2016, (c) pass a background check, and (d) have not been convicted of certain crimes or immigration violations. If individuals meet all criteria, they may be granted Conditional Permanent Resident Status (CPR) for eight years and then may apply for lawful permanent resident status after three years of CPR (United We Dream 2017).

6. As of April 2018, USCIS interpretation of SIJS has become more restrictive. Not only has USCIS been asking for more evidence in claims, but denial rates for applications of youths who were age eighteen or older at the time of application have increased (Alvarado 2018; Robbins 2018). Liz Robbins of the *New York Times* also reported that in New York City, some previously approved SIJ recipients are receiving notices of revocation. Citing the inability for state courts to grant "custody" after age eighteen, USCIS is effectively making the granting of SIJS conditional on demonstrated adult dependence. This fundamentally goes back to the question of who can be considered a "juvenile."

7. For example, I volunteered and taught English-as-a-second-language course in the basement of a Bronx Catholic Church for a local human rights organization from 2003 to 2005. I was never asked for credentials or proof of ESL training, nor was I provided with instruction or training to teach nonnative English speakers. While I taught, I was never asked for proof of student achievement, only enrollment numbers.

APPENDIX

1. In addition to unlawful entry into New York City, these youths are, to different degrees, circumventing guardianship, local school truancy, and child labor laws. Detection of just one of these violations could result in serious consequences for the youths.

2. During the first stage, I erroneously believed that fieldwork would be eased because I was kinfolk, or because I possessed familiarity based on ancestry and ethnic sameness. I soon found that a more appropriate understanding of my relationship with study participants was that of skinfolk and that only through sponsorship and continued, consistent interactions could the appropriate conditions for interviewing be established (Williams 1996).

REFERENCES

Aceves Avila, R. (2000). *El campo que nos tienen prometido . . . Notas para una nueva agenda para la organización económica del medio rural* (Estudios Agrarios Working Paper). Mexico City, D.F.: SEDATU (Secretaria de Desarrollo Agrario Territorial y Urbano) Procudaria Agraria. Retrieved from http://www.pa.gob.mx/publica/cd_estudios/Paginas/autores/aceves%20avila%20roberto%20el%20campo%20que%20nos%20tienen%20prometido.pdf.

Adato, M., and Hoddinott, J. (2007). *Conditional Cash Transfer Programs: A Magic Bullet for Reducing Poverty?* 2020 Vision Briefs BB17 [Special Edition]. International Food Policy Research Institute (IFPRI).

Aguila, M. T., and Torres B., M. E. (2009). History of Child Labor in Mexico. In H. D. Hindman (Ed.), *The World of Child Labor: A Historical and Regional Survey* (411–417). New York: Routledge.

Aguilera, M. B. (2003). The Impact of the Worker: How Social Capital and Human Capital Influence the Job Tenure of Formerly Undocumented Mexican Immigrants. *Sociological Inquiry, 73*(1), 52–83.

Aitken, S. C. (2001). Global Crises of Childhood: Rights, Justice and the Unchildlike Child. *Area, 33*(2), 119–127.

Aitken, S., Estrada, S. L., Jennings, J., and Aguirre, L. M. (2006). Reproducing Life and Labor: Global Processes and Working Children in Tijuana, Mexico. *Childhood, 13*(3), 365–387.

Alarcon-Gonzalez, D., and McKinley, T. (1999). The Adverse Effects of Structural Adjustment on Working Women in Mexico. *Latin American Perspectives, 26*(3), 103–117.

Alcala, L., Rogoff, B., Mejia-Arauz, R., Coppens, A. D., and Dexter, A. L. (2014). Children's Initiatives in Contributions to Family Work in Indigenous Heritage and Cosmopolitan Communities in Mexico. *Human Development, 57*(2–3), 96–115.

Alwin, D. F. (2012). Integrating Varieties of Life Course Concepts. *Journal of Gerontology, Series B, 67*(2), 206–220.

American Bar Association. (2016). A Humanitarian Call to Action: Unaccompanied Children in Removal Proceedings. *ABA Commission on Immigration.* Retrieved from https://www.americanbar.org/content/dam/aba/administrative/immigration/uacstatement.authcheckdam.pdf.

American Hope Act of 2017. H.R. 3591, 115th Congress, S1 (2017).

American Immigration Council. (2015, June). *A Guide to Children Arriving at the Border: Laws, Policies and Responses: Special Report.* Washington, D.C.: American Immigration Council.

American Medical Association. (2017). *AMA Adopts New Policies to Improve Health of Immigrants and Refugees.* Retrieved from https://www.ama-assn.org/ama-adopts-new-policies-improve-health-immigrants-and-refugees.

Andreas, P. (2000). *Border Games: Policing the US-Mexico Divide.* Ithaca: Cornell University Press.

Aries, P. (1962). *Centuries of Childhood: A Social History of Family Life.* New York: Vintage.

Arizpe, L. (1982). Relay Migration and the Survival of the Peasant Household. In H. I. Safa (Ed.), *Towards a Political Economy of Urbanization in Third World Countries* (19–46). London: Oxford University Press.

Arnett, J. (1997). Young People's Conceptions of the Transition to Adulthood. *Youth and Society, 29*(1), 3–23.

Arnett, J. (1999). Adolescent Storm and Stress, Reconsidered. *American Psychologist, 54*(5), 317–326.

Arnett, J. (2000). Emerging Adulthood: A Theory of Development from the Late Teens through the Twenties. *American Psychologist, 55*(5), 469–480.

Arnett, J. (2001). Conceptions of the Transition to Adulthood: Perspectives from Adolescence to Midlife. *Journal of Adult Development, 8*(2), 133–144.

Arnett, J. (2004). *Emerging Adulthood: The Winding Road from the Late Teens through the Twenties*. New York: Oxford University Press.

Arnett, J. (2006). Emerging Adulthood: Understanding the New Way of Coming of Age. In J. J. Arnett and J. L. Tanner (Eds.), *Emerging Adults in America: Coming of Age in the 21st Century* (3–19). Washington, D.C.: APA Books.

Arnett, J., and Taber, S. (1994). Adolescence Terminable and Interminable: When Does Adolescence End? *Journal of Youth and Adolescence, 23*(5), 517–537.

Ascencio, F. L. (2004). Migration Strategies from Urban Contexts: Labor Migration from Mexico City to the United States. *Migraciones Internacionales, 2*(3), 34–59.

Atkinson, W. (2016). *Beyond Bourdieu*. Malden, Mass.: Polity Press.

Bacallao, M. L., and Smokowski, P. R. (2007). The Costs of Getting Ahead: Mexican Family System Changes after Immigration. *Family Relations: Interdisciplinary Journal of Applied Family Science, 56*(1), 52–66.

Bacon, D. (2008). *Illegal People*. Boston, Mass.: Beacon Press.

Bailey, T. (1985). A Case Study of Immigrants in the Restaurant Industry. *Industrial Relations, 24*(2), 205–221.

Bailey, T., and Waldinger, R. (1991). Primary, Secondary and Enclave Labor Markets: A Training Systems Approach. *American Sociological Review, 56*(4), 432–445.

Bajack, F., and Merchant, N. (2017, July 25). Immigrants Wept, Pleaded for Water and Pounded on the Truck. *Associated Press*. Retrieved from https://www.apnews.com/cc2fe9b212b34619ab7777f2a4a830c9.

Ballinas, V. (2015, April 30). Senado establece en 15 anos la edad minima para trabajar. *La Jornada*. Retrieved from http://www.jornada.unam.mx/ultimas/2015/04/30/senado-establece-en-15-anos-la-edad-minima-para-trabajar-2825.html.

Basu, K., and Van, P. H. (1998). The Economics of Child Labor. *American Economic Review, 88*(3), 412–427.

Behrman, J. R., Parker, S. W., and Todd, P. E. (2011). Do Conditional Cash Transfers for Schooling Generate Lasting Benefits? *Journal of Human Resources, 46*(1), 93–122.

Belli, R. F., Stafford, F. P., and Alwin, D. F. (2009). *Calendar and Life Diary Methods in Life Course Research*. Los Angeles: Sage.

Belloni, M. C., and Carriero, R. (2008). Childhood: A Homogeneous Generational Group? *Comparative Social Research, 25*, 293–326.

Beoku-Betts, J. (1994). When Black Is Not Enough: Doing Field Research among Gullah. *NWSA Journal, 6*, 413–433.

Bergad, L. (2011a). *The Latino Population of New York City, 1990–2010*. Latino Data Project Report 44. New York: CLACS (Center for Latin American, Caribbean and Latino Studies).

Bergad, L. (2011b). *The Latino Population of New York City, 2009*. Latino Data Project Report 43. New York: CLACS (Center for Latin American, Caribbean and Latino Studies).

Bergad, L. (2013, May). *Demographic, Economic and Social Transformations in the Mexican-Origin Population of the New York City Metropolitan Area, 1990–2010*. Latino Data Project Report 49. New York: CLACS (Center for Latin American, Caribbean and Latino Studies).

Bernhardt, A., S. McGrath, and DeFilippis, J. (2007). *Unregulated Work in the Global City: Employment and Labor Law Violations in New York City*. New York: Brennan Center for Justice.

Bey, M. (2003). The Mexican Child: From Work with the Family to Paid Employment. *Childhood, 10*(3), 287–299.

Bhabha, J. (2014a). *Child Migration and Human Rights in a Global Age*. Princeton, N.J.: Princeton University Press.

Bhabha, J. (2014b). Introduction. In J. Bhabha (Ed.), *Human Rights and Adolescence* (1–22). Philadelphia: University of Pennsylvania Press.

Bhabha, J., and Young, W. (1999). Not Adults in Miniature: Unaccompanied Child Asylum Seekers and the New US Guidelines. *International Journal of Refugee Law, 11*(1), 84–125.

Bianet-Castellanos, M. (2007). Adolescent Migration to Cancun: Reconfiguring Maya Households and Gender Relations in Mexico's Yucatan Peninsula. *Frontiers: A Journal of Women Studies, 28*(3), 1–27.

Bianet-Castellanos, M. (2010). *A Return to Servitude: Mayan Migration and the Tourist Trade in Cancun*. Minneapolis: University of Minnesota Press.

Biemiller, L. (2010, May 27). University of Virginia Asks Court to Halt Attorney General's Demand for Documents. *Chronicle of Higher Education*. Retrieved from http://chronicle.com/article/U-of-Virginia-Asks-Court-to/65721/.

Bien, R. (2004). Nothing to Declare but Their Childhood: Reforming US Asylum Law to Declare the Rights of Children. *Journal of Law and Policy, 12*, 797–841.

Binder, M., and Scrogin, D. (1999). Labor Force Participation and Household Work of Urban Schoolchildren in Mexico: Characteristics and Consequences. *Economic Development and Cultural Change, 48*(1), 123–154.

Binford, L. (2003). Migración acelerada entre Puebla y los Estados Unidos. In E. M. Kan (Ed.), *Etnografía del Estado de Puebla* (58–67). Puebla, Mexico: Secretaría del Estado de Puebla.

Blake, J. (2012). Gang and Cartel Violence: A Reason to Grant Political Asylum from Mexico and Central America. *Yale Journal of International Law, 38*, 31–45.

Blank, S. (1998). Hearth and Home: The Living Arrangements of Mexican Immigrants and U.S.-Born Mexican Americans. *Sociological Forum, 13*(1), 35–59.

Blank, S., and Torrecilha, R. S. (1998). Understanding the Living Arrangements of Latino Immigrants: A Life Course Approach. *International Migration Review, 32*(1), 3–20.

Blecker, R. A., and Esquivel, G. (2013). Trade and the Development Gap. In P. Smith and A. Selee (Eds.), *Mexico and the United States: The Politics of Partnership* (83–110). Boulder, Colo.: Lynne Rienner.

Blum, A. S. (2009). *Domestic Economies: Family, Work and Welfare in Mexico City, 1880–1943*. Lincoln: University of Nebraska Press.

Blum, A. S. (2011). Speaking of Work and Family: Reciprocity, Child Labor and Social Reproduction, Mexico City, 1920–1940. *Hispanic American Historical Review, 91*(1), 63–95.

Blumen, I., Kogan, M., and McCarthy, P. (1955). *The Industrial Mobility of Labor as a Probability Process*. Ithaca: Cornell University Press.

Boehm, D. A. (2008). For My Children: Constructing Family and Navigating the State in the US-Mexico Transnation. *Anthropological Quarterly, 81*(4), 777–802.

Boehm, D. A. (2011). Here/Not Here: Contingent Citizenship and Transnational Mexican Children. In C. Coe, R. R. Reynolds, D. A. Boehm, J. M. Hess, and H. Rae-Espinoza (Eds.), *Everyday Ruptures: Children, Youth and Migration in a Global Perspective* (161–173). Nashville, Tenn.: Vanderbilt Press.

Boehm, D. A., Hess, J. M., Coe, C., Rae-Espinoza, H., and Reynolds, R. (2011). Introduction: Children, Youth and the Everyday Ruptures of Migration. In C. Coe, R. R. Reynolds, D. A. Boehm, J. M. Hess, and H. Rae-Espinoza (Eds.), *Everyday Ruptures: Children, Youth and Migration in a Global Perspective* (1–22). Nashville, Tenn.: Vanderbilt Press.

Borgen, L., and Rumbaut, R. G. (2011). Coming of Age in America's Finest City: Transitions to Adulthood among Children of Immigrants in San Diego. In M. Waters, P. J. Carr, M. J. Kefalas, and J. Holdaway (Eds.), *Coming of Age in America* (133–168). Berkeley: University of California Press.

Bourdieu, P. (1977a). *Algeria 1960*. Cambridge: Cambridge University Press.

Bourdieu, P. (1977b). *Outline of a Theory of Practice*. Cambridge: Cambridge University Press.

Bourdieu, P. (1983). The Field of Cultural Production, or The Economic World Reversed. *Poetics, 12* (4–5), 311–356.

Bourdieu, P. (1984). *Distinction: A Social Critique of Judgement and Taste*. Cambridge, Mass.: Harvard University Press.

Bourdieu, P. (1985). The Genesis of the Concepts Habitus and Field. *Sociocriticism*, 2(2), 11.

Bourdieu, P. (1986). The Forms of Capital. In J. Richardson (Ed.), *Handbook of Theory and Research for the Sociology of Education* (241–258). New York: Greenwood.

Bourdieu, P. (1990). *The Logic of Practice*. Oxford: Blackwell.

Bourdieu, P. (2000). *Pascalian Meditations*. Stanford, Calif.: Stanford University Press.

Bourdieu, P. (2002). Habitus. In J. Hillier and E. Rooksby (Eds.), *Habitus: A Sense of Place* (42–52), Burlington, Vt.: Ashgate.

Bourdieu, P., and Passeron, J. C. (1990). *Reproduction in Education, Society and Culture*. 2nd ed. Thousand Oaks, Calif.: Sage.

Bourdieu, P., and Wacquant, L. (1992). *An Invitation to Reflexive Sociology*. Chicago: University of Chicago Press.

Bowles, S., and Gintis, H. (1976). *Schooling in Capitalist America: Educational Reform and the Contradictions of Economic Life*. New York: Basic Books.

Boyden, J. (1997). Childhood and the Policymakers: A Comparative Perspective on the Globalization of Childhood. In A. James and J. Prout (Eds.), *Constructing and Reconstructing Childhood: Contemporary Issues in the Sociological Study of Childhood* (190–229). Bristol, Pa.: Falmer Press.

Brittain, C. (2002). *Transnational Messages: Experiences of Chinese and Mexican Immigrants in American Schools*. El Paso, Tex.: LFB Scholarly Publishing.

Brown, R. P. C., Carling, J., Fransen, S., and Siegel, M. (2014). Measuring Remittances through Surveys: Methodological and Conceptual Issues for Survey Designers and Data Analysts. *Demographic Research*, 31(41), 1243–1274.

Brownell, P. (2005, September 1). The Declining Enforcement of Employer Sanctions. *Migration Policy Institute*. Retrieved from http://www.migrationpolicy.org/article/declining-enforcement-employer-sanctions.

Bruckner, H., and Mayer, K. U. (2005). Destandardization of the Life Course: What It Might Mean and If It Means Anything, Whether It Actually Took Place. *Advances in Life Course Research*, 9, 27–53.

Buenrostro, A. M. (2011). Human Rights and Neoliberalism: An Uneasy Alliance for Protecting Children in Mexico. *Estudios Sociales, 19*(38), 10–36.

Burton, L. (1996). Age Norms, the Timing of Family Role Transitions, and Intergenerational Caregiving among Aging African American Women. *The Gerontologist, 36*, 199–208.

Burton, L., Allison, K., and Obeidallah, D. O. (1995). Social Context and Adolescence: Perspectives on Development among Inner-City African American Teens. In L. Crockett and A. Crouter (Eds.), *Pathways through Adolescence: Individual Development in Relation to Social Context* (119–138). Hillsdale, N.J.: Erlbaum.

Burton, L., Obeidallah, D. O., and Allison, K. (1996). Ethnographic Perspectives on Social Context and Adolescent Development among Inner-City African American Teens. In R. Jessor, A. Colby, and R. Schweder (Eds.), *Essays on Ethnography and Human Development* (395–418). Chicago: University of Chicago Press.

Bush, D. M., and Simmons, R. G. (1987). Gender and Coping with the Entry into Early Adolescence. In R. C. Barnett, L. Biener, and G. K. Baruch (Eds.), *Gender and Stress* (185–217). New York: Free Press.

Byrne, O., and Miller, E. (2012). *The Flow of Unaccompanied Children through the Immigration System: A Resource for Practitioners, Policymakers and Researchers.* New York: Center on Immigration and Justice, Vera Institute of Justice.

Capps, R., Fix, M., and Zong, J. (2017). *Issue Brief: The Education and Work Profiles of the DACA Population.* Migration Policy Institute. Retrieved from https://www.migrationpolicy.org/research/education-and-work-profiles-daca-population.

Carey, D., Jr. (2004). Mexico. In C. L. Schmitz, E. K. Traver, and D. Larson (Eds.), *Child Labor: A Global View* (123–142). Westport, Conn.: Greenview Press.

Carlsen, L. (2013, November 24). Under NAFTA, Mexico Suffered and the United States Felt Its Pain. *New York Times.* Retrieved from http://www.nytimes.com/roomfordebate/2013/11/24/what-weve-learned-from-nafta/under-nafta-mexico-suffered-and-the-united-states-felt-its-pain.

Carlsen, L. (2014, December 4). Mexico's Youth Under Siege. *CounterPunch.* Retrieved from https://www.counterpunch.org/2014/12/04/mexicos-youth-under-siege/.

Castañeda, E., and Buck, L. (2011). Remittances, Transnational Parenting and the Children Left Behind: Economic and Psychological Implications. *The Latin Americanist, 55*(4), 85–110.

Cavendish, B., and Cortazar, M. (2011). *Children at the Border. The Screening, Protection and Repatriation of Unaccompanied Mexican Minors.* Washington, D.C.: Appleseed Foundation. Retrieved from http://appleseednetwork.org/wp-content/uploads/2012/05/Children-At-The-Border1.pdf.

Center for Gender and Refugee Studies (CGRS). (2015). *Childhood and Migration in Central and North America: Causes, Policies, Practices and Challenges.* San Francisco: University of California Hastings College of the Law.

CEPAL. (2013). *Panorama Social de America Latina 2013.* Santiago, Chile: CEPAL. Retrieved from http://repositorio.cepal.org/bitstream/handle/11362/35904/S2013868_es.pdf?sequence=1.

Chavez, L. R. (1988). Settlers and Sojourners: The Case of Mexicans in the United States. *Human Organization, 47*(2), 95–108.

Chavez, L. R. (1992). *Shadowed Lives: Undocumented Immigrants in American Society.* New York: Holt, Rinehart and Winston.

Chavez, L., and Menjivar, C. (2010). Children without Borders: A Mapping of the Literature on Unaccompanied Migrant Children to the United States. *Migraciones Internacionales, 5*(3), 71–111.

Chen, J. (2014). An Urgent Need: Unaccompanied Children and Access to Counsel in Immigration Proceedings. *American Bar Association, Children's Rights Litigation.* Retrieved from https://www.americanbar.org/groups/litigation/committees/childrens-rights/articles/2014/urgent-need-unaccompanied-children-access-to-counsel-immigration-proceedings.html.

Chinn, S. E. (2009). *Inventing Modern Adolescence: The Children of Immigrants in Turn of the Century America.* Piscataway, N.J.: Rutgers University Press.

Chishti, M., and Hipsman, F. (2014). Dramatic Surge in the Arrival of Unaccompanied Children Has Deep Roots and No Simple Solutions. *Migration Policy Institute.* Retrieved from http://www.migrationpolicy.org/article/dramatic-surge-arrival-unaccompanied-children-has-deep-roots-and-no-simple-solutions.

Cisneros, R. G. (1997). El trabajo infantil y adolescente constancia socializadora y formadora en, para y por la vida. Master's thesis, Instituto Politecnico Naciónal, Distrito Federal.

Clausen, J. (1986). *The Life Course.* Englewood Cliffs, N.J.: Prentice Hall.

Clausen, J. (1991). Adolescent Competence and the Shaping of the Life Course. *American Journal of Sociology, 96,* 805–842.

Clausen, J. (1993). *American Lives.* New York: Free Press.

Cohen, J. H. (2001). Transnational Migration in Rural Oaxaca, Mexico: Dependency, Development and the Household. *American Anthropologist, 103*(4), 954–967.

Cohen, J. H. (2004). *The Culture of Migration in Southern Mexico.* Austin, Tex.: University of Texas Press.

Cole, J., and Durham, D. (2007). Introduction: Age, Regeneration and the Intimate Politics of Globalization. In J. Cole and D. Durham (Eds.), *Generations and Globalization: Youth Age and Family in the New World Economy* (1–28). Bloomington: Indiana University Press.

Coleman, J. S. (1990). *Foundations of Social Theory.* Cambridge, Mass.: Harvard University Press.

Comision Nacional de Derechos Humanos. (2017). *Informes especiales adolescentes: Vulnerabilidad y violencia.* Retrieved from http://www.cndh.org.mx/sites/all/doc/Informes/Especiales/Informe_adolescentes_20170118.pdf.

Comprehensive Development Initiative (CDI). (2017). *About Us.* Retrieved from https://www.cdi-ny.org/about-us.

CONAPO. (2010a). La situacion actual de los jovenes en Mexico. *Serie de documentos tecnicos.* Mexico City, D.F.: CONAPO. Retrieved from http://www.unfpa.org.mx/publicaciones/cuadro_3.pdf.

CONAPO. (2010b). *Indices de marginacion por entidad federativa y municipio 2010.* Distrito Federal: CONAPO. Retrieved from http://www.conapo.gob.mx/en/CONAPO/Indices_de_Marginacion_2010_por_entidad_federativa_y_municipio.

CONAPO. (2010c). *Indices de marginación urbana 2010.* Distrito Federal: CONAPO. Retrieved from http://www.conapo.gob.mx/es/CONAPO/Indice_de_marginacion_urbana_2010.

CONAPRED. (2010). *Documento Informativo sobre el trabajo infantil en México.* Distrito Federal: CONAPRED. Retrieved from https://www.conapred.org.mx/documentos_cedoc/DocumentoInformativo-TrabajoInfantil.pdf.

CONEVAL. (2006). *Reporta CONEVAL CIFRAS actualizadas de pobreza de ingresos 2006.* Retrieved from https://www.coneval.org.mx/rw/resource/coneval/prensa/988.pdf.

CONEVAL. (2013). *Informe de pobreza en Mexico, 2012.* Mexico City, D.F.: CONEVAL. Retrieved from http://www.coneval.org.mx/Informes/Pobreza/Informe%20de%20Pobreza%20en%20Mexico%202012/Informe%20de%20pobreza%20en%20M%C3%A9xico%202012_131025.pdf.

CONEVAL. (2014). *CONEVAL Informa los resultados de la medición de pobreza 2014*. Retrieved from https://www.coneval.org.mx/SalaPrensa/Documents/Comunicado005_Medicion_pobreza_2014.pdf.

CONEVAL. (2015). *CONEVAL Informa los resultados de la medicion de pobreza 2014*. Retrieved from https://www.coneval.org.mx/SalaPrensa/Documents/Comunicado005_Medicion_pobreza_2014.pdf.

Contreras, J. (2007, July 30). Unpaid Teens Bag Groceries for Wal-Mart. *Newsweek*. Retrieved from http://www.newsweek.com/unpaid-teens-bag-groceries-wal-mart-104021.

Coppens, A. D., Alcala, L., Mejia Arauz, R., and Rogoff, B. (2014). Children's Initiative in Family Household Work in Mexico. *Human Development, 57*(2–3), 116–130.

Corchado, A. (2014, August 29). For Some Cartels, Human Smuggling Has Taken Priority over Drugs. *Dallas Morning News*. Retrieved from http://www.dallasnews.com/news/nationworld/mexico/20140829-for-some-cartels-human-smuggling-has-taken-priority-over-drugs.ece.

Cornelius, W. (1976). *Mexican Migration to the United States: The View from Rural Sending Communities*. Cambridge, Mass.: MIT Center for International Studies.

Cornelius, W. (1982). Interviewing Undocumented Immigrants: Methodological Reflections Based on Fieldwork in Mexico and the United States. *International Migration Review, 16*(2), 378–411.

Cornelius, W. (1998). The Structural Embeddedness of Demand for Mexican Immigrant Labor: New Evidence from California. In M. Suárez-Orozco (Ed.), *Crossings: Mexican Immigration in Interdisciplinary Perspectives* (31–55). Cambridge, Mass.: Harvard University Press.

Cortina, R. (2003). Transnational Factors and School Success of Mexican Immigrants. In R. Cortina and M. Gendreau (Eds.), *Immigrants and Schooling: Mexicans in New York* (58–75). New York: Center for Migration Studies.

Cos Montiel, F. (2000). Sirviendo a las mesas del mundo: Las niñas y niños jornaleros agrícolas en México. In N. Del Lío (Ed.), *La infancia vulnerable de México en un mundo globalizado* (15–38). Mexico City, D.F.: UAM-UNICEF.

COTEIGEP. (2010a). *Fichas Municipales: Huaquechula: Comite Estatal de informacion estadistica y geografica del estado de Puebla*. Retrieved from http://www.coteigep.puebla.gob.mx/est231.php?muni=21069.

COTEIGEP. (2010b). *Fichas Municipales: Tianguismanalco: Comite Estatal de informacion estadistica y geografica del estado de Puebla*. Retrieved from http://www.coteigep.puebla.gob.mx/est231.php?muni=21175.

Cox, K. (1999). The Inevitability of Nimble Fingers? Law, Development and Child Labor. *Vanderbilt Journal of Transnational Law, 32*, 115–165.

Day, J. C., and Newberger, E. C. (2002). The Big Pay-Off: Educational Attainment and Synthetic Estimates of Work-Life Earnings. *Current Population Reports*. Washington, D.C.: Census.

De Buen, L. N. (1980). Child Labor in Mexico. *Comparative Labor Law and Policy Journal, 3*, 220–225.

De Buen Unna, C. (1996). El Trabajo de los menores y el derecho laboral. In Instituto de investigaciones jurídicas (Coords.), *Cuadernos: Memoria del coloquio multidisciplinario sobre menores, diagnosticos y propuestas* (137–149). Mexico City, D.F.: Instituto de investigaciones jurídicas-UNAM.

De Dios Palma, A. (2017, November 7). Amenazas en redes paralizan escuelas en Guerrero. *El Universal*. Retrieved from http://www.eluniversal.com.mx/estados/amenazas-en-redes-paralizan-escuelas-de-guerrero.

De Genova, N., and Ramos-Zayas, A. Y. (2003). *Latino Crossings: Mexicans, Puerto Ricans and the Politics of Race and Citizenship*. New York: Routledge.

Dehne, K. L., and Riedner, G. (2001). Adolescence—a Dynamic Concept. *Reproductive Health Matters, 9*(17), 11–15.

Delgado-Wise, R., and Cypher, J. M. (2007). The Strategic Role of Mexican Labor: Critical Perspectives on Current Economic Integration. *Annals of the American Academy of Political and Social Science, 610*(1), 119–142.

de Moya, C., Hernández, J. E., and Hernández Tapia, L. (2017, July 31). This Priest "Adopted" 27 Young People So They Don't Get Deported. *CityLab*. Retrieved from https://www.citylab.com/equity/2017/07/fabian-arias-deportation-churches-sanctuary-legal-guardianship/535002/.

Denzin, N. K. (1978). *Sociological Methods*. New York: McGraw Hill.

Desmond, M., and Lopez Turley, R. N. (2009). The Role of Familism in Explaining the Hispanic-White College Application Gap. *Social Problems, 56*(2), 311–334.

Dickson, C. (2014, July 9). How Mexican Cartels Are behind the Border Kid Crisis. *The Daily Beast*. Retrieved from http://www.thedailybeast.com/articles/2014/06/23/how-mexico-s-cartels-are-behind-the-border-kid-crisis.html.

Dinovitzer, R., Hagan, J., and Parker, P. (2003). Choice and Circumstance: Social Capital and Planful Competence in the Attainments of Immigrant Youth. *Canadian Journal of Sociology, 28*(4), 463–488.

Disare, M., and Wall, P. (2016, January 11). New York City's Graduation Rate Hits 70 Percent for the First Time. *Chalkbeat New York*. Retrieved from http://ny.chalkbeat.org/2016/01/11/new-york-citys-graduation-rate-hits-70-percent-for-first-time/#.Vw6zSTFWV1E.

Dobson, M. (2009). Unpacking Children in Migration Research. *Children's Geographies, 7*(3), 355–360.

Dominguez, M. A. (2006, December 19). Un migrante en cada hijo te dio, dicen habitantes de San Pedro Benito Juarez. *La Jornada del Oriente*. Retrieved from http://www.lajornadadeoriente.com.mx/2006/12/19/puebla/pue311.php.

Donato, K., and Bankston, C. (2008). The Origins for Employer Demand for Immigrants in a New Destination: The Salience of Soft Skills in a Volatile Economy. In D. Massey (Ed.), *New Faces in New Places: The Changing Geography of American Migration* (124–148). New York: Russell Sage Foundation.

Dornbusch, S. (1989). The Sociology of Adolescence. *Annual Review of Sociology, 15*, 233–259.

Dreby, J. (2010). *Divided by Borders: Mexican Migrants and Their Children*. Berkeley: University of California Press.

Dreby, J. (2015). *Everyday Illegal: When Policies Undermine Immigrant Families*. Berkeley: University of California Press.

Durand, J., and Massey, D. S. (1992). Mexican Migration to the United States: A Critical Review. *Latin American Research Review, 27*(2), 3–42.

Edmonds, E. V., and Pavcnik, N. (2005). Child Labor in the Global Economy. *Journal of Economic Perspectives, 19*(1), 199–220.

Elder, G. H., Jr. (1999). *Children of the Great Depression* (25th anniversary ed.). Boulder, Colo.: Westview Press.

Elder, G. H., Jr. (1994). Time, Human Agency and Change: Perspectives on the Life Course. *Social Psychology Quarterly, 57*(1), 4–15.

Elder, G. H., Jr. (1998, February). The Life Course as Developmental Theory. *Child Development, 69*(1), 1–12.

Elder, G. H., Jr., Johnson, M. K., and Crosnoe, R. (2003). The Emergence and Development of Life Course Theory. In J. T. Mortimer and M. J. Shanahan (Eds.), *Handbook of the Life Course* (3–19). Boston, Mass.: Springer.

El Diario de Mexico–New York. (2012, October 12). Diez Chavitos Migran Al Dia. *El Diario de Mexico-NY.*

El Universal. (2013, May 22). Jovenes de Huimilpan aspiran migrar al EU. *El Universal Queretaro.* Retrieved from http://m.eluniversalqueretaro.mx/politica/22-05-2013/jovenes-de-huimilpan-aspiran-migrar-eu.

Esteinou, R. (2005). La juventud y la construccion social de jovenes. In Facultad de Sciencias Sociales (Ed.), *Jovenes y niños, un enfoque sociodemografico* (25–37). Distrito Federal: UNAM.

Ewing, W. (2014, March). *The Growth of the U.S. Deportation Machine: More Immigrants Are Being Removed from the United States Than Ever Before* (Policy Brief). Washington, D.C.: Immigration Policy Center.

Executive Office of the President. (2017, October 23). Presidential Determination on Refugee Admissions for Fiscal Year 2018. *Federal Register,* 82, 203. Retrieved from https://www.govinfo.gov/content/pkg/FR-2017-10-23/pdf/2017-23140.pdf.

Falicov, C. J. (2005). Emotional Transnationalism and Family Identities. *Family Process,* 44(4), 399–406.

Farrow, C. (2007). *A Review of European Research Findings on Children in Migration.* Conference Report on Focus on Children in Migration, Warsaw, Poland.

Fernandez-Kelly, P. (1995). Social and Cultural Capital in the Urban Ghetto: Implications for the Economic Sociology of Immigration. In A. Portes (Ed.), *The Economic Sociology of Immigration* (213–247). New York: Russell Sage.

Fernandez-Kelly, P., and Massey, D. (2007). Borders for Whom: The Role of NAFTA in Mexico-US Migration. *Annals of the American Academy of Political and Social Science, 610*(1), 98–118.

Fiscal Policy Institute. (2007, November). *Working for a Better Life: A Profile of Immigrants in the New York State Economy.* New York: Fiscal Policy Institute.

Fiscal Policy Institute. (2010). *Across the Spectrum: The Wide-Range of Jobs That Immigrants Do.* New York: Fiscal Policy Institute. Retrieved from http://fiscalpolicy.org/FPI_ImmigrantsAndOccupationalDiversity.pdf.

Fitting, E. (2011). *The Struggle for Maize: Campesinos, Workers and Transgenic Corn in the Mexican Countryside.* Durham, N.C.: Duke University Press.

Flores, Y. G., Hinton, L., Barker, J. C., Franz, C. E., and Velasquez, A. (2009). Beyond Familism: A Case Study of the Ethics of Care of a Latina Caregiver of an Elderly Parent with Dementia. *Health Care for Women International,* 30(2), 1055–1072.

Flores, Z. (2014, April 3). San Lazaro aprueba elevar de 14 a 15 años edad minima de trabajo. *El Financiero.* Retrieved from http://www.elfinanciero.com.mx/economia/san-lazaro-aprueba-elevar-de-14-a-15-anos-edad-minima-de-trabajo-en-mexico.html.

Foo, L. J. (1994). The Vulnerable and Exploitable Immigrant Workforce and the Need for Strengthening Worker Protection Legislation. *Yale Law Journal, 103*(8), 2179–2212.

Foster, D., and Kramer, F. (1997, December 9). America's Secret World of Child Labor. *Associated Press.* Retrieved from http://pangaea.org/street_children/americas/AP1.htm.

Friedmann, J. (2002). Place-Making as Project? Habitus and Migration in Transnational Cities. In J. Hillsby and E. Rookier (Eds.), *Habitus: A Sense of Place* (299–316). Aldershot: Ashgate.

Fry, C. L. (2002). The Life Course as a Cultural Construct. In R. Settersten (Ed.), *Invitation to the Life Course: Toward New Understandings of Later Life* (269–294). Amityville, N.Y.: Baywood.

Fry, R. (2003). *Hispanic Youth Dropping out of U.S. Schools: Measuring the Challenge*. Washington, D.C.: Pew Hispanic Center.

Fry, R. (2005). *The Higher Dropout Rate of Foreign-Born Teens*. Washington, D.C.: Pew Research Center.

Fuchs, E. R., Warren, D., and Bayer, K. (2014). *Expanding Opportunity for Middle Class Jobs in New York City: Minority Youth Employment in the Building and Construction Trades*. New York: School of International Public Affairs, Columbia University.

Fuentes-Mayorga, N. (2011). Sorting Black and Brown Latino Workers in Gentrifying New York Neighborhoods. *Latino Studies, 9*(1), 106–125.

Fuligni, A. J., and Pedersen, S. (2002). Family Obligation and the Transition to Young Adulthood. *Developmental Psychology, 38*(5), 856–868.

Fuligni, A. J., Tseng, V., and Lam, M. (1999). Attitudes towards Family Obligations among American Adolescents with Asian, Latin American, and European Backgrounds. *Child Development, 70*(4), 1030–1044.

Furstenberg, F. F. (2000). The Sociology of Adolescence and Youth in the 1990s: A Critical Commentary. *Journal of Marriage and Family, 62*(4), 896–910.

Furstenberg, F. F. (2005). Banking on Social Capital: How Families Generate and Distribute Social Capital. *Journal of Marriage and Family, 67*, 809–821.

Furstenberg, F. F., and Hughes, M. E. (1995). Social Capital and Successful Development among at-Risk Youth. *Journal of Marriage and Family, 57*(3), 580–592.

Furstenberg, F. F., and Kaplan, S. B. (2004). Social Capital and the Family. *The Blackwell Companion to the Sociology of Families*. Retrieved from http://www.blackwellreference.com/public/tocnode?id=g9780631221586_chunk_g978063122158615.

Furstenberg, F. F., Kennedy, S., McCloyd, V. C., Rumbaut, R. G., and Settersten, R. A. (2003). *Between Adolescence and Adulthood: Expectations about the Timing of Adulthood* (The Network on the Transitions to Adulthood and Public Policy, Research Network Working Paper 1).

Fussell, E. (2004a). No Time For Youth: The Transition to Adulthood in Mexico, 1970–2000. Paper presented at the Population Association of America Annual Conference, Boston, MA, April 2004. Retrieved from https://paa2004.princeton.edu/papers/40510.

Fussell, E. (2004b). Sources of Mexico's Migration Stream: Rural, Urban and Border Migrants to the United States. *Social Forces, 82*(3), 937–967.

Fussell, E. (2005). Measuring the Early Adult Life Course in Mexico: An Application of the Entropy Index. The Structure of the Life Course: Standardized? Individualized? Differentiated? [Special issue]. *Advances in Life Course Research, 9*, 91–122.

Fussell, E., and Furstenberg, F. F. (2005). The Transition to Adulthood during the Twentieth Century: Race, Nativity and Gender. In R. Settersten, F. F. Furstenberg, and R. G. Rumbaut (Eds.), *On the Frontier of Adulthood: Theory, Research and Public Policy* (29–75). Chicago: University of Chicago Press.

Galli, C. (2017). A Rite of Reverse Passage: The Construction of Youth Migration in the US Asylum Process. *Ethnic and Racial Studies*. DOI: 10.1080/01419870.2017.1310389.

Galvez, A. (2010). *Guadalupe in New York: Devotion and the Struggle for Citizenship Rights among Mexican Immigrants*. New York: NYU Press.

Galvez, A. (2011). *Patient Citizens, Immigrant Mothers: Mexican Women, Public Prenatal Care and the Birth Weight Paradox*. New Brunswick, N.J.: Rutgers University Press.

Gandara, P., and Contreras, F. (2009). *The Latino Educational Crisis: The Consequences of Failed Social Policies*. Cambridge, Mass.: Harvard University Press.

Garabito Ballasteros, G. (2012). La Juventud en Mexico: Escenarios educativos y laborales. *Analisis Politico*. Condesa, D.F.: Friedrich Ebert Stiftung.

Garip, F., and Asad, A. L. (2016). Network Effects in Mexico-US Migration. *American Behavioral Scientist, 60*(10), 1168–1193.

Garvey, C. (1977). *Play*. Suffolk: Fontana.

Ghiselli, E. E. (1974). Some Perspectives for Industrial Psychology. *American Psychology, 29*(2), 80–87.

Giddens, A. (1993). *New Rules of Sociological Method*. Palo Alto, Calif.: Stanford University Press.

Giles, D., and Wijering, B. (2015). *New York State's Language Barrier*. New York: Center for an Urban Future.

Giorguli Saucedo, S. E. (2005). Deserción escolar, trabajo adolescente y trabajo materno en Mexico. In M. Mier y Teran and C. Rabell (Coords.), *Jovenes y niños, un enfoque demografico* (167–202). Mexico City, D.F.: Universidad Autonoma de México, FLACSO Mexico, Miguel Angel Porrua.

Giorguli Saucedo, S. E. (2006). School Dropout Rates, Adolescent Labor and Family Structures in Mexico. In J. L. Lezama and J. B. Morelos (Coords.), *Population, City and Environment in Contemporary Mexico* (223–258). Distrito Federal: El Colegio de México.

Giorguli Saucedo, S. E. (2011). Caminos Divergentes hacia la adultez en México. In G. Binstock and J. M. Viera (Coords.), *Nupcialidad y familia en America Latina actual* (123–163). Rio de Janiero: ALAP.

Gleeson, S. (2010). Labor Rights for All? The Role of Undocumented Immigrant Labor Status for Worker Claims-Making. *Law and Social Inquiry, 35*(3), 561–602.

Glick, J. E., Bean, F. D., and Van Hook, J. V. W. (1997). Immigration and Changing Patterns of Extended Family Household Structure in the United States: 1970–1990. *Journal of Marriage and Family, 59*(1), 177–191.

Glick-Schiller, N., Basch, L., and Szanton Blanc, C. (1992). Transnationalism: A New Analytic Framework for Understanding Migration. *Annals of the New York Academy of Science, 645*(1), 1–24.

Glick-Schiller, N., Basch, L., and Szanton Blanc, C. (1995). From Immigrant to Transmigrant: Theorizing Transnational Migration. *Anthropological Quarterly, 68*(1), 48–63.

Golbert, R. (2001). Transnational Orientations from Home: Constructions of Israel and Transnational Space among Ukrainian Jewish Youth. *Journal of Ethnic and Migration Studies, 27*(4), 713–731.

Goldscheider, F. K., and DaVanzo, J. (1985). Living Arrangements and Transitions to Adulthood. *Demography, 22*(4), 545–563.

Goldscheider, F. K., and Goldscheider, C. (1993). *Leaving Home before Marriage: Ethnicity, Familism, and Generational Relationships*. Madison: University of Wisconsin Press.

Gomberg-Muñoz, R. (2010). *Labor and Legality: An Ethnography of a Mexican Immigrant Network*. New York: Oxford University Press.

Gomez Cruz, M. A., and Rindermann, R. S. (2009). NAFTA's Impact on Mexican Agriculture: An Overview. In J. M. Rivera, S. Whiteford, and M. Chavez (Eds.), *NAFTA and the Campesinos: The Impact of NAFTA on Small-Scale Agricultural Producers in Mexico and the Prospects for Change* (1–20). Scranton, Pa.: University of Scranton Press.

Gonzales, R. (2011). Learning to be Illegal: Undocumented Youths and Shifting Legal Contexts in the Transition to Adulthood. *American Sociological Review, 76*(4), 602–619.

Gonzales, R. (2016). *Lives in Limbo: Undocumented and Coming of Age in America*. Berkeley: University of California Press.

Gonzales, R., and Rendon-Garcia, S. A. (2016). Understanding the Deferred Action for Childhood Arrivals (DACA) Impact on Young Adult's Well-Being. *American Psychological*

Association. Retrieved from http://www.apa.org/pi/families/resources/newsletter/2016/11/deferred-action.aspx.

Gonzales, R., Roth, B., Brant, K., Lee, J. and Valdivia, C. (2016). DACA at Year Three: Challenges and Opportunities in Accessing Higher Education and Employment. *American Immigration Council.* Retrieved from https://www.americanimmigrationcouncil.org/sites/default/files/research/daca_at_year_three.pdf.

Gonzales, R., Terriquez, V., and Ruszczyk, S. P. (2014). Becoming DACAmented: Assessing the Short-Term Benefits of Deferred Action for Childhood Arrivals. *American Behavioral Scientist, 58*(14), 1852–1872.

Gonzalez, G. (2001). The Ideology and Practice of Empire: The U.S., Mexico and the Education of Mexican Immigrants. *Cultural Logic, 4*(1), 1–9.

Gonzalez, S. (2017, March 8). What It Means That Trump Wants to Limit "Unaccompanied" Status for Minors Crossing the Border. *WNYC.* Retrieved from https://www.wnyc.org/story/unaccompanied-children-face-trump-proposals-immigration-protections/.

Gonzalez-Barrera, A. (2015, November 19). *More Mexicans Leaving Than Coming to the US.* Washington, D.C.: Pew Research Center. Retrieved from http://www.pewhispanic.org/2015/11/19/more-mexicans-leaving-than-coming-to-the-u-s/.

González-Rivera, C. (2016). *Building the Workforce of the Future.* New York: Center for an Urban Future.

Guarnizo, L. (1997). The Emergence of a Transnational Social Formation and the Mirage of Return Migration among Dominican Transmigrants. *Identities, 4*(2), 281–322.

Guarnizo, L. (2003). The Economics of Transnational Living. *International Migration Review, 37*(3), 666–699.

Gutek, G. L. (2006). *American Education in a Global Society: International and Comparative Perspectives,* Long Grove, IL: Waveland Press.

Guzman, B. G. (2007). Cambios en la division del trabajo familiar en Mexico. *Papeles de Población, 13*(53), 23–45.

Haase, C. M., Tomasik, M. J., and Silbereisen, R. K. (2008). Premature Behavioral Autonomy: Correlates in Late Adolescence and Young Adulthood. *European Psychologist, 13*(4), 255–266.

Haddal, C. (2007). *Unaccompanied Alien Children: Policies and Issues.* Washington, D.C.: Congressional Research Service Report for Congress.

Hafen, B. C., and Hafen, J. O. (1996). Abandoning Children to Their Autonomy: The United Nations Convention on the Rights of the Child. *Harvard International Law Journal, 37,* 449–465.

Hagestad, G. O., and Neugarten, B. (1985). Age and the Life Course. In R. H. Binstock and E. Shanas (Eds.), *Handbook of Aging and the Social Sciences* (2nd ed., 35–61). New York: Van Nostrand Reinhold.

Hall, G. S. (1904). *Adolescence: Its Psychology and Its Relation to Physiology, Anthropology and Sociology, Sex, Crime, Religion and Education* (Vols. 1 and 2). Englewood Cliffs, N.J.: Prentice Hall.

Halle, D., and Beveridge, A. A. (2013). New York and Los Angeles: The Uncertain Future. In D. Halle and A. A. Beveridge (Eds.), *New York and Los Angeles, the Uncertain Future* (1–32). New York: Oxford University Press.

Hamaji, K., and González-Rivera, C. (2016). *A City of Immigrant Workers: Building a Workforce Strategy to Support All New Yorkers.* New York: Center for an Urban Future.

Handel, M. J. (2003). Skills Mismatch in the Labor Market. *Annual Review of Sociology, 29,* 135–165.

Harris, E. A. (2016, January 11). New York City's Graduation Rates Top 70. *New York Times*. Retrieved from http://www.nytimes.com/2016/01/12/nyregion/new-york-citys-high-school-graduation-rate-tops-70.html?_r=0.

Hartnett, C. S., Furstenberg, F., Birditt, K., and Fingerman, K. (2013). Parental Assistance during Young Adulthood: Why Does Assistance Decline with Age? *Journal of Family Issues, 34*(7), 975–1007.

Hashim, I. (2006). *The Positives and Negatives of Independent Child Migration: Assessing the Evidence and the Debates* (Migration DRC Working Paper T16). Brighton: DRC University of Sussex. Retrieved from www.migrationdrc.org/workingpapers/WP-T16.pdf.

Heckathorn, D. D. (1997). Respondent-Driven Sampling: A New Approach to the Study of Hidden Populations. *Social Problems, 44*(2), 174–199.

Helper, S., Levine, D. I., and Woodruff, C. (2006). *How Does Economic Liberalization Affect Investment in Education?* Laboratory on International Law and Regulation, UCSD. San Diego: ILAR. Retrieved from http://ilar.ucsd.edu/assets/015/8804.pdf.

Hernandez, E. (2014, August 13). Abandonan Huimilpan 50 por ciento de jovenes. *AM de Queretaro*. Retrieved from http://amqueretaro.com/periodico-hoy/2014/08/13/abandonan-huimilpan-50-por-ciento-de-jovenes.

Hernandez, M. (2012, February 21). Migracion Afecta Cada Vez a Personas Mas Jovenes. *El Popular*. Retrieved from http://elpopular.mx/local/migracion-afecta-cada-vez-a-personas-mas-jovenes/.

Hernandez Chavez, A. (2006). *Mexico: A Brief History*. Los Angeles: University of California Press.

Hilliard, T. (2012). *Bad English*. New York: Center for an Urban Future.

Hilliard, T., and Dann-Messier, B. (2015). *Boosting Adult Education in New York*. New York: Center for an Urban Future.

Hirschfeld, L. (2002). Why Don't Anthropologists Like Children? *American Anthropologist, 104*(2), 611–627.

Hirschman, C. (2001). The Educational Enrollment of Immigrant Youth: A Test of the Segmented Assimilation Hypothesis. *Demography, 38*(3), 317–336.

Hogan, D. P. (1978). The Variable Order of Events in the Life Course. *American Sociological Review, 43*, 573–586.

Hogan, D. P., and N. M. Astone. (1986). The Transition to Adulthood. *Annual Review of Sociology, 12*, 109–130.

Holzer, H. (1996). *What Employers Want: Job Prospects for Less-Educated Workers*. New York: Russell Sage Foundation.

Human Rights First. (2017, May). Crossing the Line: US Border Agents Illegally Reject Asylum Seekers. Retrieved from https://www.humanrightsfirst.org/sites/default/files/hrf-crossing-the-line-report.pdf.

Human Rights Watch. (2014, May 13). *Tobacco's Hidden Children: Hazardous Child Labor in the United States Tobacco Farming*. Retrieved from https://www.hrw.org/report/2014/05/13/tobaccos-hidden-children/hazardous-child-labor-united-states-tobacco-farming.

Immigrant Legal Resource Center. (2017, July). *Unaccompanied Minors and New Executive Orders*. Retrieved from https://www.ilrc.org/sites/default/files/resources/uacs_under_trump_administration_final_3.21.17.pdf.

INEA. (2010). *Acciones y Programas: Nuestra Institución*. Retrieved from https://www.gob.mx/inea/acciones-y-programas/nuestra-institucion-57139.

INEE. (2009). *Panorama Educativo de Mexico 2009*. Retrieved from http://www.inee.edu.mx/Anexo_Electronico/PDF_final.pdf.

INEE. (2011). *La educacion media superior en Mexico*. Retrieved from http://publicaciones.inee.edu.mx/buscadorPub/P1/D/235/P1D235.pdf.

INEGI. (2000). *Estados Unidos Mexicanos XII Censo General de Población y Vivienda 2000. Tabuladas de la muestra censal cuestionario ampliado*. Mexico City, D.F.: INEGI. Retrieved from http://internet.contenidos.inegi.org.mx/contenidos/productos//prod_serv/contenidos/espanol/bvinegi/productos/censos/poblacion/2000/archivospdf/oportuno.pdf.

INEGI. (2004). *El Trabajo Infantil de México 1995–2002*. Aguascalientes: INEGI.

INEGI. (2005). *Encuesta nacional de ocupacion y empleo 2005: Una nueva encuesta para Mexico*. Distrito Federal: INEGI.

Internationals Network for Public Schools (INPS). (2017). *School Models*. Retrieved from http://internationalsnps.org/school-support-services/school-models/.

International Organization of Migration (IOM). (2016). *Global Migration Trends Factsheet 2015*. Retrieved from http://publications.iom.int/system/files/global_migration_trends_2015_factsheet.pdf.

Ixel Gonzalez, M. L. (2013, July 29). En Mexico viven 53.3 millones de pobres, revela CONEVAL. *El Universal*. Retrieved from http://archivo.eluniversal.com.mx/finanzas-cartera/2013/pobreza-coneval-personas-939000.html.

Izcara-Palacios, S. P. (2012). Violencia contra inmigrantes en Tamaulipas. *European Review of Latin American and Caribbean Studies (CEDLA), 93*, 3–24.

Jackson, P. B., and Berkowitz, A. (2005). The Structure of the Life Course: Gender and Racioethnic Variation in the Occurrence and Sequencing of Life Course Transitions. The Structure of the Life Course: Standardized? Individualized? Differentiated? [Special issue]. *Advances in Life Course Research, 9*, 55–90.

Jarvie, J. (2017, July 23). Ruthless Human Smugglers Blamed for Deaths of 9 People Left in a Truck in 100 Degree Texas Heat. *Los Angeles Times*. Retrieved from http://www.latimes.com/nation/nationnow/la-na-texas-trailer-20170723-story.html.

Jaschik, S. (2010, August 3). Another Subpoena for Research. *Inside Higher Education*. Retrieved from https://www.insidehighered.com/news/2010/08/13/arizona.

Jennings, J., Aitken, S., Lopez Estrada, S., and Fernandez, A. (2006). Learning and Earning: Relational Scales of Children's Work. *Area, 38*(3), 231–239.

Jimenez, M. (2009, October 1). *Humanitarian Crisis: Migrant Deaths at the U.S.-Mexico Border*. San Diego: ACLU.

Juarez, F., LeGrand, T., Lloyd, C. B., Singh, S., and Hertrich, V. (2013). Youth Migration and Transitions to Adulthood in Developing Countries. *Annals of the American Academy of Political and Social Science, 648*(1), 6–15.

Kallick, D. D. (2013). Immigration and Economic Growth in New York City. In N. Foner (Ed.), *One out of Three: Immigrant New York in the Twenty First Century* (64–89). New York: Columbia University Press.

Kanaiaupuni, S. M. (2000). Reframing the Migration Question: An Analysis of Men, Women and Gender in Mexico. *Social Forces, 78*(4), 1311–1347.

Kandel, W. A. (2017). *Unaccompanied Alien Children: An Overview*. Washington, D.C.: Congressional Research Service. Retrieved from: https://fas.org/sgp/crs/homesec/R43599.pdf.

Kandel, W. A., and Massey, D. (2002). The Culture of Mexican Migration: A Theoretical and Empirical Analysis. *Social Forces, 80*, 981–1004.

Karimi, F., Sutton, J. and Yan, H. (2017, July 24). 9 People Dead after Sweltering Tractor Trailer Found at San Antonio Walmart. *CNN*. Retrieved from https://www.cnn.com/2017/07/23/us/san-antonio-bodies-found-in-trailer/index.html.

Karjanen, D. J. (2008). Gender, Race and Nation in the Making of Mexican Migrant Labor in the United States. *Latin American Perspectives, 35*(1), 51–63.

Kasinitz, P., Mollenkopf, J. H., and Waters, M. C. (2004). *Becoming New Yorkers: Ethnographies of the Second Generation*. New York: Russell Sage Foundation.

Kasinitz, P., Mollenkopf, J. H., Waters, M. C., and Holdaway, J. (2008). *Inheriting the City: The Children of Immigrants Come of Age*. New York: Russell Sage Foundation.

Katz, C. (2004). *Growing Up Global: Economic Restructuring and Children's Everyday Lives*. Minneapolis: University of Minnesota Press.

Katz, M. S. (1976). *A History of Compulsory Education Laws*. Bloomington, Ind.: Phi Delta Kappa. Retrieved from http://files.eric.ed.gov/fulltext/ED119389.pdf.

Kawabata, M., and Gastaldo, D. (2015). The Less Said, the Better: Interpreting Silence in Qualitative Research. *International Journal of Qualitative Methods, 14*, 4.

Kelly, J. (2017, February 20). Implementing the President's Border Security and Immigration Enforcement Improvements Policies. *U.S. Department of Homeland Security*. Retrieved from https://www.dhs.gov/sites/default/files/publications/17_0220_S1_Implementing-the-Presidents-Border-Security-Immigration-Enforcement-Improvement-Policies.pdf.

Kelly, T. J. (2001). Neoliberal Reforms and Rural Poverty. *Latin American Perspectives, 28*(3), 84–103.

Kim, D. Y. (1999). Beyond Co-ethnic Solidarity: Mexican and Ecuadorean Employment in Korean-Owned Businesses in New York City. *Ethnic and Racial Studies, 22*(3), 581–605.

Kitossa, T. (2012). Habitus and Rethinking the Discourse of Youth Gangs, Crime, Violence and Urban Communities. In C. Richardson and H. A. Skott-Myhre (Eds.), *Habitus of the Hood* (121–142). Chicago: Intellect Press.

Krauze, E. (2006, November 24). What's at Stake in Mexico City. *Washington Post*. Retrieved from http://www.washingtonpost.com/wp-dyn/content/article/2006/11/24/AR2006112401097.html.

Krogstad, J. M. (2017). DACA Has Shielded Nearly 790, 000 Young Unauthorized Immigrants from Deportation. *Pew Research Center*. Retrieved from http://www.pewresearch.org/fact-tank/2017/09/01/unauthorized-immigrants-covered-by-daca-face-uncertain-future/.

Krogstad, J. M., and Gonzalez-Ibarra, A. (2014). *Number of Latino Children Caught Trying to Enter into the United States Nearly Doubles in Less Than a Year*. Washington, D.C.: Pew Research Center. http://www.pewresearch.org/fact-tank/2014/06/10/number-of-latino-children-caught-trying-to-enter-u-s-nearly-doubles-in-less-than-a-year/.

Kugel, S. (2004, February 15). Urban Tactics: Destination Neza York. *New York Times*. Retrieved from https://www.nytimes.com/2004/02/15/nyregion/urban-tactics-destination-neza-york.html.

Kuznesof, E. A. (2005). The House, the Street, Global Society: Latin American Families and Childhood in the 21st Century. *Journal of Social History, 38*(4), 859–872.

LaGuardia Community College. (2016). *New York City Welcome Back Center*. Retrieved from https://www.laguardia.edu/nycwbc/.

La Jornada. (2017, April 30). *Niñez? Tan malo el future como el presente?* Retrieved from http://www.jornada.com.mx/2017/04/30/edito.

Langton, C. E., and Berger, L. M. (2011). Family Structure and Adolescent Physical Health, Behavior, and Emotional Well-Being. *Social Service Review, 85*(3), 323–357.

Lareau, A. (2000). *Home Advantage: Social Class and Parental Intervention in Elementary Education.* Lanham, Md.: Rowman and Littlefield.

Lareau, A. (2003). *Unequal Childhoods: Class, Race and Family Life.* Berkeley: University of California Press.

Latapi, A. E., and de la Rocha, M. G. (2002). The Restructuring of Labor Markets, International Migration and Household Economies in Urban Mexico. In J. Chase (Ed.), *Spaces of Neoliberalism* (187–212). Bloomfield, Conn.: Kumarian Press.

Latapi, A. E., and de la Rocha, M. G. (2005). *Evaluacion externa del impacto del programa Oportunidades 2004.* Mexico City, D.F.: Instituto Nacional de Salud Publica.

Latapi, A. E., and Janssen, E. (2006). *Migration, the Diaspora and Development: The Case of Mexico.* Discussion Paper, International Institute for Labour Studies, Geneva Switzerland.

Latapi Sarre, P. (2005). *La SEP por dentro: Las politicas de la secretaria de la educacion publica.* Mexico City, D.F.: Fondo de Cultura Económica.

LeCompte, M. D., and Goetz, J. P. (Spring 1982). Problems of Reliability and Validity in Ethnographic Research. *Review of Educational Research, 52* (1), 31–60.

LeCompte, M. D., and Schensul, J. (1999). *Designing and Conducting Ethnographic Research: An Introduction.* Lanham, Md.: Alta Mira Press.

Lee, A. E. (2008). "Para salir adelante": The Emergence and Acceleration of International Migration in New Sending Areas of Puebla, Mexico. *Journal of Latin American and Caribbean Anthropology, 13*(1), 48–78.

Lee, J., and Zhou, M. (2014). The Success Frame and Achievement Paradox: The Costs and Consequences for Asian Americans. *Race and Social Problems, 6*(1), 38–55.

Leira, A., and Saraceno, C. (2008). Childhood: Changing Contexts. In A. Leira and C. Saraceno (Eds.), *Childhood: Changing Contexts,* Comparative Social Research Series, 25 (1–24).

Leonard, M. (2005). Children, Childhood and Social Capital: Exploring the Links. *Sociology,* 39(4), 605–622.

Levine, M. J. (2003). *Children for Hire: The Perils of Child Labor.* Westport, Conn.: Praeger.

Levinson, B. A. (1999). "Una etapa siempre dificil": Concepts of Adolescence and Secondary Education in Mexico. *Comparative Education Review,* 43(2), 129–161.

Levinson, B. A. (2001). *We Are All Equal: Student Culture and Identity at a Mexican Secondary School, 1988–1998.* Durham, N.C.: Duke University Press.

Levitt, P. (1998). Social Remittances: Migration-Driven Local Level Forms of Cultural Diffusion. *International Migration Review,* 32(4), 926–948.

Levitt, P. (2001). *The Transnational Villagers.* Berkeley: University of California Press.

Levitt, P., and Glick-Schiller, N. (2004, September). Conceptualizing Simultaneity: A Transnational Social Field Perspective on Society. *International Migration Review 38,* 1002–1039.

Lewis, J. (2002). Agrarian Change and the Privatization of Ejido Land in Northern Mexico. *Journal of Agrarian Change,* 2(3), 402–420.

Lewis, O. (1951). *Life in a Mexican Village: Tepotztlan Restudied.* Urbana: University of Illinois Press.

Ley Federal de Trabajo. (2015, June 12). Decreto de 30 de abril de 2015, por el que se reforman y derogan diversas disposiciones de la Ley Federal del Trabajo, en materia de trabajo de menores.

Ley General de Educacion. (2013, 13 July). Diario Oficial de la Federación, México: Cámara de Diputados de H. Congreso de la Unión. Retrieved from http://www.diputados.gob.mx/LeyesBiblio/ref/lge/LGE_orig_13jul93_ima.pdf.

Lin, N. (2001). *Social Capital: A Theory of Social Structure and Action.* Cambridge: Cambridge University Press.

Lincoln, Y. S., and Guba, E. G. (1985). *Naturalistic Inquiry*. Newbury Park, Calif.: Sage.

Lopez, C. (2013, June 20). Mas ninas y adolescents oaxaquenas emigrant solas a EU. *Cimacnoticias*. Retrieved from http://www.cimacnoticias.com.mx/node/63624.

Lopez, S. L. (2010). The Remittance House: Architecture of Migration in Rural Mexico. *Buildings and Landscapes: Journal of the Vernacular Architecture Form, 17*(2), 33–52.

Los Tigres del Norte. (1984). *Jaula de Oro*. Fonovisa MPCD5044, compact disc.

Louie, V. (2004). *Compelled to Excel: Immigration, Education and Opportunity among Chinese Americans*. Stanford, Calif.: Stanford University Press.

Lukes, M. (2015). *Latino Immigrant Youth and Interrupted Schooling: Dropouts, Dreamers and Alternative Pathways to College*. Buffalo: Multilingual Matters.

Mabry, D. J. (1985). Twentieth Century Mexican Education: A Review. *History of Education Quarterly, 25*, 221–226.

Macias, J. (1990). Scholastic Antecedents of Immigrant Students: Schooling in a Mexican Immigrant Sending Community. *Anthropology and Education Quarterly, 21*(4), 291–318.

MacLeod, J. (1995). *Ain't No Makin' It: Aspirations and Attainment in a Low Income Neighborhood* (2nd ed.). Boulder, Colo.: Westview Press.

Macmillan, R. (2005). The Structure of the Life Course: Classic Issues and Current Controversies. *Advances in Life Course Research, 9*, 3–24.

Macmillan, R., and Copher, R. (2005). Families in the Life Course: Interdependency of Roles, Role Configurations and Pathways. *Journal of Marriage and Family, 67*(4), 858–879.

Magaña-Salgado, J. (2017). *Policy Report: Fair Treatment Denied: The Trump Administration's Troubling Attempt to Expand Fast-Track Deportations*. San Francisco: Immigrant Legal Resource Center. Retrieved from https://www.ilrc.org/sites/default/files/resources/2017-0605_ilrc_report_fair_treatment_denied_final.pdf.

Magazine, R., and Ramirez Sanchez, M. A. (2007). Continuity and Change in San Pedro Tlalcuapan, Mexico: Childhood, Social Reproduction and Transnational Migration. In J. Cole and D. Durham (Eds.), *Generations and Globalization: Youth Age and Family in the New World Economy* (52–73). Bloomington: Indiana University Press.

Maira, S., and Soep, E. (2005). Introduction. In S. Maira and E. Soep (Eds.), *Youthscapes: The Popular, the National and the Global* (xv–xxxv). Philadelphia: University of Pennsylvania Press.

Malkin, E. (2009, June 1). Money Sent Home by Mexican Workers in U.S. Falls Sharply. *New York Times*. Retrieved from http://www.nytimes.com/2009/06/02/world/americas/02mexico.html?_r=0.

Malkin, V. (2004). We Go to Get Ahead: Gender and Status in Two Mexican Migrant Communities. *Latin American Perspectives, 31*(5), 75–99.

Manhattan Comprehensive Night and Day High School (MCNDHS). (2018). Who We Are. https://www.mcndhs.com/admissions.

Manjarrez Rosas, J. (2008). "Migración y cambios en las relaciones de genero: Un análisis circuito transnacional del San Juan Huiluco (Puebla)–New York." PhD diss., Benemérita Universidad Autonoma de Puebla.

Marini, M. M. (1984a). Age and Sequencing Norms in the Transition to Adulthood. *Social Forces, 63*(1), 229–244.

Marini, M. M. (1984b). The Order of Events in the Transition to Adulthood. *Sociology of Education, 57*(2), 63–84.

Marini, M. M. (1985). Determinants of the Timing of Adult Role Entry. *Social Science Research, 14*, 309–350.

Marini, M. M., and Chan, W., and Raymond, J. (1987). Consequences of the Process of Transition to Adulthood for Adult Economic Well-Being. *Sociology of Education and Socialization, 7*, 87–127.

Marosi, R. (2014, December 14). In Mexico's Fields, Children Toil to Harvest Crops That Make It to American Tables. *Los Angeles Times*. Retrieved from http://graphics.latimes.com/product-of-mexico-children/.

Marroni, M. G. (2003). Indigenas del Valle de Atlixco en Nueva York: Una migración internacional reciente. In E. Masferrer (Ed.), *Etnografia del Estado de Puebla* (204–212). Puebla, Mexico: Secretaría del Estado de Puebla.

Marroni, M. G. (2007). De Atlixco a Pueblayork: La migración internacional reciente y las transformaciones del campesinado. In M. A. Castillo and A. Santibanez (Coords.), *Nuevas tendencias y nuevos desafios de la migración internacional: Memorias del Seminario Permanente sobre migración internacional* (223–254). Tijuana: El Colegio de la Frontera Norte.

Marroni, M. G. (2008). Del Rebozo a la Carreola: Las Mujeres Migrantes Poblanas en Nueva York. In M. L. Rivermar Perez and B. L. Cordero Diaz (Coords.), *El Norte como destino: Circuitos migratorios Puebla–Estados Unidos* (155–186). Puebla: BUAP-Fomento Editorial.

Marroni, M. G. (2009). *Fronteras Perversa, Familias Fracturadas: Los indocumentados mexicanos y el sueño Americano*. Puebla, Mexico: BUAP.

Marroni, M. G., and Meneses, G. A. (2006). El fin del sueno Americano: Mujeres migrantes muertas en la frontera Mexico–Estados Unidos. *Migraciones Internacionales, 3*(3), 5–30.

Martin, A. J., and Steinbeck, K. (2017). The Role of Puberty in Students' Academic Motivation and Achievement. *Learning and Individual Differences, 53*, 37–46.

Martinez, I. (2006). Field Notes.

Martinez, I. (2016a). Supporting Two Households: Unaccompanied Mexican Minors and Their Absences from U.S. Schools. *Journal of Latinos and Education, 15*(3), 229–243.

Martinez, I. (2016b). Crime and the US-Mexico Border. In J. L. Morín (Ed.), *Latinos and Criminal Justice: An Encyclopedia* (158–181). Santa Barbara, Calif.: Greenwood.

Martinez, I. (2016c). Miseducating Latina Researchers: Challenges and Consequences in the Field. *Latino Studies, 14*(4), 533–544.

Martinez, M. P. (2015, July 21). La edad minima para trabajar en Mexico es de 18 años: Canacintra. *El Economista*. Retrieved from http://eleconomista.com.mx/industrias/2015/07/21/edad-minima-trabajar-mexico-18-anos-canacintra.

Massey, D. (2007). *Categorically Unequal: The American Stratification System*. New York: Russell Sage Foundation.

Massey, D. (2012a). *The New Latino Underclass: Immigration Enforcement as a Race-Making Institution*. Stanford, Calif.: Stanford Center on Poverty and Inequality. Retrieved from http://inequality.stanford.edu/_media/working_papers/massey_new-latino-underclass.pdf.

Massey, D. (2012b). Unintended Consequences of US Immigration Policy: Explaining the Post 1965 Surge from Latin America. *Population and Development Review, 38*(1), 1–29.

Massey, D., and Denton, N. (1993). *American Apartheid*. Boston, Mass.: Harvard University Press.

Massey, D., and Espinosa, K. (1997). What's Driving Mexico-US Migration? A Theoretical, Empirical, and Policy Analysis. *American Journal of Sociology, 102*(4), 939–999.

Massey, D., and Parrado, E. (1994). Migradollars: The Remittances and Savings of Mexican Migrants to the USA. *Population Research and Policy Review, 13*(1), 3–30.

Massey, D., and Pren, K. A. (2012). Origins of the New Latino Underclass. *Race and Social Problems, 4*(1), 5–17.

Mayer, K. U. (1986). Structural Constraints on the Life Course. *Human Development, 29*, 163–170.

Mayer, K. U. (2003). The Sociology of the Life Course and Lifespan Psychology: Diverging or Converging Pathways? In U. Staudinger and U. E. R. Lindenberger (Eds.), *Understanding Human Development: Dialogues with Lifespan Psychology* (463–482). New York: Kluwer Academic.

Mayer, K. U., and Schoepflin, U. (1989). The State and the Life Course. *Annual Review of Sociology, 15*, 187–209.

McDonald, S., and Mair, C. A. (2010). Social Capital across the Life Course: Age and Gendered Patterns of Network Resources. *Sociological Forum, 25*, 335–359.

McGeehan, P. (2016, April 1). New York's Path to $15 Minimum Wage: Uneven and Bumpy. *New York Times*. Retrieved from https://www.nytimes.com/2016/04/02/nyregion/new-yorks-path-to-15-minimum-wage-uneven-and-bumpy.html.

McKinley, J. C. (2008, February 1). Mexican Farmers Protest End of Corn Import Tax. *New York Times*. Retrieved from http://www.nytimes.com/2008/02/01/world/americas/01mexico.html?_r=0.

McLaughlin, C. (2017). They Don't Look like Children: Child Asylum-Seekers, the Dubs Amendment and the Politics of Childhood. *Journal of Ethnic and Migration Studies*. DOI: 10.1080/1369183X.2017.1417027.

Mejia, I. (2017). Lloran en ataud de migrante muerto en trailer de Texas. *El Universal*. Retrieved from http://www.eluniversal.com.mx/articulo/estados/2017/08/5/lloran-en-ataud-de-migrante-muerto-en-trailer-de-texas.

Melendez, C. R. P. (2015, May 19). Trabajo Infantil, rescoldos de la pobreza. *Cimacnoticias*. Retrieved from http://www.cimacnoticias.com.mx/node/69682.

Mendelson, E. G., Liebmann, T. S., and Advisory Council on Immigration Issues in Family Court. (2017). Advisory Council on Immigration Issues in Family Court Memorandum 1. *Immigrant Defense Project*. Retrieved from https://www.immigrantdefenseproject.org/wp-content/uploads/AdvCouncil-guardianshi-fingerprintSIJmemo-Final-142017.pdf.

Meneses Morales, E. (1988). *Tendencias educativas oficiales en Mexico, 1934–1964*. Distrito Federal: Centro de Estudios Educativos.

Meyer, J. W. (1986). The Institutionalization of the Life Course and Its Effects on the Self. In A. B. Sorensen, F. E. Weinert, and L. R. Sherrod (Eds.), *Human Development and the Life Course: Multidisciplinary Perspectives* (199–216). Hillsdale, N.J.: Erlbaum.

Mier y Teran y Rocha, M. M., and Rabell Romero, C. A. (2000). *El proceso de la escolarizacion de los niños en Mexico, 1960–1990*. Mexico City, D.F.: CONAPO.

Mize, R. L., and Swords, A. C. S. (2010). *Consuming Mexican Labor: From the Bracero Program to NAFTA*. Toronto: University of Toronto Press.

Modell, J. (1989). *Into One's Own: From Youth to Adulthood in the United States, 1920–1975*. Berkeley: University of California Press.

Modell, J., and Goodman, M. (1990). Historical Perspectives. In S. S. Feldman and G. R. Elliott (Eds.), *At the Threshold: The Developing Adolescent* (93–122). Cambridge, Mass.: Harvard University Press.

Mollenkopf, J. H., and Castells, M. (1992). Introduction. In J. H. Mollenkopf and M. Castells (Eds.), *Dual City: Restructuring New York* (1–22). New York: Russell Sage Foundation.

Molyneux, M. (2007). *Change and Continuity in Social Protection in Latin America*. New York: United Nations Research Institute for Social Development.

Morrow, R. A., and Torres, C. A. (1995). *Social Theory and Education: A Critique of Theories of Social and Cultural Reproduction.* Albany: State University of New York Press.

Morrow, V. (2011). *Understanding Children and Childhood.* Centre for Children and Young People, Background Briefing Series 1. Lismore: Centre for Children and Young People, Southern Cross University.

Mortimer, J. T. (2010). The Benefits and Risks of Adolescent Employment. *The Prevention Researcher, 17*(2), 8–11.

Mortimer, J. T., Oesterle, S., and Kruger, H. (2005). Age Norms, Institutional Structures and the Timing of Markers of the Transition to Adulthood. The Structure of the Life Course: Standardized? Individualized? Differentiated? [Special issue]. *Advances in Life Course Research, 9,* 175–203.

Mortimer, J. T., Staff, J., and Oesterle, S. (2003). Adolescent Work and the Early Social Career. In J. T. Mortimer and M. J. Shanahan (Eds.), *Handbook of the Life Course* (437–459). New York: Kluwer Academic/Plenum.

Moss, P., and Tilly, C. (1996). Soft Skills and Race: An Investigation of Black Men's Employment Problems. *Work and Occupations, 23*(3), 252–276.

Moss, P., and Tilly, C. (2001). *Stories Employers Tell: Race, Skill and Hiring in America.* New York: Russell Sage Foundation.

Munasinghe, L., and Sigman, K. (2003). A Hobo Syndrome? Mobility, Wages and Job Turnover. *Labour Economics, 11,* 191–218.

Muniz, P. E. (2001). La situacion escolar de niñas y niños Rurales en Mexico. *Estudios Demograficos y Urbanos, 46,* 53–83.

Muñoz Rios, P. (2005, December 1). Mas de 3 millones de niños son explotados laboralmente. *La Jornada.* Retrieved from http://www.jornada.unam.mx/2005/12/01/index.php?section=sociedad&article=054n1soc.

Muñoz Rios, P. (2017, June 21). Crece número de mexicanos con educación que viven en pobreza. *La Jornada.* Retrieved from https://www.jornada.com.mx/2017/06/21/sociedad/034n1soc.

Nakumara, D. (2017, August 16). Trump Administration Ends Obama-Era Protection Program for Central American Minors. *Washington Post.* Retrieved from https://www.washingtonpost.com/politics/trump-administration-ends-obama-era-protection-program-for-central-american-minors/2017/08/16/8101507e-82b6-11e7-ab27-1a21a8e006ab_story.html?utm_term=.51a2abd14a03.

Nathan, D. (1997). Death Comes to the Maquilas: A Border Story. *The Maquiladora Reader: Cross-Border Organizing since NAFTA.* Philadelphia: American Friends Service Committee.

National Center for Educational Statistics. (2010). *The Condition of Education 2010.* Washington, D.C.: NCES.

National Immigration Law Center. (2012, June 15). *Questions and Answers about the Administration's Announcement regarding Relief for Individuals Who Came to the United States as Children.* Retrieved from https://www.nilc.org/wp-content/uploads/2015/11/PD-children-FAQ-2012-06-15.pdf.

National Institute of Health (NIH). (2015). *Frequently Asked Questions: Certificates of Confidentiality.* Retrieved from http://grants.nih.gov/grants/policy/coc/faqs.htm#352.

Nee, V., Sanders, J. M., and Sernau, S. (1994). Job Transitions in an Immigrant Metropolis: Ethnic Boundaries and the Mixed Economy. *American Sociological Review, 59*(6), 849–872.

Negrete Prieto, R., and Leyva Parra, G. (2013). Los NINIs en México: Una aproximación crítica a su medición. *Realidad, Datos y Espacio: Revista Internacional de Estadistica y*

Geografia, 4(1), 90–121. Retrieved from https://www.inegi.org.mx/rde/RDE_08/Doctos/RDE_08_Art6.pdf.

Neugarten, B. L., and Hagestad, G. O. (1976). Age and the Life Course. In R. H. Binstock and E. Shanas (Eds.), *Handbook of Aging and the Social Sciences* (35–55). New York: Van Nostrand Reinhold.

New York Building Congress. (2010). *Outlook: New York City Construction Forecast 2008–2010*. New York: New York City Building Congress. Retrieved from http://www.buildingcongress.com/pdf/nybc-con-outlook.pdf.

New York City College of Technology Continuing Studies. (2018). *Mobile Food Vending Preparation Workshop*. Retrieved from http://www.citytechce.org/mobile-food-vending-preparation-workshop.html.

New York City Department of Education. (2010). *District 79*. Retrieved from http://proxy.nycboe.org/Offices/District79/SchoolsProgramsServices/default.htm.

New York City Department of Education. (2014). *Liberty High School*. Retrieved from http://schools.nyc.gov/OA/SchoolReports/201415/School_Quality_Snapshot_2015_HST_M550.pdf.

New York City Department of Education. (2016a). *Flushing International High School 2015–2016 School Quality Snapshot*. Retrieved from http://schools.nyc.gov/OA/SchoolReports/201516/School_Quality_Snapshot_2016_HS_Q263.pdf.

New York City Department of Education. (2016b). *Manhattan Comprehensive Night and Day High School 2015–2016 School Quality Snapshot*. Retrieved from http://schools.nyc.gov/OA/SchoolReports/2015-16/School_Quality_Snapshot_2016_HST_M575.pdf.

New York City Department of Education. (2017). *Manhattan Comprehensive Night and Day High School*. Retrieved from http://schools.nyc.gov/SchoolPortals/02/M575/default.htm.

New York State Attorney General. (2016). *Immigrant Tenant Rights*. Retrieved from https://ag.ny.gov/sites/default/files/immigration_tenants_rights_web.pdf.

New York State Department of Labor. (2013). *New York State Child Labor Law vs. Federal Law*. Retrieved from https://www.labor.ny.gov/workerprotection/laborstandards/workprot/nyvsfed.shtm.

New York State Department of Labor. (2015). *Laws Governing the Employment of Minors*. Retrieved from http://www.labor.ny.gov/workerprotection/laborstandards/workprot/minors.shtm.

New York State Department of Labor. (2016). *State Prohibited Occupations*. Retrieved from https://www.labor.ny.gov/workerprotection/laborstandards/workprot/stprhboc.shtm.

New York State Department of Labor. (2017). *Working Papers*. Retrieved from https://www.labor.ny.gov/workerprotection/laborstandards/workprot/wphmpg.shtm.

New York State Division of Human Rights. (2017). *Fair Housing Guide*. Retrieved from https://dhr.ny.gov/sites/default/files/pdf/nysdhr-fair-housing-guide.pdf.

Nofz, N., and Stevenson, M. C. (2017). The Year of Hugo Ortega, 2017 James Beard Award Winner. *Houston Hotel Magazine*. Retrieved from http://houstonhotelmagazine.com/profiles/the-year-of-hugo-ortega/.

Nolle, A. P., Gulbas, L., Kuhlberg, J. A., and Zayas, L. H. (2012). Sacrifice for the Sake of the Family: Expressions of Familism by Latina Teens in the Context of Suicide. *American Journal of Orthopsychiatry, 82*(3), 319–327.

Notimex. (2013, June 10). SEP, obligatoria, educacion, hasta nivel medio superior. *El Universal*. Retrieved from http://archivo.eluniversal.com.mx/notas/928738.html.

Nurmi, J. (1993). Adolescent Development in an Age-Graded Context: The Role of Personal Beliefs, Goals and Strategies in the Tackling of Developmental Tasks and Standards. *International Journal of Behavioral Development, 16*(2), 169–189.

OCDE. (2008). *Panorama de la educación 2008: Indicadores de la OCDE.* Paris: Organisation for Economic Cooperation and Development.

OECD. (2014). *Education at a Glance: Mexico.* OECD Briefing Note for Mexico. Retrieved from https://www.oecd.org/mexico/41277868.pdf.

O'Leary, A. O. (2009a). The ABCs of Migration Costs: Assembling, Bajadores and Coyotes. *Migration Letters, 6*(1), 27–36.

O'Leary, A. O. (2009b). In the Footsteps of Spirits: Migrant Women Testimonios in a Time of Heightened Border Enforcement. In K. Staudt, T. Payan, and Z. A. Kruszewski (Eds.), *Human Rights along the US-Mexico Border: Gendered Violence and Insecurity* (91–112). Tucson: University of Arizona Press.

O'Leary, A. O., Deeds, C. M., and Whiteford, S. (2013). Introduction. In A. O. O'Leary, C. M. Deeds, and S. Whiteford (Eds.), *Unchartered Terrains: New Directions in Border Research Methodology, Ethics, and Practice* (1–23). Tucson: University of Arizona Press.

Orellana, M., Thorne, B, Chee, A., and Lam, W. S. E. (2001). Transnational Childhoods: The Participation of Children in Processes of Family Migration. *Social Problems, 48*(4), 572–591.

Oropesa, R. S., and Landale, N. S. (2009). Why Do Immigrant Youths Who Never Enroll in US Schools Matter? An Examination of School Enrollment among Mexicans and Non-Hispanic Whites. *Sociology of Education, 82*(3), 240–266.

Orraca, P. (2014). Trabajo Infantil: Problemas de Desarrollo. *Revista Latinoamerica de Economia, 178*(45), 113–137.

Osgood, D. W., Foster, E. M., and Courtney, M. E. (2010). Vulnerable Populations and the Transition to Adulthood. *Future of Children, 20*(1), 209–229.

Osgood, D. W., Ruth, G., Eccles, J. S., Jacobs, J. E., and Barber, B. L. (2005). Six Paths to Adulthood. In R. Settersten, F. F. Furstenberg, and R. G. Rumbaut (Eds.), *On the Frontier of Adulthood: Theory, Research and Practice* (320–355). Chicago: University of Chicago Press.

Osterman, P. (1979). Education and Labor Markets at the Turn of the Century. *Politics and Society, 9*, 103–122.

Pacheco, Y. (2013, May 14). Contratan maquilas a menores de edad en Tehuacan. *El Sol de Puebla.* Retrieved from http://www.oem.com.mx/elsoldepuebla/notas/n2982187.htm.

Palan, K. M., Gentina, E., and Muratore, I. (2010). Adolescent Consumption Autonomy: A Cross-Cultural Examination. *Journal of Business Research, 63*(12), 1342–1348.

Paley, D. (2014). *Drug War Capitalism.* Oakland, Calif.: AK Press.

Pallas, A. (1993). Schooling in the Course of Human Lives: The Social Context of Education and the Transition to Adulthood in Industrial Society. *Review of Educational Research, 63*(4), 409–447.

Pallas, A. (2007). A Subjective Approach to Schooling and the Transition to Adulthood. Constructing Adulthood: Agency and Subjectivity in Adolescence and Adulthood, *Advances in Life Course Research, 11*, 173–197.

Pallas, A., and Jennings, J. L. (2009). Cumulative Knowledge about Cumulative Advantage. *Swiss Journal of Sociology, 35*, 211–229.

Parker, S. W., Rubalcava, L., Teruel, G., and Behrman, J. (2007). *The Quality of Education in Latin America and the Caribbean Region: The Mexican Case.* Washington, D.C.: Inter-American Development Bank. Retrieved from http://www.iadb.org/res/publications/pubfiles/pubs-884.pdf.

Parrado, E. A. (2005). Globalization and Transition to Adulthood in Mexico. In H. P. Blossfeld, E. Klijzing, M. Mills, and K. Kurz (Eds.), *Globalization, Uncertainty and Youth in Society* (327–348). London: Routledge.

Partlow, J. (2015, March 11). Mexican Kids Held for Months as Punishment for Border-Crossing. *Washington Post.* Retrieved from https://www.washingtonpost.com/world/the_americas/mexican-kids-held-for-months-as-punishment-for-border-crossing/2015/03/10/311d319a-b2f2-11e4-bf39-5560f3918d4b_story.html.

Partlow, J. (2017, May 30). In Mexico, the Price for America's Hunger for Heroin. *Washington Post.* Retrieved from https://www.washingtonpost.com/graphics/2017/world/violence-is-soaring-in-the-mexican-towns-that-feed-americas-heroin-habit/?utm_term=.178f405c3a03.

Passel, J. S. (2007). *Fiscal Policy Institute's Working for a Better Life.* Pew Hispanic Center, based on Pew Hispanic Center CPS data, 2000–2006.

Passel, J. S., and Cohn, D. (2009). *A Portrait of Unauthorized Immigrants in the United States.* Washington, D.C.: Pew Hispanic Center.

Passel, J. S., and Cohn, D. (2015, March 26). *Share of Unauthorized Immigrant Workers in Production, Constructions Jobs Fall since 2007.* Washington, D.C.: Pew Research Center.

Passel, J. S., Cohn, D., and Gonzalez Ibarra, A. (2012). *Net Migration from Mexico Falls to Zero—and Perhaps Less.* Washington, D.C.: Pew Hispanic Center. Retrieved from http://www.pewhispanic.org/2012/04/23/net-migration-from-mexico-falls-to-zero-and-perhaps-less/.

Patton, M. O. (1990). *Qualitative Evaluation and Research Methods.* Newbury Park, Calif.: Sage.

Pearson, E. (2014). Call This Group Fighting Hiring Scams the Truth Squad. *New York Daily News.* Retrieved from http://www.nydailynews.com/new-york/helping-immigrans-work-scammed-article-1.1750198.

Perez-Garcia, M. J. (2009). *Niños y niñas que trabajan en Mexico: Un problema persistente.* Mexico City, D.F.: UNICEF. https://www.unicef.org/mexico/spanish/Analisis_Preliminar_enoe.pdf.

Perramond, E. P. (2008). The Rise, Fall and Reconfiguration of the Mexican Ejido. *Geographical Review, 98*(3), 356–371.

Piore, M. J. (1979). *Birds of Passage: Migrant Labor and Industrial Societies.* Cambridge: Cambridge University Press.

Pizzey, N., Frederick, J., and WOLA. (2015). *Forgotten on La Frontera: Mexican Children Fleeing Violence Are Rarely Heard.* Retrieved from https://www.wola.org/analysis/forgotten-on-la-frontera-mexican-children-fleeing-violence-are-rarely-heard/.

Pleic, M., Knaul, F. M., and Berry, A. (2009). Child Labor in Mexico. In H. D. Hindman (Ed.), *The World of Child Labor: A Historical and Regional Survey* (396–415). Armonk, N.Y.: Sharpe.

Plyler v. Doe. (1982). 22 Ill. 458 U.S. 1131, 103 S. Ct. 14, 73 L. Ed. 2d 1401 (1982).

Portes, A. (1995). *The Economic Sociology of Immigration: Essays on Networks, Ethnicity and Entrepreneurship.* New York: Russell Sage Foundation.

Portes, A. (1998). Social Capital: Its Origins and Applications. *Annual Review of Sociology, 24,* 1–24.

Portes, A. (2007). Migration, Development and Segmented Assimilation: A Conceptual Review of the Evidence. *Annals of the American Academy of Political and Social Science, 610,* 73–97.

Portes, A., and Zhou, M. (1993). The New Second Generation: Segmented Assimilation and Its Variants. *Annals of the American Academy of Political and Social Science, 530,* 74–96.

Pratt Center for Community Development. (2008). *New York's Housing Underground: A Resource and a Refuge.* New York: Pratt Center for Community Development.

Proceso La Redacción. (2017, October 31). Cierran por la violencia más de 600 escuelas en Guerrero. *Proceso.* Retrieved from https://www.proceso.com.mx/509339/cierran-la-violencia-600-escuelas-en-guerrero.

Punch, S. (2002). Youth Transitions and Interdependent Adult-Child Relations in Rural Bolivia. *Journal of Rural Studies, 18*, 123–133.

Punch, S. (2003). Childhoods in the Majority World: Miniature Adults or Tribal Children? *Sociology, 37*(2), 277–295.

Punch, S. (2007). Childhood and Society: An Introduction to the Sociology of Childhood. *Children and Society, 21*(3), 235–236.

Punch, S. (2015). Youth and Migration: Negotiated and Constrained Interdependencies within and across Generations. *Journal of Youth Studies, 18*(2), 262–276.

Rama, A., and Yukhananov, A. (2015, July 23). Mexican Government Says Poverty Rate Rose to 46.2% in 2014. *Reuters*. Retrieved from https://www.reuters.com/article/us-mexico-poverty/mexican-government-says-poverty-rate-rose-to-46-2-percent-in-2014-idUSKCN0PX2B320150723.

Ramirez, H., and Hondagneu-Sotelo, P. (2009). Mexican Immigrant Gardeners: Entrepreneurs or Exploited Workers? *Social Problems, 56*(1), 70–88.

Ramirez Sanchez, M. A. (2015). Trabajo y ayuda mutual: Los niños y ñinas de San Pedro Tlalcuapan. *Cuicuilco, 22*(64), 203–222.

Reed, T. (2015). Mexico's Drug War: A New Way to Think about Mexican Organized Crime. *Stratfor Worldview*. Retrieved from https://worldview.stratfor.com/article/mexicos-drug-war-new-way-think-about-mexican-organized-crime.

Repak, T. (1994). Labor Market Incorporation of Central American Immigrants in Washington, D.C. *Social Problems, 41*(1), 114–128.

Restaurant Opportunities Centers of New York. (2005). *Behind the Kitchen Door: Pervasive Inequality in New York City's Thriving Restaurant Industry*. ROC United. Retrieved from http://rocunited.org/wp-content/uploads/2013/04/reports_bkd-ny.pdf.

Riaño-Alcalá, P., and Villa-Martínez, M. I. (2014). Forced Migration of Colombians: A Relational Perspective. In L. Rivera-Sanchez and F. L. Ascencio (Eds.), *The Practice of Research on Migration and Mobilities* (77–102). New York: Springer.

Rios, P. M. (2017, June 21). Crece numero de mexicanos con educacion que viven en pobreza. *La Jornada*. Retrieved from http://www.jornada.unam.mx/2017/06/21/sociedad/034n1soc.

Rivera, J. M., and Whiteford, S. (2009). Introduction: Mexican Agriculture and NAFTA: Prospects for Change. In J. M. Rivera, S. Whiteford, and M. Chavez (Eds.), *NAFTA and the Campesinos: The Impact of NAFTA on Small-Scale Agricultural Producers in Mexico and the Prospects for Change* (xiii–xxix). Scranton, Pa.: University of Scranton Press.

Rivera-Batiz, F. (2004). Newyorktitlan: A Socioeconomic Profile of Mexican New Yorkers. *Regional Labor Review, 6*(2), 32–43.

Robbins, L. (2018, April 18). A Rule Is Changed for Young Immigrants, and Green Card Hopes Fade. *New York Times*. Retrieved from https://www.nytimes.com/2018/04/18/nyregion/special-immigrant-juvenile-status-trump.html.

Roche, K. M., Caughy, M. O., Schuster, M. A., Bogart, L. M., Dittus, P. J., and Franzini, L. (2014). Cultural Orientations, Parental Beliefs and Practices, and Latino Adolescents' Autonomy and Independence. *Journal of Youth and Adolescence, 43*(8), 1389–1403.

Romero, M. (1992). *Maid in the U.S.A.* New York: Routledge.

Rosati, F. C., Ranzani, M., Guarcello, L., Lyon, S., Breglia, G., and Campos, P. (2012). *The Mexican Experience in Reducing Child Labor: Empirical Work and Policy Lessons*. Rome: Understanding Child's Work Programme. Retrieved from http://www.ucw-project.org/attachment/Report_Child_Labour_trends20130308_111116.pdf.

Rosenblatt, D. (2004). An Anthropology Made Safe for Culture: Patterns of Practice and the Politics of Difference in Ruth Benedict. *American Anthropologist, 106*(3), 459–472.

Rossi, A. S., and Rossi, P. H. (1990). *Of Human Bonding: Parent-Child Relations across the Life Course.* Piscataway, N.J.: Aldine Transaction.

Rowe, N. (2011). *Mexico's Oportunidades: Conditional Cash Transfers as the Solution to Global Poverty?* Claremont, Calif.: Keck Center for International and Strategic Studies.

Ruddick, S. (2003). The Politics of Aging: Globalization and the Restructuring of Youth and Childhood. *Antipode, 35*(2), 334–362.

Ruiz, A. (2012, July 25). City's Immigrant Friendly Image Tarnished by New Report on Cold ICE Practices. *New York Daily News.* Retrieved from http://www.nydailynews.com/new-york/city-immigrant-friendly-image-tarnished-new-report-cold-ice-practices-article-1.1120825.

Ruiz, A. (2014, May 25). New York Lags behind Other US Cities in Avoiding Compliance with Immigration and Customs Enforcement's Secure Communities Program. *New York Daily News.* Retrieved from http://www.nydailynews.com/new-york/new-york-lags-behind-cities-avoiding-secure-communities-program-article-1.1802775.

Ruiz, R. E. (2010). *Mexico: Why a Few Are Rich and the People Poor.* Berkeley: University of California Press.

Ruiz Marrujo, O. T. (2009). Women, Migration and Sexual Violence: Lessons from Mexico's Borders. In K. Staudt, T. Payan, and Z. A. Kruszewski (Eds.), *Human Rights along the US-Mexico Border: Gendered Violence and Insecurity* (31–47). Tucson: University of Arizona Press.

Rumbaut, R. (2005). Turning Points in the Transition to Adulthood: Determinants in Educational Attainment, Incarceration, and Early Childbearing among Children of Immigrants. *Ethnic and Racial Studies, 28*(6), 1041–1086.

Rumbaut, R., and Komaie, G. (2010). Immigration and Adult Transitions. Transitions to Adulthood [Special issue]. *The Future of Children, 20*(1), 39–63.

Salas, M. M., and de Oliviera, O. (2009). Los jovenes en el inicio de la vida adulta: Trayectorias, transiciones y subjetividades. *Estudios Sociólogicos, 27*(79), 267–279.

Salazar, F. (2000). *The Martinez Family.* Unpublished Monograph.

Sanchez, C. (2018, January 29). Nearly 9000 DACA Teachers Face an Uncertain Future. NPR. Retrieved from https://www.npr.org/sections/ed/2018/01/29/579682676/nearly-9-000-daca-teachers-face-an-uncertain-future.

Sanchez, G. (2014). *Border Crossings and Human Smuggling.* London: Routledge.

Sandoval-Cervantes, I. (2017). Uncertain Futures: The Unfinished Houses of Undocumented Migrants in Oaxaca, Mexico. *American Anthropologist, 119*(2), 209–222.

Santibanez, L., Vernez, G., and Razquin, P. (2005). *Education in Mexico: Challenges and Opportunities.* Santa Monica, Calif.: RAND.

Sassen, S. (2001). *The Global City: New York, London and Tokyo.* Princeton, N.J.: Princeton University Press.

Saucedo, L. (2006). The Employer Preference for the Subservient Worker and the Making of the Brown Collar Workplace. *Ohio State Law Journal, 67*(5), 961–1021.

Sawyer, A. (2013). The Schooling of Youth Impacted by Migration: A Binational Case Study. In B. Jensen and A. Sawyer (Eds.), *Regarding Educacion, Mexican American Schooling, Immigration and Binational Improvement* (189–212). New York: Teachers College Press.

Sawyer, A., Keyes, D., Velazquez, C., Lima, G., and Bautista, M. M. (2009). Going to School, Going to El Norte: Migration's Impact on a Tlacotepense Education. In W. Cornelius, D. Fitzgerald, J. Hernandez-Diaz, and S. Borger (Eds.), *Migration from the Mexican Mixteca: A Transnational Community between Oaxaca and California* (126–160). Boulder, Colo.: Lynne Rienner.

Schmelkes, S. (2005). La desigualdad en la calidad de la educacion primaria. *Revista Latinoamericana de Estudios Educativos (Mexico)*, 35(3–4), 9–33.

Schoeni, R., and Ross, K. (2005). Material Assistance Received from Families during the Transition to Adulthood. In R. Settersten, F. F. Furstenberg, and R. G. Rumbaut (Eds.), *On the Frontier of Adulthood: Theory, Research and Practice* (396–416). Chicago: University of Chicago Press.

Schulenberg, J., and Schoon, I. (2012). The Transition to Adulthood across Time and Space: Overview of Special Section. *Longitudinal and Life Course Studies*, 3(2), 164–172.

Schwarz, G. (2013, April 19). Why New York City Is Still the Capital of Immigrant America. *The Nation*. Retrieved from http://www.thenation.com/article/why-new-york-still-capital-immigrant-america/.

Secretaria de Educacion Publica (SEP). (2012). *Reporte de la Encuesta Nacional de Deserción en la Educación Media Superior*. Mexico City, D.F.: Secretaria de Educación Publica.

Secretaria de Seguridad Publica (SSP). (2011). *Desercion escolar y conductas de riesgo en adolescents*. Mexico City, D.F.: Gobierno Federal. Retrieved from https://www.uv.mx/dgdaie/files/2013/09/Embarazo-en-Adolescentes-del-Sureste-de-Mexico-2.pdf.

Secretaria de Trabajo y Prevision Social. (2015, June 12). *Se reforman y derogan diversas disposiciones de la ley federal del trabajo, en materia de trabajo de menores*. Retrieved from http://www.diputados.gob.mx/LeyesBiblio/ref/lft/LFT_ref27_12jun15.pdf.

SEDESOL. (2010a). *Informe anual sobre la situacion de pobreza y rezago social: Iztapalapa, Distrito Federal*. Retrieved from http://www.dof.gob.mx/SEDESOL/Distrito_Federal_007.pdf.

SEDESOL. (2010b). *Informe anual sobre la situacion de pobreza y rezago social: Distrito Federal*. Retrieved from https://www.gob.mx/cms/uploads/attachment/file/31492/Distrito_Federal_1_.pdf.

SEDESOL. (2010c). *Informe anual sobre la situacion de pobreza y rezago social: Huaquechula, Puebla*. Retrieved from http://www.sedesol.gob.mx/work/models/SEDESOL/Informes_pobreza/2014/Municipio/Puebla/Puebla_069.pdf.

SEDESOL. (2010d). *Informe anual sobre la situacion de pobreza y rezago social: Tianguismanalco, Puebla*. Retrieved from http://www.dof.gob.mx/SEDESOL/Puebla_175.pdf.

SEDESOL. (2014). *Informe anual sobre la situacion de pobreza y rezago social: Ciudad Nezahualcoyotl*. Retrieved from https://www.gob.mx/cms/uploads/attachment/file/42692/Mexico_058.pdf.

Semple, K. (2010, September 23). Mexican New Yorkers Are a Steady Force in Workplace. *New York Times*. Retrieved from http://www.nytimes.com/2010/09/23/nyregion/23mexicans.html.

Semple, K. (2011, November 24). In New York, Mexicans Lag in Education. *New York Times*. Retrieved from http://www.nytimes.com/2011/11/25/nyregion/mexicans-in-new-york-city-lag-in-education.html.

Semuels, A. (2014, December 15). How Common Is Child Labor in the U.S.? *The Atlantic*. Retrieved from http://www.theatlantic.com/business/archive/2014/12/how-common-is-chid-labor-in-the-us/383687/.

Sepulveda, L. (2013, May 21). Jovenes de Huimilpan Emigran al EU. *El Universal Queretaro*. Retrieved from http://www.eluniversalqueretaro.mx/politica/21-05-2013/jovenes-de-huimilpan-migran-eu.

Settersten, R. A., Jr. (2003). Age Structuring and the Rhythm of the Life Course. In J. T. Mortimer and M. J. Shanahan (Eds.), *Handbook of the Life Course* (81–100). New York: Kluwer Academic/Plenum.

Settersten, R. A., Jr. (2005). Social Policy and the Transition to Adulthood: Toward Stronger Institutions and Individual Capacities. In R. A. Settersten, F. F. Furstenberg, and R. G. Rumbaut (Eds.), *On the Frontier of Adulthood: Theory, Research and Public Policy* (534–560). Chicago: University of Chicago Press.

Settersten, R. A., Jr., and Hagestad, G. O. (1996). What Is the Latest? Cultural Age Deadlines for Family Transitions. *The Gerontologist, 36*(2), 178–188.

Settersten, R. A., Jr., and Mayer, K. (1997). The Measurement of Age, Age Structuring and the Life Course. *Annual Review of Sociology, 23*, 233–261.

Shanahan, M. J. (2000). Pathways to Adulthood in Changing Societies: Variability and Mechanisms in Life Course Perspective. *Annual Review of Sociology, 26*, 667–692.

Shanahan, M. J., Elder, G. H., Jr., Burchinal, M., and Conger, R. D. (1996). Adolescent Paid Labor and Relationships with Parents: Early Work-Family Linkages. *Child Development, 67*(5), 2183–2200.

Shanahan, M. J., Elder, G. H., Jr., and Meich, R. (1997). History and Agency in Men's Lives: Pathways to Achievement in the Cohort Perspective. *Sociology of Education, 70*(1), 54–67.

Shanahan, M. J., and Flaherty, B. P. (2001). Dynamic Patterns of Time-Use in Adolescence. *Child Development, 72*(2), 385–401.

Shanahan, M. J., Porfeli, E. J., Mortimer, J. T., and Erickson, L. D. (2005). Subjective Age Identity and the Transition to Adulthood: When Do Adolescents Become Adults? In R. Settersten, F. F. Furstenberg, and R. G. Rumbaut (Eds.), *On the Frontier of Adulthood: Theory, Research and Public Policy* (225–255). Chicago: University of Chicago Press.

Shanin, T. (1978). The Peasants Are Coming: Migrants Who Labour, Peasants Who Travel and Marxists Who Write. *Race and Class, 19*(3), 277–288.

Shear, M. D. (2015, November 6). Red Tape Slows US Help for Children Fleeing Central America. *New York Times*. Retrieved from https://www.nytimes.com/2015/11/06/us/politics/red-tape-slows-us-help-for-children-fleeing-central-america.html.

Smith, P. H., and Martinez-Smith, N. (2003). Educating for Bilingualism in Mexican Transnational Communities. *NABE Journal of Research and Practice, 1*(1), 138–148.

Smith, R. C. (2003). Imagining Alternative Educational Futures for Mexicans in New York City. In R. Cortina and M. Gendreau (Eds.), *The Schooling of Mexican Children in New York State* (92–124). New York: Center for Migration Studies.

Smith, R. C. (2006). *Mexican New York*. Los Angeles: University of California Press.

Sosenski Correa, S. (2010). *Niños en acción: El trabajo infantil en la ciudad de Mexico (1920–1934)*. Distrito Federal: Colegio de México.

Spener, D. (2009). *Clandestine Crossings: Migrants and Coyotes on the Texas-Mexico Border*. Ithaca: Cornell University Press.

Stanton-Salazar, R. (2001). *Manufacturing Hope and Despair: The School and Kin Support Networks of US-Mexican Youth*. New York: Teachers College Press.

Stiglitz, J. E. (2004, January 6). The Broken Promise of NAFTA. *New York Times*. Retrieved from http://www.nytimes.com/2004/01/06/opinion/the-broken-promise-of-nafta.html.

Suárez, G. (2015, April 30). Mas de 86 mil menores de edad trabajan en el DF. *El Universal*. Retrieved from http://m.eluniversal.com.mx/notas/metropoli/2015/mas-de-86-mil-menores-de-edad-trabajan-en-el-df-styfe-1096538.html.

Suárez-Orozco, C., and Suárez-Orozco, M. (1995). *Transformations: Migration, Family Life and Achievement*. Stanford, Calif.: Stanford University Press.

Suárez-Orozco, C., and Suárez-Orozco, M. (2001). *Children of Immigration*. Cambridge, Mass.: Harvard University Press.

Swartz, D. (1997). *Culture and Power: The Sociology of Pierre Bourdieu*. Chicago: University of Chicago Press.

Swartz, T. T., and O'Brien, K. B. (2009). Intergenerational Support during the Transition to Adulthood. In A. Furlong (Ed.), *Handbook of Youth and Young Adulthood: New Perspectives and Agendas* (217–225). New York: Routledge.

Tanguenco Belmonte, J. A. (2009). El Concepto de Juventud. *Revista Mexicana de Sociologia, 71*(1), 159–190.

Taracena, O. (2003). A Schooling Model for Working Children in Mexico: The Case of Children of Indian Origin Working as Agricultural Workers during the Harvest. *Childhood, 10*(3), 301–318.

Tareen, S. (2017, January 25). Restaurants May Be the Next Front for the Immigration Debate. *Associated Press*. Retrieved from https://www.apnews.com/14f3e37bf9fc45c4a8b79bca3cc6d2fe.

Terrio, S. T. (2015). *Whose Child Am I? Unaccompanied, Undocumented Children in US Immigration Custody*. Los Angeles: University of California Press.

Thomas, C. (2016, April 22). Detention for Unaccompanied Children. *Anthropology News*. Retrieved from https://ssrn.com/abstract/abstract=2799993.

Thomas, C., and Benson, L. (2016). Caught in the Web: Immigrant Children in Removal Proceedings. In Impact Center for Public Interest Law Racial Justice Project (Ed.), *Impact: Collected Essays on Expanding Access to Justice* (31–41). New York: Impact Center for Public Interest Law.

Thorne, B., Orellana, M. F., Lam, E. W. S., and Chee, A. (2003). Raising Children, and Growing Up, across National Borders: Comparative Perspectives on Age, Gender, and Migration. In P. Hondagneu-Sotelo (Ed.), *Gender and U.S. Immigration: Contemporary Trends* (241–262). Berkeley: University of California Press.

Treschan, L. (2010, October). *New York City Looks Latino*. New York: Community Service Society.

Treschan, L., and Mehrotra, A. (2013, March). *Policy Brief: Young Mexican Americans in New York City: Working More, Earning and Learning Less*. New York: Community Service Society.

Turkewitz, J. (2013, October 14). A State Inquiry Is Said to Target Job Agencies. *New York Times*. Retrieved from http://www.nytimes.com/2013/10/15/nyregion/a-state-inquiry-is-said-to-target-job-agencies.html?_r=0.

Tuttle, C. (2006). History Repeats Itself: Child Labor in Latin America. *Employee Responsibilities and Rights Journal, 18*(2), 143–154.

Tyrell, N. (2011). Children's Agency in Family Migration Decision-Making in Britain. In C. Coe, R. R. Reynolds, D. A. Boehm, J. M. Hess, and H. Rae-Espinoza (Eds.), *Everyday Ruptures: Children, Youth and Migration in a Global Perspective* (23–38). Nashville, Tenn.: Vanderbilt Press.

Ulloa, V. S., and Potter, J. (2008). "Cambio demografico y oportunidades educativos en Mexico, Brasil y Chile." Working paper presented at the III Congreso de la Asociación Latinoamericana de Población, ALAP, Córdoba–Argentina. Retrieved from http://www.alapop.org/alap/images/DOCSFINAIS_PDF/ALAP_2008_FINAL_235.pdf.

Understanding Children's Work Programme (UCW). (2012). *La Experiencia Mexicana en la reducción del trabajo infantil: Evidencia empirica y lecciones politicas*. Rome: UCW.

United Nations Department of Economic and Social Affairs (UNDESA). (2017). *International Migration Report 2017*. Geneva: United Nations. Retrieved from http://www.un.org/en/development/desa/population/migration/publications/migrationreport/docs/MigrationReport2017.pdf.

United Nations General Assembly. (1989, November 20). *Convention on the Rights of the Child*. United Nations, Treaty Series, vol. 1577, p. 3.

United Nations High Commissioner for Refugees (UNHCR). (2014). *Children on the Run: Unaccompanied Children Leaving Central America and Mexico and the Need for International Protection*. Washington, D.C.: UNHCR. Retrieved from http://www.unhcr.org/56fc266f4.html.

United Nations High Commissioner for Refugees (UNHCR). (2017). *Global Trends: Forced Displacement in 2016*. Geneva: UNHCR.

United Nations International Children's Emergency Fund (UNICEF). (2010). *The Rights of Children and Adolescents in Mexico: A Present Day Agenda*. Mexico City, D.F.: UNICEF Mexico. Retrieved from http://www.unicef.org/sitan/files/SitAn_Mexico_Eng_Jan_2011.pdf.

United Nations International Children's Emergency Fund (UNICEF). (2016). *Uprooted: The Growing Crisis for Refugee and Migrant Children*. New York: United Nations. Retrieved from https://www.unicef.org/publications/files/Uprooted_growing_crisis_for_refugee_and_migrant_children.pdf.

Urrea, L. (2004). *The Devil's Highway: A True Story*. New York: Little, Brown and Company.

Urrieta, L. (2013). Familia and Comunidad-Based Saberes: Learning in an Indigenous Heritage Community. *Anthropology and Education, 44*(3), 320–335.

U.S. Customs and Border Patrol. (2011). *United States Border Patrol, Sector Profile FY 2011*. Retrieved from https://www.cbp.gov/sites/default/files/documents/U.S.%20Border%20Patrol%20Fiscal%20Year%202011%20Sector%20Profile.pdf.

U.S. Customs and Border Patrol. (2013). *United States Border Patrol, Sector Profile FY 2013*. Retrieved from https://www.cbp.gov/sites/default/files/documents/U.S.%20Border%20Patrol%20Fiscal%20Year%202013%20Profile.pdf.

U.S. Customs and Border Patrol. (2015a). *Southwest Border Unaccompanied Alien Children Apprehension Statistics FY 2015*. Retrieved from https://www.cbp.gov/newsroom/stats/southwest-border-unaccompanied-children/fy-2015.

U.S. Customs and Border Patrol. (2015b). *Southwest Border Unaccompanied Alien Children Apprehension Statistics FY 2014*. Retrieved from https://www.cbp.gov/newsroom/stats/southwest-border-unaccompanied-children/fy-2014.

U.S. Department of Labor. (2010). *Updating Child Labor Regulations for the 21st Century*. Retrieved from https://www.dol.gov/whd/cl/whdfsCLFR.pdf.

U.S. Department of Labor. (2016). *Wages and Hour Division: Compliance Assistance and the Fair Labor Standards Act (FLSA)*. Retrieved from https://www.dol.gov/whd/flsa/.

U.S. Department of Labor. (2017). *Child Labor*. Retrieved from https://www.dol.gov/whd/childlabor.htm#Overview.

U.S. Government Accountability Office. (2002). *Child Labor: Labor Can Strengthen Its Efforts to Protect Children Who Work*. GAO-02-880. Washington, D.C. Retrieved from https://www.gao.gov/assets/240/236017.pdf.

Valdes, G. (1996). *Con Respeto: Bridging the Distances between Culturally Diverse Families and Schools, an Ethnographic Portrait*. New York: Teachers College Press.

Valenzuela, A., Jr. (2003). Day Labor Work. *Annual Review of Sociology, 29*, 307–333.

Valenzuela, A. (1999). *Subtractive Schooling*. New York: State University of New York Press.

Valenzuela, A., and Dornbusch, S. M. (1994). Familism and Social Capital in the Academic Achievement of Mexican Origin and Anglo Adolescents. *Social Science Quarterly, 75*(1), 18–36.

Van de Glind, H. (2010). *Migration and Child Labour: Exploring Child Migrant Vulnerabilities and Those of Children Left Behind*. Geneva: International Labour Office, International Programme on the Elimination of Child Labour.

Van Hook, J., and Glick, J. E. (2007). Immigration and Living Arrangements: Moving beyond Economic Need vs. Acculturation. *Demography, 44*(2), 225–249.

Velazquez, A. L. (2015). Jovenes de Cuautlancingo prefieren emigrar al EU. *Sintesis Puebla.* Retrieved from http://sintesis.mx/articulos/93383/jovenes-de-cuautlancingo-prefieren-emigrar-a-eua/puebla.

Vellos, D. (1996). Immigrant Latina Domestic Workers and Sexual Harassment. *Journal of Gender and the Law, 5*, 407–432.

Verdusco, M. A. (2013, December 5). Mexico, unico pais en AL donde crecio la pobreza: CEPAL. *El Universal.* Retrieved from http://archivo.eluniversal.com.mx/finanzas-cartera/2013/mexico-pobreza-cepal-970772.html.

Vermeulen, H. (2000). Introduction: The Role of Culture in Explanations of Social Mobility. In H. Vermeulen and J. Perlmann (Eds.), *Immigrants, Schooling and Social Mobility: Does Culture Make a Difference?* (1–21). New York: Palgrave Macmillan.

Vespa, J. (2017). *The Changing Economics and Demographics of Young Adulthood: 1975–2016.* Washington, D.C.: US Department of Commerce.

Waldinger, R. (1992). Taking Care of the Guests: The Impact of Immigrants on Services—an Industry Case Study. *International Journal of Urban and Regional Research, 16*(1), 97–113.

Waldinger, R. (1996). *Still the Promised City? African Americans and New Immigrants in Post-industrial New York.* Cambridge, Mass.: Harvard University Press.

Waldinger, R., and Perlmann, J. (1998). Second Generations: Past, Presents and Futures. *Journal of Ethnic and Migration Studies, 24*(1), 5–24.

Walsh, R. (2007). Illegal Immigrants in the Restaurant Industry. *Houston Press.* Retrieved from://www.houstonpress.com/restaurants/illegal-immigrants-in-the-restaurant-industry-6575568.

Walter, N., Bourgois, P., and Loinaz, H. M. (2004). Masculinity and Undocumented Labor Migration: Injured Latino Day Laborers in San Francisco. *Social Science and Medicine, 59*(6), 1159–1168.

Waters, M. C., Carr, P. J., and Kefalas, M. (2011). Introduction. In M. C. Waters, P. J. Carr, M. Kafalas, and J. M. Holdaway (Eds.), *Coming of Age in America: The Transition to Adulthood in the Twenty-First Century* (1–27). Berkeley: University of California Press.

Waterson, R. (2002). Enduring Landscape, Changing Habitus: The Sa'dan Toraja of Sulawesi, Indonesia. In J. Hillier and E. Rooksby (Eds.), *Habitus: A Sense of Place* (317–338). Burlington, Vt.: Ashgate.

Watters, J. K., and Biernacki, P. (1989). Targeted Sampling: Options for the Study of Hidden Populations. *Social Problems, 36*(4), 416–430.

Weisbrot, M., Lefebvre, S., and Sammut, J. (2014). Did NAFTA Help Mexico? An Assessment after 20 Years. Washington, D.C.: Center or Economic and Policy Research.

Williams, B. (1996). Skinfolk, Not Kinfolk: Comparative Reflections on the Identity of Participant-Observation in Two Field Situations. In D. L. Wolf (Ed.), *Feminist Dilemmas in Fieldwork* (72–95). Boulder, Colo.: Westview Press.

Willis, P. (1977). *Learning to Labor: How Working Class Kids Get Working Class Jobs.* New York: Columbia University Press.

Wilson, C., and Silva, G. (2013). Mexico's Latest Poverty Stats. *Wilson Center Mexico Institute.* Retrieved from https://www.wilsoncenter.org/sites/default/files/Poverty_Statistics_Mexico_2013.pdf.

Wilson, T. D. (1993). Theoretical Approaches to Mexican Wage Labor Migration. *Latin American Perspectives, 20*(3), 98–129.

Women's Refugee Commission. (2009). *Halfway Home: Unaccompanied Children in Immigration Custody*. New York: Women's Refugee Commission.

Wong, R. (2008). Are We Asking the Right Questions on Intergenerational Ties? In A. Booth, A. C. Crouter, S. M. Bianchi, and J. A. Seltzer (Eds.), *Intergenerational Caregiving* (45–52). Washington, D.C.: The Urban Institute.

World Bank. (2012). *La violencia juvenil en Mexico*. Washington, D.C.: World Bank. Retrieved from http://documents.worldbank.org/curated/en/277681468155375869/pdf/NonAsciiFileNameo.pdf.

World Bank. (2013, January 18). Children at Work in Mexico, Still a Major Issue. *World Bank*. Retrieved from http://www.worldbank.org/en/news/feature/2013/01/18/children-at-work-in-mexico-still-a-major-issue.

Young, A. A., Jr. (2004). *The Minds of Marginalized Black Men: Making Sense of Mobility, Opportunity and Future Life Chances*. Princeton, N.J.: Princeton University Press.

Yuñez-Naude, A. (2003). El TLCAN y la agricultura Mexicana. In H. Sobarzo and E. Casares (Eds.), *Diez Años de TLCAN en Mexico*. Distrito Federal: El Trimestre Economico.

Zapata, B. (2013). La falta de espacios complica la meta de bachillerato obligatorio. *CNN-Mexico*. Retrieved from http://expansion.mx/nacional/2013/07/12/la-falta-de-espacios-complica-la-meta-de-bachillerato-obligatorio.

Zavella, P. (1993). Feminist Insider Dilemmas: Constructing Ethnic Identity with Chicana Informants. *Frontiers: A Journal of Women Studies, 13*(3), 53–76.

Zelizer, V. A. (1994). *Pricing the Priceless Child: The Changing Social Value of Children*. Princeton, N.J.: Princeton University Press.

Zenteno, R., Giorguli, S. E., and Gutierrez, E. (2013). Mexican Adolescent Migration to the United States and Transitions to Adulthood. *Annals of the American Academy of Political and Social Science, 648*(1), 18–37.

Zong, J., and Batalova, J. (2017). Refugees and Asylees in the United States. *Migration Policy Institute*. Retrieved from https://www.migrationpolicy.org/article/refugees-and-asylees-united-states.

Zong, J., Ruiz Soto, A. G., Batalova, J., Gelatt, J., and Capps, R. (2017). A Profile of Current DACA Recipients by Education, Industry and Occupation. *Migration Policy Institute*. Retrieved from https://www.migrationpolicy.org/research/profile-current-daca-recipients-education-industry-and-occupation.

Zuñiga, V., and Leon-Hernandez, R. (2006). Introduction. In V. Zuñiga and R. Hernandez-Leon (Eds.), *New Destinations: Mexican Immigration in the United States* (1–22). New York: Russell Sage Foundation.

INDEX

ABOUT THE AUTHOR

ISABEL MARTINEZ is an assistant professor of Latin American and Latina/o studies at John Jay College of Criminal Justice. She is the recipient of numerous awards and fellowships, including the Woodrow Wilson National Foundation Fellowship, and her work has been featured in the *Journal of Latinos and Education* and *Latino Studies*.

Available titles in the Latinidad: Transnational Cultures in the United States series:

María Acosta Cruz, *Dream Nation: Puerto Rican Culture and the Fictions of Independence*

Rodolfo F. Acuña, *The Making of Chicana/o Studies: In the Trenches of Academe*

Mike Anastario, *Parcels: Memories of Salvadoran Migration*

Xóchitl Bada, *Mexican Hometown Associations in Chicagoacán: From Local to Transnational Civic Engagement*

Maritza E. Cárdenas, *Constituting Central American–Americans: Transnational Identities and the Politics of Dislocation*

Adriana Cruz-Manjarrez, *Zapotecs on the Move: Cultural, Social, and Political Processes in Transnational Perspective*

T. Jackie Cuevas, *Post-Borderlandia: Chicana Literature and Gender Variant Critique*

Marivel T. Danielson, *Homecoming Queers: Desire and Difference in Chicana Latina Cultural Production*

Allison E. Fagan, *From the Edge: Chicana/o Border Literature and the Politics of Print*

Jerry González, *In Search of the Mexican Beverly Hills: Latino Suburbanization in Postwar Los Angeles*

Rudy P. Guevarra Jr., *Becoming Mexipino: Multiethnic Identities and Communities in San Diego*

Colin Gunckel, *Mexico on Main Street: Transnational Film Culture in Los Angeles before World War II*

Marie-Theresa Hernández, *The Virgin of Guadalupe and the Conversos: Uncovering Hidden Influences from Spain to Mexico*

Anita Huizar-Hernández, *Forging Arizona: A History of the Peralta Land Grant and Racial Identity in the West*

Lisa Jarvinen, *The Rise of Spanish-Language Filmmaking: Out from Hollywood's Shadow, 1929–1939*

Regina M. Marchi, *Day of the Dead in the USA: The Migration and Transformation of a Cultural Phenomenon*

Desirée A. Martín, *Borderlands Saints: Secular Sanctity in Chicano/a and Mexican Culture*

Isabel Martinez, *Becoming Transnational Youth Workers: Independent Mexican Teenage Migrants and Pathways of Survival and Social Mobility*

Marci R. McMahon, *Domestic Negotiations: Gender, Nation, and Self-Fashioning in US Mexicana and Chicana Literature and Art*

A. Gabriel Meléndez, *Hidden Chicano Cinema: Film Dramas in the Borderlands*

Priscilla Peña Ovalle, *Dance and the Hollywood Latina: Race, Sex, and Stardom*

Amalia Pallares, *Family Activism: Immigrant Struggles and the Politics of Noncitizenship*

Luis F. B. Plascencia, *Disenchanting Citizenship: Mexican Migrants and the Boundaries of Belonging*

Cecilia M. Rivas, *Salvadoran Imaginaries: Mediated Identities and Cultures of Consumption*

Jayson Gonzales Sae-Saue, *Southwest Asia: The Transpacific Geographies of Chicana/o Literature*

Mario Jimenez Sifuentez, *Of Forest and Fields: Mexican Labor in the Pacific Northwest*

Maya Socolovsky, *Troubling Nationhood in U.S. Latina Literature: Explorations of Place and Belonging*

Susan Thananopavarn, *LatinAsian Cartographies*